PUERTO RICO

3RD EDITION

Where to Stay and Eat for All Budgets

Must-See Sights and Local Secrets

Ratings You Can Trust

Fodor's Travel Publications New York, Toronto, London, Sydney, Auckland
www.fodors.com

FODOR'S PUERTO RICO
Editor: Douglas Stallings

Editorial Production: David Downing
Editorial Contributors: Isabel Abisláiman, Martin G. Delfin, John Marino, Kevin Mead
Maps: David Lindroth, *cartographer*; Bob Blake and Rebecca Baer, *map editors*
Design: Fabrizio La Rocca, *creative director*; Guido Caroti, *art director*; Moon Sun Kim, *cover designer*; Melanie Marin, *senior photo editor*
Production/Manufacturing: Angela L. McLean
Cover Photo (Festival of Santiago Apostol, Loiza): Tony Arruza/Corbis

COPYRIGHT

Third Edition

ISBN 1-4000-1427-1

ISSN 1531-0396

SPECIAL SALES

This book is available for special discounts for bulk purchases for sales promotions or premiums. Special editions, including personalized covers, excerpts of existing books, and corporate imprints, can be created in large quantities for special needs. For more information, write to Special Markets/Premium Sales, 1745 Broadway, MD 6-2, New York, New York 10019, or e-mail specialmarkets@randomhouse.com.

AN IMPORTANT TIP & AN INVITATION

Although all prices, opening times, and other details in this book are based on information supplied to us at press time, changes occur all the time in the travel world, and Fodor's cannot accept responsibility for facts that become outdated or for inadvertent errors or omissions. So **always confirm information when it matters,** especially if you're making a detour to visit a specific place. Your experiences—positive and negative—matter to us. If we have missed or misstated something, **please write to us.** We follow up on all suggestions. Contact the Puerto Rico editor at editors@fodors.com or c/o Fodor's at 1745 Broadway, New York, NY 10019.

PRINTED IN THE UNITED STATES OF AMERICA

10 9 8 7 6 5 4 3 2 1

DESTINATION PUERTO RICO

Puerto Rico is unique among Caribbean destinations because of the sheer breadth of experiences available to you. If you crave a luxury resort, you'll find several world-class options to choose from. If you're a nature lover, you'll find an abundance of wonders to explore. If you're a surfer or an art aficionado, a golfer or a history buff, a deep-sea diver or a gourmet, you'll find satisfaction here. And perhaps foremost, lending a distinctive flavor to any Puerto Rico experience, you'll find a sophisticated, centuries-old culture—a mix of Native American, Spanish, African, and contemporary U.S. influences. San Juan's rapid pulse is what distinguishes life there from life *en la isla* (out on the island), the term Puerto Ricans use for everything that's not part of the city. The distinction is as much psychological as geographical; it implies a freedom from stress, an embrace of tradition, and the power and beauty of nature. If all you want is to sit on the sand and enjoy a piña colada, there's no better place to do it. But if you want something more, this island is rich with possibilities. Have a great trip!

Tim Jarrell, Publisher

CONTENTS

About This Book *F6*
On the Road with Fodor's *F8*
What's Where *F9*
Great Itineraries *F16*
When to Go *F18*
On the Calendar *F19*
Pleasures & Pastimes *F23*
Fodor's Choice *F25*
Smart Travel Tips *F28*

1 San Juan *1*

Exploring San Juan *2*
Where to Eat *23*
Where to Stay *39*
Nightlife & the Arts *47*
Sports & the Outdoors *56*
Shopping *62*
San Juan A to Z *68*

2 Eastern Puerto Rico *75*

The Northeast & El Yunque *78*
Vieques & Culebra *100*
The Southeastern Coast *111*
Eastern Puerto Rico A to Z *114*

3 Southern Puerto Rico *119*

Central Southern Puerto Rico *122*
Ponce *133*
Southwest Puerto Rico *143*
Southern Puerto Rico A to Z *154*

4 Northwestern Puerto Rico *158*

The North Coast *160*
West-Central Inlands *171*
The West Coast *177*
Northwestern Puerto Rico A to Z *187*

Understanding Puerto Rico *192*

Puerto Rico at a Glance *193*
Cocina Criolla *195*
The State of the Arts in Puerto Rico *198*
Chronology *200*
A Gambling Primer *205*
Spanish Vocabulary *213*

Index *220*

Maps

Puerto Rico *F12–F13*
The Caribbean *F14–F15*
San Juan
Exploring Old San Juan *8–9*
Exploring Greater San Juan *18–19*
Where to Stay & Eat in Old San Juan *26–27*
Where to Stay & Eat in Greater San Juan *34–35*
Eastern Puerto Rico *80–81*
El Yunque *92*
Southern Puerto Rico *124*
Ponce Centro *135*
Greater Ponce *138*
San Germán *149*
Northwestern Puerto Rico *164–165*

CloseUps

Peaceful Music *15*
Art Invasion *21*
On the Menu *28*
Design Lions *67*
144 Parrots & Counting *93*
Vieques Libre *102*
Masked Mischief *136*
Lives of the Santos *150*
The Abominable Chupacabra *169*
Modern-Day Taínos? *173*
Coffee—Puerto Rico's Black Gold *175*

ABOUT THIS BOOK

	The best source for travel advice is a like-minded friend who's just been where you're headed. But with or without that friend, you'll be in great shape to find your way around your destination once you learn to find your way around your Fodor's guide.
SELECTION	Our goal is to cover the best properties, sights, and activities in their category, as well as the most interesting communities to visit. We make a point of including local food lovers' hot spots as well as neighborhood options, and we avoid all that's touristy unless it's really worth your time. You can go on the assumption that everything in this book is recommended wholeheartedly by our writers and editors. Flip to **On the Road with Fodor's** to learn more about who they are. It goes without saying that no property pays to be included.
RATINGS	Orange stars ★ denote sights and properties that our editors and writers consider the very best in the area covered by the entire book. These, the best of the best, are listed in the **Fodor's Choice** section in the front of the book. Black stars ★ highlight the sights and properties we deem **Highly Recommended,** the don't-miss sights within any region. In cities, sights pinpointed with numbered map bullets ❻ in the margins tend to be more important than those without bullets.
SPECIAL SPOTS	**Pleasures & Pastimes** and text on chapter title pages focus on experiences that reveal the spirit of the destination. Also watch for **Off the Beaten Path** sights. Some are out of the way, some are quirky, and all are worth while. When the munchies hit, look for **Need a Break?** suggestions.
TIME IT RIGHT	Check **On the Calendar** up front and chapters' **Timing** sections for weather and crowd overviews and best days and times to visit.
SEE IT ALL	Use Fodor's exclusive **Great Itineraries** as a model for your trip. Either follow those that begin the book, or mix regional itineraries from several chapters. In cities, **Good Walks** guide you to important sights in each neighborhood; ⚑ indicates the starting points of walks and itineraries in the text and on the map.
BUDGET WELL	Hotel and restaurant price categories from **¢ to $$$$** are defined in the opening pages of each chapter—expect to find a balanced selection for every budget. For attractions, we always give standard adult admission fees; reductions are usually available for children, students, and senior citizens.
BASIC INFO	**Smart Travel Tips** lists travel essentials for the entire area covered by the book; city- and region-specific basics end each chapter. To find the best way to get around, see the transportation section; see individual modes of travel ("By Car," "By Train") for details.

ON THE MAPS	Maps throughout the book show you what's where and help you find your way around. Black and orange numbered bullets ❻ ❻ in the text correlate to bullets on maps.
BACKGROUND	We give background information within the chapters in the course of explaining sights as well as in the CloseUp boxes and in Understanding Puerto Rico at the end of the book. The vocabulary can be invaluable.
FIND IT FAST	Within the book, chapters are arranged in a roughly clockwise direction starting with San Juan. Chapters are divided into small regions, within which towns are covered in logical geographical order; attractive routes and interesting places between towns are flagged as En Route. Heads at the top of each page help you find what you need within a chapter.
DON'T FORGET	Restaurants are open for lunch and dinner daily unless we state otherwise; we mention dress only when there's a specific requirement and reservations only when they're essential or not accepted—it's always best to book ahead. Hotels have private baths, phone, TVs, and air-conditioning and operate on the European Plan (a.k.a. EP, meaning without meals). We always list facilities but not whether you'll be charged extra to use them, so when pricing accommodations, find out what's included.

SYMBOLS

Many Listings

- ★ Fodor's Choice
- ★ Highly recommended
- ✉ Physical address
- ✣ Directions
- 📫 Mailing address
- ☎ Telephone
- 📠 Fax
- 🌐 On the Web
- ✉ E-mail
- 🎟 Admission fee
- ⏲ Open/closed times
- ⚑ Start of walk/itinerary
- Ⓜ Metro stations
- 💳 Credit cards

Outdoors

- ⛳ Golf
- ⛺ Camping

Hotels & Restaurants

- 🏨 Hotel
- 🛏 Number of rooms
- 👍 Facilities
- 🍽 Meal plans
- ✕ Restaurant
- ✍ Reservations
- 👔 Dress code
- 🚬 Smoking
- 🍷 BYOB
- ✕🏨 Hotel with restaurant that warrants a visit

Other

- 👶 Family-friendly
- ℹ Contact information
- ⇨ See also
- ✉ Branch address
- ☞ Take note

ON THE ROAD WITH FODOR'S

A trip takes you out of yourself. Concerns of life at home completely disappear, driven away by more immediate thoughts—about, say, what marvels will beguile the next day, or where you'll have dinner. That's where Fodor's comes in. We make sure that you know all your options, so that you don't miss something that's around the next bend just because you didn't know it was there. Because the best memories of your trip might well have nothing to do with what you came to Puerto Rico to see, we guide you to sights large and small all over the region. You might set out to relax on the island's great beaches, but back at home you find yourself unable to forget the bioluminescent Bahía Mosquito in Vieques or the Río Camuy caves. With Fodor's at your side, serendipitous discoveries are never far away.

Our success in showing you every corner of Puerto Rico is a credit to our extraordinary writers. Although there's no substitute for travel advice from a good friend who knows your style, our contributors are the next best thing—the kind of people you would poll for travel advice if you knew them.

Isabel Abislaimán, a writer-photographer who also happens to be a litigation lawyer, put her talents to work covering sights, hotels, sports outfitters, fashion, art and cuisine traditions, and shops in San Juan. She also revised the chapter's A to Z section. Isabel has contributed to the travel section of Spanish-language newspaper, *El Nuevo Día*, and collaborated with National Geographic. In 2003, she had an individual exhibit at the Liga de Estudiantes de Arte de San Juan. Her photographs have appeared in collective exhibits such as the Puerto Rico National Art Exhibit and Photography Biennial.

A native of San Antonio, Texas, journalist and broadcaster **Martin G. Delfin** has written about Puerto Rico and Latin America for various media outlets, including *The New York Times,* Agence France-Presse, and the *Boston Globe.* His news reports on Puerto Rico have been transmitted by the Voice of America and National Public Radio. He lives in San Juan, where he writes regularly for the *San Juan Star* and is a panelist on a new analysis program broadcast on the local PBS affiliate. He covered Southern Puerto Rico for this book.

John Marino, who reviewed San Juan restaurants and nightclubs and explored Eastern Puerto Rico for us, is managing editor at the *San Juan Star.* He has written extensively about Puerto Rico and the Caribbean for several publications, including the *Washington Post, New York Times, Gourmet, New York Newsday,* and Reuters. He lives with his wife and son in San Juan.

Kevin Mead, who updated the Northwestern Puerto Rico chapter, is the assistant city editor for the *San Juan Star* and a frequent contributor to the paper's Portfolio section covering travel and entertainment.

WHAT'S WHERE

Destination chapters in *Fodor's Puerto Rico* are arranged geographically. They start with San Juan, the first destination for most visitors, and move to the inland rain forest and coastal regions of the east, on to the southern mountains and shores, and around to the island's northwestern reaches.

1 San Juan

San Juan, buffed by Atlantic Ocean currents and gentle trade winds, sits on the island's northeast coast, a bit more than a two-hour drive from the west coast, about an hour's drive from the eastern shores, and about an hour from the town of Ponce, on the south coast. It's generally a flat town, with mountain ranges to the east and to the south, near the island's center. Most flights to the island land at Aeropuerto Internacional Louis Muñoz Marín. San Juan is where you'll find the island's densest concentration of high-rise hotels, not to mention bustling beaches, a lively, rejuvenated nightlife scene, and excellent restaurants. No visit to the island would be complete without at least a stroll down the cobblestone streets of Old San Juan, San Juan's oldest district, which also has some of San Juan's finest restaurants and hippest night spots. Condado, east of Old San Juan, is a thin strip of beachfront, where you'll find some of the island's most venerable hotels, such as the Wyndham Condado Plaza and the San Juan Marriott, not to mention some of the finest restaurants. East of Condado is the lower-rise neighborhood of Ocean Park, which is primarily residential but still has several small hotels and guesthouses and a good beach. Beyond Ocean Park is Isla Verde, where there's another string of luxury high-rises along the city's finest stretch of beachfront, including the Ritz-Carlton and the Wyndham El San Juan. Miramar, south of Condado, is a residential area filled with turn-of-the-20th-century homes and some good restaurants and small hotels. The city's financial and business center is Hato Rey; along with Santurce—the historical downtown area—it's become a new nightlife center. San Juan is one of the Caribbean's busiest cruise-ship ports.

2 Eastern Puerto Rico

Although eastern Puerto Rico encompasses several thriving communities, all have a slow pace and a somewhat provincial outlook on life. They also tend to hang on to traditions, something that's reflected in the music, food, and art of the region. The east coast begins just outside San Juan and follows the Atlantic Ocean down to where it meets the Caribbean. Piñones, the first community east of San Juan, is well known for its open-air seafood restaurants that play music, especially on weekend nights. Loíza is a traditional community of some 30,000 residents steeped in African heritage and famous for its festivals. The stretch of coast from Loíza to Fajardo is best known for its excellent beaches and several sprawling resorts, including the Westin Río Mar, the new Paradisus Puerto Rico, and the El Conquistador. The shore is placid in some spots, banked by the remains of coconut plantations, and rugged in others, especially north of Fajardo, where bluffs overlook the ocean. The outer island Vieques sits squarely off the central coast and has been known for years for its excellent beaches, bioluminiscent bay, and naval bombing ranges; now that the Navy has departed, much of the island has been turned into a wildlife refuge, beaches have been reopened to the public, and development is improving the island's infrastructure, including its first full-scale resort, the Wyndham Martineau Bay. Its smaller sister island Culebra floats east of the northeasternmost corner of the "main island," a quiet and romantic haven for day-trippers, who come to enjoy the island's excellent, powdery soft beaches, or for those looking for a quieter vacation. Much of this region lies in the foothills of mountains, including El Yunque rain forest, the only tropical forest in the U.S. National Forest system.

3 Southern Puerto Rico

Stretching from Puerto Rico's central mountains to the Caribbean Sea and some 90 mi along the southern coast, southern Puerto Rico encompasses lush forests, such as in the Bosque Estatal Carite in the southeastern part of the island, as well as tropical dry forests such as the Bosque Estatal de Guánica on the southwestern coast. In general, this area is drier than other parts of the island, and numerous forms of cacti are abundant. You'll find homes scattered through the area, picturesque mountain towns, seaside fishing villages, and Puerto Rico's second-largest urban hub, Ponce. Although the south has a few resorts, including the large Hilton in Ponce and the Copamarina Beach Resort in Guánica, this part of the island is known more for its small hotels and paradores. La Parguera, in the southwest, is the island's second bioluminiscent bay, although it's not as spectacular as the one on Vieques. The south also has one of island's most historic towns, San Germán, also known for its *santeros,* who specialize in carving the wooden figures of saints. The region's best beaches are in the southwest, including those on Gilligan's Island—just offshore near Guánica—and the beaches of the Cabo Rojo peninsula.

4 Northwestern Puerto Rico

The north coast, which skirts the Atlantic Ocean, was formerly the home of many coconut and fruit plantations, and trees are still abundant in the area. One of these former plantations is now a large resort, the Hyatt Dorado Beach Resort, a family favorite and the largest on the north coast. The jagged coastline is also known for its world-class surfing beaches, particularly near Rincón, a laid-back town with several small hotels and a couple of medium-size resorts. The area just inland is dominated by limestone karst terrain, where huge cliffs and sinkholes in the porous ground create a surreal feeling. Winding deep underground is Río Camuy and its famous caves, one of the island's many natural wonders. Tropical vegetation fills the area still farther inland, near the Cordillera Central, where the island's tallest peak, Cerro de Punta, looms 4,390 feet above sea level. A casual, laid-back atmosphere is the norm in this region, which is dotted with small hotels and restaurants. New flights to the airport in Aguadilla make it a quick and easy trip for surfers and vacationers coming down for the weekend from the East Coast of the United States.

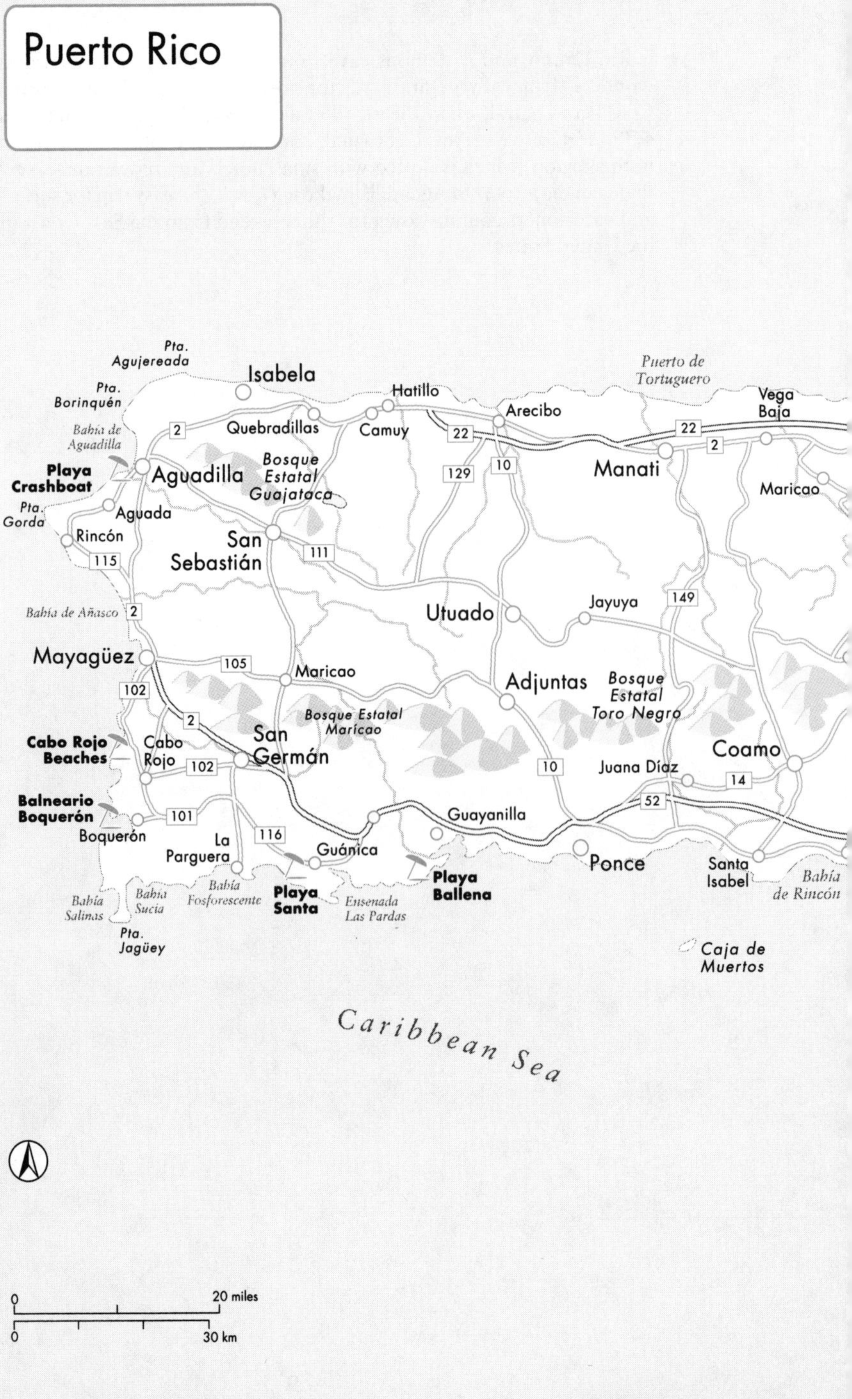

Puerto Rico

Pta. Agujereada
Isabela
Pta. Borinquén
Hatillo
Puerto de Tortuguero
Vega Baja
Arecibo
Bahía de Aguadilla
2
Quebradillas
Camuy
22
22
2
Manati
Playa Crashboat
Aguadilla
Bosque Estatal Guajataca
129
10
Maricao
Pta. Gorda
Aguada
Rincón
San Sebastián
111
115
Bahía de Añasco
2
Utuado
Jayuya
149
Mayagüez
105
Maricao
Adjuntas
Bosque Estatal Toro Negro
102
2
Bosque Estatal Maricao
Cabo Rojo Beaches
Cabo Rojo
San Germán
102
10
Juana Díaz
Coamo
14
Balneario Boquerón
101
52
Guayanilla
Boquerón
116
La Parguera
Guánica
Ponce
Santa Isabel
Playa Ballena
Bahía de Rincón
Bahía Salinas
Bahía Sucia
Bahía Fosforescente
Playa Santa
Ensenada Las Pardas
Pta. Jagüey
Caja de Muertos

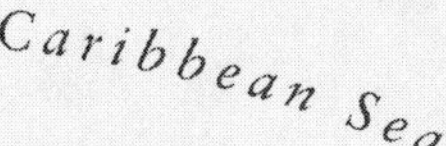

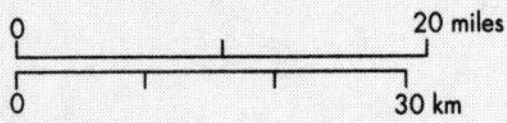

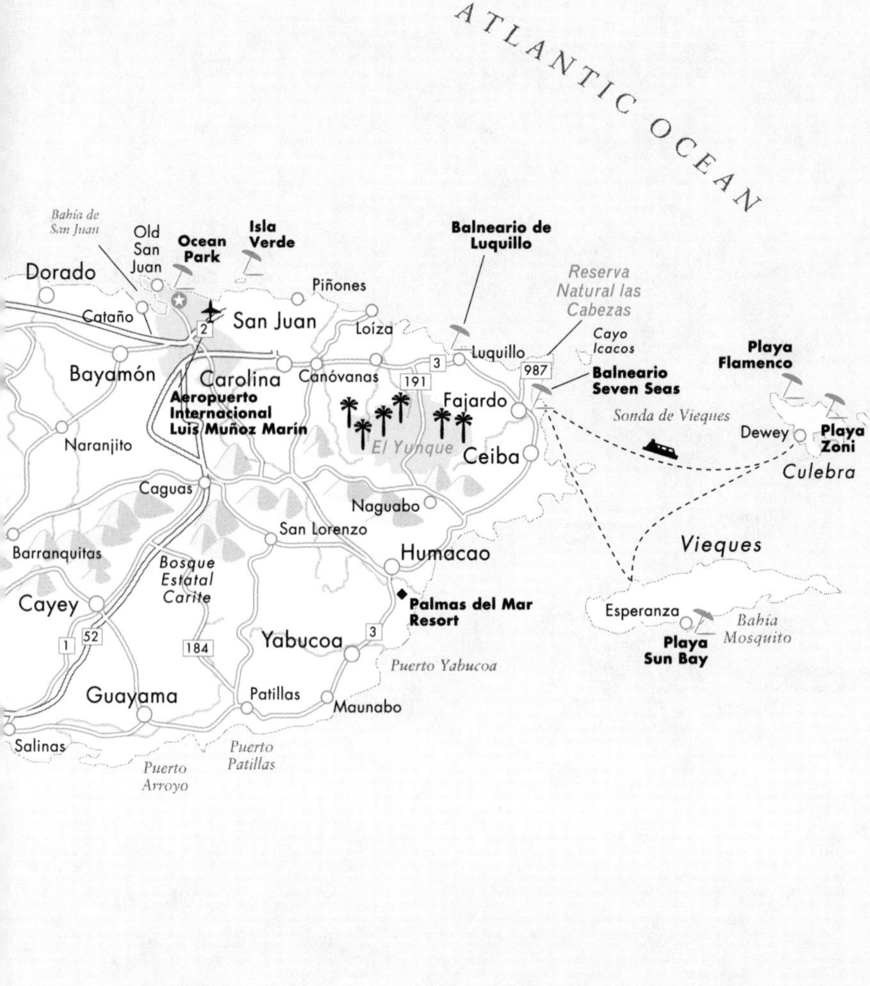

ATLANTIC OCEAN

Bahía de San Juan
Old San Juan
Ocean Park
Isla Verde
Dorado
Cataño
San Juan
Piñones
Loíza
Balneario de Luquillo
Luquillo
Reserva Natural las Cabezas
Cayo Icacos
Balneario Seven Seas
Playa Flamenco
Bayamón
Carolina
Canóvanas
Aeropuerto Internacional Luis Muñoz Marín
Fajardo
Sonda de Vieques
Dewey
Playa Zoni
Culebra
Naranjito
El Yunque
Ceiba
Caguas
Naguabo
San Lorenzo
Barranquitas
Humacao
Vieques
Bosque Estatal Carite
Palmas del Mar Resort
Cayey
Esperanza
Bahía Mosquito
Playa Sun Bay
Yabucoa
Puerto Yabucoa
Guayama
Patillas
Maunabo
Salinas
Puerto Patillas
Puerto Arroyo
2
3
191
987
1
52
184

KEY
Rainforest

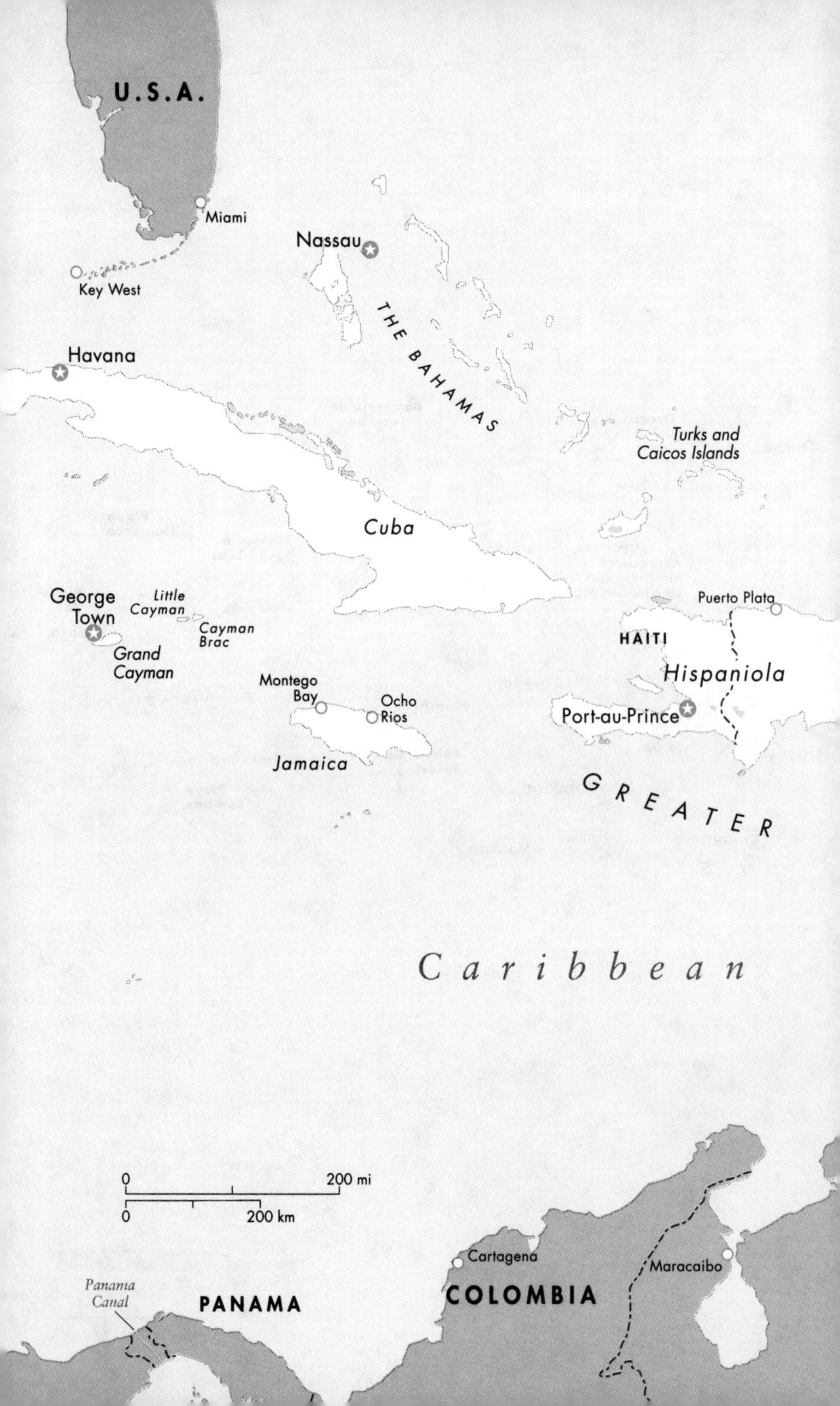

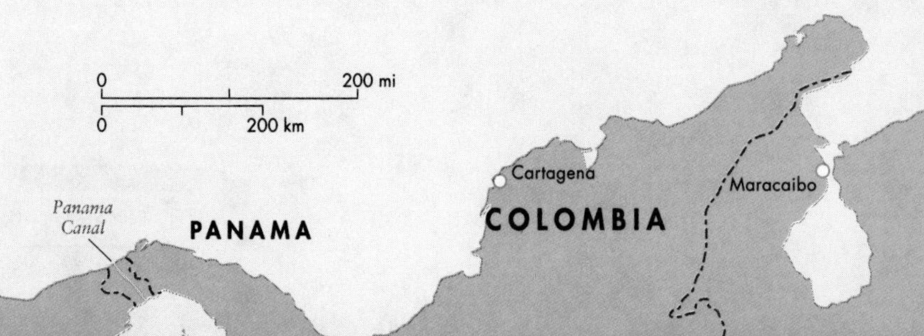
U.S.A.
Miami
Key West
Nassau
THE BAHAMAS
Havana
Cuba
Turks and
Caicos Islands
George
Town
Little
Cayman
Cayman
Brac
Grand
Cayman
Montego
Bay
Ocho
Rios
Jamaica
HAITI
Puerto Plata
Hispaniola
Port-au-Prince
GREATER
Caribbean
0
200 mi
0
200 km
Cartagena
Maracaibo
Panama
Canal
PANAMA
COLOMBIA

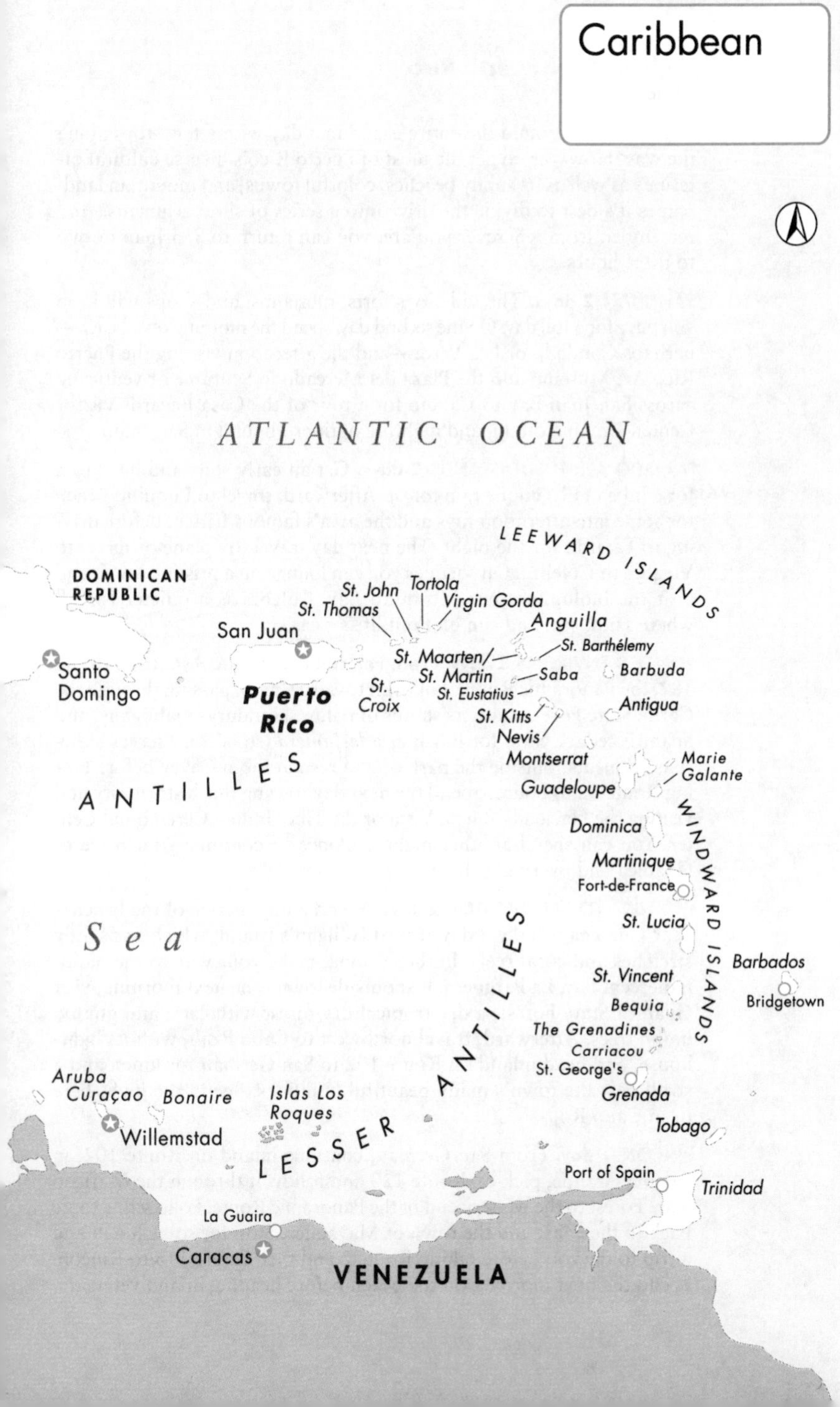

Caribbean

ATLANTIC OCEAN

LEEWARD ISLANDS

DOMINICAN REPUBLIC

St. John

Tortola

Virgin Gorda

St. Thomas

Anguilla

San Juan

St. Barthélemy

St. Maarten/ St. Martin

Saba

Barbuda

Santo Domingo

St. Croix

St. Eustatius

Antigua

Puerto Rico

St. Kitts

Nevis

Montserrat

Marie Galante

Guadeloupe

ANTILLES

Dominica

Martinique

Fort-de-France

WINDWARD ISLANDS

St. Lucia

Sea

Barbados

St. Vincent

Bridgetown

Bequia

The Grenadines

Carriacou

St. George's

Aruba

Curaçao

Bonaire

Islas Los Roques

Grenada

LESSER ANTILLES

Willemstad

Tobago

Port of Spain

Trinidad

La Guaira

Caracas

VENEZUELA

Highlights of Puerto Rico

11 days

You can loop around the entire island in a day with a few stops along the way. However, to get the most of Puerto Rico's diverse cultural offerings as well as its sunny beaches, colorful towns, and mountain landscapes it's best to divide the drive into a series of short segments. And remember, from wherever you are, you can return to San Juan in two to three hours.

SAN JUAN **2 days.** The old city's forts, museums, and shops will keep you busy for a full day. On the second day, spend the morning on a beach—perhaps Condado or Isla Verde—and the afternoon visiting the Puerto Rico Art Museum and the Plaza del Mercado in Santurce or venturing across San Juan Bay to Cataño for a tour of the Casa Bacardí Visitor Center. Evening dining and nightlife options abound in San Juan.

FAJARDO & THE OUT ISLANDS **2 days.** Get an early start and head east for a hike in El Yunque rain forest. Afterward, travel to Luquillo Beach for some late-afternoon rays and the area's famous fritters before driving to Fajardo for the night. The next day travel (by plane or ferry) to Vieques or Culebra. On Vieques you can lounge on a pristine beach and visit the bioluminescent Mosquito Bay. Culebra is a quieter island, where sand, sea, and sun blot out life's cares.

PONCE & ENVIRONS **2 days.** From Fajardo take Route 3 south to Route 182, the Panoramic Route. Follow it toward Cayey, passing through the Carite State Forest, with its stands of palms, Honduras mahogany, and Spanish cedars. Stop for lunch at a *lechonera* (stand that serves slow-roasted meats) outside the park or at a restaurant in Cayey before taking Route 52 to Ponce. Spend the next day touring this historic city and visiting the Hacienda Buena Vista or the Tibes Indian Ceremonial Center. You can spend another night in Ponce or continue your drive to Guánica and overnight there.

GUÁNICA TO SAN GERMÁN **2 days.** Spend a day on one of the beaches near Guánica or take a day-trip to Gilligan's Island, which has sandy stretches and coral reefs. In the evening, make your way to the bioluminescent bay, La Parguera, just outside town. The next morning, visit Guánica State Forest, a dry tropical dry forest with cacti and gumbo limbo trees. Afterward, travel northwest to Cabo Rojo, with its lighthouse, and head inland on Route 102 to San Germán for lunch and a stroll past the town's many beautiful buildings. Spend the night here or in Cabo Rojo.

RINCÓN **1 day.** From San Germán, continue inland on Route 102; in Sábana Grande, pick up Route 120 and follow it through the Maricao State Forest to the western end of the Panoramic Route. Follow this route back to the coast and the town of Mayagüez. Stop for some lunch and a trip to the zoo before taking Route 2 and then Route 115 to Rincón. Spend the next morning on the beach before heading inland yet again.

JAYUYA TO SAN JUAN **2 days.** From Rincón, work your way back to Route 2, and follow it to the scenic Route 111. Make a brief stop in Lares before visiting Río Camuy Cave Park and/or the Caguana Indian Ceremonial Center. Head inland still farther to Utuado or Jayuya, both of which are good places to spend the night. The next day, visit the Toro Negro State Forest, learn more about the Taíno Indians at the Museo Cemí, and see the petroglyphs on La Piedra Escrita. In the afternoon, return west along Route 111 and pick up Route 129 north to the Arecibo Observatory. Make your way north to the town of Arecibo and return to San Juan on Route 22.

WHEN TO GO

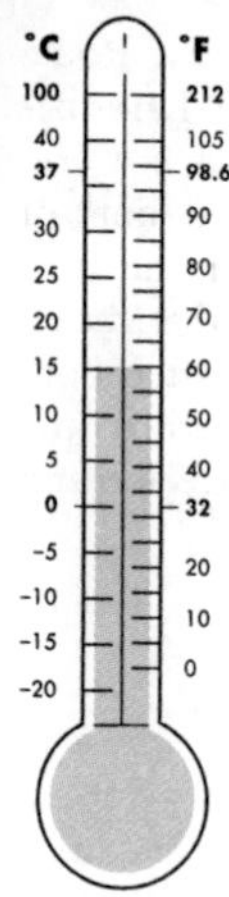

High season runs from mid-December through mid-April. Winter hotel rates are 25% to 40% higher than off-season rates, and hotels tend to be packed. San Juan is also a commercial town, and hotels, except for the short season around Christmas and New Year's, are busy year-round with international business travelers. This doesn't mean the island won't have rooms in winter—rarely is space completely unavailable—but if you plan to beat that winter sleet in Duluth, make arrangements for flights and hotel space at least a few weeks ahead of time. A fun and often less expensive time to visit is during the "shoulder" seasons of fall and spring. The weather is—still—perfect, and the tourist crush is less intense.

Climate

Puerto Rico's weather is moderate and tropical year-round, with an average temperature of about 82°F (26°C). Essentially, there are no seasonal changes, although winter sees cooling (not cold) breezes from the north, and temperatures in higher elevations drop by as much as 20 degrees. Hurricane season in the Caribbean runs July through November.

The following are average daily maximum and minimum temperatures.

Forecasts **Puerto Rico Weather** ☎ 787/253-4586. **The Weather Channel** www.weather.com.

SAN JUAN

Jan.	70F	21C	May	74F	23C	Sept.	75F	24C
	80	27		84	29		86	30
Feb.	70F	21C	June	75F	24C	Oct.	75F	24C
	80	27		85	29		85	29
Mar.	70F	21C	July	75F	24C	Nov.	73F	23C
	81	27		85	29		84	29
Apr.	72F	22C	Aug.	76F	24C	Dec.	72F	22C
	82	28		85	29		81	27

ON THE CALENDAR

Puerto Rico's top seasonal events are listed below, and any one of them could provide the stuff of lasting memories. Contact local tourism authorities for exact dates and for further information.

ONGOING

Feb.–early Mar.	The weeks preceding Lent have special significance for Catholicism and other religions, and Puerto Rico celebrates its **Carnivales** with vigor. The flamboyant celebrations, held island-wide but with particular energy in Ponce, are complete with float parades, folk music, local foods, Carnival Queen pageants, and music competitions.
Late May–early June	The annual **Heineken JazzFest** attracts some 15,000 aficionados to San Juan for four days of outdoor concerts by the likes of David Sánchez, George Benson, Nestor Torres, and Spyro Gyra.
Late Aug.–early Sept.	Anglers of all stripes try their hand at snagging blue marlin and other game fish in the largest fishing competition in Puerto Rico, the **International Billfish Tournament**, which is hosted by the Club Náutico de San Juan. The strongest tackle might prevail—marlins can weigh as much as 900 pounds.
Nov.–Jan.	The boys of summer are actually the boys of winter in Puerto Rico: in October the **baseball season** commences. Fans follow the games, played at various island stadiums, with the fervor of sports enthusiasts anywhere. Major-league players often travel to Puerto Rico to play with the island's six pro teams.

WINTER

Dec.	The Puerto Rico National Folkloric Ballet performs its highly anticipated **Annual Criollísimo Show** regularly during the month. The dance blends modern ballet with Puerto Rican and Caribbean music and themes. Look to the Teatro Tapia in Old San Juan or the Centro de Bellas Artes Luis A. Ferré in Santurce for schedules.
Early Dec.	For 10 days in early December, **Humacao's Fiesta Patronale** celebrates the Virgin of the Immaculate Conception; the festival coincides with the city's sprucing up for Christmas.
Mid-Dec.	Cataño's Casa Bacardí Visitor Center hosts the **Bacardí Artisan's Fair.** With local crafts, children's activities, folk bands, and food and drink kiosks, it's arguably the largest event of its kind in the Caribbean.
	If you've got a hankering for loud engines and sea spray, visit the exciting **Puerto Rico International Offshore Cup** speed-boat races held every year in Fajardo, where local and international teams compete for prize money and prestige.

	Fortaleza Street in Old San Juan is closed to traffic for the annual "South of Fortaleza" **SOFO Culinary Week,** when more than 20 restaurants set their chairs, tables, and bars outside on the street.
Late Dec.	The annual **Hatillo Festival de los Mascaras** honors the mask-making traditions of the northwestern town of Hatillo, where colorful masks used in religious processions have been crafted for centuries.
	Navidades, or Christmas, features costumed nativity processions, music concerts, and other festivities island-wide during the week leading to one of the busiest holidays of the year.
Jan.	The annual season of the **Puerto Rico Symphony Orchestra** begins with classical and pop performances by the island's finest orchestra. Concerts are held in San Juan.
Jan. 6	The traditional **El Día de los Tres Reyes** (Three Kings Day) is a time of gift-giving and celebration. Sculptures of the gift-bearing three wise men, in wood or wire decorated with Christmas lights, appear in towns around the island, accompanied by music, puppet shows for children, and feasts. Be aware that the traditional Governor's mansion reception and gifts handed out to the public creates traffic congestion and overcrowds the streets of Old San Juan.
Late Jan.	The annual **Las Fiestas de la Calle San Sebastián** (San Sebastián Street Festival), named after the street in Old San Juan where the festival originated, features several nights of live music in the plazas as well as food festivals and *cabezudos* parades, where folk legends are caricatured in oversize masks.
Late Jan.–early Feb.	Each year the Puerto Rico film industry picks talent to honor in the **Puerto Rico International Film Festival.** International stars such as Benicio Del Toro and Chita Rivera attest to the power of Puerto Rican influence in the arts, and the San Juan film festival showcases island-made films and works from around the world.
Early Feb.	Coamo's **San Blas de Illescas Half Marathon** has been running, literally, since 1957. The race, in honor of the town's patron saint and part of its fiesta patronale, covers 21 km (13 mi) in the hills of the central town; it's so popular that competitors come from the world over, and the streets are lined with some 200,000 spectators.
Mid-Feb.	Ponce's **Danza Week** of cultural activities celebrates the *danza,* a colonial-era dance similar to the waltz.
Late Feb.	The mountain towns of Maricao and Yauco, centers of the island's coffee-growing region, host the annual **Festival de Café** (Coffee Harvest Festival), honoring both crops and farmers. It takes place at the towns' plazas, with exhibits of coffee and harvesting equipment as well as with local bands, folk crafts, and food and drink kiosks.

SPRING	
Mar.	The two-day Dulce Sueño Paso Fino Fair, showcasing the island's famous Paso Fino horses, is held in the town of Guayama. Paso Finos are bred and trained to walk with a distinctive, smooth gait, and the horses and their trainers are held in high regard.
Mid-Mar.	The Puerto Rico Tourism Company sponsors the annual International Artisans' Festival, with folk art, carvings, leather work, and other crafts from islanders and international artists.
Apr.	Fajardo's Festival de Chiringas (Kite Festival) features demonstrations and flying competitions, as well as food and drink booths.
	The annual Regata de Veleros Copa Kelly (Kelly Cup Sailboat Regatta) takes place off the coast of Fajardo.
	Not only for professionals in the tourism industry, the Puerto Rico Tourism Fair, held at La Guancha in Ponce, highlights island attractions and activities, as well as local crafts and artisans' creations.
Late Apr.–May	Isabela's Festival de Mundillo (Bobbin Lace Festival) showcases delicate, woven lace with demonstrations and exhibits.
May	Bayamón's Chicharrón Festival celebrates the island's famous puffy, pork-rind fritter. The city has become known for this treat thanks to the many *chicharronero* carts that line Route 2 on the way into town.
	The Fajardo Festival de Bomba y Plena turns the spotlight on Puerto Rico's lively Afro-influenced music and dance.
SUMMER	
June	In San Juan, the Fiesta de San Juan Bautista or Noche de San Juan (San Juan Bautista Festival) honors city patron St. John the Baptist with a week of parades, music, dance, and, ultimately, a traditional backward walk into the ocean to bring good luck in the ensuing year.
Early June	The annual Casals Festival in San Juan honors the late, great cellist Pablo Casals, who lived in Old San Juan. The 10 days of classical-music performances feature the Puerto Rico Symphony Orchestra as well as soloists from the island and around the world.
Late June–July	Gardenias, lilies, begonias, and thousands of tropical plants are showcased at Aibonito's annual Fiesta de Flores (Flower Festival).
July	Loíza's Fiesta de Santiago Apóstal (St. James Festival), held in July, honors Puerto Rico's African traditions and the apostle St. James with a carnival of street parades, music, and dancing.
Early July	Río Grande celebrates its Carnivale, between the first and second week of July with music competitions, parades, and feasts.

Mid-July	The Barranquitas Feria de Artesanía (Barranquitas Artisans' Fair) offers spots to more than 200 local artisans to display their pottery, wood carvings, leather bags and belts, basketry, and other handiwork.
	Around July 16, such coastal towns as Naguabo, Ceiba, and Humacao conduct religious processions honoring the Virgen del Carmen. Offerings of flowers from the *flamboyán* tree are made to this virgin, the patron saint of the fishermen, and festivities continue into the evening.
FALL	
Oct.	Arecibo, on the north coast, holds the Cetí Festival, named after a tiny, sardinelike fish found in the area and considered a culinary delicacy.
Early Oct.	Naguabo's fiesta patronale honors Our Lady of the Rosary the first 10 days of October.
Late Oct.	The northern town of Corozal hosts the Festival del Platano (Plantain Festival), which highlights this versatile staple of Puerto Rican cuisine.
Mid-Nov.	The Festival of Puerto Rican Music, held in San Juan and other locations, celebrates the vibrancy of the island's folk music, highlighted by a contest featuring the *cuatro,* a traditional guitar with five double strings.
Late Nov.	Luquillo hosts the three-day Festival de Platos Típicos (Festival of Typical Dishes), highlighting food and drink prepared with coconut.
	The central mountain areas hold an annual Jayuya Indian Festival, honoring the island's indigenous Taíno culture with crafts demonstrations, ceremonies, and guided visits to Taíno sites in the area.

PLEASURES & PASTIMES

Beaches

Beaches rim the island. Sanjuaneros often pack the sandy stretches lining the neighborhoods of Puerta de Tierra, Condado, Ocean Park, and Isla Verde as well as such east-coast beaches as Luquillo. Those seeking solitude will find it on the outer islands of Vieques and Culebra, where the beaches are wide, spectacular, and often uncrowded. To the south, several strands are broad and inviting, with plenty of seaside bars and restaurants where you can while away the hours. The west coast near the town of Rincón is noted for its big waves and is popular with surfers.

Dining

Many Puerto Rican chefs have taken cues from the international set, and "world cuisine" is the buzzword at trend-conscious restaurants. Throughout the island you'll find everything from French haute cuisine to sushi bars, as well as superb local eateries serving *comidas criollas,* traditional Caribbean-creole meals. If you're looking for authentic Puerto Rican cuisine, one indication is the *mesón gastronómico* label used by the government to recognize restaurants that preserve culinary traditions. There are more than 40 such establishments island-wide.

Festivals

Puerto Rico's festivals are colorful and inclined toward lots of music and feasting. The towns and villages are particularly loyal to their patron saints, and every year each of the island's 78 municipalities celebrates a *fiesta patronale* (patron-saint festival). Though religious in origin, these festivities feature processions, sports events, folklore shows, feasting, music, and dance, and they often highlight local crafts (such as the delicate *mundillo* lace of Aguadilla). Festivities last about 10 days, with more activities on weekends than on weekdays. Several towns and regions also have pre-Lenten Carnivals, complete with parades, folk music, local dishes, a Carnival Queen pageant, and music competitions. All are in early to late February, sometimes into March. The island calendar is also full year-round with street fêtes, sporting competitions, and cultural and arts festivals.

Gambling

The time when one of the main tourism activities in Puerto Rico was gambling has passed, but casinos still draw crowds. Today, rather than high rollers out for a week of intense dice and card games, the casinos tend to be filled with couples looking for fun and a chance to hit the jackpot. Games generally include slot machines, blackjack, roulette, craps, Caribbean stud poker (a five-card stud game), and *pai gow* poker (a combination of American poker and the ancient Chinese game of pai gow, which employs cards and dice). Hotels that house casinos have live entertainment most weekends, restaurants, and bars.

Music

Music is the heart and soul of Puerto Rico. Take the instruments from the days of the Taíno Indians—the *guiro* (scratch gourd) and the *fotuto* (conch shell)—and blend them with the drums and rhythms of Africa that took root on the island's sugarcane-lined coasts. To this mixture, stir in the Spanish-Moorish–influenced music of the inland farmers and mountain folk—the *trovadores,* who still perform their improvised songs accompanied by the *cuatro* (five-double-string Spanish guitar). Let all this simmer for a couple centuries, and there you have it.

The island's brash Latin sound is best exemplified by the highly danceable salsa, especially as interpreted by such entertainers as the late, great Tito Puente and pop sensation Ricky Martin. Salsa, Spanish for "sauce" (as in the sauce that energizes the party) is a fusion of West African percussion and jazz with a swing beat. Two of its predecessors, *bomba* and *plena,* can still be heard today. Bomba is African-based drum and dance music in which a lead singer often leads a chorus of singers in a call-and-response interplay, similar to Cuba's rumba music. Plena is a more melodic country music that makes use of the cuatro as well of scratch gourds.

Other Latin beats heard on the island, with origins in the Caribbean, Latin America, and Spain, are mambo, merengue, flamenco, cha-cha, and rumba. Increasingly, young musicians are experimenting with new forms, including urban dance music, rap, and Spanish-language rock and pop. Fiel a la Vega and Sol de Menta compose and perform danceable rock tunes without losing their island roots, and heavy metal band Puya has been making its marks in stateside markets. Vico C is one of the island's most famous rappers, known for weaving urban tales with a positive message.

FODOR'S CHOICE

Fodor'sChoice ★

The sights, restaurants, hotels, and other travel experiences on these pages are our editors' top picks—our Fodor's Choices. They're the best of their type in the area covered by the book—not to be missed and always worth your time. In the destination chapters that follow, you will find all the details.

LODGING

$$$$ **Wyndham El Conquistador Resort & Golden Door Spa, Fajardo.** Hanging off a bluff just above the Atlantic Ocean this giant, self-contained complex aims to meet all of your needs—and succeeds.

$$$$ **Wyndham El San Juan Hotel & Casino, San Juan.** Put on your dancing gear and salsa the night away in the immense, mahogany-paneled lobby of the landmark El San Juan, where on Saturday night it's the place to see and be seen. This is also one of San Juan's finest hotels.

$$$$ **Horned Dorset Primavera, Rincón.** This west-coast inn is the place to go to get away from it all in luxury. There are no phones, TVs, or radios in the antique-trimmed rooms, a secluded beach is steps away, and plunge pools dot the manicured grounds.

$$–$$$$ **El Convento Hotel, Old San Juan.** You wouldn't recognize the El Convento as the Carmelite convent it was 350 years ago; today it's luxurious and hip, a fine example of what sensitive planning and a good decorator can achieve.

$$–$$$ **Hacienda Tamarindo, Vieques.** A tamarind tree rises up through three stories in the lobby, and the outdoor pool is touted as one of Puerto Rico's most beautiful, sitting on a hilltop overlooking Vieques. It's a formula for whimsical bliss.

$$–$$$ **Inn on the Blue Horizon, Vieques.** No phones, no televisions, no noise—just privacy and pampering at this hotel made up of six villas and a main house.

$–$$ **Villas del Mar Hau, Isabela.** A row of brightly colored cottages lines the Montones Beach, and the whole area is dotted with palm and pine trees. There are outdoor sports facilities where active children and adults can work up a sweat, and horseback riding is available.

$ **Mary Lee's by the Sea, Guánica.** Tranquillity reigns at this colorful complex of apartments and suites with fully equipped kitchenettes. It's a wonderful place to escape after a day of sun and sea.

RESTAURANTS

$$–$$$$ **Ajili Mojili, San Juan.** Here you'll find classic Puerto Rican dishes given an upscale twist and served with a mix of efficiency and island charm.

$$$ **Café Media Luna, Vieques.** For lovers of exotic spices, this local favorite is heaven. Everything from Asian to Middle Eastern fare joins tropical cuisine for a meld that is incomparable.

$$-$$$ **Mark's at the Meliá, Ponce.** This restaurant gets points for being right in the center of town in the Meliá Hotel on Plaza las Delicias. Award-winning chef Mark French serves up consistently outstanding food—an eclectic mix of Caribbean and international cuisine.

$$-$$$ **Parrot Club, Old San Juan.** The relaxed yet stylish environment here seems to have struck a chord with sanjuaneros, who are quickly turning this Nuevo Latino restaurant into an institution.

$$-$$$ **Sand and the Sea, Cayey.** The open balcony at this mountaintop restaurant may have the best view on the island—it's especially breathtaking at sunset. Piano music, a fireplace, and good food make for a memorable experience.

$-$$$ **El Picoteo, Old San Juan.** El Convento Hotel's stylish tapas bar is nothing if not flexible—stop in for an early cocktail and an appetizer, have a full meal, or end the evening with dessert or a nightcap.

$-$$ **La Fonda del Jibarito, Old San Juan.** There are excellent family-run restaurants serving traditional Puerto Rican fare all over the island–this happens to be one of the best.

HISTORY

Fuerte San Felipe del Morro, Old San Juan. El Morro is solid as a rock and even today seems impenetrable. Take a guided tour and see why San Juan was able to fend off invaders for 400 years.

Hacienda Buena Vista, Ponce. The grounds of this former coffee plantation are meticulously maintained, and the guided tours, offered in English and Spanish, are as informative as they come. You'll know how it felt to be a settler taming the wilderness.

Museo de las Américas, Old San Juan. The Museum of the Americas, housed in the impressive 1864 Cuartel de Ballajá military barracks in Old San Juan, has extraordinary folk art collected from throughout North and South America.

Museo de Arte de Ponce, Ponce. The breadth and quality of both European and Puerto Rican art found here is astounding. The collection of Pre-Raphaelite paintings is truly world-class.

Museo de Arte de Puerto Rico, San Juan. The island's premier art museum scours the island for interesting pieces, displays works by contemporary local artists, hosts retrospectives of such island masters as Rafael Tufiño, and mounts shows by international artists.

NATURE

Bahía Mosquito, Vieques. The magnificence of gliding through the sparkling sea creatures at this bioluminescent bay is almost beyond description. Forget special effects and high-tech trickery; here nature beats them hands down.

Bosque Estatal de Guánica. This dry forest is an amazing site with its various forms of cacti and abundant bird life. Hiking here may not be for everyone—it's hot and arid—but you'll love it if you're interested in exotic flora and birds.

Parque de las Cavernas de Río Camuy, Arecibo. The caves are nestled in the island's limestone karst country just south of Arecibo. The tram ride down to them—through wild bamboo and banana plants—is worth the price of admission alone. The large Clara Cave de Empalme is a natural wonder of stalactites, stalagmites, and unique cave life.

El Yunque. With 100 billion gallons of precipitation annually, this protected area truly is a rain forest. Among its sights are 240 tree species and 68 types of birds, including the endangered Puerto Rican green parrot.

BEACHES

Balneario Boquerón, Cabo Rojo. The best of the Cabo Rojo beaches is also a favorite of Puerto Ricans looking for a bit of sand. It's one of the island's most beautiful beaches.

Balneario de Luquillo, Luquillo. This beautiful beach has all the trimmings—including lifeguards, changing rooms, and nearby kiosks where you can find tasty local cuisine and piña coladas. It also has something extra: ocean access for wheelchair users.

El Combate, Cabo Rojo. Especially popular with college students, this beach is lined with interesting rustic restaurants and the scene of frequent summer concerts and festivals.

Playa Crashboat, Aguadilla. The picturesque boats lining the shores here are just part of the appeal. The water has a shimmering, glasslike look and is great for swimming and snorkeling. The shoreline has picnic tables and playground areas.

Playa Flamenco, Culebra. Imagine a long curve of white sand and azure-tinted water. Palm trees wave in the wind. No one is there to claim the spot as theirs. That's what you'll find at this Culebra beach.

Playa de Isla Verde, San Juan. There's a reason this spot is the site for some of the toniest resorts in San Juan—the beach, wide and warm and kissed by the surf, seems to go on forever.

SMART TRAVEL TIPS

Air Travel
Airports & Transfers
Boat & Ferry Travel
Bus Travel
Cameras & Photography
Car Rental
Car Travel
Children in Puerto Rico
Computers on the Road
Consumer Protection
Cruise Travel
Customs & Duties
Disabilities & Accessibility
Discounts & Deals
Eating & Drinking
Ecotourism
Electricity
Embassies & Consulates
Emergencies
English-Language Media
Etiquette & Behavior
Gay & Lesbian Travel
Health
Holidays
Insurance
Language
Lodging
Mail & Shipping
Money Matters
Packing
Passports & Visas
Restrooms
Safety
Senior-Citizen Travel
Shopping
Sports & the Outdoors
Students in Puerto Rico
Taxes
Telephones
Time
Tipping
Tours & Packages
Train Travel
Travel Agencies
Visitor Information
Web Sites

Finding out about your destination before you leave home means you won't squander time organizing everyday minutiae once you've arrived. You'll be more streetwise when you hit the ground as well, better prepared to explore the aspects of Puerto Rico that drew you here in the first place. The organizations in this section can provide information to supplement this guide; contact them for up-to-the-minute details, and consult the A to Z sections that end each chapter for facts on the various topics as they relate to the island's many regions. Happy landings!

AIR TRAVEL

There are many daily flights to Puerto Rico from the United States, and connections are particularly good from the east coast and Midwest; there are even a few nonstop flights from California and London. San Juan's airport is a major hub for travel elsewhere in the Caribbean, so many travelers will make connections there if they don't change planes in Miami. Because of the number of flights, fares to San Juan are among the most reasonably priced to the Caribbean region.

BOOKING

When you book, look for nonstop flights and remember that "direct" flights stop at least once. Try to avoid connecting flights, which require a change of plane. Two airlines may operate a connecting flight jointly, so ask whether your airline operates every segment of the trip; you may find that the carrier you prefer flies you only part of the way. To find more booking tips and to check prices and make online flight reservations, log on to www.fodors.com.

CARRIERS

San Juan's busy Aeropuerto Internacional Luis Muñoz Marín is the Caribbean hub of American Airlines, which flies nonstop from Baltimore, Boston, Chicago, Dallas, Fort Lauderdale, Hartford, Los Angeles, Miami, Newark, New York–JFK, St. Louis, and Washington, DC–Dulles. Continental Airlines flies nonstop from Cleveland, Houston, and Newark (and to

Aguadilla from Newark). Delta flies nonstop from Atlanta and New York–JFK. JetBlue flies nonstop from New York–JFK (and to Aguadilla from New York–JFK, as well). Northwest flies nonstop from Detroit. Spirit Air flies nonstop from Fort Lauderdale and Orlando. United flies nonstop from Chicago, New York–JFK, and Washington, DC–Dulles. US Airways flies nonstop from Baltimore Boston, Charlotte, Philadelphia, and Washington, DC–Dulles.

International carriers serving San Juan include Air Canada from Toronto, Air France from Paris, and British Airways from London.

Puerto Rico is also a good spot from which to hop to other Caribbean islands. American Eagle serves many islands in the Caribbean; Cape Air connects San Juan to St. Thomas and St. Croix, not to mention Ponce; LIAT, based in Antigua, flies to nearly all the Lesser Antilles islands. Vieques Air-Link connects San Juan with Vieques and Culebra.

Airlines **Air Canada** ☎ 888/247-2262 🌐 www.aircanada.com. **Air France** ☎ 800/237-2747 🌐 www.airfrance.com. **American Airlines/American Eagle** ☎ 800/433-7300, 787/791-5050 in San Juan 🌐 www.aa.com. **British Airways** ☎ 800/247-9297 🌐 www.britishairways.com. **Cape Air** ☎ 800/352-0714 🌐 www.flycapeair.com. **Continental** ☎ 800/231-0856 🌐 www.continental.com. **Delta** ☎ 800/221-1212 🌐 www.delta.com. **JetBlue** ☎ 800/538-2583, 787/253-3300 in San Juan 🌐 www.jetblue.com. **LIAT** ☎ 888/844-5428 🌐 www.liatairline.com. **Song** ☎ 800/359-7664 🌐 www.flysong.com. **Spirit Air** ☎ 800/772-7117 🌐 www.spiritair.com. **United Airlines** ☎ 800/864-8331 🌐 www.united.com. **US Airways** ☎ 800/428-4322 🌐 www.usairways.com. **Vieques Air Link** ☎ 787/722-3736 or 888/901-9247 🌐 www.vieques-island.com/val.

CHECK-IN & BOARDING

Always **find out your carrier's check-in policy.** Plan to arrive at the airport about two hours before your scheduled departure time for domestic flights and 2½ to 3 hours before international flights. You may need to arrive earlier if you're flying from one of the busier airports or during peak air-traffic times. To avoid delays at airport-security checkpoints, try not to wear any metal. Jewelry, belt and other buckles, steel-toe shoes, barrettes, and underwire bras are among the items that can set off detectors.

Assuming that not everyone with a ticket will show up, airlines routinely overbook planes. When everyone does, airlines ask for volunteers to give up their seats. In return, these volunteers usually get a several-hundred-dollar flight voucher, which can be used toward the purchase of another ticket, and are rebooked on the next flight out. If there are not enough volunteers, the airline must choose who will be denied boarding. The first to get bumped are passengers who checked in late and those flying on discounted tickets, so get to the gate and check in as early as possible, especially during peak periods.

Always **bring a government-issued photo ID** to the airport; even when it's not required, a passport is best.

CUTTING COSTS

The least expensive airfares to Puerto Rico are priced for round-trip travel and must usually be purchased in advance. Airlines generally allow you to change your return date for a fee; most low-fare tickets, however, are nonrefundable. It's smart to call a number of airlines and check the Internet; when you are quoted a good price, book it on the spot—the same fare may not be available the next day, or even the next hour. Always check different routings and look into using alternate airports. Also, price off-peak flights, which may be significantly less expensive than others. Travel agents, especially low-fare specialists (⇨ Discounts & Deals), are helpful.

Consolidators are another good source. They buy tickets for scheduled flights at reduced rates from the airlines, then sell them at prices that beat the best fare available directly from the airlines. (Many also offer reduced car-rental and hotel rates.) Sometimes you can even get your money back if you need to return the ticket. Carefully read the fine print detailing penalties for changes and cancellations, purchase the ticket with a credit card, and confirm your consolidator reservation with the airline.

If you plan to use Puerto Rico as a base for exploring other Caribbean islands, **look for special island-hopping fares.** LIAT's Caribbean Super Explorer includes unlimited travel for 30 days to any LIAT destination; other passes allow a certain number of additional stopovers during a 21-day period.

Consolidators **AirlineConsolidator.com** ☎ 888/468-5385 🌐 www.airlineconsolidator.com, for international tickets. **Best Fares** ☎ 800/880-1234 or 800/576-8255 🌐 www.bestfares.com; $59.90 annual membership. **Cheap Tickets** ☎ 800/377-1000 or 800/652-4327 🌐 www.cheaptickets.com. **Expedia** ☎ 800/397-3342 or 404/728-8787 🌐 www.expedia.com. **Hotwire** ☎ 866/468-9473 or 920/330-9418 🌐 www.hotwire.com. **Now Voyager Travel** ✉ 45 W. 21st St., Suite 5A New York, NY 10010 ☎ 212/459-1616 📠 212/243-2711 🌐 www.nowvoyagertravel.com. **Onetravel.com** 🌐 www.onetravel.com. **Orbitz** ☎ 888/656-4546 🌐 www.orbitz.com. **Priceline.com** 🌐 www.priceline.com. **Travelocity** ☎ 888/709-5983, 877/282-2925 in Canada, 0870/876-3876 in U.K. 🌐 www.travelocity.com.

Discount Passes **LIAT** ☎ 888/844-5428 🌐 www.liatairline.com.

ENJOYING THE FLIGHT

State your seat preference when purchasing your ticket, and then repeat it when you confirm and when you check in. For more legroom, you can request one of the few emergency-aisle seats at check-in, if you're capable of moving obstacles comparable in weight to an airplane exit door (usually between 35 pounds and 60 pounds)—a Federal Aviation Administration requirement of passengers in these seats. Seats behind a bulkhead also offer more legroom, but they don't have underseat storage. Don't sit in the row in front of the emergency aisle or in front of a bulkhead, where seats may not recline.

Ask the airline whether a snack or meal is served on the flight. If you have dietary concerns, request special meals when booking. These can be vegetarian, low-cholesterol, or kosher, for example. It's a good idea to pack some healthful snacks and a small (plastic) bottle of water in your carry-on bag. On long flights, try to maintain a normal routine, to help fight jet lag. At night, get some sleep. By day, eat light meals, drink water (not alcohol), and **move around the cabin** to stretch your legs. For additional jet-lag tips consult *Fodor's FYI: Travel Fit & Healthy* (available at bookstores everywhere).

Smoking policies vary from carrier to carrier. Many airlines prohibit smoking on all of their flights; others allow smoking only on certain routes or certain departures. Ask your carrier about its policy.

FLYING TIMES

Nonstop flights to San Juan from New York are 3¾ hours; from Miami, 2½ hours; from Atlanta, 3½ hours; from Boston, 4 hours; from Chicago, 4¾ hours; from Los Angeles, 8 hours; from the United Kingdom, 5 hours; from Germany, 9¾ hours.

HOW TO COMPLAIN

If your baggage goes astray or your flight goes awry, complain right away. Most carriers require that you **file a claim immediately.** The Aviation Consumer Protection Division of the Department of Transportation publishes *Fly-Rights,* which discusses airlines and consumer issues and is available online. You can also find articles and information on mytravelrights.com, the Web site of the nonprofit Consumer Travel Rights Center.

Airline Complaints **Aviation Consumer Protection Division** ✉ U.S. Department of Transportation, Office of Aviation Enforcement and Proceedings, C-75, Room 4107, 400 7th St. SW, Washington, DC 20590 ☎ 202/366-2220 🌐 airconsumer.ost.dot.gov. **Federal Aviation Administration Consumer Hotline** ✉ for inquiries: FAA, 800 Independence Ave. SW, Washington, DC 20591 ☎ 800/322-7873 🌐 www.faa.gov.

RECONFIRMING

Check the status of your flight before you leave for the airport. You can do this on your carrier's Web site, by linking to a flight-status checker (many Web booking services offer these), or by calling your carrier or travel agent. Always confirm international flights at least 72 hours ahead of the scheduled departure time.

AIRPORTS & TRANSFERS

The Aeropuerto Internacional Luis Muñoz Marín (airline code SJU) is minutes east of downtown San Juan along the Baldorioty de Castro Highway (Route 26) in the coastal section of Isla Verde. San Juan's other airport, the small Aeropuerto Fernando L. Ribas Dominicci (also known as the Isla Grande Airport), is near the city's Miramar section. From here you can catch Vieques Air-Link flights to Culebra, Vieques, and other destinations on Puerto Rico and throughout the Caribbean. (Note that although the Dominicci airport was still operating at this writing, its future was uncertain.) Other Puerto Rican airports include Mercedita in the south coast town of Ponce, Eugenio María de Hostos in the west coast community of Mayagüez, Rafael Hernández in the northwestern town of Aguadilla (which has the only other direct flights from the U.S. mainland), Antonio Rivera Rodríguez on Vieques, and Benjamín Rivera Noriega on Culebra.

Airport Information **Aeropuerto Antonio Rivera Rodríguez** ☎ 787/741-8358. **Aeropuerto Benjamín Rivera Noriega** ☎ 787/742-0022. **Aeropuerto Eugenio María de Hostos** ☎ 787/833-0148. **Aeropuerto Fernando L. Ribas Dominicci** ☎ 787/729-8711. **Aeropuerto Internacional Luis Muñoz Marín** ☎ 787/791-3840. **Aeropuerto Mercedita** ☎ 787/842-6292. **Aeropuerto Rafael Hernández** ☎ 787/891-2286.

AIRPORT TRANSFERS

From the Aeropuerto Internacional Luis Muñoz Marín into San Juan, *taxis turísticos* charge set rates based on zones. Uniformed and badged officials will help you find a cab (look for the tourism company booth) and hand you a slip with your fare, which you present to your driver. To Isla Verde, the fare is $8; to Condado, $12; to Old San Juan, $16. Prices may be adjusted upward seasonally. The fare will, however, be officially established. Outside the designated tourist areas, make sure the driver sets the meter or else you're at his or her mercy.

Airport Limousine Service provides exclusive prepaid town car service to Isla Verde ($50), Condado ($60), and Old San Juan ($75). The rates are by the trip, not per person. You can also arrange to have the driver take you to other parts of the island. Limousines of Dorado Transport Co-op serve hotels and villas in the Dorado area for $22 per person.

Many hotels offer guests transportation from the airport (either free or at a cost); when booking your room, get the lowdown. You should do the same if you're heading directly out onto the island and don't want to rent a car; many of the larger resorts run regular shuttles.

Taxis & Shuttles **Airport Limousine Service** ☎ 787/791-4745. **Dorado Transport Co-op** ☎ 787/796-1214. **Taxis Turísticos** ☎ 787/721-2400.

DUTY-FREE SHOPPING

Puerto Rico isn't a duty-free island, but you'll find duty-free shops at Luis Muñoz Marín International Airport in San Juan. They're in the terminal boarding areas, and you'll have to show your boarding pass before loading up on watches, liquor, and perfume.

BOAT & FERRY TRAVEL

The Autoridad de los Puertos (Port Authority) ferry between Old San Juan (Pier 2) and Cataño costs a mere 50¢ one-way. It runs daily every 15 or 30 minutes from 5:45 AM until 10 PM. The Fajardo port authority's 400-passenger ferries run between that east coast town and the out islands of Vieques and Culebra; both trips take 90 minutes. The vessels carry cargo and passengers to Vieques three times daily ($2 one-way) and to Culebra twice daily ($2.25 one-way). Additional vessels carry vehicles and large cargo to both islands each weekday morning at 9:30 AM and at 4 PM. Overnight Ferries del Caribe ferries also connect Mayagüez and Santo Domingo. Ships leave from the Zona Portuaria (Ports Zone), past the Holiday Inn on Highway 2.

FARES & SCHEDULES

Get schedules for the Culebra and Vieques ferries by calling the port authority in Fajardo, Vieques, or Culebra. You buy tickets at the ferry dock. Reservations aren't necessary unless you're transporting a vehicle, in which case you should make a reservation at least two weeks in advance and arrive one hour before the departure time. Tickets for the Mayaguëz–Santo Domingo ferry are usually available, but reserve well in advance if you're bringing your car. Most of the year, fares are around $149 per person and an additional $146 for cars; fares are higher from December to January.

Autoridad de los Puertos ☎ 787/788-1155 in San Juan, 787/863-4560 in Fajardo, 787/742-3161 in Culebra, 787/741-4761 in Vieques. **Ferries del Caribe** ☎ 787/832-4800.

BUSINESS HOURS

BANKS & OFFICES

Bank hours are generally weekdays from 8 to 4 or 9 to 5, though a few branches are open Saturday from 9 to noon or 1. Post offices are open weekdays from 7:30 to 4:30 and Saturday from 8 to noon. Government offices are open weekdays from 9 to 5.

GAS STATIONS

Most stations are open daily from early in the morning until 10 or 11 PM. Numerous stations in urban areas are open 24 hours.

MUSEUMS & SIGHTS

As a rule, San Juan area museums are closed on Monday, and in some cases, Sunday. Hours otherwise are 9 or 10 AM to 5 PM, often with an hour off for lunch between noon and 2. Sights managed by the National Parks Service, such as Fuerte San Felipe del Morro and San Cristóbal, are open daily from 9 to 5.

PHARMACIES

In cities, pharmacies are generally open from 9 to 6 or 7 weekdays and on Saturday. Walgreens operates numerous pharmacies around the island; some are open 24 hours.

SHOPS

Street shops are open Monday through Saturday from 9 to 6 (9 to 9 during Christmas holidays); mall stores tend to stay open to 9 or so. Count on convenience stores staying open late into the night, seven days a week. Supermarkets are often closed on Sunday, although some remain open 24-hours, seven days a week.

BUS TRAVEL

The Autoridad Metropolitana de Autobuses (AMA, or Metropolitan Bus Authority) operates *guaguas* (buses) that thread through San Juan, running in exclusive lanes on major thoroughfares and stopping at signs marked PARADA or PARADA DE GUAGUAS. The main terminals are at the Covadonga parking lot and Plaza de Colón in Old San Juan and the Capetillo Terminal in Río Piedras, next to the central business district. Most buses are air-conditioned and have wheelchair lifts and lock-downs.

Bus travel to outlying areas is less than comprehensive. Your best bet for travel to other parts of the island is by rental car or by *públicos*—"public cars," though most are actually 17-passenger vans. They have yellow license plates ending in "P" or "PD," and they scoot to towns throughout the island, stopping in each community's main plaza. They operate primarily during the day; routes and fares are fixed by the public service commission, but schedules aren't set, so you have to call ahead.

In San Juan, the main terminals are at Aeropuerto Internacional Luis Muñoz Marín and at Plaza Colón on the waterfront in Old San Juan. San Juan–based público companies include Blue Line for trips to Aguadilla and the northwest coast, Choferes Unidos de Ponce for Ponce, Línea Caborrojeña for Cabo Rojo and the southwest coast, Línea Boricua for the interior and the southwest, Línea Sultana for Mayagüez and the west coast, and Terminal de Transportación Pública for Fajardo and the east.

FARES & SCHEDULES

In San Juan, bus fares are 25¢ or 50¢, depending on the route, and are paid in exact change upon entering the bus. Buses adhere to their routes, but schedules are fluid, to say the least. Count on a bus passing your stop every 20 to 30 minutes, less frequently on Sunday and holidays. Service starts at around 6 AM and generally lasts until 9 PM. For more information, call the AMA or pick up a schedule at the nearest bus station. The government plans to integrate bus services to work together with the urban train (Tren Urbano), which is was still being built at this writing. Some

AMA buses already have a prepaid fare card that will work on both transportation systems.

AMA ☎ 787/729-1512 or 787/767-7979. **Blue Line** ☎ 787/765-7733. **Choferes Unidos de Ponce** ☎ 787/764-0540. **Línea Boricua** ☎ 787/765-1908. **Línea Caborrojeña** ☎ 787/723-9155. **Línea Sultana** ☎ 787/765-9377. **Terminal de Transportación Pública** ☎ 787/250-0717.

CAMERAS & PHOTOGRAPHY

Frothy waves in a turquoise sea and palm-lined crescents of beach are relatively easy to capture on film or digitally if you don't let the brightness of the sun on sand and water fool your light meter. You must compensate or else work early or late in the day when the light isn't as brilliant and contrast isn't such a problem. Try to capture expansive views of waterfront, beach, or village scenes; consider shooting down onto the shore from a clearing on a hillside or from a rock on the beach. Or zoom in on something colorful, such as a delicate tropical flower or a craftsman at work—but always **ask permission to take pictures of locals or their property.** Use a disposable underwater camera to make your snorkeling and diving adventures more memorable. The *Kodak Guide to Shooting Great Travel Pictures* (available at bookstores everywhere) is loaded with tips.

Photo Help **Kodak Information Center** ☎ 800/242-2424 www.kodak.com.

EQUIPMENT PRECAUTIONS

Don't pack film or equipment in checked luggage, where it is much more susceptible to damage. X-ray machines used to view checked luggage are extremely powerful and therefore are likely to ruin your film. Try to ask for hand inspection of film, which becomes clouded after repeated exposure to airport X-ray machines, and keep videotapes and computer disks away from metal detectors. Always keep film, tape, and computer disks out of the sun. Carry an extra supply of batteries, and be prepared to turn on your camera, camcorder, or laptop to prove to airport security personnel that the device is real.

On the beach, be wary of sand and salt spray—keep your camera and film in a sealed container or bag when not in use. Also, don't leave your camera locked in your rental car's trunk all day—heat can reduce the quality of the film. Never leave your gear unattended on the seats of your car or on the beach, and lock it in your hotel room safe when you go out.

FILM & DEVELOPING

Film of all types is widely available in supermarkets, drugstores, souvenir shops, and photo shops. Count on paying about $7 for a 24-exposure roll of color-print film. In San Juan and other urban areas, numerous film-developing shops and drugstores will get your prints made promptly, although seldom within the one-hour time frame that they advertise.

VIDEOS

The local standard for video players is the same as on the U.S. mainland–NTSC. Travelers from Australia, Britain, and New Zealand, where PAL is the standard, will have to wait until returning home to view their vacation.

CAR RENTAL

Rates start as low as $35 a day (plus insurance), with unlimited mileage. Discounts are often offered for long-term rentals, for cars that are booked more than 72 hours in advance, and to automobile association members. In addition, if you pay using an American Express or many other credit cards, you may not need to buy insurance (check with your credit-card company). All major U.S. car-rental agencies are represented on the island, but be sure to look into local companies. Most are reliable and some offer competitive rates.

If you're visiting during peak season or over holiday weekends reserve your car before arriving on the island—not only because of possible discounts but also to ensure that you get a car and that it's a reliable one. Faced with high demand, the agencies may be forced to drag out the worst of their fleet; waiting unil the last minute could leave you stranded without a car or stranded with one on the side of the road.

You'll find offices for dozens of agencies at San Juan's Aeropuerto Internacional Luis

Muñoz Marín, and a majority of them have shuttle service to and from the airport and the pickup point. Most rental cars are available with automatic or standard transmission. Four-wheel-drive vehicles aren't necessary unless you plan to go way off the beaten path or along the steep, rocky roads of Culebra or Vieques; in most cases a standard compact car will do the trick. If you are given a choice always opt for air-conditioning. You'll be glad you did when it's high noon and you're in a San Juan traffic jam.

Major Agencies **Alamo** ☎ 800/327-9633 🌐 www.alamo.com. **Avis** ☎ 800/331-1212, 800/879-2847 or 800/272-5871 in Canada, 0870/606-0100 in U.K., 02/9353-9000 in Australia, 09/526-2847 in New Zealand 🌐 www.avis.com. **Budget** ☎ 800/527-0700, 0870/156-5656 in U.K. 🌐 www.budget.com. **Dollar** ☎ 800/800-4000, 0800/085-4578 in U.K. 🌐 www.dollar.com. **Hertz** ☎ 800/654-3131, 800/263-0600 in Canada, 0870/844-8844 in U.K., 02/9669-2444 in Australia, 09/256-8690 in New Zealand 🌐 www.hertz.com. **National Car Rental** ☎ 800/227-7368, 0870/600-6666 in U.K. 🌐 www.nationalcar.com.

CUTTING COSTS

For a good deal, book through a travel agent who will shop around. Also, price local car-rental companies—whose prices may be lower still, although their service and maintenance may not be as good as those of major rental agencies—and research rates on the Internet. Consolidators that specialize in air travel can offer good rates on cars as well (⇨ Air Travel). Remember to ask about required deposits, cancellation penalties, and drop-off charges if you're planning to pick up the car in one city and leave it in another. If you're traveling during a holiday period, also make sure that a confirmed reservation guarantees you a car.

Local Agencies **Charlie Car Rental** ☎ 787/791-1101 or 800/289-1227 🌐 www.charliecars.com. **L & M Car Rental** ☎ 787/791-1160 or 800/666-0807. **Target** ☎ 787/728-1447 or 800/934-6457.

INSURANCE

When driving a rented car you are generally responsible for any damage to or loss of the vehicle. You also may be liable for any property damage or personal injury that you may cause while driving. Before you rent, see what coverage you already have under the terms of your personal auto-insurance policy and credit cards.

For about $9 to $25 a day, rental companies sell protection, known as a collision- or loss-damage waiver (CDW or LDW), that eliminates your liability for damage to the car; it's always optional and should never be automatically added to your bill. However, **make sure you have enough coverage to pay for the car.** If you do not have auto insurance or an umbrella policy that covers damage to third parties, purchasing liability insurance and a CDW or LDW is highly recommended.

REQUIREMENTS & RESTRICTIONS

A valid driver's license from your native country can be used in Puerto Rico for three months. In some cases the driver must be at least 25 years old.

SURCHARGES

Before you pick up a car in one city and leave it in another, ask about drop-off charges or one-way service fees, which can be substantial. Also inquire about early-return policies; some rental agencies charge extra if you return the car before the time specified in your contract, whereas others give you a refund for the days not used. To avoid a hefty refueling fee, fill the tank just before you turn in the car, but be aware that gas stations near the rental outlet may overcharge. It's almost never a deal to buy the tank of gas that's in the car when you rent it; the understanding is that you'll return it empty, but some fuel usually remains. Surcharges may apply if you're under 25 or if you take the car outside the area approved by the rental agency. You'll pay extra for child seats (about $8 a day), which are compulsory for children under five, and usually for additional drivers (up to $25 a day, depending on location).

CAR TRAVEL

Several well-marked multilane highways link population centers. Route 26 is the main artery through San Juan, connecting Condado and Old San Juan to Isla Verde and the airport. Route 22, which runs east–west between San Juan and Camuy, and the Luis A. Ferré Expressway (Route 52), which runs north–south between San Juan and Ponce, are toll roads (35¢–50¢). Route 2, a smaller highway, travels along the west coast, and routes 3 and 53 traverse the east shore.

Five highways are particularly noteworthy thanks to their scenery and vistas. The island's tourism authorities have even given them special names. Ruta Panorámica (Panoramic Route) runs east–west through the central mountains. Ruta Cotorra (Puerto Rican Parrot Route) travels along the north coast. Ruta Paso Fino (Paso Fino Horse Route, after a horse breed) takes you north–south and west along the south coast. Ruta Coquí, named for the famous Puerto Rican tree frog, runs along the east coast. Ruta Flamboyán, named after the island tree, goes from San Juan through the mountains to the east coast.

EMERGENCY SERVICES

In an emergency, dial 911. If your car breaks down, call the rental company for a replacement. Before renting, make sure you investigate the company's policy regarding replacement vehicles and repairs out on the island, and ask about surcharges that might be incurred if you break down in a rural area and need a new car.

GASOLINE

All types of fuel—unleaded regular, unleaded super-premium, diesel—are available by the liter. Most stations have both full- and self-service. Hours vary, but stations generally operate daily from early in the morning until 10 or 11 PM; in metro areas many are open 24 hours. Stations are few and far between in the central mountains and other rural areas; plan accordingly. In cities, you can pay with cash and bank or credit cards; in the hinterlands cash is often your only option.

ROAD CONDITIONS

Puerto Rico has some of the Caribbean's best roads. That said, potholes, sharp turns, speed bumps, sudden gradient changes, and poor lighting can make driving difficult. Be especially cautious when driving after heavy rains or hurricanes; roads and bridges might be washed out or damaged. Many of the mountain roads are very narrow and steep, with unmarked curves and cliffs. Locals are familiar with such roads and often drive at high speeds, which can give you quite a scare. When traveling on a narrow, curving road, it's best to honk your horn as you take any sharp turn.

Traffic around cities—particularly San Juan, Ponce, and Mayagüez—is heavy at rush hours (weekdays from 7 to 10 and 4 to 7).

ROAD MAPS

Most car-rental agencies give you a free map with your car; more detailed maps are available in bookstores, drugstores, and souvenir shops. Look for the *Puerto Rico Mapa de Carreteras* (about $7), by Metro Data Maps, which features an island map; a large metro map of San Juan; and insets of Aguadilla, Mayagüez, Arecibo, Ponce, and other large towns. Also, look for the free *Puerto Rico Travel Maps* at tourism company offices and information booths.

RULES OF THE ROAD

U.S. driving laws apply in Puerto Rico, and you'll find no problem with signage or directionals. Street and highway signs are most often in Spanish but use international symbols; brushing up on a few key Spanish terms before your trip will help. The following words and phrases are especially useful: *calle* (street), *calle sin salida* (dead end, no exit), *cruce de peatones* (pedestrian crossing), *cuidado* (caution), *desvío* (detour), *estación de peaje* (toll booth), *no entre* (do not enter), *prohibido adelantar* (no passing), *salida* (exit), *tránsito* (one way), *zona escolar* (school zone).

Distances are posted in kilometers (1.6 km to 1 mi), whereas speed limits are posted in miles per hour. Speeding and drunk-driving penalties are much the same here as on the mainland. Police cars often travel with their lights flashing, so it's difficult to know when they're trying to pull you over. If the siren is on, move to the right to get out of their way. If the lights are on, it's best to pull over—just be sure that the vehicle is a *marked* police car before doing so.

CHILDREN IN PUERTO RICO

With miles of beach and plenty of outdoor activities, the island is a good family destination, and Puerto Ricans themselves are very family-oriented. The Puerto Rico Tourism Company's free publication *Qué Pasa*—available at all their offices—lists children's events. If you are renting a car, don't forget to arrange for a car seat when you reserve. For general advice about traveling with children, consult *Fodor's FYI: Travel with Your Baby* (available in bookstores everywhere).

FLYING

If your children are two or older, ask about children's airfares. As a general rule, infants under two not occupying a seat fly at greatly reduced fares or even for free. But if you want to guarantee a seat for an infant, you have to pay full fare. Consider flying during off-peak days and times; most airlines will grant an infant a seat without a ticket if there are available seats. When booking, confirm carry-on allowances if you're traveling with infants. In general, for babies charged 10% to 50% of the adult fare you are allowed one carry-on bag and a collapsible stroller; if the flight is full, the stroller may have to be checked or you may be limited to less.

Experts agree that it's a good idea to use safety seats aloft for children weighing less than 40 pounds. Airlines set their own policies: if you use a safety seat, U.S. carriers usually require that the child be ticketed, even if he or she is young enough to ride free, because the seats must be strapped into regular seats. And even if you pay the full adult fare for the seat, it may be worth it, especially on longer trips. Do **check your airline's policy about using safety seats during takeoff and landing.** Safety seats are not allowed everywhere in the plane, so get your seat assignments as early as possible.

When reserving, request children's meals or a freestanding bassinet (not available at all airlines) if you need them. But note that bulkhead seats, where you must sit to use the bassinet, may lack an overhead bin or storage space on the floor.

FOOD

Children tend to enjoy many Puerto Rican dishes, but there are plenty of options for those who shy away from new or different foods. You're never far from a Burger King or a Pizza Hut, and island supermarkets stock familiar brands of cereals, snacks, and other items. When thoroughly washed and/or peeled, fresh fruit is often a treat for even the most finicky eaters.

Many restaurants, including those in hotels, offer children's menus. Note that the legal drinking age on Puerto Rico is a loosely enforced 18.

LODGING

In general, kids are welcome at island resorts and hotels, many of which have children's activity centers or programs, wading pools, and babysitting services. Some resorts also have video games rooms, in-room videos, or in-room "movies on demand" with films for children and safeguards that allow you to block out adult flicks. When reserving your hotel room ask about children's programs and amenities.

Most hotels in Puerto Rico allow children under a certain age to stay in their parents' room at no extra charge, but others charge for them as extra adults; be sure to find out the cutoff age for children's discounts.

Best Choices **Copamarina Beach Resort** ✉ Rte. 333, Km 6.5, Box 805, Guánica 00653 ☎ 787/821-0505 or 800/468-4553 📠 787/821-0070 🌐 www.copamarina.com. **Hyatt Dorado Beach Resort & Country Club** ✉ Rte. 693, Km 10.8, Dorado 00646 ☎ 787/796-1234 or 800/233-1234 🌐 www.doradobeach.hyatt.com. **Westin Río Mar Beach Resort** ✉ 6000 Río Mar Blvd., Box 2006, Barrio Palmer, Río Grande 00721 ☎ 787/888-6000 🌐 www.starwood.com. **Wyndham Condado Plaza Hotel & Casino** ✉ 999 Av. Ashford, Condado, San Juan 00902 ☎ 787/721-1000 or 800/468-8588, 800/624-0420 🌐 www.wyndham.com. **Wyndham El Conquistador Resort & Country Club** ✉ 1000 Av. El Conquistador, Box 70001, Fajardo 00738 ☎ 787/863-1000, 800/996-3426, or 800/468-5228 🌐 www.wyndham.com. **Wyndham El San Juan**

Hotel & Casino ✉ 6063 Av. Isla Verde, Box 2872, Isla Verde, San Juan 00902 ☎ 787/791-1000, 800/468-2818, or 800/996-3426.

PRECAUTIONS

The sun can be the greatest danger to children. Be sure to stock up on sun screen with a high SPF. Some island flowers—which are very bright and attractive to children—are actually poisonous. It's best to encourage your kids to look but not touch. At the beach, watch out for jellyfish, which are particularly abundant in winter, in the water or on the sand and spiky sea urchins, which are often embedded in rocks under water.

SIGHTS & ATTRACTIONS

Puerto Rico offers many sights and attractions that are particularly suitable for kids. Places that are especially appealing to children are indicated by a rubber-duckie icon (🐤) in the margin.

The Museo del Niño (Children's Museum) in Old San Juan has interactive exhibits. The Parque de las Cavernas del Río Camuy (Río Camuy Cave Park) offers an educational video and a trolley ride through a cave system. The Parque de las Ciencias Luis A. Ferré (Luis A. Ferré Science Park) has a planetarium, educational exhibits, and a small zoo. The Parque Zoológico de Puerto Rico (Puerto Rico Zoo) in Mayagüez houses a wide array of animals. There's also a lot to be said for flying kites at El Morro and feeding pigeons at Parque de Palomas in Old San Juan as well as splashing about or building sand castles at a beach just about anywhere on the island.

Best Choices **Museo del Niño** ✉ 150 Calle Cristo, Old San Juan, San Juan ☎ 787/722-3791. **Parque de las Cavernas del Río Camuy** ✉ Rte. 129, Km 18.9, Arecibo ☎ 787/898-3100. **Parque de las Ciencias Luis A. Ferré** ✉ Rte. 167, Bayamón ☎ 787/740-6878. **Parque Zoológico de Puerto Rico** ✉ Rte. 108, Miradero Sector, Mayagüez ☎ 787/834-8110.

SUPPLIES & EQUIPMENT

American brands of baby food, diapers, and other infant necessities are easy to find in any grocery store, drug store, or American chain such as Walmart, Sams, or Kmart. Baby formula is available in premixed and powdered form. Note that most supplies are more expensive than in the United States; some premixed formulas cost twice as much as they would on the mainland.

COMPUTERS ON THE ROAD

It's easy to plug in at many hotels, which are now frequently equipped with dedicated fax/modem lines and plenty of outlets. Still, it's a good idea to carry an extra battery as well as a small extension cord for those cases when the only outlet is behind the headboard of the bed.

More and more copy shops and cybercafés are popping up, especially in San Juan. Although service in such places is reliable, your hotel's business center is probably the best place to surf the Web. Many of the big hotels in San Juan now offer wireless Internet service, though usually for a fee.

Internet Access **Cigar Box** ✉ Plazoleta de Isla Verde #6150, L-15, Isla Verde, San Juan ☎ 787/253-2336. **CyberNet Café** ✉ 1128 Av. Ashford, Condado, San Juan ☎ 787/724-4033 ✉ 5575 Av. Isla Verde, Isla Verde, San Juan ☎ 787/791-3138. **Diner's Restaurant** ✉ 357 Calle San Francisco, Old San Juan, San Juan ☎ 787/723-4616.

CONSUMER PROTECTION

Whether you're shopping for gifts or purchasing travel services, **pay with a major credit card** whenever possible, so you can cancel payment or get reimbursed if there's a problem (and you can provide documentation). If you're doing business with a particular company for the first time, contact your local Better Business Bureau and the attorney general's offices in your state and (for U.S. businesses) the company's home state as well. Have any complaints been filed? Finally, if you're buying a package or tour, always consider travel insurance that includes default coverage (⇨ Insurance).

BBBs **Council of Better Business Bureaus** ✉ 4200 Wilson Blvd., Suite 800, Arlington, VA 22203 ☎ 703/276-0100 📠 703/525-8277 🌐 www.bbb.org.

CRUISE TRAVEL

Puerto Rico is a major cruise destination and a common port of embarkation for cruises on southern Caribbean routes. Cruising is a relaxing and convenient way to tour this beautiful part of the world. You get all of the amenities of a luxury hotel and enough activities to guarantee fun, even on the occasional rainy day. All your important decisions are made long before you board. Your itinerary is set, and you know the total cost of your vacation beforehand.

Ships usually call at several ports on a single voyage but are at each port for only one day. Thus, although you may be exposed to several islands, you don't get much of a feel for any one of them.

To learn how to plan, choose, and book a cruise-ship voyage, consult *Fodor's FYI: Plan & Enjoy Your Cruise* (available in bookstores everywhere).

Puerto Rico's main cruise-ship docks are in the San Juan metropolitan area. Most of the time, vessels dock at the piers in Old San Juan, though during the busy high season they often must dock at Isla Grande's Pan American Pier or Puerta de Tierra's Frontier Pier. Públicos, taxis, and tour buses meet passengers at the piers. Públicos have fixed fees from the piers to main tourist areas: $16 to and from the airport and Isla Verde, $10 to and from Condado and Miramar, and $6 to and from Old San Juan and Puerta de Tierra. Monday and Tuesday are big days for ships to dock in the old city.

Cruise Lines **Carnival Cruise Lines** ✉ 3655 N. W. 87th Ave., Miami, FL 33178 ☎ 305/599-2600 or 888/227-6482 🌐 www.carnival.com. **Celebrity Cruises** ✉ 1050 Caribbean Way, Miami, FL 33122 ☎ 305/539-6000 or 800/221-4789, 800/668-6166 in Canada 🌐 www.celebrity.com. **Costa Cruise Lines** ✉ 200 South Park Rd., Suite 200, Hollywood, FL 33021 ☎ 954/266-5600 or 800/332-6782 🌐 www.costacruises.com. **Cunard Line** ✉ 6100 Blue Lagoon Dr., Suite 400, Miami, FL 33126 ☎ 305/463-3000 or 800/728-6273 🌐 www.cunardline.com. **Holland America Line** ✉ 300 Elliott Ave. W, Seattle, WA 98119 ☎ 206/281-3535 or 800/626-9900 🌐 www.hollandamerica.com. **Norwegian Cruise Line** ✉ 7665 Corporate Center Dr., Miami, FL 33126 ☎ 305/436-4000 or 800/323-1308 🌐 www.ncl.com. **Princess Cruises** ✉ 24303 Town Center Dr., Santa Clarita, CA 91355 ☎ 661/753-0000 or 800/774-6237 🌐 www.princesscruises.com. **Radisson Seven Seas Cruises** ✉ 600 Corporate Dr., Suite 410, Fort Lauderdale, FL 33334 ☎ 954/776-6123 or 800/285-1835 🌐 www.rssc.com. **Royal Caribbean International** ✉ 1050 Caribbean Way, Miami, FL 33132 ☎ 305/539-6000 or 800/327-6700 🌐 www.royalcaribbean.com. **The Yachts of Seabourn** ✉ 6100 Blue Lagoon Dr., Suite 400, Miami, FL 33126 ☎ 305/463-3000 or 800/929-9395 🌐 www.seabourn.com.

Organization **Cruise Lines International Association** ✉ 500 5th Ave., Suite 1407, New York, NY 10010 ☎ 212/921-0066.

Port Information **Autoridad de Puertos de Puerto Rico** ☎ 787/723-2260. **Terminal de San Juan** ☎ 787/729-8714.

CUSTOMS & DUTIES

When shopping abroad, keep receipts for all purchases. Upon reentering the country, **be ready to show customs officials what you've bought.** Pack purchases together in an easily accessible place. If you think a duty is incorrect, appeal the assessment. If you object to the way your clearance was handled, note the inspector's badge number. In either case, first ask to see a supervisor. If the problem isn't resolved, write to the appropriate authorities, beginning with the port director at your point of entry.

IN AUSTRALIA

Australian residents who are 18 or older may bring home A$400 worth of souvenirs and gifts (including jewelry), 250 cigarettes or 250 grams of cigars or other tobacco products, and 1,125 ml of alcohol (including wine, beer, and spirits). Residents under 18 may bring back A$200 worth of goods. Members of the same family traveling together may pool their allowances. Prohibited items include meat products. Seeds, plants, and fruits need to be declared upon arrival.

Australian Customs Service Regional Director, Box 8, Sydney, NSW 2001 ☎ 02/9213-2000 or 1300/363263, 02/9364-7222 or 1800/020-504 quarantine-inquiry line 📠 02/9213-4043 🌐 www.customs.gov.au.

IN CANADA

Canadian residents who have been out of Canada for at least seven days may bring in C$750 worth of goods duty-free. If you've been away fewer than seven days but more than 48 hours, the duty-free allowance drops to C$200. If your trip lasts 24 to 48 hours, the allowance is C$50. You may not pool allowances with family members. Goods claimed under the C$750 exemption may follow you by mail; those claimed under the lesser exemptions must accompany you. Alcohol and tobacco products may be included in the seven-day and 48-hour exemptions but not in the 24-hour exemption. If you meet the age requirements of the province or territory through which you reenter Canada, you may bring in, duty-free, 1.5 liters of wine *or* 1.14 liters (40 imperial ounces) of liquor *or* 24 12-ounce cans or bottles of beer or ale. Also, if you meet the local age requirement for tobacco products, you may bring in, duty-free, 200 cigarettes and 50 cigars. Check ahead of time with the Canada Customs and Revenue Agency or the Department of Agriculture for policies regarding meat products, seeds, plants, and fruits.

You may send an unlimited number of gifts (only one gift per recipient, however) worth up to C$60 each duty-free to Canada. Label the package UNSOLICITED GIFT—VALUE UNDER $60. Alcohol and tobacco are excluded.

Canada Customs and Revenue Agency ✉ 2265 St. Laurent Blvd., Ottawa, Ontario K1G 4K3 ☎ 800/461-9999 in Canada, 204/983-3500, 506/636-5064 🌐 www.ccra.gc.ca.

IN NEW ZEALAND

All homeward-bound residents may bring back NZ$700 worth of souvenirs and gifts; passengers may not pool their allowances, and children can claim only the concession on goods intended for their own use. For those 17 or older, the duty-free allowance also includes 4.5 liters of wine or beer; one 1,125-ml bottle of spirits; and either 200 cigarettes, 250 grams of tobacco, 50 cigars, *or* a combination of the three up to 250 grams. Meat products, seeds, plants, and fruits must be declared upon arrival to the Agricultural Services Department.

New Zealand Customs ✉ Head office: The Customhouse, 17-21 Whitmore St., Box 2218, Wellington ☎ 09/300-5399 or 0800/428-786 🌐 www.customs.govt.nz.

IN PUERTO RICO

U.S. citizens and legal residents need not clear customs in Puerto Rico when arriving from the mainland. Otherwise, clearing U.S. Customs in Puerto Rico is fast and efficient, provided you've filled out all customs forms and declared all items, including fruits and vegetables, plants and plant products, meat and meat products, and live animals and wildlife products. Pets and birds can enter Puerto Rico subject to certification, permits, inspection, and quarantine rules that vary with the animal and its origin.

When leaving Puerto Rico for the mainland, you must pass your bag through a checkpoint of the U.S. Department of Agriculture's (USDA) Animal and Plant Health Inspection Service (APHIS). The list of organic products that can be transported from Puerto Rico to the States includes avocados, bananas, breadfruits, citrus fruits, ginger, papayas, and plantains.

U.S. Customs and Border Protection ✉ For inquiries and equipment registration, 1300 Pennsylvania Ave. NW, Washington, DC 20229 🌐 www.cbp.gov ☎ 877/287-8667, or 202/354-1000 ✉ For complaints, Customer Satisfaction Unit, 1300 Pennsylvania Ave. NW, Room 5.2C, Washington, DC 20229.

IN THE U.K.

From countries outside the European Union, including Puerto Rico, you may bring home, duty-free, 200 cigarettes, 50 cigars, 100 cigarillos, or 250 grams of tobacco; 1 liter of spirits or 2 liters of fortified or sparkling wine or liqueurs; 2 liters of still table wine; 60 ml of perfume; 250 ml of toilet water; plus £145 worth of other goods, including gifts and souvenirs. Prohibited items include meat and dairy products, seeds, plants, and fruits.

HM Customs and Excise ✉ Portcullis House, 21 Cowbridge Rd. E, Cardiff CF11 9SS ☎ 0845/010-9000, 0208/929-0152 advice service, 0208/929-6731, 0208/910-3602 complaints 🌐 www.hmce.gov.uk.

DISABILITIES & ACCESSIBILITY

As a commonwealth of the United States, Puerto Rico complies with regulations of the Americans with Disabilities Act (ADA). For information on accessibility in Puerto Rico, contact the Northeast Disability &

Business Technical Assistance Center of the United Cerebral Palsy Associations of New Jersey.

Parking for travelers with disabilities is readily available in most places, and many towns have curbs cut to accommodate wheelchairs. Note that Old San Juan's cobblestone streets, narrow alleys, and steep hills are problematic for travelers in wheelchairs.

Local Resources **Northeast Disability & Business Technical Assistance Center** ✉ 354 S. Broad St., Trenton, NJ 08608 ☎ 800/949-4232.

LODGING

Despite the Americans with Disabilities Act, the definition of accessibility seems to differ from hotel to hotel. Some properties may be accessible by ADA standards for people with mobility problems but not for people with hearing or vision impairments, for example.

If you have mobility problems, ask for the lowest floor on which accessible services are offered. If you have a hearing impairment, check whether the hotel has devices to alert you visually to the ring of the telephone, a knock at the door, and a fire/emergency alarm. Some hotels provide these devices without charge. Discuss your needs with hotel personnel if this equipment isn't available, so that a staff member can personally alert you in the event of an emergency.

If you're bringing a guide dog, get authorization ahead of time and write down the name of the person with whom you spoke.

RESERVATIONS

When discussing accessibility with an operator or reservations agent, ask hard questions. Are there any stairs, inside *or* out? Are there grab bars next to the toilet *and* in the shower/tub? How wide is the doorway to the room? To the bathroom? For the most extensive facilities meeting the latest legal specifications, opt for newer accommodations. If you reserve through a toll-free number, consider also calling the hotel's local number to confirm the information from the central reservations office. Get confirmation in writing when you can.

SIGHTS & ATTRACTIONS

Public attractions—including beaches as well as museums and galleries—are subject to ADA regulations. In some cases, however, phones, rest rooms, displays, and trails or other parts of a given sight aren't fully accessible to people with mobility, vision, or hearing problems.

In a quick survey of the island's top attractions, the following have limited accessibility: Hacienda Buena Vista in Ponce, Las Cabezas de San Juan in Las Croabas, El Morro and the Catedral de San Juan in Old San Juan, and the Bosque Nacional del Caribe (Caribbean National Forest), commonly known as El Yunque, in eastern Puerto Rico. (Note that a wheelchair-accessible trail with Braille markers is on the drawing board for El Yunque).

One of the most accessible sights for travelers with mobility problems is Balneario de Luquillo, a palm-lined public beach in eastern Puerto Rico. Its Mar Sin Barreras (Sea Without Barriers) includes a ramp that enables wheelchair users to take a dip.

TRANSPORTATION

San Juan's Luis Muñoz Marín International Airport is well equipped for travelers with disabilities. You disembark on jetways straight into the airport, thus avoiding the steep airplane stairways common in the Caribbean. Public rest rooms and phones are accessible, and, if necessary, airport personnel can help you through long walkways, through baggage claim, and through customs and immigration. Just be sure to request wheelchairs and escorts when booking your flights.

Most public buses are equipped with wheelchair lifts and lockdowns, and taxis and públicos can fit chairs in their trunks. Public parking lots have designated spots for travelers with disabilities, and although car-rental agencies don't issue tags or placards, you can use yours from home. With advance notice (at least a week) major car-rental agencies like Avis can equip vehicles with hand controls and other devices and deliver the car to you at the arrivals area. Wheelchair Getaway in San Juan offers transportation from airports and cruise-ship docks to San Juan hotels. The company also has city sightseeing tours.

Complaints **Aviation Consumer Protection Division** (⇨ Air Travel) for airline-related problems. **Departmental Office of Civil Rights** ✉ For general inquiries, U.S. Department of Transportation, S-30, 400 7th St. SW, Room 10215, Washington, DC 20590 ☎ 202/366-4648 ⎙ 202/366-9371 🌐 www.dot.gov/ost/docr/index.htm. **Disability Rights Section** ✉ NYAV, U.S. Department of Justice, Civil Rights Division, 950 Pennsylvania Ave. NW, Washington, DC 20530 ☎ ADA information line 202/514-0301, 800/514-0301, 202/514-0383 TTY, 800/514-0383 TTY 🌐 www.ada.gov. **U.S. Department of Transportation Hotline** ☎ For disability-related air-travel problems, 800/778-4838, 800/455-9880 TTY.

Local Contacts **Wheelchair Getaway** ☎ 800/868-8028 or 787/883-0131.

TRAVEL AGENCIES

In the United States, the Americans with Disabilities Act requires that travel firms serve the needs of all travelers. Some agencies specialize in working with people with disabilities.

Travelers with Mobility Problems **Access Adventures/B. Roberts Travel** ✉ 206 Chestnut Ridge Rd., Scottsville, NY 14624 ☎ 585/889-9096 🌐 www.brobertstravel.com ✉ dltravel@prodigy.net, run by a former physical-rehabilitation counselor. **CareVacations** ✉ No. 5, 5110-50 Ave., Leduc, Alberta, Canada, T9E 6V4 ☎ 780/986-6404 or 877/478-7827 ⎙ 780/986-8332 🌐 www.carevacations.com, for group tours and cruise vacations. **Flying Wheels Travel** ✉ 143 W. Bridge St., Box 382, Owatonna, MN 55060 ☎ 507/451-5005 ⎙ 507/451-1685 🌐 www.flyingwheelstravel.com.

Travelers with Developmental Disabilities **New Directions** ✉ 5276 Hollister Ave., Suite 207, Santa Barbara, CA 93111 ☎ 805/967-2841 or 888/967-2841 ⎙ 805/964-7344 🌐 www.newdirectionstravel.com. **Sprout** ✉ 893 Amsterdam Ave., New York, NY 10025 ☎ 212/222-9575 or 888/222-9575 ⎙ 212/222-9768 🌐 www.gosprout.org.

DISCOUNTS & DEALS

Be a smart shopper and compare all your options before making decisions. A plane ticket bought with a promotional coupon from travel clubs, coupon books, and direct-mail offers or purchased on the Internet may not be cheaper than the least expensive fare from a discount ticket agency. And always keep in mind that what you get is just as important as what you save.

DISCOUNT RESERVATIONS

To save money, look into discount reservations services with Web sites and toll-free numbers, which use their buying power to get a better price on hotels, airline tickets (⇨ Air Travel), even car rentals. When booking a room, always **call the hotel's local toll-free number** (if one is available) rather than the central reservations number—you'll often get a better price. Always ask about special packages or corporate rates.

Airline Tickets **Air 4 Less** ☎ 800/AIR4LESS; low-fare specialist.

Hotel Rooms **Accommodations Express** ☎ 800/444-7666 or 800/277-1064 🌐 www.acex.net. **Hotels.com** ☎ 800/246-8357 🌐 www.hotels.com. **Quikbook** ☎ 800/789-9887 🌐 www.quikbook.com. **Turbotrip.com** ☎ 800/473-7829 🌐 www.turbotrip.com.

PACKAGE DEALS

Don't confuse packages and guided tours. When you buy a package, you travel on your own, just as though you had planned the trip yourself. Fly–drive packages, which combine airfare and car rental, are often a good deal. In cities, ask the local visitor's bureau about hotel and local transportation packages that include tickets to major museum exhibits or other special events.

EATING & DRINKING

Throughout the island you'll find everything from French haute cuisine to sushi bars, as well as superb local eateries serving *comidas criollas,* traditional Caribbean-creole meals. Note that the *mesón gastronómico* label is used by the government to recognize restaurants that preserve culinary traditions. The restaurants we list are the cream of the crop in each price category. Properties indicated by a ✕🏨 are lodging establishments whose restaurant warrants a special trip.

MEAL TIMES

Puerto Ricans' eating habits mirror those of their counterparts on the mainland United States: they eat breakfast, lunch, and dinner, though they don't tend to down coffee all day long. Instead, islanders like a steaming, high-test cup in the morning and another between 2 and 4 PM. They may finish a meal with coffee, but they never drink coffee *during* a meal.

Unless otherwise noted, the restaurants listed in this guide are open daily for lunch and dinner. People tend to eat dinner late in Puerto Rico; you may find yourself alone in the restaurant if you eat at 5 PM; at 6, business will pick up a little, and from 7 to 10, it may be quite busy.

RESERVATIONS & DRESS

Reservations are always a good idea; we mention them only when they're essential or not accepted. Book as far ahead as you can, and reconfirm as soon as you arrive. (Large parties should always call ahead to check the reservations policy.) We mention dress only when men are required to wear a jacket or a jacket and tie. Puerto Ricans generally dress up to go out, particularly in the evenings. And always remember: beach attire is only for the beach.

SPECIALTIES

Puerto Rican cooking uses lots of local vegetables: plantains are cooked a hundred different ways—as *tostones* (fried green), *amarillos* (baked ripe), and as chips. Rice and beans with tostones or amarillos are basic accompaniments to every dish. Locals cook white rice with *habichuelas* (red beans), *achiote* (annatto seeds), or saffron; brown rice with *gandules* (pigeon peas); and *morro* (black rice) with frijoles *negros* (black beans). Garbanzos and white beans are served in many daily specials. Assorted yams and other root vegetables such as yucca and yautía are served baked, fried, stuffed, boiled, mashed, and whole. *Sofrito*—a garlic, onion, sweet pepper, coriander, oregano, and tomato puree—is used as a base for practically everything.

Beef, chicken, pork, and seafood are rubbed with *adobo,* a garlic-oregano marinade, before cooking; the practice is said to date from the time of the Taínos. *Arroz con pollo* (chicken with rice), *sancocho* (beef or chicken and tuber soup), *asopao* (a soupy rice gumbo with chicken or seafood), and *encebollado* (steak smothered in onions) are all typical plates. Other traditional favorites, found in abundance during the Christmas holidays, are *lechón* (roast pork) and *pastelles,* a kind of Puerto Rican tamale made of meat and condiment stuffed inside plantain paste, which is then wrapped in a plantain leaf and tied off for boiling. The Cayey barrio of Guavaté, a pleasant 45-minute drive from San Juan, is known for its roast pork, and another favorite, *morcilla,* a black spicy sausage.

Fritters are a Puerto Rican specialty served in snack bars along the highways and beaches as well as at cocktail parties. You may find *empanadillas* (stuffed fried turnovers), *sorullitos* (cheese-stuffed corn sticks), *alcapurrias* (stuffed green banana croquettes), and *bacalaítos* (codfish fritters).

Caribbean lobster (not as sweet as the Maine variety) is available mainly at small coastal restaurants, and there's always lots of fresh dolphinfish and red snapper. Conch is prepared in a chilled ceviche salad or stuffed inside fritters with tomato sauce. Local *pan de agua* is an excellent French-style bread, best hot out of the oven. It's also good toasted and should be tried as part of a *cubano* sandwich (roast pork, ham, Swiss cheese, pickles, and mustard). Local desserts include flans, puddings, and fruit pastes served with native white cheese. The renowned locally grown coffee is excellent served espresso-black or generously cut *con leche* (with hot milk).

WINE, BEER & SPIRITS

Puerto Rico isn't a notable producer of wine, but there are several well-crafted local beers to choose from. Legends trace the birthplace of the piña colada to any number of San Juan establishments, from the Caribe Hilton to a Calle La Fortaleza bar. Puerto Rican rum is popular mixed with cola (known as a *cuba libre*), soda, tonic, juices, or water, or served on the rocks or even straight up. Rums range from light mixers to dark, aged sipping liqueurs. Look for Bacardí, Don Q, Ron Rico, Palo Viejo, and Barrilito. The drinking age in Puerto Rico is 18.

ECOTOURISM

The Puerto Rico government and numerous private organizations are combatting the depletion of the island's natural resources. The Conservation Trust of Puerto Rico has acquired lands with ecological and historical significance. Among them are Las Cabezas de San Juan in Las Croabas—which contains several ecosystems common to Puerto Rico—and sections of the Bahía Fosforescente (Phosphorescent Bay) in La Parguera. El Yunque's 28,000 acres are managed by the U.S. Forest Service.

ELECTRICITY

Puerto Rico uses the same 110-volt AC (60-cycle), two-prong-outlet electrical system as in North America. Plugs have two flat pins set parallel to each another. European visitors should bring adapters and converters, or call ahead to to see whether their hotel has them on hand.

EMBASSIES & CONSULATES

There are no foreign embassies in Puerto Rico, but Canada and the United Kingdom have consulates in San Juan. Australia and New Zealand don't have consulates on Puerto Rico.

British Consulate ✉ Bank Trust Plaza, Suite 807, 265 Av. Ponce de León, Hato Rey, San Juan 00917 ☎ 787/758-9828. **Canadian Consulate** ✉ 33 Calle Bolivia, Hato Rey, San Juan 00917 ☎ 787/794-1205.

EMERGENCIES

Emergencies are handled by dialing 911. You can expect a quick response by police, fire, and medical personnel, most of whom speak at least some English. San Juan's Tourist Zone Police are particularly helpful to visitors.

Ambulance, police, and fire ☎ 911. **Air Ambulance Service** ☎ 800/633-3590 or 787/756-3424. **Dental Emergencies** ☎ 787/722-2351 or 787/795-0320. **Fire Department** ☎ 787/343-2330. **Medical Emergency** ☎ 787/754-2222. **Police** ☎ 787/343-2020. **Tourist Zone Police** ☎ 787/726-7020, 787/726-7015 for Condado, 787/728-4770 or 787/726-2981 for Isla Verde. **Travelers' Aid** ☎ 787/791-1054 or 787/791-1034.

ENGLISH-LANGUAGE MEDIA

BOOKS

Most bookstores carry books in both English and Spanish, and you'll find the standard English-language paperbacks at supermarkets and drugstores, with prices comparable to those in the United States.

Bookstores **Bell Book & Candle** ✉ 102 Av. de Diego, Santurce, San Juan ☎ 787/728-5000. **Borders** ✉ Plaza Las Américas, 525 Av. Franklin Delano Roosevelt, Hato Rey, San Juan ☎ 787/777-0916. **Castle Books** ✉ San Patricio Plaza, Guaynabo ☎ 787/774-1790. **Cronopios** ✉ 255 Calle San José, Old San Juan, San Juan ☎ 787/724-1815. **La Tertulia** ✉ Calle Amalia Marín y González, Río Piedras ☎ 787/765-1148. **Thekes** ✉ Plaza Las Américas, 525 Av. Franklin Delano Roosevelt, Hato Rey, San Juan ☎ 787/765-1539.

NEWSPAPERS & MAGAZINES

Puerto Rico's Pulitzer prize–winning *San Juan Star* is printed daily (45¢) in Spanish and English. It carries local and syndicated columnists as well as a good mix of local and international news. *Caribbean Business* offers a comprehensive weekly lowdown on major local and international business issues. In addition, you can get copies of the *Wall Street Journal, New York Times, USA Today, Miami Herald,* and other nationally distributed U.S. newspapers, most often at hotels and drugstores. For the most comprehensive weekly listing of activities and events in the San Juan metropolitan area, pick up a copy of *Voices,* the region's alternative newsweekly. Although most of the editorial content is in Spanish, the entertainment listings are completely in English.

RADIO & TELEVISION

Most local TV programs are in Spanish, and consist of the usual mix of news, game shows, movies, soaps, and music videos. Some local shows broadcast in English, but the majority of English programming comes from cable-transmitted HBO, CNN, and others.

Radio programs run the gamut of Spanish talk shows, Miami-based English news broadcasts, evangelical religious broadcasts, and music of all sorts in both

English and Spanish. Radio WOSO (1030 AM) is a local English-language radio station.

ETIQUETTE & BEHAVIOR

In general, islanders have a strong sense of religion—as evidenced by the numerous Catholic patron-saint festivals held throughout the year. Family ties are also strong, and it's not unusual to see families piling onto the beaches on weekends for a day of fun and barbecue. Puerto Ricans tend to proffer a great deal of respect to their elders, in formal greetings, language, and general attitude.

Many islanders are conservative in dress and manners, despite a penchant for frenetic music and dance. Typical greetings between female friends and male and female friends and relatives is a kiss on the cheek, and the greetings "*Buenos días*" ("Good day"), "*Buenos tardes*" ("Good afternoon"), and "*Buenas noches*" ("Good evening") are among a host of formal and less formal colloquial greetings. The phrases are also said in departing.

Although you may be spending a great deal of time on the beach, it's important to wear a shirt and shoes when entering any indoor business establishments. It's considered highly disrespectful to enter a store or a restaurant in a bathing suit or other inappropriate attire.

Islanders' knowledge of U.S. culture is thorough. Many Puerto Ricans have spent a great deal of time stateside, and those who haven't inevitably have relatives or friends living on the mainland. U.S. music, dress, and attitudes have infiltrated the culture, especially among the young, but the overriding cues are Spanish-Caribbean. Indeed, Puerto Ricans have a strong sense of identity, marked by often-ferocious debates over the island's political destiny.

GAY & LESBIAN TRAVEL

Although prevailing local attitudes toward same-sex couples are similar to those in the states, normal precautions regarding overt behavior stand: Puerto Ricans tend to be conservative in matters of sexuality and dress. You aren't likely to have any difficulty with the staff at hotels or restaurants, though you may have a negative response from other patrons. Also be aware that other types of businesses may have practices that discriminate in more subtle ways (e.g., any man wearing an earring may be barred from entering).

In sophisticated San Juan, gays and lesbians will find it easy to mingle. There are gay-friendly hotels, restaurants, and clubs throughout the city, the beaches at Condado and Ocean Park tend to attract a gay crowd, and the first Sunday in June sees a gay pride parade in Condado that's preceded by a week of events. The bohemian Old San Juan crowd is particularly friendly and—just as in Ocean Park and Condado—many businesses there are owned by gays or lesbians. Some also have a weekly "gay night." Other welcoming areas of the island include Boquerón in the southwest and the town of Fajardo and the out islands of Vieques and Culebra in the east. To find out more about events and gay-friendly businesses, pick up a copy of the *Puerto Rico Breeze,* the island's gay and lesbian newspaper.

Gay- & Lesbian-Friendly Travel Agencies **Different Roads Travel** ✉ 8383 Wilshire Blvd., Suite 520, Beverly Hills, CA 90211 ☎ 323/651-5557 or 800/429-8747 (Ext. 14 for both) 323/651-5454 lgernert@tzell.com. **Kennedy Travel** ✉ 130 W. 42nd St., Suite 401, New York, NY 10036 ☎ 212/840-8659 or 800/237-7433 212/730-2269 www.kennedytravel.com. **Now, Voyager** ✉ 4406 18th St., San Francisco, CA 94114 ☎ 415/626-1169 or 800/255-6951 415/626-8626 www.nowvoyager.com. **Skylink Travel and Tour/Flying Dutchmen Travel** ✉ 1455 N. Dutton Ave., Suite A, Santa Rosa, CA 95401 ☎ 707/546-9888 or 800/225-5759 707/636-0951, serving lesbian travelers.

HEALTH

Health care in Puerto Rico is among the best in the Caribbean, but expect long waits and often a less-than-pleasant bedside manner. At all hospitals and medical centers you'll find English-speaking medical staff, and many large hotels have an English-speaking doctor on call.

DIVERS' ALERT

Do not fly within 24 hours of scuba diving.

FOOD & DRINK

Tap water is generally fine on the island; just avoid drinking it after storms (when the water supply can become mixed with sewage). Thoroughly wash or peel produce you buy in markets before eating it.

MEDICAL PLANS

No one plans to get sick while traveling, but it happens, so consider signing up with a medical-assistance company. Members get doctor referrals, emergency evacuation or repatriation, hot lines for medical consultation, cash for emergencies, and other assistance.

Medical-Assistance Companies International SOS Assistance www.internationalsos.com 8 Neshaminy Interplex, Suite 207, Trevose, PA 19053 215/245-4707 or 800/523-6586 215/244-9617 Landmark House, Hammersmith Bridge Rd., 6th fl., London, W6 9DP 20/8762-8008 20/8748-7744 12 Chemin Riantbosson, 1217 Meyrin 1, Geneva, Switzerland 22/785-6464 22/785-6424 331 N. Bridge Rd., 17-00, Odeon Towers, Singapore 188720 6338-7800 6338-7611.

OVER-THE-COUNTER REMEDIES

All the U.S. brands of sunscreen and over-the-counter medicines (Tylenol, Advil, Robitussin, Nyquil, etc.) are available in pharmacies, supermarkets, and convenience stores.

PESTS & OTHER HAZARDS

Most health problems encountered by visitors involve the trio of rum, sun, and blisters. Overindulgence has probably sidelined more travelers than any other health hazard. Use common sense. The sun is hot, so take precautions whether you're on the beach or hiking through a rain forest. Limit your time in the sun, wear a T-shirt and/or a hat when the rays become too powerful, and use a strong sunscreen. To prevent dehydration, drink plenty of water and monitor your intake of caffeine and alcohol, both of which hasten the dehydration process.

The ocean presents its own hazards. Some beaches along the north and west coasts have strong waves and undertows. Signs are often posted where and when the waves make it too dangerous to swim, but ask about the undertow conditions, which vary from season to season.

Avoid black, long-spined sea urchins, often found in shallow water near shore, hidden among coral and rocks. Their strong barbs can pierce the skin and break off, resulting in painful swelling. Remove the fragments immediately, soak the injured area, and treat it with an antiseptic as soon as possible. Then see a doctor. Also, stay clear of all forms of jellyfish, which often wash up on shore, particularly in winter. Their tentacles are equipped with stinging organisms that detach when brushed. Splash the affected area with drying agents such as alcohol, talcum powder, or even sand, but avoid rubbing your skin or you may activate detached stingers. Then see a doctor.

When snorkeling or diving, avoid touching live coral, for the organism's safety as well as your own. All corals can be harmful, either causing a slow-healing gash or releasing toxins on contact. Fire and stinging corals do what their names suggest. If you accidentally touch them, seek treatment. Further, breaking coral, kicking it with your fins, or brushing it with your underwater camera can traumatize a reef's delicate ecological balance.

Bugs are, primarily, annoying—mosquitoes and sand gnats (no-see-ums) are the biggest problems, particularly around sunrise and sunset. They can be warded off with a good repellent with DEET, available in all drugstores and pharmacies. Mosquito coils are also sold throughout the island. Some mosquitoes carry dengue fever; if you develop a fever, fatigue, pin-size red spots, diarrhea, or nausea, see a doctor.

Health Warnings National Centers for Disease Control and Prevention (CDC) Office of Health Communication, National Center for Infectious Diseases, Division of Quarantine, Travelers' Health, 1600 Clifton Rd. NE, Atlanta, GA 30333 877/394-8747 international travelers' health line, 800/311-3435 other inquiries, 404/498-1600 Division of Quarantine 888/232-3299 www.cdc.gov/travel. **World Health Organization** (WHO) www.who.int.

HOLIDAYS

Puerto Rico observes all U.S. federal holidays, as well as many local holidays. Most government offices and businesses shut down on holidays, with the exception of convenience stores and some supermarkets, pharmacies, and restaurants. Public transportation runs on abbreviated schedules, just as on Sunday. Public holidays in Puerto Rico include: New Year's Day, Three Kings Day (Jan. 6), Eugenio María de Hostos Day (Jan. 8), Dr. Martin Luther King Jr. Day (3rd Mon. in Jan.), Presidents' Day (3rd Mon. in Feb.), Palm Sunday, Good Friday, Easter Sunday, Memorial Day (last Mon. in May), Independence Day (July 4), Luis Muñoz Rivera Day (July 16), Constitution Day (July 25), José Celso Barbosa Day (July 27), Labor Day (1st Mon. in Sept.), Columbus Day (2nd Mon. in Oct.), Veterans' Day (Nov. 11), Puerto Rico Discovery Day (Nov. 19), Thanksgiving Day, and Christmas.

INSURANCE

The most useful travel-insurance plan is a comprehensive policy that includes coverage for trip cancellation and interruption, default, trip delay, and medical expenses (with a waiver for preexisting conditions).

Without insurance you'll lose all or most of your money if you cancel your trip, regardless of the reason. Default insurance covers you if your tour operator, airline, or cruise line goes out of business—the chances of which have been increasing. Trip-delay covers expenses that arise because of bad weather or mechanical delays. Study the fine print when comparing policies.

If you're traveling internationally, a key component of travel insurance is coverage for medical bills incurred if you get sick on the road. Such expenses aren't generally covered by Medicare or private policies. U.K. residents can buy a travel-insurance policy valid for most vacations taken during the year in which it's purchased (but check preexisting-condition coverage). British and Australian citizens need extra medical coverage when traveling overseas.

Always **buy travel policies directly from the insurance company**; if you buy them from a cruise line, airline, or tour operator that goes out of business you probably won't be covered for the agency or operator's default, a major risk. Before making any purchase, review your existing health and home-owner's policies to find what they cover away from home.

Travel Insurers In the U.S.: **Access America** ✉ 2805 N. Parham Rd., Richmond, VA 23294 ☎ 800/284-8300 🖷 804/673-1491 or 800/346-9265 🌐 www.accessamerica.com. **Travel Guard International** ✉ 1145 Clark St., Stevens Point, WI 54481 ☎ 715/345-0505 or 800/826-1300 🖷 800/955-8785 🌐 www.travelguard.com.

In the U.K.: **Association of British Insurers** ✉ 51 Gresham St., London EC2V 7HQ ☎ 020/7600-3333 🖷 020/7696-8999 🌐 www.abi.org.uk. In Canada: **RBC Insurance** ✉ 6880 Financial Dr., Mississauga, Ontario L5N 7Y5 ☎ 800/668-4342 or 905/816-2400 🖷 905/813-4704 🌐 www.rbcinsurance.com. In Australia: **Insurance Council of Australia** ✉ Insurance Enquiries and Complaints, Level 12, Box 561, Collins St. W, Melbourne, VIC 8007 ☎ 1300/780808 or 03/9629-4109 🖷 03/9621-2060 🌐 www.iecltd.com.au. In New Zealand: **Insurance Council of New Zealand** ✉ Level 7, 111-115 Customhouse Quay, Box 474, Wellington ☎ 04/472-5230 🖷 04/473-3011 🌐 www.icnz.org.nz.

LANGUAGE

The official languages are Spanish and English, in that order. Spanish prevails in everyday conversation, in commerce, and in the media. And although English is widely spoken, you'll probably want to take a Spanish phrase book along, particularly outside of San Juan. Hotel front desk staffs and restaurant staffs in large facilities speak English. Most business and government phones are manned by people who speak English (or will find someone who does), and telephone answering systems are bilingual. If you're stumped, call the Tourist Information line or the Traveler's Aid line.

Tourist Information Line ☎ 787/766-7777. **Traveler's Aid Line** ☎ 787/791-1054.

LANGUAGES FOR TRAVELERS

A phrase book and language-tape set can help get you started. *Fodor's Spanish for Travelers* (available at bookstores everywhere) is excellent.

LODGING

San Juan's high-rise hotels on the Condado and Isla Verde beach strips cater primarily to the cruise-ship and casino crowd, though several target business travelers. Outside San Juan, particularly on the east coast, you'll find self-contained luxury resorts that cover hundreds of acres. In the west, southwest, and south—as well as on the islands of Vieques and Culebra—smaller inns, villas, condominiums, and government-sponsored *paradores* are the norm.

Before booking a room consider (and make a list of) your needs. Is it worth paying extra for a room overlooking the beach or the pool? Must the hotel even be on the beach? Rooms with garden or mountain views and properties away from the shore entirely often cost less. Which in-room amenities—air-conditioning, mini-bars, safes, etc.—and on-site facilities are important to you? Do you want able to open your room windows and control the air-conditioning yourself? Do you need cable TV to keep up with world events? Are you concerned about children's programs? Do you want a hotel with a dance club or a casino, or are you seeking peace? These are just some of the questions you should ask yourself.

The lodgings we list are the cream of the crop in each price category. We always list the facilities that are available, but we don't specify whether they cost extra; when pricing accommodations, always ask what's included and what costs extra. Properties are assigned price categories based on the range between their least and most expensive standard double rooms at high season (excluding holidays). Properties marked ✕ are lodging establishments whose restaurants warrant a special trip. Assume that hotels operate on the European Plan (EP, with no meals) unless we specify that they use either the Continental Plan (CP, with a Continental breakfast), Breakfast Plan (BP, with a full breakfast), or the Modified American Plan (MAP, with breakfast and dinner) or are all-inclusive (including all meals and most activities).

APARTMENT & VILLA RENTALS

If you want a home base that's roomy enough for a family and comes with cooking facilities, consider a furnished rental. These can save you money, especially if you're traveling with a group. Home-exchange directories sometimes list rentals as well as exchanges.

International Agents **At Home Abroad** 163 Third Ave., No. 319, New York, NY 10003 212/421-9165 212/533-0095 www.athomeabroadinc.com. **Hideaways International** 767 Islington St., Portsmouth, NH 03801 603/430-4433 or 800/843-4433 603/430-4444 www.hideaways.com, annual membership $145. **Vacation Home Rentals Worldwide** 235 Kensington Ave., Norwood, NJ 07648 201/767-9393 or 800/633-3284 201/767-5510 www.vhrww.com. **Villanet** 1251 N.W. 116th St., Seattle, WA 98177 206/417-3444 or 800/964-1891 206/417-1832 www.rentavilla.com. **Villas & Apartments Abroad** 183 Madison Ave., Suite 201, New York, NY 10016 212/213-6435 or 800/433-3020 212/213-8252 www.vaanyc.com. **Villas International** 4340 Redwood Hwy., Suite D309, San Rafael, CA 94903 415/499-9490 or 800/221-2260 415/499-9491 www.villasintl.com.

Local Agents **Caleta Realty** 11 Caleta de las Monjas Old San Juan, San Juan 00901 787/725-5347 787/977-5642 www.thecaleta.com. **Coconut Palms** 2734 Calle 8, Rincón 00677 787/823-0147 www.coconutpalmsinn.com. **Connections** Box 358, Esperanza, Vieques 00765 787/741-0023. **Island West Properties & Beach Rentals** Rte. 413, Km 1.3 Box 700, Rincón 00677 787/823-2323 787/823-3254. **Puerto Rico Vacation Apartments** Marbella del Caribe Oeste S-5, Av. Isla Verde, Isla Verde, San Juan 00979 787/727-1591 or 800/266-3639 787/268-3604.

CAMPING

It's not safe or legal to simply to pitch a tent in the woods or on a deserted beach. The island's designated campgrounds—for tents and/or RVs—are most often found at balnearios. Most have cooking grills and bath houses. Weekend camping at balnearios is popular among Puerto Ricans, and you'll find that the crowds are usually in a party mood, with lots of music and general merriment—not a setting for peaceful communion with nature.

Other areas include a few private camps along the north and northeast coast and grounds in the Carite, Guilarte, Toro Nego, Río Abajo, and other state forests. To camp in nature reserves or state forests, you must get a permit from the Department of Natural and Environmental Resources. Request the permit at least three weeks in advance.

Department of Natural & Environmental Resources ✉ Avenida Fernández Juncos, San Juan, next to the Club Náutico ☎ 787/724-3724 or 787/724-3647. **Department of Sports & Recreation** ☎ 787/721-2800 or 787/636-6340. **Tourist Information Line** ☎ 787/766-7777.

HOME EXCHANGES

If you would like to exchange your home for someone else's, join a home-exchange organization, which will send you its updated listings of available exchanges for a year and will include your own listing in at least one of them. It's up to you to make specific arrangements.

Exchange Clubs **HomeLink International** Box 47747, Tampa, FL 33647 ☎ 813/975-9825 or 800/638-3841 813/910-8144 www.homelink.org; $110 yearly for a listing, online access, and catalog; $70 without catalog. **Intervac U.S.** ✉ 30 Corte San Fernando, Tiburon, CA 94920 ☎ 800/756-4663 415/435-7440 www.intervacus.com; $125 yearly for a listing, online access, and a catalog; $65 without catalog.

HOSTELS

Currently, no hostels in Puerto Rico, youth or otherwise, are sanctioned by local or international organizations.

HOTELS

In the most expensive hotels, your room will be large enough for two to move around comfortably, with two double beds (*camas matrimoniales*) or one queen- or king-size bed, air-conditioning (*aire acondicionado*), a phone (*teléfono*), a private bath (*baño particular*), an in-room safe, cable TV, a hair dryer, iron and ironing board, room service (*servicio de habitación*), shampoo and toiletries, and possibly a view of the water (*vista al mar*). There will be a concierge and at least one hotel restaurant and lounge, a pool, a shop, and an exercise room or spa. In Puerto Rico's smaller inns, rooms will have private baths with hot water (*agua caliente*), air-conditioning or fans, a double to king-size bed, possibly room service, and breakfast (continental or full) included in the rates. In some hotels, several rooms share baths—it's a good idea to ask before booking. All hotels listed in this guide have private baths unless otherwise noted.

RESERVING A ROOM

Toll-Free Numbers **Best Western** ☎ 800/528-1234 www.bestwestern.com. **Choice Hotels** ☎ 800/424-6423 www.choicehotels.com. **Comfort Inn** ☎ 800/424-6423 www.choicehotels.com. **Days Inn** ☎ 800/325-2525 www.daysinn.com. **Doubletree Hotels** ☎ 800/222-8733 www.doubletree.com. **Embassy Suites** ☎ 800/362-2779 www.embassysuites.com. **Hilton** ☎ 800/445-8667 www.hilton.com. **Holiday Inn** ☎ 800/465-4329 www.ichotelsgroup.com. **Howard Johnson** ☎ 800/446-4656 www.hojo.com. **Hyatt Hotels & Resorts** ☎ 800/233-1234 www.hyatt.com. **Inter-Continental** ☎ 800/327-0200 www.ichotelsgroup.com. **Marriott** ☎ 800/228-9290 www.marriott.com. **Ritz-Carlton** ☎ 800/241-3333 www.ritzcarlton.com. **Sheraton** ☎ 800/325-3535 www.starwood.com/sheraton. **Westin Hotels & Resorts** ☎ 800/228-3000 www.starwood.com/westin. **Wyndham Hotels & Resorts** ☎ 800/822-4200 www.wyndham.com.

PARADORES

Some paradores are rural inns offering no-frills apartments, and others are large hotels; all must meet certain standards, such as proximity to an attraction or beach. Most have a small restaurant that serves local cuisine. They're great bargains (from $60 to $125 for a double room). You can make reservations by contacting the tourist board's Paradores of Puerto Rico. Small Inns of Puerto Rico, a branch of the Puerto Rico Hotel & Tourism Association, is a marketing arm for some 25 small hotels island-wide. The organization occasionally has package deals including casino coupons and LeLoLai (a cultural show) tickets.

Paradores of Puerto Rico ☎ 800/866-7827 www.prtourism.com. **Small Inns of Puerto Rico** ☎ 787/725-2901 www.prhtasmallhotels.com.

MAIL & SHIPPING

Puerto Rico uses the U.S. postal system, and all addresses on the island carry zip codes. However, mail between Puerto Rico and the U.S. mainland can take more than a week.

Major Post Offices **U.S. Post Office** ✉ 153 Calle Fortaleza, Old San Juan, San Juan ✉ 163 Av. Fernández Juncos, San Juan ✉ 102 Calle Garrido Morales, Fajardo ✉ 60 Calle McKinley, Mayagüez ✉ 94 Calle Atocha, Ponce.

OVERNIGHT SERVICES

Post offices in major Puerto Rican cities offer express mail (next-day) service to the U.S. mainland and to Puerto Rican destinations. In addition, you can send overnight letters and packages via FedEx or UPS. Ask at the concierge desk of your hotel; most have regular courier pick-ups or can call for one. They might also be able to direct you to a store like Mailboxes, Etc., where you can arrange shipment through a variety of different companies. Hotels that offer business services will take care of the entire ordeal for you. Caveat emptor: courier delivery and pick-up is not available on Saturday, and "overnight" packages often take two to three days to reach the U.S. mainland.

FedEx ☎ 787/793-9300. **UPS** ☎ 787/253-2877.

POSTAL RATES

For mail sent within the United States, you need a 37¢ stamp for first-class letters weighing up to 1 ounce (23¢ for each additional ounce) and 23¢ for postcards. You pay 80¢ for 1-ounce airmail letters and 70¢ for airmail postcards to most other countries; to Canada and Mexico, you need a 60¢ stamp for a 1-ounce letter and 50¢ for a postcard. An aerogram—a single sheet of lightweight blue paper that folds into its own envelope, stamped for overseas airmail—costs 70¢.

SHIPPING PARCELS

Many shops—particularly those in Old San Juan and Condado—will ship purchases for you. Shipping services are especially common at art galleries. Pay by credit card, and save your receipts. Make sure the proprietor insures the package against loss or damage, and ships it first-class or by courier. Grab a business card with the proprietor's name and phone number so you can readily follow up with him or her if needed.

MONEY MATTERS

Puerto Rico, which is a commonwealth of the United States, uses the U.S. dollar as its official currency. Prices for most items are stable and comparable to those in the States, and that includes restaurants and hotel rates. As in many places, city prices tend to be higher than those in rural areas, but you're not going to go broke staying in the city: soft drinks or a cup of coffee run about $1; a local beer in a bar, $2.75; museum admission, $2.

Prices throughout this guide are given for adults. Substantially reduced fees are almost always available for children, students, and senior citizens. For information on taxes, *see* Taxes.

ATMS

Automated Teller Machines (ATMs; known as or ATHs here) are readily available and reliable in the cities; many are attached to banks, but you can also find them on the streets and in supermarkets. Just about every casino has one—the better to keep people in the game—as do many of the larger hotels, but these can carry large surcharges, so check before you withdraw money. ATMs are found less frequently in rural areas. Look to local banks, such as Banco Popular.

CREDIT CARDS

Throughout this guide, the following abbreviations are used: **AE,** American Express; **D,** Discover; **DC,** Diners Club; **MC,** MasterCard; and **V,** Visa.

Reporting Lost Cards **American Express** ☎ 800/992-3404. **Diners Club** ☎ 800/234-6377. **Discover** ☎ 800/347-2683. **MasterCard** ☎ 800/622-7747. **Visa** ☎ 800/ 847-2911.

TRAVELER'S CHECKS

Do you need traveler's checks? It depends on where you're headed. If you're going to rural areas and small towns, go with cash; traveler's checks are best used in cities. Lost or stolen checks can usually be replaced within 24 hours. To ensure a speedy refund, buy your own traveler's checks—don't let someone else pay for them: irregularities like this can cause delays. The person who bought the checks should make the call to request a refund.

PACKING

Although "casual" is the operative word for vacation clothes, wearing resort attire outside the hotel or at the casino will peg you as a tourist. Puerto Ricans, particularly in the cities, dress up to go out. Pack some dressy casual slacks and shirts, summer skirts for women, casual clothes for the resort, at least two bathing suits (to avoid having to wear that wet one from yesterday), and sturdy shoes for walking. A light sweater or jacket isn't a bad idea either.

In your carry-on luggage, pack an extra pair of eyeglasses or contact lenses and enough of any medication you take to last a few days longer than the entire trip. You may also ask your doctor to write a spare prescription using the drug's generic name, as brand names may vary from country to country. In luggage to be checked, **never pack prescription drugs, valuables, or undeveloped film.** And don't forget to carry with you the addresses of offices that handle refunds of lost traveler's checks. Check *Fodor's How to Pack* (available at online retailers and bookstores everywhere) for more tips.

To avoid customs and security delays, carry medications in their original packaging. Don't pack any sharp objects in your carry-on luggage, including knives of any size or material, scissors, nail clippers, and corkscrews, or anything else that might arouse suspicion.

To avoid having your checked luggage chosen for hand inspection, don't cram bags full. The U.S. Transportation Security Administration suggests packing shoes on top and placing personal items you don't want touched in clear plastic bags.

CHECKING LUGGAGE

You're allowed to carry aboard one bag and one personal article, such as a purse or a laptop computer. Make sure what you carry on fits under your seat or in the overhead bin. Get to the gate early, so you can board as soon as possible, before the overhead bins fill up.

Baggage allowances vary by carrier, destination, and ticket class. On international flights, you're usually allowed to check two bags weighing up to 70 pounds (32 kilograms) each, although a few airlines allow checked bags of up to 88 pounds (40 kilograms) in first class. Some international carriers don't allow more than 66 pounds (30 kilograms) per bag in business class and 44 pounds (20 kilograms) in economy. On domestic flights, the limit is usually 50 to 70 pounds (23 to 32 kilograms) per bag. In general, carry-on bags shouldn't exceed 40 pounds (18 kilograms). Most airlines won't accept bags that weigh more than 100 pounds (45 kilograms) on domestic or international flights. Expect to pay a fee for baggage that exceeds weight limits. Check baggage restrictions with your carrier before you pack.

Airline liability for baggage is limited to $2,500 per person on flights within the United States. On international flights it amounts to $9.07 per pound or $20 per kilogram for checked baggage (roughly $640 per 70-pound bag), with a maximum of $634.90 per piece, and $400 per passenger for unchecked baggage. You can buy additional coverage at check-in for about $10 per $1,000 of coverage, but it often excludes a rather extensive list of items, shown on your airline ticket.

Before departure, itemize your bags' contents and their worth, and label the bags with your name, address, and phone number. (If you use your home address, cover it so potential thieves can't see it readily.) Include a label inside each bag and **pack a copy of your itinerary.** At check-in, make sure each bag is correctly tagged with the destination airport's three-letter code. Because some checked bags will be opened for hand inspection, the U.S. Transportation Security Administration recommends that you leave luggage unlocked or use the plastic locks offered at check-in. TSA screeners place an inspection notice inside searched bags, which are re-sealed with a special lock.

If your bag has been searched and contents are missing or damaged, file a claim with the TSA Consumer Response Center as soon as possible. If your bags arrive damaged or fail to arrive at all, file a written report with the airline before leaving the airport.

Complaints **U.S. Transportation Security Administration Contact Center** ☎ 866/289-9673 🌐 www.tsa.gov.

PASSPORTS & VISAS

When traveling internationally, carry your passport even if you don't need one (it's always the best form of ID) and **make two photocopies of the data page** (one for someone at home and another for you, carried separately from your passport). If you lose your passport, promptly call the nearest embassy or consulate and the local police.

ENTERING PUERTO RICO

U.S. citizens don't need passports to visit Puerto Rico, but you should always carry some form of identification—a passport, or a driver's license along with an original copy of a birth certificate—to evidence U.S. citizenship or nationality. We strongly recommend that you carry a valid passport when traveling to Puerto Rico, even though it's not required. Canadians need proof of citizenship (preferably a valid passport; otherwise bring a birth certificate with a raised seal along with a government-issued photo ID). Citizens of Australia, New Zealand, and the United Kingdom must have passports but don't need visas for stays of fewer than 90 days.

PASSPORT OFFICES

The best time to apply for a passport or to renew is in fall and winter. Before any trip, check your passport's expiration date, and, if necessary, renew it as soon as possible.

Australian Citizens **Passports Australia** Australian Department of Foreign Affairs and Trade ☎ 131-232 🌐 www.passports.gov.au.

Canadian Citizens **Passport Office** ✉ To mail in applications: 200 Promenade du Portage, Hull, Québec J8X 4B7 ☎ 819/994-3500 or 800/567-6868 🌐 www.ppt.gc.ca.

New Zealand Citizens **New Zealand Passports Office** ☎ 0800/22-5050 or 04/474-8100 🌐 www.passports.govt.nz.

U.K. Citizens **U.K. Passport Service** ☎ 0870/521-0410 🌐 www.passport.gov.uk.

RESTROOMS

Restrooms you encounter in Puerto Rico will be not unlike those at home—some clean, some not so clean. Most public restrooms at government facilities will be accessible for travelers with disabilities. Spanish for toilet is *baño*; men's room doors are labeled *caballeros,* ladies' room doors *damas*.

SAFETY

San Juan and Ponce, like most big cities, have their share of crime, so guard your wallet or purse on the city streets. Avoid beaches at night, when muggings have been known to occur even on posh stretches, such as those in Condado and Isla Verde. Don't leave anything unattended on the beach. Lock your valuables in the hotel safe, and stick to the fenced-in beach areas of your hotel. Always lock your car; if you must keep valuables in your vehicle, put them in the trunk.

Don't wear a money belt or a waist pack, both of which peg you as a tourist. Distribute your cash and any valuables (including your credit cards and passport) between a deep front pocket, an inside jacket or vest pocket, and a hidden money pouch. Do not reach for the money pouch once you're in public.

WOMEN IN PUERTO RICO

If you carry a purse, choose one with a zipper and a thick strap that you can drape across your body; adjust the length so that the purse sits in front of you at or above hip level. (Don't wear a money belt or a waist pack.) Store only enough money in the purse to cover casual spending. Distribute the rest of your cash and any valuables between deep front pockets, inside jacket or vest pockets, and a concealed money pouch.

In the cities, women traveling solo are less likely to attract attention than elsewhere. Even so, men might still attempt to make conversation. Be polite but firm. A simple

"*No, gracias*" ("No, thanks") is usually enough to discourage them. Avoid drinking alone in bars and walking on deserted beaches—day or at night—or along dark, empty streets. Getting into an unmarked car identified by the driver as a taxi is a bad idea. It's also best not to don revealing attire or to wear swimsuits anywhere but at the beach or by the pool.

SENIOR-CITIZEN TRAVEL

To qualify for age-related discounts, mention your senior-citizen status up front when booking hotel reservations (not when checking out) and before you're seated in restaurants (not when paying the bill). Be sure to have identification on hand. When renting a car, ask about promotional car-rental discounts, which can be cheaper than senior-citizen rates.

Educational Programs **Elderhostel** ✉ 11 Ave. de Lafayette, Boston, MA 02111-1746 ☎ 877/426-8056, 978/323-4141 international callers, 877/426-2167 TTY 📠 877/426-2166 🌐 www.elderhostel.org. **Interhostel** ✉ University of New Hampshire, 6 Garrison Ave., Durham, NH 03824 ☎ 603/862-1147 or 800/733-9753 📠 603/862-1113 🌐 www.learn.unh.edu.

SHOPPING

Shopping in Puerto Rico differs little from shopping in North America: cash, of course, is always accepted, and in most cases traveler's checks and major credit cards are fine. Street vendors selling crafts and other items are likely to accept cash only; they're also open to bargaining, which isn't a common practice in shops and boutiques.

Although there are a few duty-free shops in the terminal boarding areas at San Juan's Luis Muñoz Marín International Airport, Puerto Rico isn't a duty-free island. You can, however, still find excellent prices on china, crystal, jewelry, and designer fashions.

SMART SOUVENIRS

Shopping for local crafts can be gratifying: you'll run across a lot of tacky items, but you can also find some treasures, and in many cases you can watch the artisans at work. For guidance, contact the Puerto Rico Tourism Company's Asuntos Culturales (Cultural Affairs Office). Popular items include *santos* (small hand-carved figures of saints or religious scenes), hand-rolled cigars, Panama hats, handmade *mundillo* lace from Aguadilla, *veijigantes* (colorful festival masks made of papier-mâché and/or coconut husks), and fancy men's shirts called *guayaberas*. Also, some folks swear that Puerto Rican rum is the best in the world, and locally grown and processed coffee is of a very high quality.

Puerto Rico Tourism Company's Asuntos Culturales ☎ 787/723-0692.

WATCH OUT

Remember, Puerto Rico is not duty-free, and shopkeepers who tell you otherwise are trying to scam you.

SPORTS & THE OUTDOORS

BEACHES

An island visit isn't complete without some time in the sand and sun. By law, everyone is welcome on Puerto Rico's *playas* (beaches), some of which—called balnearios—are maintained by the government. There are more than a dozen such beaches around the island, with dressing rooms; lifeguards; parking; and, in some cases, picnic tables, playgrounds, and camping facilities. Admission is free, and parking runs $2 to $3. Hours vary, but most balnearios are open from 9 to 5 daily in summer and Tuesday through Sunday the rest of the year.

BICYCLING

Selected areas—small towns, the central mountains, the southern coast—lend themselves to bike travel. In the San Juan, it is a fairly safe and enjoyable ride from Ocean Park or Condado to Old San Juan through the Third Millenium or Muñoz Rivera park. In general, however, the roads are congested and distances vast. Avoid main city thoroughfares, such as Fernández Juncos, Ponce de León, and Muñoz Rivera avenues, where the traffic is too heavy. East of the city, beginning just past the Isla Verde area of San Juan, the bike trails in Piñones provide a beautiful beach-front escape. The entire southwest coast of Cabo Rojo also makes for good biking, particularly the broad beach at Boquerón. Vieques and Culebra are ideal for biking, as there's little traffic. If you're looking for a more challenging ride, head to the central mountains, particularly the Bosque Estatal de Toro Negro (Toro Negro State Forest) in Jayuya. The Puerto Rico Mountain Bike Association schedules events from March to October. Road bike events are organized throughout the year by the Federación Puertorriqueña de Ciclismo.

Most airlines accommodate bikes as luggage, provided they are dismantled and boxed. For bike boxes, often free at bike shops, you'll pay about $5 from airlines (at least $100 for bike bags). International travelers can sometimes substitute a bike for a piece of checked luggage at no charge; otherwise, the cost is about $100. Domestic and Canadian airlines charge $25 to $50.

Federación Puertorriqueña de Ciclismo www.federacionciclismopr.com.

DIVING & SNORKELING

The diving is excellent off Puerto Rico's south, east, and west coasts as well as around its offshore islands. Popular among divers is tiny Desecheo Island, about 24 km (15 mi) off the coast of Rincón in the west. At depths of 20 to 120 feet, the rocky ocean floor around the base of the islet is full of coral and tropical fish, as well as several rock terraces and caverns. In the south, several reef-bordered cays lie off the Cabo Rojo area near walls that drop to 100 feet. In the east, many divers head to Fajardo, which is the jumping off point for Vieques and Culebra; the waters around these islets are full of diving possibilities. The nearest hyperbaric chamber is at the Hospital Universitario (University Hospital) in Río Piedras.

Emergencies **Hospital Universitario** 787/758-7910.

Culebra Divers 4 Pedro Marquez, Dewey, Culebra 787/742-0803. **Desecheo Dive Shop** Rte. 413, Km 2.5, Rincón 787/823-0390. **Sea Ventures Pro Dive Center** Puerto del Rey Marina, Rte. 3, Km 51.4, Fajardo 787/863-3483 or 800/739-3483 www.divepuertorico.com. **Tour Marine** Rte. 101, Km 14.1, Joyuda Sector, Puerto Real, Cabo Rojo 787/851-9259.

HIKING

In the east, El Yunque's 13 hiking trails loop past giant ferns, exotic orchids, sibilant streams and waterfalls, and broad trees reaching for the sun. You can even hike to the top of El Toro, the highest peak in the forest at 3,532 feet. The northwest's Bosque Estatal de Toro Negro and the south's Bosque Estatal de Guánica are also great places to hike.

Bosque Estatal de Guánica Rte. 333 or 334, Guánica 787/821-5706. **Bosque Estatal de Toro Negro** Rte. 143, Km 31.8, Jayuya 787/867-3040. **El Yunque** Centro de Información El Portal Rte. 191, Km 4.3, off Rte. 3, El Yunque 787/888-1880.

GOLF

For aficionados worldwide, Puerto Rico is known as the birthplace of golf legend Chi Chi Rodríguez, whose new 18-hole golf course on Route 173 outside of Guayama in the south was scheduled, at this writing, to open in late 2004. Currently you'll find nearly 20 courses on the island, including several championship links. None of the courses is public, though plans for public facilities are on the table. Always call ahead for details on reserving tee times; hours vary and several hotel courses give preference to guests or allow only allow guests to play. The Puerto Rican Golf Association is a good general source for information on courses and tournaments.

Puerto Rican Golf Association 58 Calle Caribe, San Juan 787/721-7742 www.prga.org.

STUDENTS IN PUERTO RICO

Puerto Rico is well within the budget of students and is tailor-made for the adventurous. To beat the costs of traveling alone, hook up with educational institutions that use the island for research. Educational trips where you help out in projects are often inexpensive but might require a time commitment of several weeks.

IDs & Services **STA Travel** 10 Downing St., New York, NY 10014 212/627-3111, 800/777-0112 24-hr service center 212/627-3387 www.sta.com. **Travel Cuts** 187 College St., Toronto, Ontario M5T 1P7, Canada 800/592-2887 in U.S., 416/979-2406 or 866/246-9762 in Canada 416/979-8167 www.travelcuts.com.

TAXES

You must pay a tax on your hotel room rate: for hotels with casinos it's 11%, for other hotels it's 9%, and for government-approved paradores it's 7%. Ask your hotel before booking. The tax, in addition to each hotel's discretionary service charge (which usually ranges from 5% to 12%), can add a hefty 12% to 23% to your bill. There's no sales tax on Puerto Rico. Airport departure taxes are usually included in the cost of your plane ticket rather than being collected at the airport.

TELEPHONES

All Puerto Rican phone numbers—like those throughout the United States—consist of a three-digit area code and a seven-digit local number. Puerto Rico's area codes are 787 and 939. Toll-free numbers (prefix 800, 888, or 877) are widely used in Puerto Rico, and many can be accessed from North America. You can also access many North American toll-free numbers from the island.

Cell phones are a viable alternative to using local service if you need to keep records of your bills. Call your cell-phone company before departing to get information about activation and roaming charges. Companies that have service on the island include Cellular One and Sprint.

DIRECTORY & OPERATOR ASSISTANCE

Dial 411 for directory assistance, and dial 0 for operator-assisted calls. Operators generally speak English.

INTERNATIONAL CALLS

For direct international calls to the United Kingdom, Australia, New Zealand, and elsewhere dial "011" followed by the country code, area code, and number. Dial 00 for the international long-distance operator.

LOCAL CALLS

You must always dial the area code and the number when making calls on the island.

LONG-DISTANCE CALLS

If the call is outside of your zone but still on the island or it's to (or from) the United States or Canada, simply dial a "1" before the area code and the number. The same procedure applies for calls to many other Caribbean islands.

LONG-DISTANCE SERVICES

AT&T, MCI, and Sprint access codes make calling long-distance relatively convenient, but you may find the local access number blocked in many hotel rooms. First ask the hotel operator to connect you. If the hotel operator balks, ask for an international operator, or dial the international operator yourself. One way to improve your odds of getting connected to your long-distance carrier is to travel with more than one company's calling card (a hotel may block Sprint, for example, but not MCI). If all else fails, call from a pay phone.

Access Codes **AT&T Direct** ☎ 787/725-0300. **Cellular One** ☎ 787/505-2273 or 787/505-4636. **MCI WorldPhone** ☎ 787/782-6244 or 800/939-7624. **Sprint International Access** ☎ 800/473-3037 or 800/298-3266.

PHONE CARDS

Phone cards are widely available. The Puerto Rico Telephone Company sells its "Ring Cards" in various denominations that can be used for both local and international calls. They're available in shops, supermarkets, and drugstores as well as from the phone company.

Ring Cards ☎ 800/981-9105.

PUBLIC PHONES

Pay phones, which are abundant in tourist areas, use coins or prepaid phone cards; some accept credit cards. Local calls run 10¢ to 25¢, and on-island, long-distance calls cost about 50¢.

TIME

Puerto Rico operates on Atlantic standard time, which is one hour later than the U.S. Eastern standard time in winter. The island does not keep U.S. Daylight Savings time. This means that when it's noon on a winter day in New York, it's 1 PM in Puerto Rico. In summer, Puerto Rico and the east coast of the United States are on the same time, and three hours ahead of the west coast. Sydney is 14 hours ahead of Puerto

Rico, Auckland is 16 hours ahead, and London is 4 hours ahead.

TIPPING

Some hotels automatically add a 5% to 12% service charge to your bill. Check ahead to confirm whether this charge is built into the room rate or will be tacked on at check out. Some smaller hotels might charge extra (as much as $5 per day) for use of air-conditioning, called an "energy tax." Tips are expected, and appreciated, by restaurant waitstaff (15% to 20% if a service charge isn't included), hotel porters ($1 per bag), maids ($1 to $2 a day), and taxi drivers (10% to 15%).

TOURS & PACKAGES

Because everything is prearranged on a prepackaged tour or independent vacation, you spend less time planning—and often get it all at a good price.

BOOKING WITH AN AGENT

Travel agents are excellent resources. But it's a good idea to collect brochures from several agencies, as some agents' suggestions may be influenced by relationships with tour and package firms that reward them for volume sales. If you have a special interest, find an agent with expertise in that area; the American Society of Travel Agents (ASTA; ⇨ Travel Agencies) has a database of specialists worldwide. You can log on to the group's Web site to find an ASTA travel agent in your neighborhood.

Make sure your travel agent knows the accommodations and other services of the place being recommended. Ask about the hotel's location, room size, beds, and whether it has a pool, room service, or programs for children, if you care about these. Has your agent been there in person or sent others whom you can contact?

Do some homework on your own, too: local tourism boards can provide information about lesser-known and small-niche operators, some of which may sell only direct.

BUYER BEWARE

Each year consumers are stranded or lose their money when tour operators—even large ones with excellent reputations—go out of business. So check out the operator. Ask several travel agents about its reputation, and try to **book with a company that has a consumer-protection program.** (Look for information in the company's brochure.) In the United States, members of the U.S. Tour Operators Association are required to set aside funds ($1 million) to help eligible customers cover payments and travel arrangements in the event that the company defaults. It's also a good idea to choose a company that participates in the American Society of Travel Agents' Tour Operator Program; ASTA will act as mediator in any disputes between you and your tour operator.

Remember that the more your package or tour includes, the better you can predict the ultimate cost of your vacation. Make sure you know exactly what is covered, and beware of hidden costs. Are taxes, tips, and transfers included? Entertainment and excursions? These can add up.

Tour-Operator Recommendations **American Society of Travel Agents** (⇨ Travel Agencies). **National Tour Association** (NTA) ✉ 546 E. Main St., Lexington, KY 40508 ☎ 859/226-4444 or 800/682-8886 📠 859/226-4404 🌐 www.ntaonline.com. **United States Tour Operators Association** (USTOA) ✉ 275 Madison Ave., Suite 2014, New York, NY 10016 ☎ 212/599-6599 📠 212/599-6744 🌐 www.ustoa.com.

TRAIN TRAVEL

San Juan is constructing an elevated light-rail system. Once completed, it will connect the city with the suburbs of Bayamón, Guaynabo, Santurce, Río Piedras, and Carolina. The system is slated to have 16 city stops and will also serve Aeropuerto Internacional Luis Muñoz Marín. The ultimate goal is an integrated transport system in coordination with buses that will be called "ATI", but at this writing the system was still not open.

TRAVEL AGENCIES

A good travel agent puts your needs first. Look for an agency that has been in business at least five years, emphasizes customer service, and has someone on staff who specializes in your destination. In addition, **make sure the agency belongs to a professional trade organization.** The American Society of Travel Agents (ASTA)—the largest and most influential in the field with more than 20,000 members in some 140 countries—maintains and enforces a strict code of ethics and will step in to help mediate any agent-client disputes involving ASTA members if necessary. ASTA (whose motto is "Without a travel agent, you're on your own") also maintains a Web site that includes a directory of agents. (If a travel agency is also acting as your tour operator, *see* Buyer Beware *in* Tours & Packages.)

Local Agent Referrals **American Society of Travel Agents** (ASTA) ✉ 1101 King St., Suite 200, Alexandria, VA 22314 ☎ 703/739-2782 or 800/965-2782 24-hr hotline 📠 703/684-8319 🌐 www.astanet.com. **Association of British Travel Agents** ✉ 68-71 Newman St., London W1T 3AH ☎ 020/7637-2444 📠 020/7637-0713 🌐 www.abta.com. **Association of Canadian Travel Agencies** ✉ 130 Albert St., Suite 1705, Ottawa, Ontario K1P 5G4 ☎ 613/237-3657 📠 613/237-7052 🌐 www.acta.ca. **Australian Federation of Travel Agents** ✉ Level 3, 309 Pitt St., Sydney, NSW 2000 ☎ 02/9264-3299 or 1300/363-416 📠 02/9264-1085 🌐 www.afta.com.au. **Travel Agents' Association of New Zealand** ✉ Level 5, Tourism and Travel House, 79 Boulcott St., Box 1888, Wellington 6001 ☎ 04/499-0104 📠 04/499-0786 🌐 www.taanz.org.nz.

VISITOR INFORMATION

In addition to the Puerto Rico Tourism Company's *Qué Pasa*, pick up the Puerto Rico Hotel and Tourism Association's *Bienvenidos* and *Places to Go*. Among them you'll find a wealth of information about the island and its activities. All are free and available at tourism offices and hotel desks. The Puerto Rico Tourism Company has information centers at the airport, Old San Juan, Ponce, Aguadilla, and Cabo Rojo. Most island towns also have a tourism office in their city hall.

Learn more about foreign destinations by checking government-issued travel advisories and country information. For a broader picture, consider information from more than one country.

Tourist Information **Puerto Rico Tourism Company** ✉ Box 902-3960, Old San Juan Station, San Juan, PR 00902-3960 ☎ 787/721-2400 or 800/223-6530 in U.S. 🌐 www.gotopuertorico.com ✉ 3575 W. Cahuenga Blvd., Suite 560, Los Angeles, CA 90068 ☎ 213/874-5991 ✉ 901 Ponce de León Blvd., Suite 101, Coral Gables, FL 33134 ☎ 305/445-9112.

Government Advisories **U.S. Department of State** ✉ Overseas Citizens Services Office, 2100 Pennsylvania Ave. NW, 4th fl., Washington, DC 20520 ☎ 202/647-5225 interactive hotline or 888/407-4747 🌐 www.travel.state.gov. **Consular Affairs Bureau of Canada** ☎ 800/267-6788 or 613/944-6788 🌐 www.voyage.gc.ca. **U.K. Foreign and Commonwealth Office** ✉ Travel Advice Unit, Consular Division, Old Admiralty Bldg., London SW1A 2PA ☎ 0870/606-0290 or 020/7008-1500 🌐 www.fco.gov.uk/travel. **Australian Department of Foreign Affairs and Trade** ☎ 300/139-281 travel advice, 02/6261-1299 Consular Travel Advice Faxback Service 🌐 www.dfat.gov.au. **New Zealand Ministry of Foreign Affairs and Trade** ☎ 04/439-8000 🌐 www.mft.govt.nz.

WEB SITES

Do check out the World Wide Web when planning your trip. You'll find everything from weather forecasts to virtual tours of famous cities. Be sure to visit Fodors.com (🌐 www.fodors.com), a complete travel-planning site. You can research prices and book plane tickets, hotel rooms, rental cars, vacation packages, and more. In addition, you can post your pressing questions in the Travel Talk section. Other planning tools include a currency converter and weather reports, and there are loads of links to travel resources.

You can get basic information about Puerto Rico from 🌐 www.puertoricowow.com and 🌐 www.gotopuertorico.com. Maps are available at 🌐 www.travelmaps.com. For information on conferences and conventions, see the Puerto Rico Convention Center Web site at 🌐 www.prconvention.com or the Puerto Rico Convention Bureau at 🌐 www.meetpuertorico.com. In addition, many of the hotels and attractions throughout the island have their own Web sites.

SAN JUAN

1

TRY SOME COMIDA CRIOLLA
at Ajili Mojili ⇨ *p.32*

GET THEE TO A NUNNERY
El Convento Hotel, which was once a Carmelite convent ⇨ *p.40*

SHOP FOR ART AND LOCAL DESIGNS
in San Juan's great boutiques ⇨ *p.62*

GAZE AT THE MASTERWORKS
in the Museo de Arte de Puerto Rico ⇨ *p.17*

LAY OUT ON THE CITY'S BEST BEACH
Playa de Isla Verde ⇨ *p.57*

JUMP-START YOUR TASTE BUDS
at the Parrot Club, where the passion-fruit cocktail is a cool start ⇨ *p.29*

Updated by John Marino and Isabel Abislaimán

SAN JUAN IS PARADISE'S BABY IN AN URBAN COMFORTER. Puerto Rico's sprawling capital is bordered to the north by the Atlantic and to the east and west by bays and lagoons. More than ⅓ of the island's 4 million citizens are proud to call themselves *sanjuaneros*. They go about their business surrounded by the antique and the modern, the commercial and the residential, the man-made and the natural.

By 1508 the explorer Juan Ponce de León had established a colony in an area now known as Caparra, southeast of present-day San Juan. He later moved the settlement north to a more hospitable peninsular location. In 1521, after he became the first colonial governor, Ponce de León switched the name of the island—which was called San Juan Bautista in honor of St. John the Baptist—with that of the settlement of Puerto Rico (Rich Port). The capital of paradise was born.

Defended by the imposing Fuerte San Felipe del Morro (El Morro), Puerto Rico's administrative and population center helped to keep the island firmly in Spain's hands until 1898, when it came under U.S. control after the Spanish-American War. Centuries of Spanish rule left an indelible imprint on the city, particularly in the walled area now known as Old San Juan. Its cobblestone streets are lined with brightly painted, well-preserved colonial structures, and the area has been a U.S. National Historic Zone since 1950.

Old San Juan is a monument to the past, but the rest of the city is firmly in the here and now. It draws migrants from elsewhere on the island to jobs in its businesses and industries. It captivates both residents and visitors with its vibrant lifestyle as well as its balmy beaches, pulsing nightclubs, and mesmerizing museums. Wrap yourself up in even one small patch of the urban comforter, and you may never want to leave this baby.

A new Puerto Rico Convention Center is expected to create a singular destination for conventions and trade shows in San Juan. It's being built on a 113-acre site in Isla Grande, a former U.S. naval base, immediately southeast of the Ribas Dominicci Regional Airport. The area is near Condado and the neighborhood of Miramar. At this writing, the center was expected to open in late 2005.

EXPLORING SAN JUAN

San Juan's metro area stretches for 12 mi along the north coast, and defining the city is rather like assembling a puzzle. Its neighborhoods are irregular and sometimes overlapping—not easily pieced together.

West from Luis Muñoz Marín Airport is Isla Verde, a stretch of high-rise-apartment complexes and hotels, many of which sit directly on a superb, sandy beach. West of Isla Verde is the more sedate Ocean Park, a residential neighborhood of low-lying buildings on another fine patch of beach, with several outstanding small hotels and restaurants and a few shops. South of Ocean Park lies Santurce, a combined residential and business district with wide roads, plenty of commercial activity, and a growing artistic vitality thanks to the Museo de Arte de Puerto Rico on De Diego Avenue. The city's core is several miles south of Santurce,

If you have 3 days

It's only fitting that you spend the first day on a *playa* (beach). Choose from the city's finest at Condado, Ocean Park, or Isla Verde, and park yourself in a rented chair with a good book, a cold drink, and plenty of sunscreen. In the evening, make sure you enjoy the warm weather dining al fresco. On the second day, take a walking tour of Old San Juan. Ramble through the cobblestone streets and get caught up in the many shops and sights, but save plenty of time for exploring the turrets, towers, and dungeons of **El Morro** 21, the original fortress on a rocky promontory at the old city's northwestern tip. Walk along Norzagaray to do the same in **Fuerte San Cristóbal** 22, or stop at the very good **Museo de las Américas** 19. Spend the morning of the third day back on the beach. Return to Old San Juan for an early lunch and some shopping along Calle Fortaleza and Calle Cristo. Hop the ferry across the bay to Cataño for a tour of the **Casa Bacardí Visitor Center** 33; the last tour is at 4, and if you time it right, you'll catch beautiful sunset views of Viejo San Juan from Morgan's, with a cuba libre in hand—but remember the last ferry is at 9 PM. Of course, if you start with Bacardí on your first day, you may want to reverse the order of this itinerary and spend your last day at the beach.

If you have 5 days

Nothing is more restful than sun, sand, and sea waves, especially after long night out in San Juan. Regardless of your personal tastes, it is highly likely that you will need to spend at least one full day on the beach recuperating from the night before. That said, you will need at least one to two days to explore Old San Juan and tour the **Casa Bacardí Visitor Center** 33 in Cataño. At some point—in between sunbathing and sightseeing—make arrangements to visit the 28,000-acre Bosque Nacional del Caribe (Caribbean National Forest) **El Yunque** on the fourth day (*see* ⇨ Chapter 2). You can either rent a car and head out yourself or sign on to a tour through your hotel. El Yunque, as this park is affectionately known, is 43 km (26 mi) southeast of San Juan (about an hour's drive). It has 100-foot trees, dramatic mountain ranges, and walking trails leading to cool, soothing waterfalls. On your way back from El Yunque, stop at the kiosks in **Luquillo.** There's nothing like fritters and cold beer after a rain-forest outing. Alternatively, you could head east for a day of golf on one of the region's championship courses. Leave one evening free so that you can go kayaking on the phosphorescent bay in **Bahía de Mosquito** in Vieques. Several companies organize excursions from San Juan (*see* ⇨ Kayaking *in* Sports & the Outdoors). Several companies offer organized tours from San Juan. If you are ambitious, you can plan another day trip, but if you are entranced by the lively metropolitan casinos, bars, and discos, on the fifth day, it's back to the beach for some (more) well-deserved rest.

If you have 7 days

Follow the five-day itinerary above, adding a walk along the **Paseo de la Princesa** 25 and the outer wall of **El Morro** 21. On the sixth day, head for the Santurce district, and immerse yourself in island art at the **Museo de Arte Contemporáneo de Puerto Rico** 30, the **Museo de Arte de Puerto Rico** 28, or both. Afterward, wander through the produce at the Plaza del Mercado in Santurce, with a fresh papaya or soursop shake in hand, and have your palm read. Be sure to note the giant bronze sculptures of avocados by artist by Annex Burgos. On the morning of the seventh day, hit the beach once more, then head to Avenida Ashford in Condado for an afternoon of shopping in its ritzy boutiques or visit the Jardin Botánico on the campus of the **Universidad de Puerto Rico** 31 in the Río Pedras district.

---

in a collection of neighborhoods including Hato Rey, a busy financial district where you'll find the large Plaza las Américas Mall, and the mostly residential Río Piedras area, home of the Universidad de Puerto Rico (University of Puerto Rico) and its museum and botanical garden.

Back along the north coast and west of Ocean Park is Condado, on a thin strip of land between the ocean and the Laguna del Condado (Condado Lagoon). Here the buzz is all about tourism: hotels crowd the beach, and tony shops and restaurants line the main drag, Avenida Ashford. Heading west from Condado will bring you to the Puerta de Tierra peninsula, between the ocean to the north and Bahía de San Juan (San Juan Bay) to the south, where there are several resort hotels and two noteworthy parks, the Parque de Tercer Milenio (Third Millennium Park) and the Parque Muñoz Rivera. Finally, west of Puerta de Tierra is famous Old San Juan, the focal point and showplace of the island's rich history, where you will find the city's finest museums and shops, as well as excellent dining and lodging. It's a soulful feast, indeed.

When to Tour San Juan

The high season is roughly mid-December through mid-April. Winter hotel rates are 25% to 40% higher than in the off-season, and hotels tend to be packed, though rarely entirely full. A winter visit may allow you to participate in several colorful annual events on the San Juan social calendar. The January San Sebastián Street Festival, held in Old San Juan, consists of several nights of live music in the plazas, food festivals, and *cabezudos* (parades), in which folk legends are caricatured using oversize masks. A near-winter festival, the mid-November Festival of Puerto Rican Music, is held both in San Juan venues and out on the island. The festival celebrates Puerto Rico's traditional *plena* and *bomba* folk music with competitions and concerts.

A less expensive time to visit San Juan is during the "shoulder" seasons of fall and spring, when the weather is still fantastic and the tourist crush is less intense. Weather in San Juan is moderate and tropical year-round, with an average temperature of about 82°F (26°C). And although it's true that much of the summer encompasses the hurricane season, San Juan is still an attractive destination during those months—many accommodations charge the lowest rates of the year, restaurant reservations are easier to come by, and the streets are free of tourists.

Old San Juan

Old San Juan is compelling. Its 16th-century cobblestone streets, ornate Spanish town houses with wrought-iron balconies, busy plazas, and museums are all the repositories of the island's history. Founded in 1521 by the Spanish explorer Juan Ponce de León, Old San Juan (*Viejo San Juan*) sits on a peninsula separated from "new" San Juan by a couple of miles and a couple of centuries. Ironically, it's youthful and vibrant. It has a culture unto itself, reflecting the sensibilities of the stylish professionals, the bohemian art crowd, and the skateboarding teenagers who populate its streets. You'll find more streetside cafés and restaurants, more contemporary art galleries, more musicians playing in plazas, than anywhere else in San Juan.

At the northwest end of Old San Juan, Calle Norzagaray leads to El Morro, the old city's defense bastion. On the north side of Calle Norzagaray, you'll note a small neighborhood at the foot of an embankment, bordering the ocean—this is La Perla, a rough neighborhood that you would do best to avoid. The west end of the old city faces San Juan Bay, and it's here that the stone walls of the original city are most in evidence. On Old San Juan's south side, you'll find the commercial and cruise-ship piers that jut into San Juan Harbor.

Numbers in the text correspond to numbers in the margin and on the Old San Juan map.

a good walk

Start at the central **Plaza de Armas** ❶ ⚑, bordered by calles San Francisco, San José, and Cruz. From here you can branch out, much like following the spokes of a wheel, to various parts of the old city. On the north side of the plaza is the **Alcaldía** ❷, the former city hall built between 1604 and 1789. On the west side of the plaza, the regal **La Intendencia** ❸, once the Spanish Treasury building, now houses Puerto Rico's State Department.

A block to the west is Calle Cristo and its many galleries and clothing outlets. Head south on Cristo and follow it to its end and the **Capilla del Cristo** ❹, an ornate 18th-century chapel. You can gaze through the gates at the ornate altar, but note that it's open only on Tuesday. To the right of the chapel is the **Parque de las Palomas** ❺, roost for many of the city's pigeons. A few steps north, also on Calle Cristo, is the **Casa del Libro** ❻, home to rare books and exhibits on bookbinding. Next door, the **Centro Nacional de Artes Populares y Artesanías** ❼ displays island crafts. Walk north on Calle Cristo from the Casa del Libro to Calle Fortaleza, where you should turn left and then, after a block, right on Calle Recinto Oeste to reach **La Fortaleza** ❽, the imposing former bastion now used as the governor's residence. Backtrack east on Calle Fortaleza and south on Calle Cristo to the Parque de las Palomas. A block and a half east of here, along Calle Tetuán, is the **Casa de Ramón Power y Giralt** ❾, the restored home of an 18th-century naval hero and politician.

From Casa de Ramón Power y Giralt, head back west to Calle Cristo and walk north for two blocks to find the looming **Catedral de San Juan** ❿. Across the street from the cathedral is one of the city's premier hotels, El Convento, which was once a Carmelite convent. Adjacent to the hotel on the west side of Plaza de Catedral is the small but absolutely child-friendly **Museo del Niño** ⓫, which has natural-history exhibits and educational interactive displays. If you go west from the Museo del Niño on Caleta de las Monjas, you'll find a small plaza, the **Plazuela de la Rogativa** 12. The statue here of a priest and three women commemorates the historic moment when British attackers were frightened off by torches of a religious procession, or *rogativa,* which they mistook for Spanish reinforcements.

Keep going north on Calle Cristo until you reach the white stucco **Iglesia de San José** 13, one of the oldest churches in the western hemisphere, on the far side of Plaza San José. On the plaza's east side are two museums: the two-story **Museo Pablo Casals** 14, which celebrates the life and art of the famous cellist, and the **Museo de Nuestra Raíz Africana** 15, which investigates African influences on Puerto Rico's culture. Also on the plaza, to the west of the church, is the 1532 **Convento de los Dominicos** 16, now home to the bookshop of the Instituto de Cultura Puertorriqueña (Institute of Puerto Rican Culture), where you can buy folk crafts. A short walk west on Calle San Sebastián will bring you to the **Casa Blanca** 17, built in 1521 as a home for Ponce de León, and rebuilt in 1523 after a hurricane destroyed the original.

Traveling north on Calle Cristo from Plaza San José will bring you to Calle Norzagaray; to the east is the **Museo de Arte y Historia de San Juan** 18, once a bustling marketplace and now an art and history museum. West on Calle Norzagaray, you'll pass the large Plaza de Quinto Centenario, a tribute to the quincentennial of Columbus's voyages. On its west side is the Cuartel de Ballajá, a three-story structure that once served as a military barracks. Today the second floor is home to the **Museo de las Américas** 19 and its rotating exhibits of Latin American art. The next building west of the Cuartel is the old Asilo de Beneficencia, once a hospital for indigents and now the headquarters of the Instituto de Cultura Puertorriqueña. On its first floor is the tiny **Museo del Indio** 20, a museum that traces the indigenous Taíno culture of Puerto Rico through artifacts and a short video presentation. Finally, look to the northwest across a wide field. The massive stone structure on the hill is **Fuerte San Felipe del Morro** 21, also known as El Morro, the city's premier defense bastion, built between 1540 and 1783 and well worth a visit.

East of El Morro on Calle Norzagaray is Old San Juan's second fort. **Fuerte San Cristóbal** 22, built in the 18th century, guarded the north end of the city. Near its base is the **Plaza de Colón** 23, bordered by Calle San Francisco and Calle O'Donell and adorned with a large statue of Christopher Columbus. On the south side of the plaza, across Calle Fortaleza on Calle Recinto Sur, stands the **Teatro Tapia** 24, which has been hosting performances since 1832. If you were to head south and west on Calle Recinto Sur, you'll pass La Princesa, once the old city's jail and now the offices of the Puerto Rican Tourism Company. On the south side of the building is **Paseo de la Princesa** 25, a long, wide promenade that stretches to the Bahía de San Juan.

TIMING & PRECAUTIONS Old San Juan is, in effect, a small neighborhood, approximately seven city blocks square with numerous side streets, alleys, and hidden plazas. In strictly geographical terms, it's easily traversed in a day, but lingering is what Old San Juan is all about. To truly appreciate the numerous museums, galleries, and cafés requires two or three days—and the walk

Architecture San Juan has been under construction for nearly 500 years. The old city's colonial Spanish–row houses—brick with plaster fronts painted in pastel blues, oranges, and yellows—line narrow streets and alleys paved with *adoquines* (blue-gray stones originally used as ballast in Spanish ships). Several churches, including the Catedral de San Juan, were built in the ornate Spanish Gothic style of the 16th century. The massive, white-marble El Capitolio, home of Puerto Rico's legislature, was completed in 1929. The gleaming high-rise resorts along the beaches in Condado and Isla Verde and the glistening steel-and-glass towers in the business and financial district of Hato Rey belong to the end of the 20th century.

Beaches Just because you're staying in the city doesn't mean you'll have to forgo time on the *playa* (beach). San Juan's beaches are among the island's best, and Condado, Isla Verde, and Ocean Park—to name just a few sandy stretches—are always abuzz. The government maintains 13 *balnearios* (public beaches), including two in the San Juan–metro area. They're gated and have dressing rooms, lifeguards, parking, and in some cases picnic tables, playgrounds, and camping facilities. Admission is free; hours are generally daily from 9 to 5 in summer and Tuesday through Sunday from 9 to 5 during the rest of the year.

Music Music is a source of Puerto Rican pride, and it seems that, increasingly, everyone wants to live that *vida loca* (crazy life) espoused by Puerto Rico's own Ricky Martin. The brash Latin sound is best characterized by the music–dance form salsa, which shares not only its name with the word "sauce," but also its zesty, hot flavor. This fusion of West African percussion, jazz (especially swing and Big Band), and other Latin beats (mambo, merengue, flamenco, cha-cha, rumba) is sexy and primal. Dancing to it is a chance to let go of inhibitions.

Nightlife Almost a big city, San Juan boasts a wide variety of restaurants and bars for people of all palates and party habits. Old San Juan and Condado, in particular, are big night-time destinations. Many of the newer establishments have set their tables on terraces, on the beach, on indoor patios, or simply streetside to take advantage of the late-night atmosphere. Many clubs and discos open until the wee hours of the morning, though some discos attract violent crowds, so caution should be exercised at these sometimes raucous places. Casinos are also a big attraction, mostly for visitors. Locals tend to test their luck after a wedding reception in a big hotel, unless they're regulars at the slot machines.

---

described above is designed with that in mind. If you're limited to a day, you'll need to pick and choose sights according to your interests. It can be done—it's just not quite so rewarding.

Don't consider driving in Old San Juan unless you have a penchant for sitting in traffic jams for much of the waking day. Old San Juan is a walking city, with narrow one-way streets, narrower alleys, sparse parking,

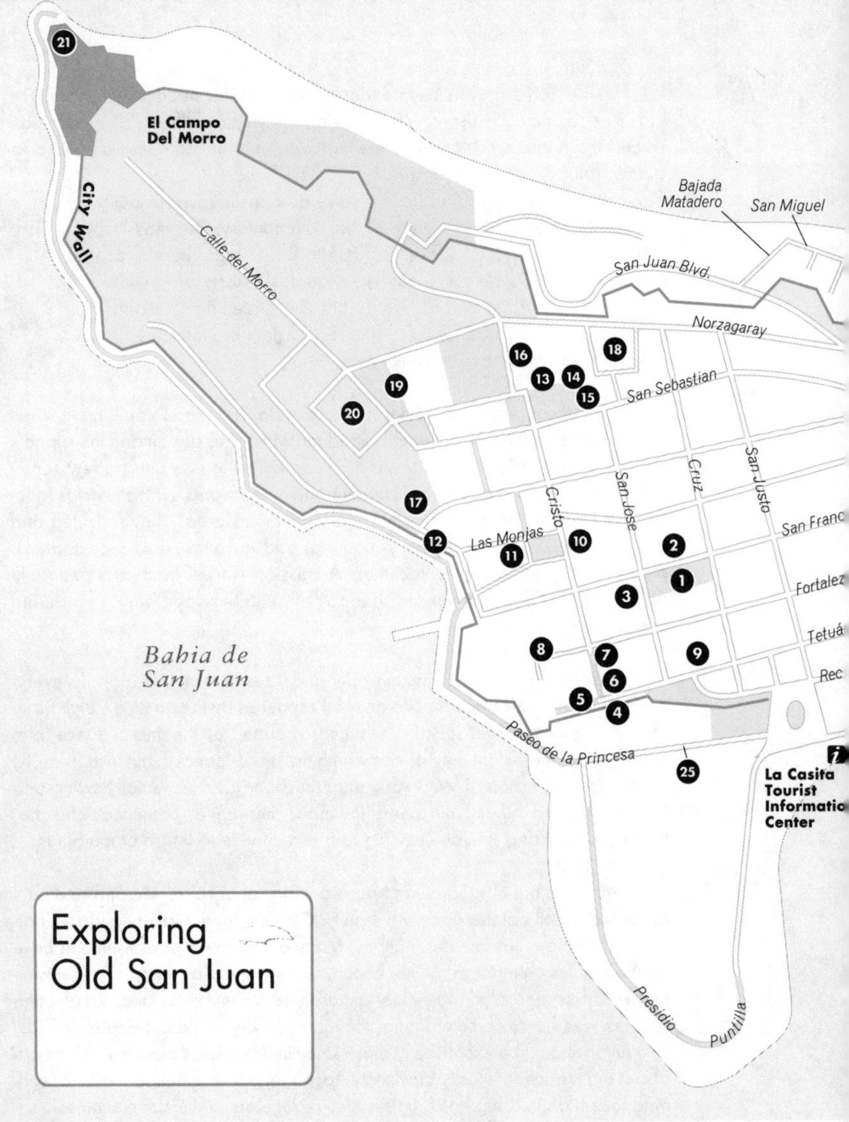

Alcaldía **2**
Capilla del Cristo **4**
Casa Blanca **17**
Casa del Libro **6**
Casa de Ramón Power y Giralt **9**
Catedral de San Juan **10**
Centro Nacional de Artes Populares y Artesanías **7**
Convento de los Dominicos **16**
La Fortaleza **8**
Fuerte San Cristóbal **22**
Fuerte San Felipe del Morro (El Morro) **21**
Iglesia de San José **13**

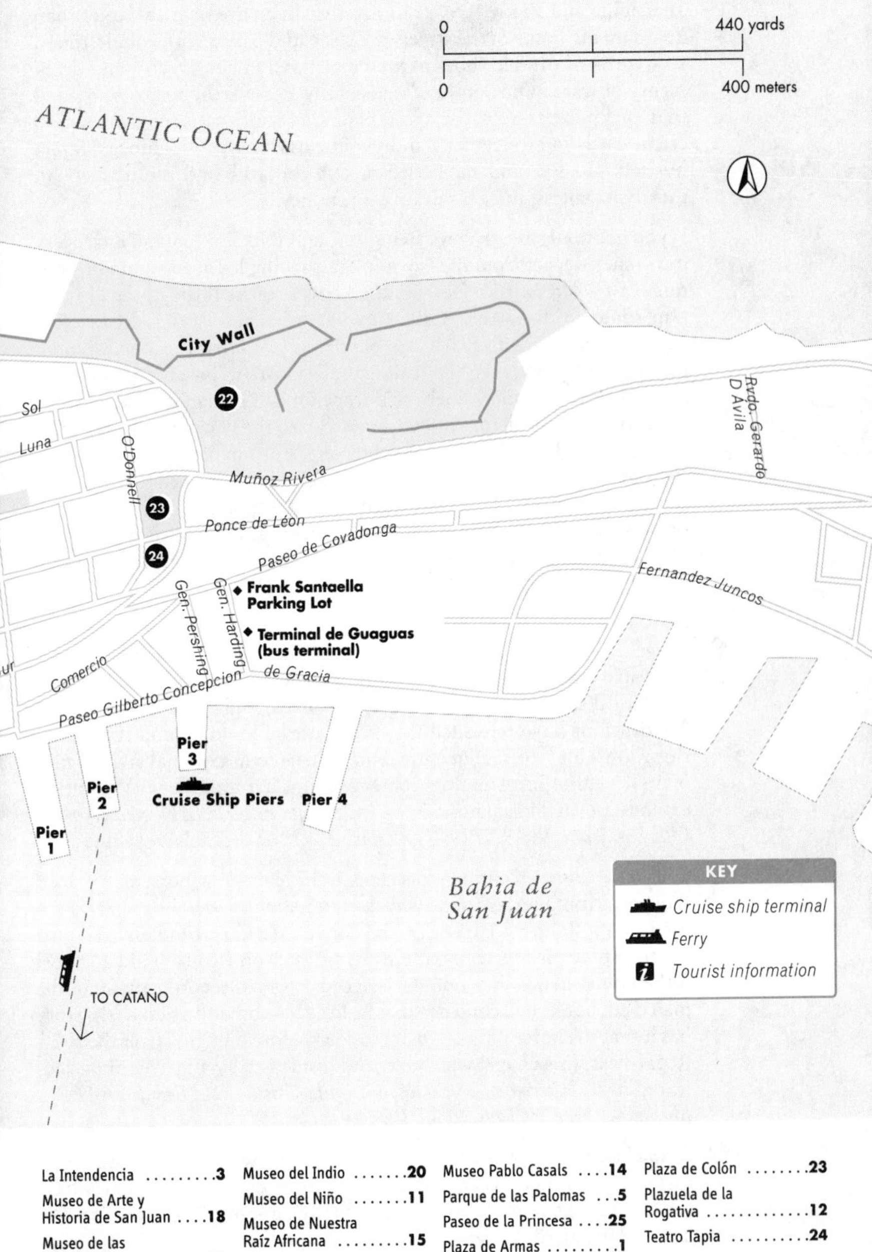

La Intendencia 3
Museo de Arte y Historia de San Juan 18
Museo de las Américas 19
Museo del Indio 20
Museo del Niño 11
Museo de Nuestra Raíz Africana 15
Museo Pablo Casals 14
Parque de las Palomas . . . 5
Paseo de la Princesa 25
Plaza de Armas 1
Plaza de Colón 23
Plazuela de la Rogativa 12
Teatro Tapia 24

and sights and shops all packed together in an area hardly larger than ½ square mi. Some of the streets are steep and paved with cobblestones, so wear comfortable shoes as well as a hat and sunscreen—and drink plenty of water. Old San Juan is generally a safe area, but keep in mind that pickpockets visit the same places as tourists. Keep money and credit cards in money belts and avoid carrying open handbags. Street hustlers are few and far between, but you will find the occasional, mostly harmless, indigent asking for money.

If you get tired, free trolleys swing through Old San Juan all day, every day—they depart from the Covadonga parking lot at the main bus terminal area across from Pier 4 and take two routes through the old city. One route heads north to Calle Norzagaray then west to El Morro (the trolley doesn't go into El Morro, but drops you off at the long footpath leading to the fort), then south along Calle Cristo to Fortaleza, San Justo, and back along Calle Gilberto Concepción de Gracia (also called Calle la Marina) to the piers. Another takes you to the Plaza de Armas, south on Calle San José, then back to the piers. Both make regular stops (at signs marked PARADA) on their routes. When you're finished touring, taxis can be found in several spots: in front of Pier 2, on the Plaza de Armas, or on Calle O'Donell near the Plaza de Colón. Puerto Ricans do a lot of internal tourism on the weekends, so expect these sites to be more crowded on weekend days.

What to See

2 **Alcaldía.** San Juan's city hall was built between 1604 and 1789. In 1841 extensive alterations were made so that it would resemble the city hall in Madrid's, with arcades, towers, balconies, and an inner courtyard. Renovations have refreshed the facade of the building and some interior rooms, but the architecture remains true to its colonial style. A municipal tourist-information center and an art gallery with rotating exhibits are on the first floor. ✉ *153 Calle San Francisco, Plaza de Armas, Old San Juan* ☎ *787/724–7171 Ext. 2391* 💰 *Free* ⏲ *Weekdays 8–4.*

4 **Capilla del Cristo.** According to legend, in 1753 a young horseman named Baltazar Montañez, carried away during festivities in honor of San Juan Bautista (St. John the Baptist), raced down Calle Cristo and plunged over its steep precipice. A witness to the tragedy promised to build a chapel if the young man's life could be saved. Historical records maintain the man died, but legend contends that he lived. (Another version of the story has it that the horse miraculously stopped before plunging over the cliff.) Regardless, this chapel was built, and inside is a small silver altar dedicated to the Christ of Miracles. ✉ *Calle Cristo, Old San Juan* ☎ *No phone* 💰 *Free* ⏲ *Tues. 10–3:30.*

17 **Casa Blanca.** The original structure on this site was a frame house built in 1521 as a home for Ponce de León. But he died in Cuba, never having lived in the home, which was virtually destroyed by a hurricane in 1523. Afterward, his son-in-law had the present masonry home built. His descendants occupied the house for 250 years. From the end of the Spanish-American War in 1898 to 1966, it housed the U.S. Army commander in Puerto Rico. A museum devoted to archaeology is on the

second floor. Select rooms, with period furniture, are open for viewing as well. The surrounding garden, cooled by fountains, is a tranquil spot for a restorative pause. ✉ *1 Calle San Sebastián, Old San Juan* ☎ *787/724–4102* 🌐 *www.icp.gobierno.pr* 🎫 *$2* 🕓 *Tues.–Sat. 9–noon and 1–4:30.*

6 **Casa del Libro.** This 18th-century building contains exhibits of books and bookbinding techniques—it's dedicated to the artistry of the printed word. The museum's 6,000 books, sketches, and illustrations include some 200 rare volumes produced before 1501, as well as what appears to be legal writing on a fragment of clay, thought to date from the time of Christ. Also on hand are several antique printing presses, one constructed in 1812 in France and brought to Puerto Rico in the mid-19th century. ✉ *255 Calle Cristo* ☎ *787/723–0354* 🌐 *www.lacasadellibro.org* 🎫 *$2 donation suggested* 🕓 *Tues.–Sat. 11–4:30.*

9 **Casa de Ramón Power y Giralt.** The restored home of 18th-century naval hero Don Ramón Power y Giralt is now the headquarters of the Conservation Trust of Puerto Rico. On-site are several displays highlighting the physical, cultural, and historical importance of land and properties on the island under the trust's aegis. You'll find a display of musical instruments that you can play, a bird diorama with recorded bird songs, an active beehive, and a seven-minute movie discussing the trust's efforts. Displays are in Spanish; the movie is in English or Spanish. A gift shop sells toys and Puerto Rican candies. ✉ *155 Calle Tetuán, Old San Juan* ☎ *787/722–5834* 🎫 *Free* 🕓 *Tues.–Sat. 10–4.*

10 **Catedral de San Juan.** The Catholic shrine of Puerto Rico had humble beginnings in the early 1520s as a thatch-top, wooden structure. Hurricane winds tore off the thatch and destroyed the church. It was reconstructed in 1540, when it was given a graceful circular staircase and vaulted Gothic ceilings. Most of the work on the present cathedral, however, was done in the 19th century. The remains of Ponce de León are in a marble tomb near the transept. ✉ *153 Calle Cristo, Old San Juan* ☎ *787/722–0861* 🌐 *www.catedralsanjuan.com* 🎫 *$1 donation suggested* 🕓 *Weekdays 8:30–4; masses Sat. at 7 PM, Sun. at 9 AM and 11 AM, weekdays at 12:15 PM.*

7 **Centro Nacional de Artes Populares y Artesanías.** Run by the Institute of Puerto Rican Culture, the Popular Arts and Crafts Center is in a colonial building next to the Casa del Libro, and is a superb repository of island crafts, some of which are for sale. ✉ *253 Calle Cristo* ☎ *787/722–0621* 🎫 *Free* 🕓 *Mon.–Sat. 9–5.*

16 **Convento de los Dominicos.** Built by Dominican friars in 1523, this convent often served as a shelter during Carib Indian attacks and, more recently, as headquarters for the Antilles command of the U.S. Army. Now home to some offices of the Institute of Puerto Rican Culture, the beautifully restored building contains religious manuscripts, artifacts, and art. The institute also maintains a book and music shop on the premises. Classical concerts are held here occasionally. ✉ *98 Calle Norzagaray, Old San Juan* ☎ *787/721–6866* 🎫 *Free* 🕓 *Mon.–Sat. 9–5.*

8 **La Fortaleza.** Sitting on a hill overlooking the harbor, La Fortaleza, the western hemisphere's oldest executive mansion in continuous use, was built as a fortress. It was attacked numerous times and taken twice, by the British in 1598 and by the Dutch in 1625. Numerous changes to the original primitive structure, constructed in 1540, over the past four centuries have resulted in the present collection of marble and mahogany, medieval towers, and stained-glass galleries. The building is still the official residence of the island's governor, and much of its interior is closed to visitors. Guided tours of the extensive gardens and selected rooms are conducted every hour on the hour in English, on the half hour in Spanish; both include a short video presentation. ✉ *Calle Recinto Oeste, Old San Juan* ☎ *787/721–7000 Ext. 2211 or 2358* 🌐 *www.fortaleza.gobierno.pr* 🎟 *Free* ⏲ *Weekdays 9–4.*

need a break?

On your hike up hilly Calle Cristo, stop at **Ben & Jerry's** (✉ 61 Calle Cristo, Old San Juan ☎ 787/977–6882) at the corner of Calle Sol. You can savor Vermont ice cream under a palm tree or enjoy fresh-fruit smoothies next to a Green Mountain cow—depending on how you look at it. Olympic gymnast Michelle Campi and her mother, Celí Williams, have made this ice-cream parlor one of the friendliest hangouts in Old San Juan.

22 **Fuerte San Cristóbal.** This stone fortress, built between 1634 and 1785, guarded the city from land attacks. Even larger in structure (but not in area covered) than El Morro, San Cristóbal was known in the 17th and 18th centuries as the Gibraltar of the West Indies. Five free-standing structures are connected by tunnels, and restored units include an 18th-century barracks. You're free to explore the gun turrets, officers' quarters, and passageways. Along with El Morro, San Cristóbal is a National Historic Site administered by the U.S. Park Service; it's a UN World Heritage Site as well. Rangers conduct tours in Spanish and English. ✉ *Calle Norzagaray, Old San Juan* ☎ *787/729–6960* 🌐 *www.nps.gov/saju* 🎟 *$3; combo ticket with El Morro $5* ⏲ *Daily 9–5.*

21 Fodor's Choice ★ **Fuerte San Felipe del Morro.** On a rocky promontory at the northwestern tip of the old city is El Morro (which translates as "promontory"), a fortress built by the Spaniards between 1540 and 1783. Rising 140 feet above the sea, the massive six-level fortress covers enough territory to accommodate a 9-hole golf course. It is a labyrinth of dungeons, ramps, barracks, turrets, towers, and tunnels. Built to protect the port, El Morro has a commanding view of the harbor. You're free to wander throughout. The cannon emplacement walls are thick as a child's arm is long, and the dank secret passageways are a wonder of engineering. The fort's small but enlightening museum displays ancient Spanish guns and other armaments, military uniforms, and blueprints for Spanish forts in the Americas. There's also a gift shop. The fort is a National H&istoric Site administered by the U.S. Park Service; it's a UN World Heritage Site as well. Tours and a video are available in English. ✉ *Calle Norzagaray, Old San Juan* ☎ *787/729–6960* 🌐 *www.nps.gov/saju* 🎟 *$3; combo ticket with El Morro $5* ⏲ *Daily 9–5.*

13 **Iglesia de San José.** With its vaulted ceilings, this church is a splendid example of 16th-century Spanish Gothic architecture. It was built under the supervision of Dominican friars in 1532, making it one of the oldest churches in the western hemisphere. The body of Ponce de León, the Spanish explorer who came to the New World seeking the Fountain of Youth, was buried here for almost three centuries before being moved to the Catedral de San Juan in 1913. *Calle San Sebastián, Plaza de San José 787/725–7501 $1 donation suggested Mon.–Sat. 8:30–4; mass Sun. at 12:15 PM.*

3 **La Intendencia.** From 1851 to 1898, this three-story neoclassical building was home to the Spanish treasury; now it's the headquarters of Puerto Rico's State Department. You can go inside, where the wide interior courtyard, typical of colonial architectural, is framed by the high arcades of the perimeter walkways. *200 Calle San José, at Calle San Francisco, Old San Juan 787/722–2121 Ext. 230 Free Weekdays 8–noon and 1–4:30 Tours in Spanish at 2 and 3, in English at 4.*

18 **Museo de Arte y Historia de San Juan.** A bustling marketplace in 1855, this handsome building is now the modern San Juan Museum of Art and History. You'll find exhibits of Puerto Rican art and audiovisual shows that present the island's history. Concerts and other cultural events take place in the huge interior courtyard. *150 Calle Norzagaray, at Calle MacArthur, Old San Juan 787/724–1875 Free Tues.–Sun. 10–4.*

19 **Museo de las Américas.** One of the finest collections of its type in Puerto Rico, the Museum of the Americas is on the second floor of the imposing former military barracks, Cuartel de Ballajá. Most exhibits rotate, but the focus is on the popular and folk art of Latin America. The permanent exhibit, "Las Artes Populares en las Américas," has religious figures, musical instruments, basketwork, costumes, farming, and other implements of the Americas. The old military barracks, big and boxy in a neoclassical style and painted green and peach, was built between 1854 and 1864, and its immense inner courtyard is used for concerts and private events such as weddings. With a little notice, the staff can take you on a guided tour. *Calle Norzagaray and Calle del Morro, Old San Juan 787/724–5052 www.museolasamericas.org Free Tues.–Fri. 10–4, weekends 11–5.*

Fodor's Choice ★

20 **Museo del Indio.** The Instituto de Cultura Puertorriqueña (Institute of Puerto Rican Culture) maintains the small Museum of the Indian as a repository of ancient Taíno artifacts and information regarding Taíno life some 500 years ago. The short tour starts with a five-minute video describing the island's geophysical origins, and displays include Taíno religious figures carved from rock, digging and fishing implements, and a replica of a Taíno home. The museum is in the institute's headquarters in the Asilo de Beneficencia, once a hospital for the poor. *Calle Beneficencia at Calle del Morro 787/724–0700 $1 Tues.–Sat. 10–4.*

11 **Museo del Niño.** This three-floor, hands-on "museum" is pure fun for kids. There are games to play, clothes for dress-up, a mock plaza with market, even a barber shop where children can play (no real scissors

here). One of the newer exhibits is an immense food-groups pyramid, where children can climb to place magnets representing different foods. Older children will appreciate the top-floor garden where bugs and plants are on display, and the little ones can pretend to go shopping or to work at a construction site. For toddlers, there's a playground. Note that the museum's ticket window closes an hour before the museum. ✉ *150 Calle Cristo* ☎ *787/722–3791* 🌐 *www.museodelninopr.org* *$4, $5 for children* ⏱ *Tues.–Thurs. 9–3:30, Fri. 9–5, weekends 12:30–5.*

15 **Museo de Nuestra Raíz Africana.** The Institute of Puerto Rican Culture created this museum to help Puerto Ricans understand African influences in island culture. On display over two floors are African musical instruments, documents relating to the slave trade, and a list of African words that have made it into popular Puerto Rican culture. ✉ *101 Calle San Sebastián, Plaza de San José, Old San Juan* ☎ *787/724–0700 Ext. 4239* 🌐 *www.icp.gobierno.pr* *Free* ⏱ *Tues.–Sat. 8:30–4:20.*

14 **Museo Pablo Casals.** The small, two-story museum contains memorabilia of the famed cellist, who made his home in Puerto Rico from 1956 until his death in 1973. Manuscripts, photographs, and his favorite cellos are on display, in addition to recordings and videotapes (shown on request) of Casals Festival concerts, which he instituted in 1957. The festival is held annually in June. ✉ *101 Calle San Sebastián, Plaza de San José, Old San Juan* ☎ *787/723–9185* *$1* ⏱ *Tues.–Sat. 9:30–5:30.*

5 **Parque de las Palomas.** Never have birds had it so good. The small shaded park bordering Old San Juan's Capilla del Cristo has a large stone wall with pigeonholes cut into it. Hundreds of *palomas* (pigeons) roost here, and the park is full of cooing local children chasing the well-fed birds. There's a small kiosk where you can buy refreshments and bags of seed to feed the palomas. Stop to enjoy the wide views over the bay.

25 **Paseo de la Princesa.** This street down at the port is spruced up with flowers, trees, benches, street lamps, and a striking fountain depicting the various ethnic groups of Puerto Rico. Take a seat and watch the boats zip across the water. At the west end of the paseo, beyond the fountain, is the beginning of a shoreline path that hugs Old San Juan's walls and leads to the city gate at Calle San Juan.

1 **Plaza de Armas.** The old city's original main square was once used as military drilling grounds. Bordered by calles San Francisco, Rafael Codero, San José, and Cruz, it has a fountain with 19th-century statues representing the four seasons, as well as a bandstand and a small café. This is a central meeting place in Old San Juan, and you're likely to encounter everything from local bands to artists sketching caricatures to street preachers imploring the wicked to repent.

need a break?

At **Café 4 Estaciones,** on the Plaza de Armas in Old San Juan, tables and chairs sit under a canvas canopy surrounded by potted plants. It's the perfect spot to put down your shopping bags and rest your tired feet. Grab a *café con leche* (coffee with hot milk), an espresso, or cold drink, and watch the children chase the pigeons.

PEACEFUL MUSIC

C**ELLIST PABLO CASALS** *was one of the 20th century's most influential musicians. Born in Catalonia in 1876, he studied in Spain and Belgium, settled for a time in Paris, then returned to Barcelona. Tours in Europe, the United States, and South America brought him artistic and financial success and opportunities to collaborate with other prominent musicians.*

By the advent of the Spanish Civil War, he was an internationally famous musician, teacher, and conductor. He was also an outspoken supporter of a democratic Spain. Forced into exile by Franco's regime, Casals arrived in Puerto Rico, his mother's birthplace, in 1956. There, the 81-year-old maestro continued to work and teach. He established the Casals Festival of Classical Music, making it a home for sublime orchestral and chamber works. During two weeks each June, the Puerto Rico Symphony Orchestra is joined by musicians from all over the world.

In Catalan, Casal's first name is "Pau," which appropriately enough means "peace." He and his friend Albert Schweitzer appealed to the world powers to stop the arms race, and he made what many experts say is his greatest work—an oratorio titled "The Manger"—his personal message of peace. Casals died in Puerto Rico in 1973, but his many legacies live on. His favorite instruments, his recordings, and some of his many awards, are preserved at the Museo Pablo Casals.

— Karen English

23 **Plaza de Colón.** A statue of Christopher Columbus stands atop a high pedestal in this bustling Old San Juan square. Originally called St. James Square, it was renamed in honor of Columbus on the 400th anniversary of his arrival in Puerto Rico. Bronze plaques on the statue's base relate various episodes in the life of the great explorer. On the north side of the plaza is a terminal for buses to and from San Juan.

12 **Plazuela de la Rogativa.** According to legend, the British, while laying siege to the city in 1797, mistook the flaming torches of a *rogativa*—religious processions—for Spanish reinforcements, and beat a hasty retreat. In this little plaza, statues of a bishop and three women commemorate the legend. The monument was created in 1971 by the artist Lindsay Daen to mark the old city's 450th anniversary. ✉ *Caleta de las Monjas, Old San Juan.*

24 **Teatro Tapia.** Named after the Puerto Rican playwright Alejandro Tapia y Rivera, this municipal theater was built in 1832 and remodeled in 1949 and again in 1987. It showcases ballets, plays, and operettas. Stop by the box office to find out what's showing. ✉ *Calle Fortaleza, Plaza de Colón, Old San Juan* ☎ *787/722–0407.*

Greater San Juan

Modern San Juan is a study in congested highways and cement-block housing complexes, as well as the ritzy resorts of the Condado and Isla Verde shoreline. Sightseeing in the modern city requires more effort than it does in Old San Juan—the sights are scattered in the suburbs, accessible by taxi, bus, or a rental car, but not by foot.

Avenidas Muñoz Rivera, Ponce de León, and Fernández Juncos are the main thoroughfares that cross Puerta de Tierra, just east of Old San Juan, to the business and tourist districts of Condado and Isla Verde. Puente Dos Hermanos (Bridge of the Brothers) connects Puerta de Tierra with Condado's avenidas Ashford and Isla Verde, which goes through Ocean Park and on to Isla Verde. The G. Esteves and San Antonio bridges also connect Puerta de Tierra to "new" San Juan.

Due south of the Laguna del Condado is Miramar, a residential area with fashionable turn-of-the-20th-century homes and a few hotels and restaurants. East of Miramar and south of Ocean Park is Santurce, another business and residential area characterized by high-rise office and apartment complexes. South of that is the Golden Mile—Hato Rey, the city's financial and banking hub. Isla Verde, with its glittering beachfront hotels, casinos, discos, and public beach, is to the east, near the airport.

Numbers in the text correspond to numbers in the margin and on the Greater San Juan map.

a good tour

East of Old San Juan on Avenida Ponce de León you'll find **El Capitolio** 26 ►, Puerto Rico's magnificent capitol building. At the east end of Puerta de Tierra is the Caribe Hilton hotel, where you'll find the small bastion **Fuerte San Gerónimo** 27, which once guarded an entrance to San Juan Bay. Avenida Baldorioty de Castro (Route 26) leads into Miramar, then Santurce, where the Route 37 exit (Avenida José de Diego) brings you to the **Museo de Arte de Puerto Rico** 28, a former hospital that has been transformed into the island's most ambitious art museum. Farther south on José de Diego at Avenida Ponce de León is the **Centro de Bellas Artes Luis A. Ferré** 29, the boxy, white performing-arts center.

Minutes from the arts center, west on Avenida Fernández Juncos, then left on Calle Sagrado Corazón, is the Universidad del Sagrado Corazón (Sacred Heart University) and its **Museo de Arte Contemporáneo de Puerto Rico** 30, with a fine collection of contemporary Puerto Rican art. From the university, it's a straight ride south on Avenida Ponce de León (Route 25) to the Río Piedras district, where you'll find the **Universidad de Puerto Rico** 31 and its Museo de Historia, Antropología y Arte. Less than 1 mi to the west, at the junction of routes 1 and 847, is the university's Jardín Botánico, a 75-acre garden. If you're looking for a place to jog or play tennis, visit the **Parque Central Municipo de San Juan** 32 in Miramar, at the Calle Cerra exit off Avenida John F. Kennedy (Route 2), northwest of the university.

TIMING Depending on what mode of transportation you choose, you can see these sights in a day; if you linger in the museums, exploring the Greater San

Juan area might require two days. Buses are the least expensive but most time-consuming way to travel. Taxis are more convenient and you won't get lost—consider hiring a taxi by the hour and covering your selected sights in a couple of hours. Taxis charge $30 per hour for city tours, but the rate can be negotiable for long stretches of time. If you choose to rent a car, get a good map. San Juan's roads are well marked, but one-way streets pop up out of nowhere, and traffic jams at rush hour are frequent.

What to See

26 **El Capitolio.** Puerto Rico's capitol is a white marble building with Corinthian columns that dates from the 1920s. The grand rotunda, with mosaics and friezes, was completed in the late 1990s. The seat of the island's bicameral legislature, the capitol contains Puerto Rico's constitution and is flanked by the modern buildings of the Senate and the House of Representatives. There are spectacular views from the observation plaza on the capitol's sea side. Pick up a booklet about the building from the House Secretariat on the second floor. Guided tours are by appointment only. You can also watch the legislature in action—note that the action is in Spanish—on select days, most often Monday and Tuesday. ⊠ *Av. Ponce de León, Puerta de Tierra* ☎ *787/724–8979* 🎫 *Free* ⏲ *Daily 8:30–5.*

29 **Centro de Bellas Artes Luis A. Ferré.** This completely modern facility, the largest of its kind in the Caribbean, hosts the yearly Pablo Casals Festival in June and has a full schedule of concerts, plays, and operas throughout the year. The entrance wall is characterized by an immense mural by artist Jaime Suárez. Stop by the ticket office for a list of current shows. ⊠ *Av. José de Diego and Av. Ponce de León, Santurce* ☎ *787/725–7334* 🌐 *www.cba.gobierno.pr.*

27 **Fuerte San Gerónimo.** At Puerta de Tierra's eastern tip, behind the splashy Caribe Hilton, this tiny fort is perched over the Atlantic like an afterthought. Added to San Juan's fortifications in the 18th century, it barely survived the British attack of 1797. Restored in 1983 by the Institute of Puerto Rican Culture, it's now leased by the Caribe Hilton for private functions. The buildings are empty and the structure itself is the attraction, but it's free and open to the public (accessed from the Caribe Hilton entrance). ⊠ *Calle Rosales, Puerta de Tierra* ☎ *787/724–5477.*

★ 30 **Museo de Arte Contemporáneo de Puerto Rico.** The museum opened in this renovated historic building in early 2003. The red-brick, Georgian-style structure displays a dynamic range of painting, sculpture, photography, and new-media art by both established and up-and-coming Puerto Rican and Latin American artists. Exhibits, movies, conferences, and workshops are scheduled throughout the year. ⊠ *Av. Ponce de León, corner of Av. R. H. Todd, Santurce* ☎ *787/977–4030* 🌐 *www.museocontemporaneopr.org* 🎫 *Free* ⏲ *Tues.–Sat. 10–4, Sun. 1–4.*

28 **Museo de Arte de Puerto Rico.** The west wing of this ambitious 130,000-square-foot museum is the former San Juan Municipal Hospital, a 1920s neoclassical building that contains a permanent collection of Puerto Rican art dating from the 17th century to the present. The newly

Fodor's Choice ★

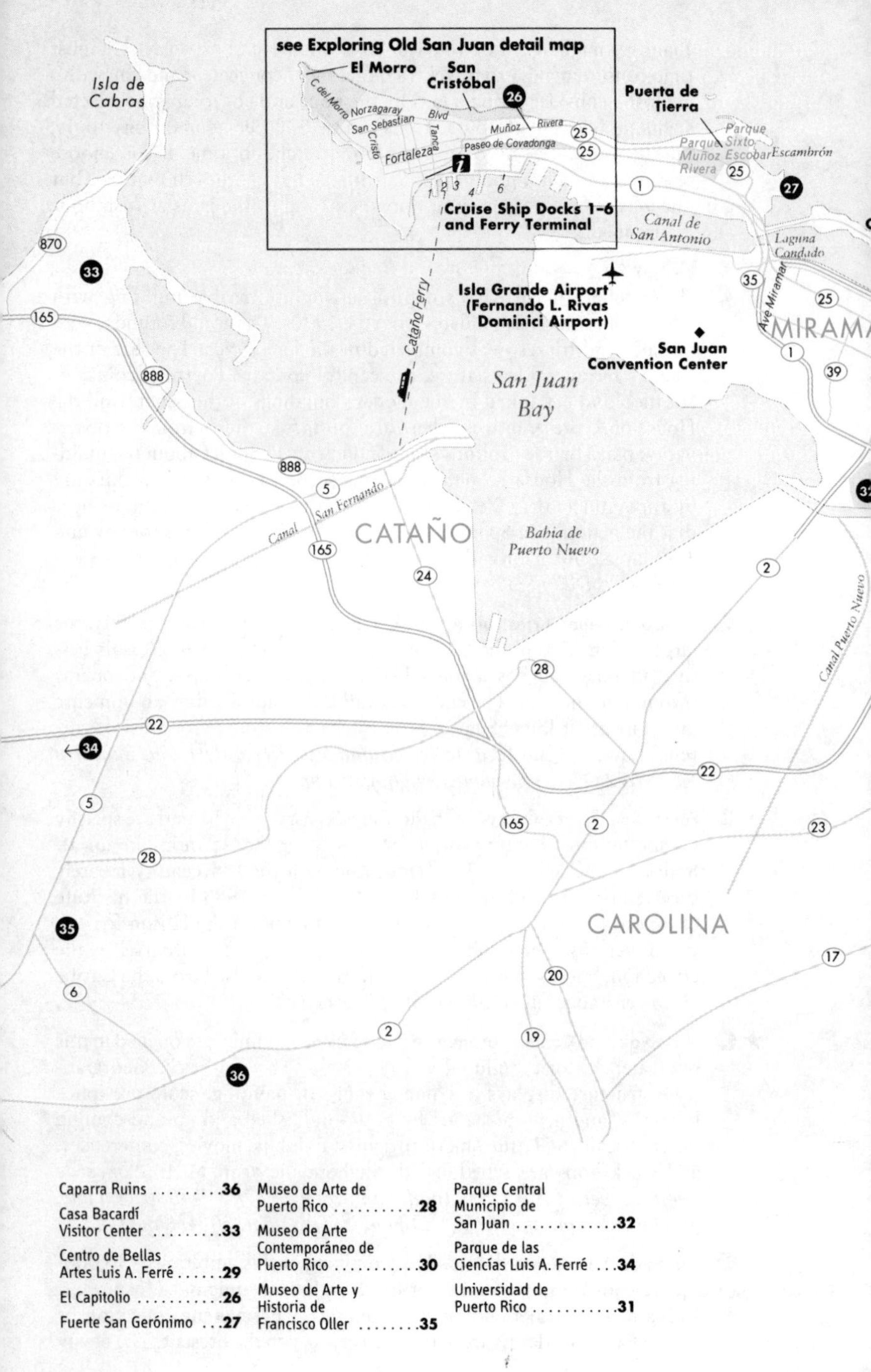

Caparra Ruins 36
Casa Bacardí Visitor Center 33
Centro de Bellas Artes Luis A. Ferré 29
El Capitolio 26
Fuerte San Gerónimo . . .27
Museo de Arte de Puerto Rico 28
Museo de Arte Contemporáneo de Puerto Rico 30
Museo de Arte y Historia de Francisco Oller 35
Parque Central Municipio de San Juan 32
Parque de las Ciencias Luis A. Ferré . . .34
Universidad de Puerto Rico 31

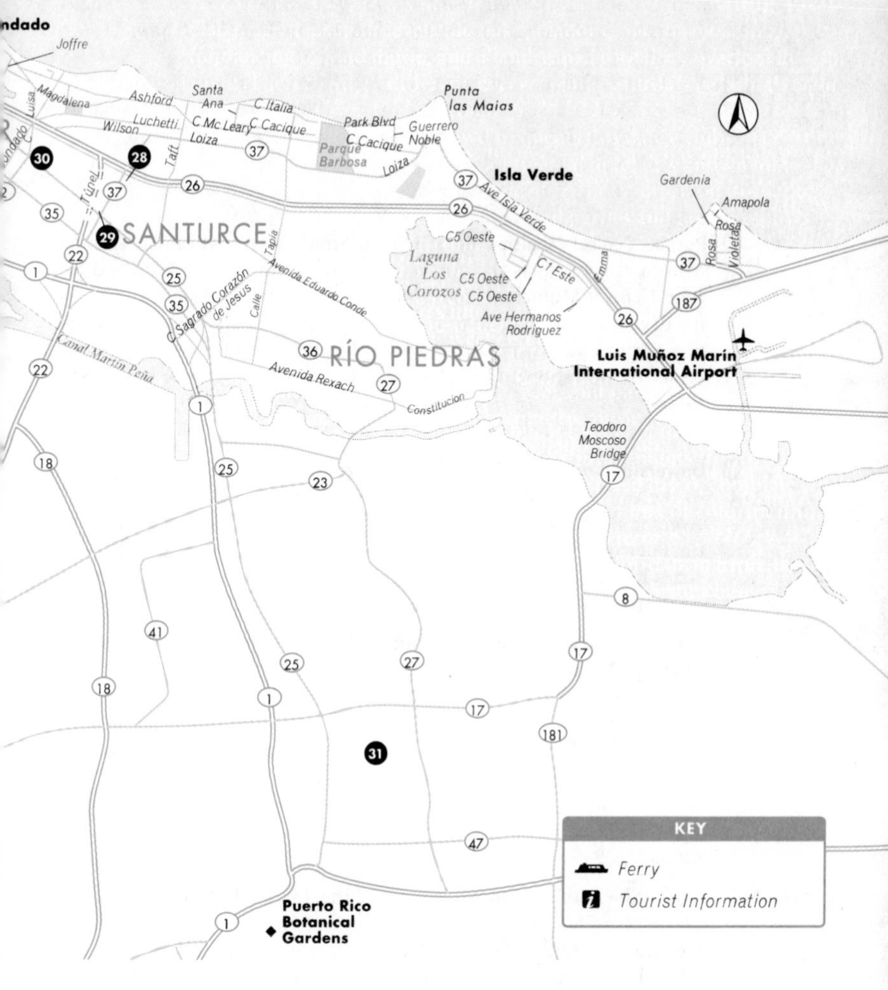

Exploring
Greater San Juan
ATLANTIC OCEAN
Joffre
Magdalena
Luisa
Ashford
Santa Ana
C Italia
Luchetti
Wilson
C Mc Leary
C Cacique
Loiza
Park Blvd
C Cacique
Guerrero Noble
Punta las Maias
Parque Barbosa
Loiza
Taft
Túnel
Isla Verde
Ave Isla Verde
Gardenia
Amapola
Rosa
Rosa
Violeta
SANTURCE
Tapia
C5 Oeste
Laguna Los Corozos
C5 Oeste
C5 Oeste
C1 Este
Emma
Avenida Eduardo Conde
C Sagrado Corazón de Jesus
Calle
Ave Hermanos Rodriguez
Canal Martín Peña
RÍO PIEDRAS
Avenida Rexach
Constitucion
Luis Muñoz Marín International Airport
Teodoro Moscoso Bridge
Puerto Rico Botanical Gardens
KEY
Ferry
Tourist Information

constructed east wing is dominated by a five-story-tall stained-glass window, the work of local artist Eric Tabales, which towers over the museum's Grand Hall and faces a 5-acre garden. In the east wing there are galleries for changing exhibits, an interactive Family Gallery, and a 400-seat theater that's worth seeing for the stage's remarkable lace curtain alone. The garden has a sculpture trail, a pond, and a variety of native flora. *300 Av. José De Diego, Santurce* *787/977–6277* *www.mapr.org* *$5* *Tues.–Sat. 10–5, Wed. 10–8, Sun. 11–6.*

need a break?

While in Santurce, drop by **Plaza del Mercado,** a produce market surrounded by restaurants where you can have fresh fish for lunch at reasonable prices. The area also has many *botánicas,* small stores that sell herbs, candles, and religious items. There may even be an in-house card- or palm-reader ready to show you your future.

32 **Parque Central Municipo de San Juan.** Southeast of Miramar, Avenida Muñoz Rivera skirts the northern side of the mangrove-bordered San Juan Central Municipal Park. Built for the 1979 Pan-American Games, it's dry and dusty but, with several miles of trails and inexpensive tennis courts, it's a good place to work off some of San Juan's rich desserts. It has a sports shop and a cafeteria. *Calle Cerra, exit on Rte. 2, Santurce* *787/722–1646* *75¢ per vehicle* *Mon. 2–10, Tues.–Thurs. 6:30 AM–10 PM, Fri. 6:30 AM–9 PM, weekends 6:30 AM–6 PM.*

31 **Universidad de Puerto Rico.** The southern district of Río Piedras is home to the University of Puerto Rico, between Avenida Ponce de León and Avenida Barbosa. The campus is one of the two performance venues for the Puerto Rico Symphony Orchestra (the other is the Centro de Bellas Artes Luis A. Ferré in Santurce). Theatrical productions and other concerts are also scheduled here.

The university's **Museo de Historia, Antropología y Arte** (Museum of History, Anthropology and Art) has archaeological and historical exhibits that deal with the Native American influence on the island and the Caribbean, the colonial era, and the history of slavery. Art displays are occasionally mounted; the museum's prize exhibit is the painting *El Velorio* (*The Wake*), by the 19th-century artist Francisco Oller. *Next to main university entrance on Av. Ponce de León, Río Piedras* *787/764–0000 Ext. 2452* *Free* *Mon.–Wed. and Fri. 9–4:30, Thurs. 9–9, weekends 9–3.*

The university's main attraction is the **Jardín Botánico** (Botanical Garden), a 75-acre forest of more than 200 species of tropical and subtropical vegetation. Gravel footpaths lead to a graceful lotus lagoon, a bamboo promenade, an orchid garden with some 30,000 plants, and a palm garden. Signs are in Spanish and English. Trail maps are available at the entrance gate, and groups of 10 or more can arrange guided tours ($25). *Intersection of Rtes. 1 and 847 at entrance to Barrio Venezuela, Río Piedras* *787/767–1710* *www.upr.clu.edu* *Free* *Daily 9–4:30.*

ART INVASION

PUBLIC ART IS TRANSFORMING *the Puerto Rican capital: here, a monolithic metal dove; there, avocados so big you can stretch out on them. The stained-glass blades of a windmill spin above an oceanfront drive. A bright red jack towers over children at play in a park. These are just some of the 25 works by local artists that the city commissioned from 1996 to 2000, when Governor Sila Marí Calderón was its mayor. Part of a $3 million urban-art project, the pieces range from realistic to abstract, and many were installed as part of larger renovations of parks, plazas, and markets.*

Often the works seem perfectly at home in their environments. Platanal, *by Imel Sierra Cabreras, has translucent panels that run across the ceiling of the restored Plaza del Mercado in Santurce. The avocados in* My Favorite Fruit *by Annex Burgos seem to spill from the entrance of this marketplace and across its front plaza. Although the large jack by María Elena Perales is a bit surreal, it's an appropriate addition to a playground in Parque Central Municipo de San Juan.*

Some pieces attempt to soften or enliven their surroundings. Carmen Inés Blondet, whose Fire Dance *is a collection of 28- to 35-foot spirals, seems an abstract forest in the midst of the concrete jungle. The iron spirals are interspersed with benches across a small plaza beneath an expressway. Crabs were once a common sight in Santurce (hence the name of the baseball team, the Santurce Crabbers), so Adelino González's benches for the area are bronze crabs.* Windmills of San Juan, *by Eric Tables, is a whimsical tribute to the coast and its ocean breezes. The steel tower, with its rotating wheel of color, is on a restored oceanside drive in Ocean Park.*

The works haven't been without controversy. Many residents found Paloma, *the metallic dove that towers over a busy Condado intersection ugly; others went so far as to assert that it was the cause of traffic jams. Mayor Jorge Santini even threatened to remove it during his campaign. But it appears to be here to stay. To soften the piece, a fountain was added to its base and it's now especially beautiful at night when the water is illuminated.*

As a whole, however, the statues have made San Juan more interesting. And public art is about to go islandwide. In January 2002 Governor Calderón unveiled plans for the Puerto Rico Public Art Project. Its budget of $15 million is slated to fund about 100 new works over the course of three years. Twenty-one locations have been selected by an independent committee of art experts. In San Juan, these include stations of the still-under-construction urban train, the Luis Muñoz Marín International Airport, and several government buildings and city parks. The committee also envisions installing works at nature reserves, along highways, and in school playgrounds across the island. Soon, perhaps, that new bus stop, lifeguard station, or street-vendor stand you see will truly be a work of art.

— John Marino

San Juan Environs

The metro suburbs of Cataño, Bayamón, and Guaynabo, west and south of San Juan, are separate municipalities but in many ways are indistinguishable from the city itself. Cataño, bordered by the Bahía de San Juan in the north, is an industrial suburb, perhaps most noted for its Bacardí Rum Plant. Bayamón, 15 to 30 minutes from central San Juan, depending on traffic, has an attractive central park bordered by historic buildings. Guaynabo is a mix of residential and industrial areas and is worth visiting for its historical importance—Juan Ponce de León established the island's first settlement here in Caparra, and you can visit the ruins of the original fortification.

a good tour

Make your way to Old San Juan and Pier 2 at the south end of the old city for the ferry to Cataño. Once there, take a quick taxi or bus ride to the **Casa Bacardí Visitor Center** 33 ⚑. The plant tour will lead you through the process of distilling the spirits; its new multimedia museum displays the history of the Bacardí family.

To reach the 42-acre **Parque de las Ciencias Luis A. Ferré** 34, take Route 22 south from San Juan's Avenida Ponce de León to Bayamón and head south on Route 167. A great stop for children, the park has a planetarium and a science and physics museum examining the wonders of space. Bayamón's central park on Calle Santiago Veve contains several historic buildings and a church, as well as the **Museo de Arte y Historia de Francisco Oller** 35, which is in the old city hall and dedicated to the life and work of the famous Puerto Rican artist. From the science park, head south again on Route 167, then left (east) on Route 2 into Guaynabo. You'll come to the **Caparra Ruins** 36, the site of one of San Juan's first settlements, with its small museum.

TIMING A tour of the Bacardí plant takes at least half a day, including the time required to travel to it. It's best to visit the sights in Bayamón and Guaynabo on a separate day. They're about 30 minutes from central San Juan, and you'll need a rental car or taxi to reach them. Be advised of the infamous traffic known as *el tapón de Bayamón* (Bayamón's traffic jam), which also rhymes with *chicharrón de Bayamón* (the area's famous pig-skin fritters).

What to See

33 **Casa Bacardí Visitor Center.** In 2003 Bacardí inaugurated its new multimedia center to declare Puerto Rico the Rum Capital of the World. Exiled from Cuba, the Bacardí family built the Puerto Rico plant in the 1950s. It's one of the world's largest, with the capacity to produce 100,000 gallons of spirits a day and 221 million cases a year. You can take a 45-minute tour of the bottling plant, museum (called the Cathedral of Rum), and distillery, and there's a gift shop. Yes, you'll be offered a sample. If you don't want to drive, you can reach the factory by taking the ferry from Pier 2 for 50¢ each way and then a public car from the ferry pier to the factory for about $2 or $3 per person. ✉ *Bay View Industrial Park, Rte. 888, Km 2.6, Cataño* ☎ *787/788–1500 or 787/788–8400* 🌐 *www.casabacardi.org* 🎫 *Free* ⏲ *Mon.–Sat. 8:30–5:30, Sun. 10–5. Tours every 45 min.*

need a break?

A *cuba libre* (Coca-Cola with rum and lime) is the perfect complement to the view of El Morro and Old San Juan across the bay from the bar window at **Morgan's Steak & Sea Food** (✉ 94 Av. Las Nereidas, Cataño ☎ 787/275–0850). If you come at sunset, you might be tempted to have two. And beware of the charms of the *música bohemia* (nostalgic, sultry music) or you might miss the last ferry back to the old city.

36 **Caparra Ruins.** In 1508 Ponce de León established the island's first settlement here. The ruins—a few crumbling walls—are what remains of an ancient fort. The small Museo de la Conquista y Colonización de Puerto Rico (Museum of the Conquest and Colonization of Puerto Rico) contains historical documents, exhibits, and excavated artifacts, though you can see the museum's contents in less time than it takes to say the name. Both the ruins and the museum are maintained by the Puerto Rican government's museums and parks division. ✉ *Rte. 2, Km 6.6, Guaynabo* ☎ *787/781–4795* 🌐 *www.icp.gobierno.pr* *Free* *Tues.–Sat. 8:30–4:30.*

35 **Museo de Arte y Historia de Francisco Oller.** In Bayamón's central park you'll find the 18th-century Catholic church of Santa Cruz and the neoclassical former city hall, which now houses the Francisco Oller Art and History Museum. Oller (1833–1917) was one of the most accomplished artists of his time, and in Puerto Rico is best known for his painting *El Velorio* (*The Wake*, on display at the Museo de Historia, Antropolgía y Arte at the University of Puerto Rico), which depicts the futility of a wake for a peasant child. ✉ *Calle Santiago Veve, Bayamón* ☎ *787/787–8620* *Free* *Tues.–Sat. 9–4.*

34 **Parque de las Ciencias Luis A. Ferré.** The 42-acre Luis A. Ferré Science Park contains a collection of intriguing activities and displays. The Transportation Museum has antique cars and the island's oldest bicycle. In the Rocket Plaza, children can experience a flight simulator, and in the planetarium, the solar system is projected on the ceiling. Also onsite are a small zoo and a natural-science exhibit. The park is popular with Puerto Rican schoolchildren, and, although it's a bit of a drive from central San Juan, it's a good activity for the family. ✉ *Rte. 167, Bayamón* ☎ *787/740–6878* *$5* *Wed.–Fri. 9–4, weekends and holidays 10–6.*

WHERE TO EAT

In cosmopolitan San Juan, European, Asian, and Middle Eastern eateries vie for your attention with family-owned restaurants specializing in seafood or *comida criolla* (creole cooking). U.S. chains such as McDonald's and Pizzeria Uno compete with chains like Pollo Tropical specializing in local cuisine. Although each of the city's large hotels has two or more fine restaurants, the best dining is often in stand-alone establishments—don't be shy about venturing to such places.

Dress codes vary greatly, though a restaurant's price category is a good indicator of its formality. For less expensive places, anything but beachwear is fine. Ritzier spots will expect collared shirts for men (jacket and tie requirements are rare) and chic attire for women. When in doubt, do as the Puerto Ricans often do and dress up.

For breakfast outside of your hotel, cafés are your best bet. Although it's rare for such establishments to close between breakfast and lunch, it's slightly more common for restaurants to close between lunch and dinner. Dinner is generally served late; if you arrive at a restaurant before 7 PM, you may be the only diners. Although some places don't accept reservations, it's always a good idea to make them for dinner whenever possible. This is especially true during the busy season from November through April and on weekends at any time of the year.

WHAT IT COSTS In U.S. dollars

	$$$$	$$$	$$	$	¢
AT DINNER	over $30	$20–$30	$12–$20	$8–$12	under $8

Prices are per person for a main course at dinner.

Old San Juan

Cafés

$$–$$$ ✕ **Café Berlin.** Tasty vegetarian fare prevails at this spot overlooking Plaza Colón. Long known for its fresh-baked pastries, breads, and fruit juices, the café has added a small bar, which is one of the few places in Puerto Rico that serves draft beer. The tofu steak, served in a mushroom Marsala sauce, is every bit as flavorful as the real thing. The turkey Berlin is a fileted breast in a mustard-curry sauce, served with an ample helping of vegetables and a salad of local root vegetables. It's a perfect stop after you tour Old San Juan. ✉ *407 Calle San Francisco, Old San Juan* ☎ *787/722–5205* ▭ *AE, MC, V.*

★ $–$$ ✕ **Cafeteria Mallorca.** The specialty here is the *mallorca,* a sweet pastry that's buttered, grilled, and then sprinkled with powdered sugar. Wash one down with a terrific cup of *café con leche* (coffee with milk). For something more substantial, try the breakfast mallorca, which has ham and cheese. The waitstaff—all dressed in crisp green uniforms and caps—are attentive. ✉ *300 Calle San Francisco, Old San Juan* ☎ *787/724–4607* ▭ *MC, V* ⊗ *Closed Sun.*

¢–$$ ✕ **La Bombonera.** Strong coffee and excellent pastries make this café, a landmark that was established in 1903, very popular in the morning—particularly on Sunday. All this even though the waiters are grumpy and give the appearance of having worked here since day one. It's open from 7:30 AM to early evening, and full breakfasts are served until 11 AM. ✉ *259 Calle San Francisco, Old San Juan* ☎ *787/722–0658* ▭ *AE, MC, V.*

Caribbean

$$–$$$ ✕ **Ají.** This restaurant done up in red and earth tones specializes in contemporary, creative versions of Caribbean cuisine. In many dishes, sugar cane, mango, tomato, and sweet red peppers are used in inventive combinations. In *de patillas a Cabo Rojo,* steak-and-shrimp kebabs are crusted, respectively, in cinnamon and sugar cane and served with a side

of Caribbean pesto linguine. Fresh fish comes in a garbanzo coconut sauce, and a baked hen comes with Mamposteao rice. Pork medallions are served in a mashed-plantain casserole with apple and olive gravy. On most nights you can hear live flamenco and jazz sounds. ✉ *315 Calle Recinto Sur, Old San Juan* ☎ *787/723–3514* 💳 *AE, D, MC, V* ⏲ *Closed Sun. and Mon. No lunch Sat.*

$$–$$$ ✕ **Casa Borinquen.** A portrait of independence leader Pedro Albizu Campos adorns the building's facade, a holdover from before restoration work, when a group of artists turned the crumbling walls into the "Museo sin Techo" ("Roofless Museum"). Today it's a bright, attractive restaurant serving radically delicious local cuisine. The vegetarian dishes are made with local produce, shrimp is served with a sauce made from *acerola* (a local fruit similar to a cherry but not as sweet) and mashed casava, and pork loin comes with fresh corn relish. ✉ *109 Calle San Sebastián, Old San Juan* ☎ *787/725–0888* 💳 *AE, D, MC, V* ⏲ *Closed Mon.*

$–$$ ✕ **La Fonda del Jibarito.** Sanjuaneros have favored this casual, family-run restaurant for years. The back porch is filled with plants, the dining room is filled with fanciful depictions of Calle Sol (the street outside), and the ever-present owner, Pedro J. Ruiz, is filled with the desire to ensure that everyone is happy. The conch ceviche and chicken fricassee are among the specialties. ✉ *280 Calle Sol, Old San Juan* ☎ *787/725–8375* ✍ *Reservations not accepted* 💳 *AE, MC, V.*

Fodor'sChoice ★

Contemporary

$$–$$$ ✕ **Amadeus.** A trendy crowd enjoys such nouvelle Caribbean appetizers as buffalo wings or plantain mousse with shrimp, and entrées such as ravioli with a goat-cheese and walnut sauce or Cajun-grilled mahimahi. The front dining room is attractive—whitewashed walls, dark wood, white tablecloths, ceiling fans—and an interior courtyard leads to a romantic back dining room with printed tablecloths, candles, and exposed brick. There's also a seating area on Plaza San José. ✉ *106 Calle San Sebastián, Old San Juan* ☎ *787/722–8635* 💳 *AE, MC, V* ⏲ *No lunch Mon.*

$$–$$$ ✕ **Avocat.** This dining option on Plaza Colón, new in late 2003, is housed in classy surroundings, and its blend of Caribbean-Mediterranean cuisine is strong competition for its better known neighbors. There's plenty of Latin grilled dishes and seafood platters—a house churrasco platter, of course—as well as Italian and Middle Eastern influences in the pork osso buco, served with a plantain–wild mushroom timbal, and grilled rack of lamb served in a mint demi-glace with malanga mash and sautéed spinach. On weekends diners are treated to soothing live jazz. ✉ *200 O'Donnell, Old San Juan* ☎ *787/721–7175* 💳 *AE, MC, V* ⏲ *Closed Mon.*

$$–$$$ ✕ **Barú** This restaurant-lounge is in a plushly renovated historic residence. The blend of Mediterranean and Caribbean cuisines has earned it a solid reputation among sanjuaneros and savvy visitors, so it's often crowded. The menu ranges effortlessly from Middle Eastern to Asian to Caribbean. Appetizers are wide-ranging, including a shellfish platter with Asian, citrus, and cocktail sauces; a fine selection of risottos, including seafood and asparagus; plus fine beef, tuna, and salmon carpaccios. Main courses prance from filet mignon with horseradish mashed potatoes and red-

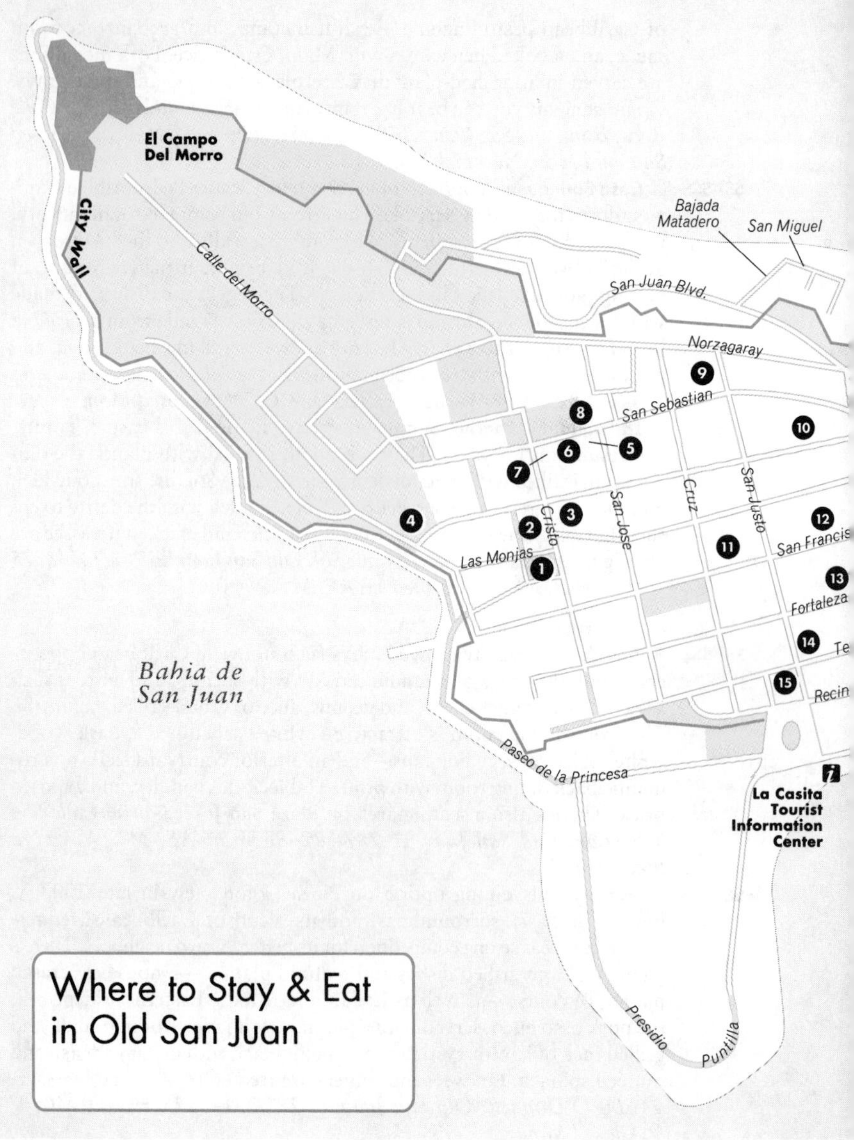

Where to Stay & Eat in Old San Juan

Restaurants ▼

- Aguaviva Seaside Latino Cuisine **21**
- Aji **17**
- Amadeus **6**
- Avocat **24**
- Barú **7**
- La Bella Piazza **25**
- La Bombonera **11**
- Café Berlin **26**
- Cafeteria Mallorca **12**
- Carli Café Concierto **15**
- Casa Borinquen **8**
- La Chaumière **19**
- Dragonfly **22**
- La Fonda del Jibarito **10**
- La Mallorquina **14**
- La Ostra Cosa **1**
- Parrot Club **23**
- El Patio de Sam **5**

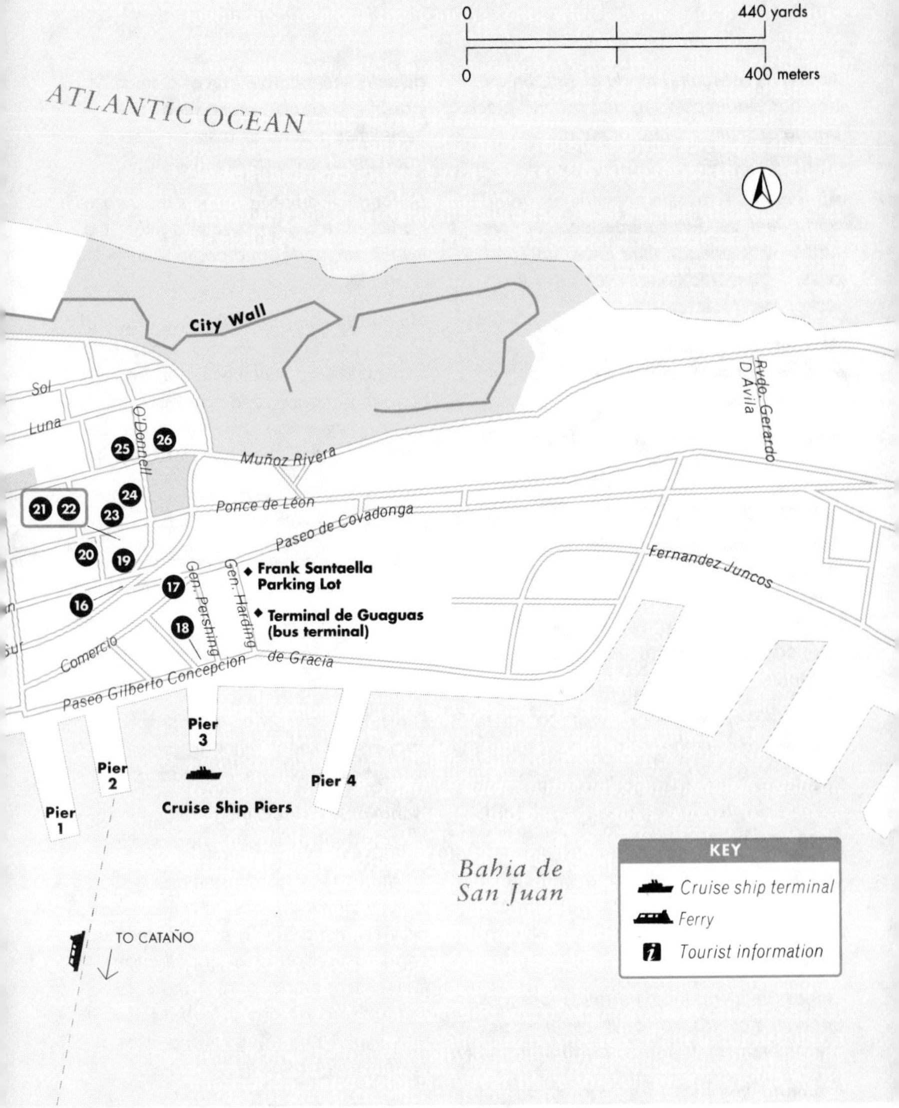

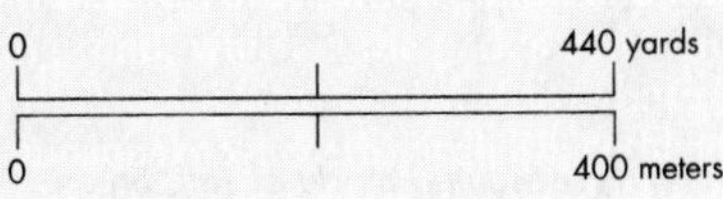

Il Perugino **3**
El Picoteo **2**
Tantra **20**
Transylvania **16**

Hotels
Caleta Guesthouse **4**
El Convento Hotel **2**
Gallery Inn **9**
Hotel Milano **13**
Wyndham Old San Juan Hotel & Casino **18**

CloseUp

ON THE MENU

Adobo. *A seasoning made of salt, onion powder, garlic powder, and ground black pepper, usually rubbed on meats before they are roasted.*

Aji-li-mojili. *A dressing combining garlic and sweet, seeded chili peppers, flavored further with vinegar, lime juice, salt, and olive oil; it is traditionally served with* lechón asado.

Alcapurrias. *Banana croquettes stuffed with beef or pork, which are very popular as a fast-food.*

Amarillos. *Fried ripe, yellow-plantain slices, a common side dish.*

Arepas. *Fried corn or bread cakes.*

Asopao. *A gumbo made with fish or chicken, flavored with spices such as garlic, paprika, and oregano as well as salt pork, cured ham, green peppers, chili peppers, onions, tomatoes, chorizo, and pimentos.*

Batido. *A tropical fruit-and-milk shake; basically, a smoothie.*

Bacalaítos. *Deep-fried codfish fritters, which are often served as an appetizer for lunch or dinner.*

Chimichurri. *An herb sauce of finely chopped cilantro or parsley with garlic, lemon, and oil that is usually served with grilled meats.*

Chinas. *In Puerto Rico,* naranjas *(oranges) are called chinas, so you'll see "jugo de china" on many breakfast menus.*

Empanadillas. *Turnovers, bigger than* pastelillos, *filled with beef, crabmeat, conch, or even lobster.*

Jueyes. *Land crab, which is often boiled or served in a stew.*

Lechón asado. *A slow-roasted, garlic-studded whole pig, marinated in sour orange juice and coloring made from achiote, the inedible fruit of a small Caribbean shrub, whose seeds are sometimes ground as a spice; it's traditionally served with* aji-li-mojili.

Mofongo. *A mix of plantains mashed with garlic, olive oil, and salt in a* pilón, *the traditional mortar and pestle used in the Puerto Rican kitchen.*

Mojo or Mojito Isleño. *A sauce made of olives and olive oil, onions, pimientos, capers, tomato sauce, vinegar, and a flavoring of garlic and bay leaves that is usually served with fried fish (not to be confused with Cuban rum drink,* mojito*).*

Pasteles. *Corn or yucca wrapped in a plantain leaf with various fillings.*

Pastelillos. *Deep-fried cheese and meat turnovers, which are a popular fast-food snack.*

Picadillo. *Spicy ground meat, which is used for stuffing or eaten with rice.*

Pique. *A condiment consisting of hot peppers soaked in vinegar, sometimes with garlic or other spices added.*

Pionono. *A slice of ripe plantain wrap filled with picadillo, breaded and fried.*

Sofrito. *A seasoned base made with pureed tomatoes, sautéed onions, bell peppers, tomatoes, sweet red chili peppers, herbs and spices, cilantro (coriander), recao, garlic, and colored with achiote (annato seeds); it's used in rice, soups, and stews, giving them a bright yellow coloring.*

Tembleque. *A coconut custard, which is a popular dessert; when served, it's usually sprinkled with cinnamon or nutmeg.*

Tostones. *Crushed fried green plantains, usually served as an appetizer.*

wine sauce to paprika-pineapple lamb chops to chicken kabobs in a peanut green-curry sauce. ✉ *150 Calle San Sebastián, Old San Juan* ☎ *787/977–7107* ▭ *AE, MC, V* ⊙ *No lunch.*

★ **$$–$$$** ✕ **Carli Café Concierto.** The Banco Popular building dominates the Old San Juan skyline. On its ground floor, you'll find this intimate bistro, with rust-hue walls and black-marble tables. Have a seat indoors or on the streetside patio, and dine on such international savories such as seared loin of lamb or spinach-and-ricotta ravioli in pesto sauce. The genial owner and host, Carli Muñoz, is a pianist who toured with the Beach Boys (note the gold album on the wall). Many evenings he plays the Steinway grand piano, often accompanied by singers and musicians who happen to drop in. ✉ *Plazoleta Rafael Carrión, Calle Recinto Sur and Calle San Justo, Old San Juan* ☎ *787/725–4927* ▭ *AE, MC, V.*

$$–$$$ Fodor'sChoice ★ ✕ **Parrot Club.** The cuisine at this hot spot is inventive, the decor colorful, and the staff casual but efficient. Stop by the bar for a passion-fruit cocktail before moving to the adjacent dining room or the back courtyard. The menu has contemporary variations of Cuban and Puerto Rican classics. You might start with mouthwatering crabcakes or tamarind-barbecued ribs, followed by blackened tuna in a dark rum sauce or *churrasco* (barbecued steak) with *chimichurri* (a green sauce made with herbs, garlic, and tomatoes). ✉ *363 Calle Fortaleza, Old San Juan* ☎ *787/725–7370* *Reservations not accepted* ▭ *AE, DC, MC, V.*

$–$$$ ✕ **Dragonfly.** Many visitors don't want to leave town without eating here. With Chinese-red furnishings and a charming staff outfitted in kimonos and satin shirts, this hip little restaurant has the feel of an elegant opium den. Surely the frequent lines outside its door attest to the seductive power of chef Roberto Trevino's Latin-Asian cuisine. The *platos* (large appetizers) are meant to be shared and include pork-and-plantain dumplings with an orange dipping sauce; spicy, perfectly fried calimari; and Peking-duck nachos with wasabi sour cream. ✉ *364 Calle La Fortaleza, Old San Juan* ☎ *787/977–3886* *Reservations not accepted* ▭ *AE, MC, V.*

Eclectic

$$–$$$$ ✕ **El Patio de Sam.** A warm interior of dark wood and faux brick and a great selection of beers make Sam's a popular late-night spot. The menu consists mostly of steaks and seafood, with a few native dishes mixed in. Try the Samuel's Special pizza—mozzarella, tomato sauce, beef, pepperoni, and black olives—which feeds two or three people. The flan melts in your mouth. There's entertainment (usually a guitarist singing old Spanish standards) every night but Sunday. ✉ *102 Calle San Sebastián, Old San Juan* ☎ *787/723–1149* ▭ *AE, D, DC, MC, V.*

$$ ✕ **La Ostra Cosa.** The menu here includes everything from oysters to burgers, but most people come for the large, succulent prawns, which are grilled and served with garlic butter. Opt for a seat in the back courtyard: with bougainvillea and moonlight, it's one of the city's prettiest alfresco dining spots. The gregarious owner, Alberto Nazario, brother of pop star Ednita Nazario, genuinely enjoys seeing his guests satisfied. ✉ *154 Calle Cristo, Old San Juan* ☎ *787/722–2672* ▭ *AE, MC, V.*

French

$$$–$$$$ ✕ **La Chaumière.** With black-and-white floor tiles, a beamed ceiling, and floral-print curtains, this two-story restaurant evokes rural France. It has been under the same management since 1969, and with all that experience the service is smooth. Daily specials augment a menu of stellar French classics, including onion soup, rack of lamb, scallops Provençale, and chateaubriand for two. ✉ *367 Calle Tetuan, Old San Juan* ☎ *787/722–3330* ▭ *AE, DC, MC, V* ⏲ *Closed Sun. No lunch.*

Indian

$$–$$$$ ✕ **Tantra.** San Juan's first Indian restaurant is in the up-and-coming area known as SoFo (south Fortaleza Street). The menu has traditional tandoori and curry dishes as well as such inventive surprises as salmon-stuffed beef tenderloin in a casava puree. The earthtone interior invites you to linger, and many patrons do so for an after-dinner puff on an Asian water pipe. ✉ *356 Calle La Fortaleza, Old San Juan* ☎ *787/977–8141* ▭ *AE, MC, V* ⏲ *Closed Mon.*

Italian

★ **$$$–$$$$** ✕ **Il Perugino.** The intimate 200-year-old building seems the perfect place to dine on classic carpaccios, homemade pastas, hearty main courses, and exquisite desserts. Try the black fettuccine with crayfish and baby eels or the rack of lamb in a red-wine sauce with aromatic herbs. The extensive wine cellar, housed in the former cistern, is sure to contain the perfect complement to your meal. ✉ *105 Calle Cristo, Old San Juan* ☎ *787/722–5481* ▭ *MC, V.*

$$–$$$ ✕ **La Bella Piazza.** The narrow dining room has Roman columns, gold-leaf flourishes, and arched doorways that lead to an interior terrace. You'll find such quintessentially Italian appetizers as calamari *in padella* (lightly breaded and sautéed in olive oil, parsley, and garlic) and such archetypal pasta dishes as fusilli *amatriciana* (in a crushed bacon, tomato, and red-pepper sauce). Main courses include *saltinbocca alla romana* (veal and prosciutto in a sage, white-wine, and butter sauce) and *medaglioni al Chianti* (beef medallions in a spicy Chianti sauce). ✉ *355 Calle San Francisco, Old San Juan* ☎ *787/721–0396* ▭ *AE, MC, V* ⏲ *Closed Wed.*

Latin

$$–$$$$ ✕ **La Mallorquina.** It's said to date from 1848 and may be the island's oldest restaurant. The food consists of such basic Puerto Rican and Spanish fare as *asopao* (a stew with rice and seafood) and paella, but the atmosphere is what really recommends the place. Friendly, nattily attired staffers zip between tables amid the peach-color walls and the whir of ceiling fans. ✉ *207 Calle San Justo, Old San Juan* ☎ *787/722–3261* ▭ *AE, MC, V* ⏲ *Closed Sun.*

Romanian

$$–$$$ ✕ **Transylvania.** Despite the portraits of Vlad-like characters and the medieval weaponry on its stone walls, this Romanian restaurant is welcoming—this is, after all, the sunny Caribbean. There's goulash, a red-meat lover's platter called Dracula's Feast, and such surprisingly contemporary dishes as walnut-crusted chicken in a caper cream sauce. The bar attracts an affable expatriot crowd. ✉ *317 Calle Recinto Sur, Old San Juan* ☎ *787/977–2328* ▭ *AE, MC, V.*

Seafood

$$$–$$$$ ✕ **Aguaviva Seaside Latino Cuisine.** This ultramodern seafood restaurant bathed in blue and white is from the same team that created the Parrot Club and Dragonfly. Split oysters and elegantly groomed ceviches float on cracked ice along the raw bar; you can enjoy your selection with a large, sparling martini. The extensive menu is alive with inventive citrus-based ceviches and fresh takes on classics like paella and oysters Rockefeller. Try dorado in a shrimp, tomato, and coconut sauce or with mango herb salsa, or a meaty fish like tuna with diced tomatoes, herbs, and olives. There's also mixed-seafood enchiladas and grouper and chorizo kebabs. ✉ *364 Calle La Fortaleza, Old San Juan* ☎ *787/722–0665* ✍ *No reservations* ▭ *AE, D, MC, V* ⊙ *No lunch.*

Spanish

$–$$$ ✕ **El Picoteo.** Many patrons make a meal of the appetizers that dominate the menu at this chic tapas bar. Entrées such as paella are also noteworthy. There's a long, lively bar inside; one dining area overlooks the hotel El Convento's courtyard, and the other takes in the action along Calle Cristo. Even if you have dinner plans elsewhere, consider stopping here for a cocktail or a nightcap. ✉ *El Convento Hotel, 100 Calle Cristo, Old San Juan* ☎ *787/723–9621* ▭ *AE, D, DC, MC, V.*

Fodor'sChoice ★

Greater San Juan

Cafés

$–$$ ✕ **Kasalta Bakery, Inc.** Make your selection from the display cases full of luscious pastries and other tempting treats. Walk up to the counter and order a sandwich (try the Cubano) or such items as the meltingly tender octopus salad and the savory *caldo gallego* (a soup of fresh vegetables, sausage, and potatoes). Wash everything down with a cold drink or a café con leche that's guaranteed to be strong. ✉ *1966 Calle McLeary, Ocean Park* ☎ *787/727–7340* ▭ *AE, MC, V.*

¢–$$ ✕ **La Patisserie.** Everything—from the pastries to the pastas—is delicious at this café on a quiet stretch of the Condado strip. For breakfast there are wonderful omelets stuffed with fresh vegetables and imported cheeses. For lunch or an early dinner there are sandwiches—from pastrami to king crab, on croissants, baguettes, or other breads—as well as pasta dishes and salads. There's a second location in Plaza Las Américas mall. ✉ *1504 Av. Ashford, Condado* ☎ *787/728–5508* ▭ *AE, MC, V.*

¢–$ ✕ **Frutti Mar.** This bright luncheonette off bustling Loíza Street has great vegetarian fare, baked goods, and fruit frappés. There are tasty garden burgers, and eggplant, hummus and tofu sandwiches and platters. The Saturday special, vegetarian *sancocho* is a hearty blend of tubers and vegetables, slow-cooked in a sweet-herb sofrito. The natural carrot muffins, pistachio coffee cake, and Arabian desserts will have you carrying paper bags out of the place. It's open only until 6 PM. ✉ *101 Diez de Andino, Ocean Park* ☎ *787/722–4103* ▭ *No credit cards* ⊙ *Closed Sun. No dinner.*

¢–$ ✕ **Pinky's.** This tiny café near the beach is known for its gourmet wraps and sandwiches, fresh fruit frappés, and big breakfasts. The pink sub is a blend of turkey, salami, and mozzarella, with a fresh dijon vinaigrette and mix of chopped tomatoes, olives, and basil. The surfer wrap is a mix of grilled turkey, mozarella, chopped tomato, and avocado with basil mayonnaise. Seating is limited, but takeout and delivery are available. Or place your order from the beach itself, where servers in black T-shirts emblazoned with the pink "Eat Me" slogan tend to your hunger pangs. ✉ *51 Calle María Moczo, Ocean Park* ☎ *787/727–3347* ▭ *MC, V* ⊙ *Closed Mon. No dinner.*

Caribbean

$$–$$$$ Fodor's Choice ★ ✕ **Ajili Mojili.** Traditional Puerto Rican food is prepared here with a flourish and served in an attractive plantation-style setting. Sample the fried cheese and *yautía* (a tuber similar to a potato) dumplings with the house sauce, a tomato, herb, garlic, and shaved-almond concoction. The *mofongo,* mashed-plantain casserole with seafood or meat, is wonderful, as is the plantain-crusted shrimp in a white-wine herb sauce. ✉ *1006 Av. Ashford, Condado* ☎ *787/725–9195* ▭ *AE, DC, MC, V* ⊙ *No lunch Sat.*

$$–$$$$ ✕ **Casa Dante.** The self-proclaimed "casa del mofongo" is a good place to try this Puerto Rican specialty of plantains mashed with garlic and other ingredients. You can get it with seafood, chicken, or beef in a red sauce, or as a side dish to a churrasco or sautéed red snapper. The bright dining room has tourist photos of Puerto Rico covering its walls and is a favorite of families. ✉ *39 Calle Loíza, Punta Las Marías* ☎ *787/726–7310* ▭ *AE, MC, V* ⊙ *Closed Mon.*

$$–$$$ ✕ **Yerba Buena.** This so-called "corner of South Beach in the Condado" serves Latin-Caribbean food in contemporary trappings. The Cuban classic *ropa vieja* (meat cooked so slowly that it becomes tender shreds) comes in a stylish plantain nest. The shrimp has a coconut-and-ginger sauce, the halibut filet one of mango and Grand Marnier. The restaurant claims to use the "original" recipe for its *mojito,* Cuba's tasty rum, lime, and mint drink. Live Latin jazz is played many nights. Some tables on the outdoor terrace are outfitted atop sliding porch swings, making your meal a relaxing experience. ✉ *1350 Av. Ashford, Condado* ☎ *787/721–5700* ▭ *AE, MC, V* ⊙ *Closed Mon.*

$–$$$ ✕ **Tropical Restaurant.** For years, locals have favored this unpretentious Cuban restaurant for its reasonably priced Latin classics. Years of experience at preparing steak in brandy sauce, lobster stew, and chicken in rice show up in the final product. For dessert, the *dulce de leche* (a sweet milk pudding) and the flan are good bets. ✉ *1214 Av. Ashford, Condado* ☎ *787/724–3760* ▭ *AE, MC, V.*

Chinese

$$–$$$$ ✕ **Great Taste Chinese Restaurant.** The kitchen is open until 2 AM, and the menu has dim sum offerings and several regional classics whose quality rivals that of anything served in New York City's Chinatown. The setting—in a faded condominium complex with canned disco music playing through cheap speakers—might seem less than enchanting at first, but the view over the Laguna del Condado is beautiful. ✉ *1018 Av. Ashford, Condado* ☎ *787/721–8111* ▭ *AE, D, DC, MC, V.*

$–$$$$ ✕ **Oriental Palace.** Located in what locals refer simply to as " Plaza," the largest shopping mall in the Caribbean, this casual eatery has some of the best-quality Chinese food in San Juan, served quickly and at reasonable prices. Nobody can touch the dumplings, Szehcuan noodles, and other classic staples. It's in the new wing, near Macy's and Borders. ✉ *Plaza Las Américas, Av. Roosevelt, Hato Rey* ☎ *787/767–2736* 💳 *AE, D, DC, MC, V.*

Contemporary

$$$–$$$$ ✕ **Pikayo.** Chef Wilo Benet artfully fuses classic French, Caribbean-creole, and California-nouvelle nuances at this delightful museum restaurant. A changing selection of paintings wraps around the main dining room, and a plasma television broadcasts the kitchen action above the silver and black bar. The regularly changing menu is a feast for the eye as well as the palate and might include perfectly shaped tostones stuffed with oven-dried tomatoes, or mofongo topped with saffron shrimp. Veal and prosciutto are served in a swirl of sweet-pea couscous, and beef medallions are served with crumbled blue cheese and a dark oriental sauce. ✉ *Museo de Arte de Puerto Rico, 300 Av. José de Diego, Santurce* ☎ *787/721–6194* 💳 *AE, MC, V* ⏲ *Closed Mon.*

★ **$$–$$$** ✕ **Chayote.** Although it's slightly off the beaten path, this chic eatery—all earthtones and contemporary Puerto Rican art—is definitely an "in" spot. The chef gives haute international dishes tropical panache. Starters include *sopa del día* (soup of the day) made with local produce, chayote stuffed with prosciutto, and corn tamales with shrimp in a coconut sauce. Half the entrées are seafood dishes, including an excellent pan-seared tuna with Asian ginger sauce. The ginger flan is a must for dessert. ✉ *Hotel Olimpo Court, 603 Av. Miramar, Miramar* ☎ *787/722–9385* 💳 *AE, MC, V* ⏲ *Closed Sun. and Mon. No lunch Sat.*

$$–$$$ ✕ **Tangerine.** The dining room spills onto a terrace fronting the Atlantic, whose steady breezes and distant roiling are as much a part of the dreamy scene as the muted-orange lighting and cream walls. Asian-European fusion dishes appear under the provocative menu titles "Foreplay" (appetizers), "Loss of Innocence" (entrées), and "Sensuous Pleasures" (desserts). Appetizers such as Asiatic baby greens in a tangerine dressing or grilled scallops with mushrooms and noodles in a basil-cilantro sauce are seductive. Artful entrées include pork chops in tangerine vinaigrette with sage-potato puree and a pan-seared sea bass with sea-urchin butter sauce and mushroom couscous. ✉ *Water Club, 2 Calle Tartak, Isla Verde* ☎ *787/728–3666* 💳 *AE, MC, V.*

$$–$$$ ✕ **Zabor Creative Cuisine.** In a restored plantation with a pastoral front yard, this inventive restaurant seems as if it's out on the island somewhere rather than just off Avenida Ashford. One of the main pastimes here is grazing, particularly among the good appetizers—such as breaded calamari in a tomato-basil sauce—which you can share your dinner companions. Of the notable main courses, try the veal chops stuffed with provolone, pancetta, and herbs and served with a garlic-merlot sauce, or the catch of the day over yellow-raisin couscous in a mango-rosemary curry. ✉ *14 Calle Candida, Condado* ☎ *787/725–9494* 💳 *AE, D, DC, MC, V* ⏲ *Closed Sun. and Mon. No lunch Tues.–Thurs. and Sat.*

Continental

$$$–$$$$ ✕ **Augusto's Cuisine.** Austrian-born chef Augusto Schreiner, a graduate of the Salzburg Culinary School, regularly wins awards for his classic

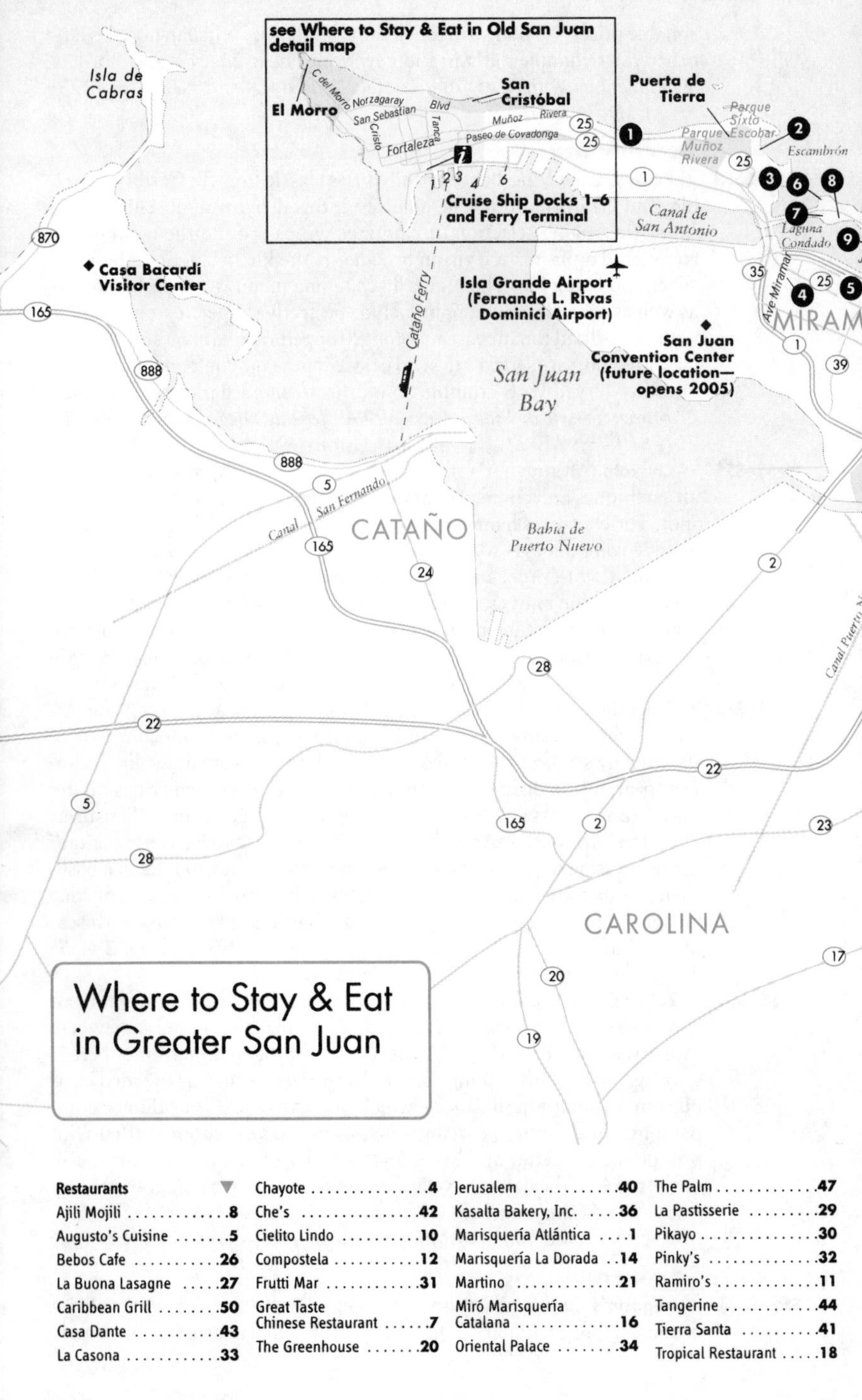

Where to Stay & Eat in Greater San Juan

Restaurants

- Ajili Mojili **8**
- Augusto's Cuisine **5**
- Bebos Cafe **26**
- La Buona Lasagne **27**
- Caribbean Grill **50**
- Casa Dante **43**
- La Casona **33**
- Chayote **4**
- Che's **42**
- Cielito Lindo **10**
- Compostela **12**
- Frutti Mar **31**
- Great Taste Chinese Restaurant **7**
- The Greenhouse **20**
- Jerusalem **40**
- Kasalta Bakery, Inc. **36**
- Marisquería Atlántica **1**
- Marisquería La Dorada . . **14**
- Martino **21**
- Miró Marisquería Catalana **16**
- Oriental Palace **34**
- The Palm **47**
- La Pastisserie **29**
- Pikayo **30**
- Pinky's **32**
- Ramiro's **11**
- Tangerine **44**
- Tierra Santa **41**
- Tropical Restaurant **18**

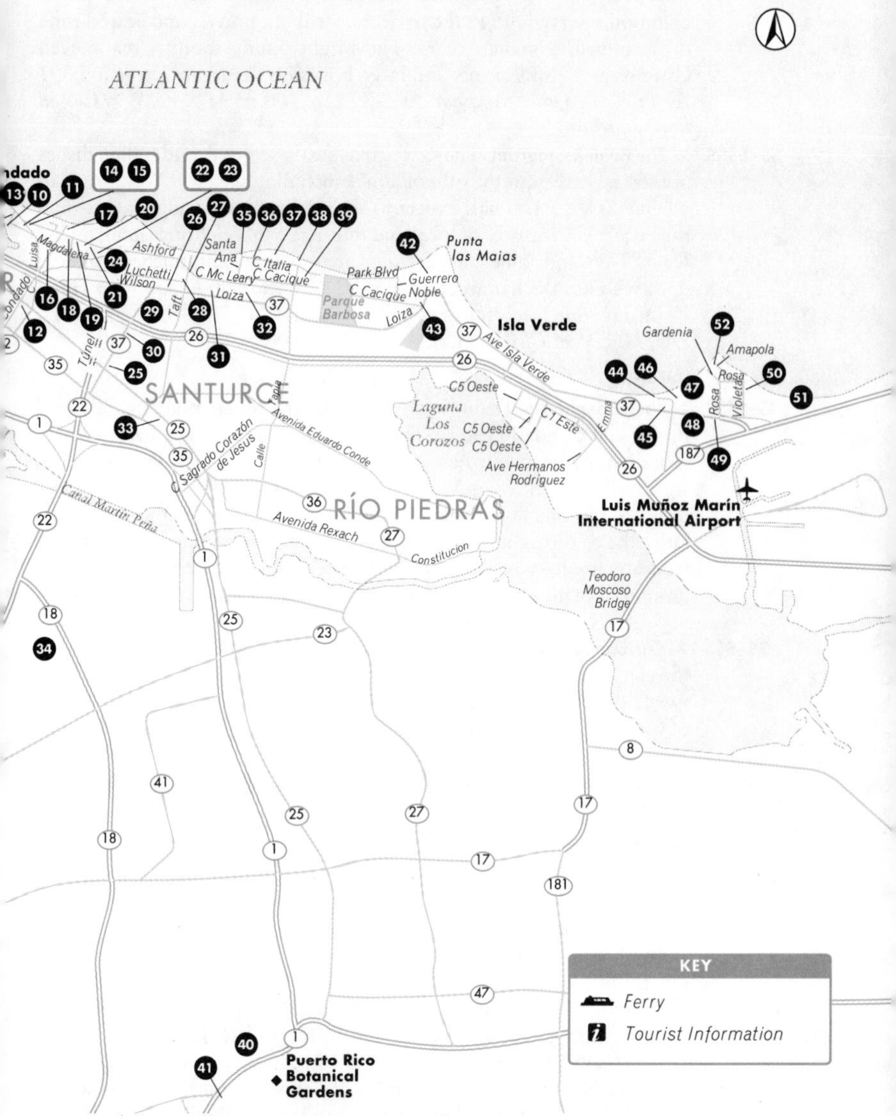

Urdin 15
Via Appia 24
La Vista Restaurant 17
Yerba Buena 23
Zabor Creative Cuisine . .22

Hotels

At Wind Chimes Inn 28
El Canario by the Sea . . .13
Caribe Hilton 3
Casa del Caribe 19
El Consulado 9
Courtyard Isla Verde 51
Embassy Suites 45
L'Habitation Beach Guest House 37
Hampton Inn & Suites . . .48
Hostería del Mar 38
Hotel La Playa 52
Hotel Olimpo Court 4
Howard Johnson 49
Inter-Continental 46
Numero Uno 35
Park Plaza Normandie 2
Radisson Ambassador Plaza 25
Ritz-Carlton 50
San Juan Marriott 17
Tu Casa 39
The Water Club 44
Wyndham Condado Plaza . .6
Wyndham El San Juan . . .47

European cuisine. His menu changes seasonally; some of the dishes commonly served are veal carpaccio, steak au poivre, and seared tuna or shrimp in a mango curry. The bright dining room is made even cheerier with floral prints and large bouquets. ✉ *Hotel Excelsior, 801 Av. Ponce de León, Miramar* ☎ *787/725–7700* ▭ *AE, MC, V* ⊙ *Closed Sun. and Mon.*

$$–$$$$ ✕ **The Palm Restaurant.** The same great steak, seafood, and Italian dishes are served here as at the other Palm's, including the New York original; when you leave you half expect to see the Brooklyn Bridge rather than the beach. Caricatures of local and international celebrities hang on the walls. They and some glass dividers are the only light touches amid the dark wood of the bar and the booths. ✉ *Wyndham El San Juan Hotel & Casino, 6063 Av. Isla Verde, Isla Verde* ☎ *787/791–1000* ▭ *AE, D, DC, MC, V* ⊙ *Closed Mon.*

Eclectic

$$–$$$$ ✕ **The Greenhouse.** From lunch to wee hours, diners pour steadily into this casual Condado eatery. The late-night hours draw a lively crowd. A wide-ranging menu has such standards as burgers, French onion soup, grilled-chicken sandwiches, and omelets as well as more ambitious dishes like lobster tail or baked salmon. The desserts, from the rich chocolate cake to the light fruit sorbet, are divine. Everything is consistently well prepared—as well it should be given that the restaurant has been around since the late 1970s. ✉ *1200 Av. Ashford, Condado* ☎ *787/725–4036* ▭ *AE, D, MC, V.*

$$–$$$ ✕ **Caribbean Grill Restaurant.** This restaurant in the Ritz-Carlton takes the elegance associated with the chain's name and gives it a Caribbean twist. The menu emphasizes a variety of grilled seafood; there's a mix of Caribbean and North American fare. Overall, it has some of the city's most consistently first-rate cuisine. ✉ *Ritz-Carlton San Juan Hotel, Spa & Casino, Av. Las Gobernadores (Rte. 187), Isla Verde* ☎ *787/253–1700* ▭ *AE, D, DC, MC, V.*

Italian

$$–$$$$ ✕ **Martino.** Beneath a glass atrium on the top floor of the Black Diamond Hotel, Martino is a San Juan favorite for its classic northern Italian cuisine and its spectacular view of the Condado beach district. Start off with a hot seafood antipasto, followed by osso buco or one of the several fine pasta dishes, which are meals in themselves. Chef Martin Acosta's creations taste like they've come direct from the mother country to your table. ✉ *Black Diamond Hotel, 55 Av. Condado, Condado* ☎ *787/722–5356* ▭ *AE, DC, MC, V* ⊙ *No lunch weekends.*

$–$$ ✕ **Via Appia.** The food at this no-frills café is just as authentic and as tasty—from the pizza to the veal and peppers to house red wine—as its higher-priced *paisanos*. The outdoor-seating area looks out on Condado's busy Ashford Avenue, which is usually filled with people coming from and going to the beach. Indoors there's air-conditioning but very little ambience. ✉ *1350 Av. Ashford, Condado* ☎ *787/725–8711* ▭ *AE, MC, V.*

$–$$ ✕ **La Buona Lasagne.** Don't let the elegance fool you. The prices are truly reasonable at this restaurant far from the well-trodden areas and in a restored art-deco structure with tile floors, large picture windows, and pastel walls. The menu includes about 30 pasta dishes, all freshly made with top-quality ingredients. The basic meat lasagne is just as good as the more elaborate penne with smoked salmon and a cream sauce. ✉ *176 Calle Delbrey, at Baldorioty de Castro Expressway, Santurce* ☎ *787/721–7488* ▭ *AE, MC, V* ⊗ *Closed Sun. No dinner Mon.–Wed.*

Latin

$$–$$$$ ✕ **Che's.** Juicy churrasco, lemon chicken, and grilled sweetbreads are specialties at this casual Argentine restaurant. The hamburgers are huge, and the french fries are fresh. The Chilean and Argentine wine list is also good. ✉ *35 Calle Caoba, Punta Las Marías* ☎ *787/726–7202* ▭ *AE, D, DC, MC, V.*

$–$$$ ✕ **Bebos Cafe.** Smiling *dominicanas* bring you delicious comida criolla made fresh and served quickly. The tasty fare, friendly service, and low prices are good reasons the place is always packed. The menu includes everything from grilled flank steak to seafood-stuffed mofongo to chicken stew to barbecued ribs. The selection of good local desserts includes flan and dense, moist *tres leches* cake. Breakfast is also served. ✉ *1600 Calle Loiza, Santurce* ☎ *787/268–5087* ▭ *AE, MC, V.*

$–$$$ ✕ **La Vista Restaurant & Ocean Terrace.** You can choose from a wide-ranging menu while enjoying an ocean view at this 24-hour restaurant in the San Juan Marriott. Mexican, seafood, Puerto Rican, Caribbean, and Argentinian specials are featured on different nights of the week. The regular menu includes such appetizers as crabcakes and an *arepa* (a light flour biscuit often filled with seafood) salad. For an entrée, try the shrimp with garlic, papaya, and cilantro. ✉ *San Juan Marriott Resort & Stellaris Casino, 1309 Av. Ashford, Condado* ☎ *787/722–7000* ▭ *AE, MC, V.*

¢–$$ ✕ **Cielito Lindo.** There's a beach-shack quality to this Mexican restaurant, but it serves a good mole, juicy flank steaks, and awesome enchiladas. There's also a wide selection of South of the Border brews, each one iced to perfection and served with a lime wedge. ✉ *1108 Av. Magdalena, Condado* ☎ *787/723–5597* ▭ *AE, MC, V.*

Middle Eastern

$$ ✕ **Jerusalem.** You feel as if you're in an Arabian tent at one of San Juan's oldest Middle Eastern restaurants. Hypnotic music is piped in over the sound system, and belly dancers put on a great show. Although the spectacle may seem contrived, the food is straightforward and delicious. The *baba ghanoush* (eggplant puree with tahini, olive oil, lemon juice, and garlic) and tabbouleh make good starters; consider following them with grilled chicken kebabs or baked lamb. Entrées are served with Arabian rice, which is mixed with parsley and almonds, and a cucumber-and-tomato salad. For dessert, the baklava is unrivaled. ✉ *1109 Av. Roosevelt, Hato Rey* ☎ *787/783–8332* ▭ *AE, D, MC, V.*

$$ ✕ **Tierra Santa.** San Juan's small community of Middle Eastern immigrants isn't large enough to explain the local affection for that region's cuisine—or the popularity of belly dancing (performers gyrate here on Friday and Saturday nights). You can contemplate these mysteries as you dine on such starters as hummus and falafel, and on entrées such as roasted halibut in almond, lime, and garlic, or lamb curry with oranges and onions. ✉ *284 Av. Roosevelt, Hato Rey* ☎ *787/754–6865* ▭ *AE, MC, V.*

Seafood

$$–$$$$ ✕ **Marisquería Atlántica.** At this restaurant and fish market, the seafood is fresh and reasonably priced. Stop in for a cool drink at the bar and a side dish of calamari, served lightly breaded and in a spicy sauce. Specialties include fresh Maine lobster, grilled red snapper in a garlic sauce, and paella loaded with scallops, clams, shrimp, squid, and fish. ✉ *7 Calle Lugo Viñas, Puerta de Tierra* ☎ *787/722–0890* ▭ *AE, MC, V* ⏲ *Closed Mon.*

$–$$$ ✕ **Marisquería La Dorada.** This fine seafood establishment on Condado's restaurant row is surprisingly affordable. The grilled seafood platter is the specialty, but there are also excellent pastas and other fish dinners, including mahimahi in caper sauce and codfish in green sauce. The friendly waitstaff makes you feel genuinely welcome. ✉ *1105 Av. Magdalena, Condado* ☎ *787/722–9583* ▭ *AE, D, MC, V.*

Spanish

$$$–$$$$ ✕ **La Casona.** San Juan's moneyed class comes here for power lunches, but it's also a nice spot for a romantic dinner. The restored Spanish colonial residence has well-appointed rooms and blooming gardens. The menu is based solidly in Spain, but has many creative flourishes—start with the duck pâté or smoked salmon and move on to the duck breast in a raspberry sauce or the rack of lamb, which is first baked and then sautéed with brandy and fruit. ✉ *609 Calle San Jorge, Santurce* ☎ *787/727–2717* ▭ *AE, D, DC, MC, V* ⏲ *Closed Sun.*

$$$–$$$$ ✕ **Compostela.** Contemporary Spanish food and a 10,000-bottle wine cellar are the draws here. The dining room is pleasant, with bright colors and many plants, and the kitchen is often honored in local competitions for specialties such as mushroom pâté, port *pastelillo* (wild-mushroom turnover), grouper fillet with scallops in salsa verde, rack of lamb, duck with orange and ginger sauce, and paella. ✉ *106 Av. Condado, Santurce* ☎ *787/724–6088* ▭ *AE, DC, MC, V* ⏲ *Closed Sun. No lunch Sat.*

$$–$$$$ ✕ **Miró Marisquería Catalana.** Like its namesake, the painter Joan Miró, this small restaurant draws its inspiration from the Catalan region of Spain, where the cuisine is heavy on seafood and hearty tapas. Prints by the artist hang on the walls, and the overall design, dominated by bright hues and brass, is also influenced by Miró. Start off with braised chorizo and peppers, or steamed clams with garlic. Main courses include delicious lamb chops, as well as grilled tuna or codfish in a red-pepper-and-eggplant sauce. ✉ *74 Av. Condado, Condado* ☎ *787/723–9593* ▭ *AE, MC, V.*

★ **$$–$$$$** ✕ **Ramiro's.** The smell of chef-owner Jesus Ramiro's imaginative Castilian cooking fills the sea-green dining room here. Ramiro is also known for his artistic presentation: flower-shaped peppers filled with fish mousse, a mix of seafood caught under a vegetable net, roast duckling with sugarcane honey, and, if you can stand more, a kiwi dessert sculpted to resemble twin palms. ✉ *1106 Av. Magdalena, Condado* ☎ *787/721–9049* ▭ *AE, DC, MC, V* ⏲ *No lunch Sat.*

$$–$$$$ ✕ **Urdin.** The owners, who include Julían Gil, a well-known model and actor, describe the menu here as Spanish with a Caribbean touch. The soup and seafood appetizers are particularly good, and a highly recommended entrée is *chillo urdin de lujo* (red snapper sautéed with clams, mussels, and shrimp in a tomato, herb, and wine sauce). The name of the restaurant comes from the Basque word for "blue," which is the dining room's dominant color. ✉ *1105 Av. Magdalena, Condado* ☎ *787/724–0420* 💳 *AE, MC, V.*

WHERE TO STAY

San Juan prides itself on its clean, comfortable, plentiful accommodations, and hoteliers, by and large, aim to please. Big hotels and resorts, several with casinos, and a few smaller establishments line the sandy strands along Condado and Isla Verde. Between these two neighborhoods, the Ocean Park area has homey inns, as do the districts of Miramar and Santurce, although the latter two areas aren't directly on the beach. Old San Juan has only a few noteworthy hotels, one of which has a casino.

Staying in a self-catering apartment or condo has advantages over a resort, especially for families. You can cook when and what you want, and you can enjoy considerable autonomy. Several companies represent such properties in San Juan. When booking, be sure ask about maid service, swimming pools, and any other amenities that are important to you. The small, government-sponsored inns, called *paradores* are primarily *en la isla* (out on the island) rather than in San Juan.

At this writing, the Wyndham Old San Juan Hotel was scheduled to become a Sheraton in early 2005. Until then, it will remain a part of the Wyndham chain.

Prices

The city's rooms aren't inexpensive: for a high-end beach-resort room, expect to pay at least $200 to $300 for a double in high season—roughly mid-November through mid-April. For smaller inns and hotels, doubles start at $100 to $150. As a rule, if your room is less than $50 in high season, then the quality of the hotel might be questionable. Although most hotels operate on the European plan (EP, no meals included), a few larger establishments offer other meal plans and/or all-inclusive packages; there's only one true all-inclusive hotel in Puerto Rico, and it's not in San Juan.

WHAT IT COSTS In U.S. dollars

	$$$$	$$$	$$	$	¢
FOR 2 PEOPLE	over $350	$250–$350	$150–$250	$80–$150	under $80

Prices are for a double room in high season, excluding 9% tax (11% for hotels with casinos, 7% for paradores) and typical 5%–12% service charge.

Apartment Rentals

Investigate rates at high-end condominiums through **Condo World** (✉ 300 17th Ave. S, North Myrtle Beach, SC 29582 ☎ 843/272–7011 or 800/753–4537 📠 843/272–8200). **Puerto Rico Vacation Apartments** (✉ Calle Marbella del Caribe Oeste S-5, Isla Verde 00979 ☎ 787/727–1591 or

800/266–3639 787/268–3604 www.sanjuanvacations.com) represents some 200 properties in Condado and Isla Verde.

Old San Juan

$$–$$$$ Fodor'sChoice ★ **El Convento Hotel.** Once a Carmelite convent, this 350-year-old building is a prime example of the right way to blend old-world gentility with modern luxury. Much of the original architecture is intact, including a colonial interior courtyard. Rooms have a Spanish-deco look, with dark woods, wrought-iron lamps, and ornate furniture. Complimentary wine and hors d'oeuvres are served before dinner, and there's an honor bar that's open until 4 AM. The courtyard's El Picoteo, street-side Café Bohemio, and indoor patio Café del Níspero are among the dining choices. *100 Calle Cristo, Old San Juan Box 1048, 00902 787/723–9020 or 800/468–2779 787/721–2877 www.elconvento.com 54 rooms, 4 suites 3 restaurants, in-room data ports, in-room safes, cable TV, in-room VCRs, pool, gym, 2 bars, library, shop, dry cleaning, laundry service, concierge, business services, meeting room, parking (fee), no-smoking rooms AE, D, DC, MC, V CP.*

$$$ **Wyndham Old San Juan Hotel & Casino.** The gleaming Wyndham blends classic Spanish-colonial lines with a modern, triangular shape that subtly echoes the cruise ships docked nearby. The lobby, adjacent to the casino, shines with multihue tiles and mahogany. Each standard room—with honey-color rugs, floral prints, and light woods—has a two-line phone, a coffeemaker, and a hair dryer. Spacious suites also have sitting rooms and extra TVs. On the ninth floor you'll find a small patio pool and whirlpool bath; the seventh-floor concierge level provides hassle-free check-ins, continental breakfasts, and evening hors d'oeuvres. At this writing, the Wyndham had been purchased by Starwood and was slated to be renovated and become a Sheraton in early 2005. *100 Calle Brumbaugh, Old San Juan 00901 787/721–5100 or 800/996–3426 787/721–1111 www.wyndham.com 185 rooms, 55 suites Restaurant, room service, in-room data ports, in-room safes, some minibars, cable TV, pool, gym, hot tub, 2 bars, casino, dry cleaning, laundry service, concierge floor, business services, meeting rooms, travel services, parking (fee), no-smoking floors AE, D, DC, MC, V CP, EP.*

★ **$$–$$$** **Gallery Inn.** Jan D'Esopo and Manuco Gandia transformed this rambling colonial house into an inn that's full of comforts and quirky details: winding, uneven stairs; a music room with a Steinway grand piano; courtyard gardens, where Jan's pet macaws and cockatoos hang out. Each room has a look all its own; several have whirlpool baths. From the rooftop deck there's a spectacular view of the forts and the Atlantic. The first-floor Galería San Juan displays artwork by Jan and others. There's no restaurant, but meals for groups can be prepared upon request. *204–206 Calle Norzagaray, Old San Juan 00901 787/722–1808 787/724–7360 www.thegalleryinn.com 13 rooms, 10 suites Some refrigerators, piano, no-smoking rooms; no a/c in some rooms, no room TVs AE, DC, MC, V CP.*

$ **Hotel Milano.** This clean affordable hotel is just steps from the old city's plazas, shops, and museums. Caribbean floral prints fill the guest rooms, many of which have two double beds. In Old San Juan noise is a way of life; for less clamor, opt for a room at the back. The rooftop restaurant, Panorama, provides expansive views of the city and the pier. ✉ *307 Calle Fortaleza, Old San Juan 00901* ☎ *787/729–9050 or 877/729–9050* 📠 *787/722–3379* 🌐 *home.coqui.net/hmilano* *30 rooms* *Restaurant, refrigerators, cable TV, bar, no-smoking rooms* 💳 *AE, MC, V* 🍽 *CP.*

¢–$ **The Caleta Guesthouse.** In an area overlooking the Bahía de San Juan, this guesthouse gives you the sense of what it would be like to live in Old San Juan. Narrow stairs and hallways lead to the seven studios, each of which has its own character and can accommodate up to four people. Some suites have balconies; all have phones with answering machines. Returning guests often request the Sunshine Studio, with its warm light and outstanding views. Noise can sometimes be a problem here. Although proprietor Michael Giessler usually requires a two-night minimum stay, he can arrange daily rates with a month's notice. ✉ *151 Clara Lair St., Old San Juan 00901* ☎ *787/725–5347* 📠 *787/977–5642* 🌐 *www.thecaleta.com* *8 studios* *Fans, kitchenettes, cable TV, dry cleaning, laundry facilities; no a/c in some rooms, no smoking* 💳 *AE, MC, V* 🍽 *EP.*

San Juan

$$$$ **InterContinental San Juan Resort & Casino.** The spacious rooms in this 16-story hotel have pleasant views of the ocean, the San José Lagoon, or the city; suites overlook the pool. The jangling casino is just off the lobby, and on-site restaurants include the poolside Restaurant Ciao Mediterraneo, Ruth's Chris Steak House, and the Grand Market Café. ✉ *5961 Av. Isla Verde, Isla Verde 00979* ☎ *787/791–6100 or 800/443–2009* 📠 *787/253–2510* 🌐 *www.ichotelsgroup.com* *380 rooms, 22 suites* *6 restaurants, room service, in-room data ports, some in-room hot tubs, minibars, in-room safes, cable TV with movies and video games, pool, gym, hair salon, hot tub, spa, beach, boating, 3 bars, casino, nightclub, shops, dry cleaning, laundry facilities, laundry service, concierge, business services, meeting rooms, car rental, travel services, no-smoking rooms* 💳 *AE, D, MC, V* 🍽 *EP.*

$$$$ Fodor'sChoice ★ **Wyndham El San Juan Hotel & Casino.** An immense antique chandelier illuminates the hand-carved mahogany paneling, Italian rose marble, and 250-year-old French tapestries in the huge lobby of this resort on the Isla Verde beach. You'll be hard pressed to decide whether you want a main tower suite with a whirlpool bath and a wet bar; a garden room with a whirlpool bath and a patio; or a casita with a sunken Roman bath. All rooms have such amenities as walk-in closets, irons, and CD players. Relax at the lobby's Cigar Bar or take dinner at the Ranch, a rooftop country-western bar and grill. ✉ *6063 Av. Isla Verde, Isla Verde 00902* ☎ *787/791–1000, 800/468–2818, or 800/996–3426* 📠 *787/791–0390* 🌐 *www.wyndham.com* *332 rooms, 57 suites* *8 restaurants, room service, in-room data ports, in-room safes, minibars, cable TV, in-room VCRs, 3 tennis courts, 2 pools, wading pool, health club, 5 hot tubs, beach, 14 bars, casino, nightclub, shops, children's programs (ages 5–17), dry cleaning, laundry service, concierge, business services, meeting rooms, travel services, parking (fee), no-smoking rooms* 💳 *AE, DC, MC, V* 🍽 *EP.*

$$$–$$$$ **Caribe Hilton San Juan.** Beyond the lobby, your eyes are gently led to the Atlantic blue past the edge of the infinity pool. The beach, the only private one in San Juan, was expanded in 2002. The open-air lobby's sunken bar looks out over the gentle cascades of a tri-level pool, which is adjacent to a wading pool and an area with whirlpool tubs. Rooms have ocean or lagoon views, and those on the executive floor include such services as private check-in and check-out and free Continental breakfast and evening cocktails. Local businesspeople often frequent the on-site Morton's of Chicago restaurant. *Calle Los Rosales, San Gerónimo Grounds, Puerta de Tierra 00901 787/721–0303 or 800/468–8585 787/725–8849 www.hilton.com 602 rooms, 44 suites 6 restaurants, room service, in-room data ports, in-room safes, minibars, cable TV, 3 tennis courts, pool, wading pool, health club, hair salon, outdoor hot tub, spa, beach, bar, shops, children's programs (ages 4–12), video game room, dry cleaning, laundry service, concierge, business services, meeting rooms, parking (fee), no-smoking floors AE, D, DC, MC, V EP.*

★ $$$–$$$$ **Ritz-Carlton San Juan Hotel, Spa & Casino.** The Ritz's signature elegance won't undermine the feeling that this is a true beach getaway. The hotel's sandy stretch is lovely, as is the cruciform pool, which is surrounded by a garden overlooking the ocean. Works by Latin American artists adorn the lobby lounge and the hallways leading to the well-equipped business center. Rooms have a mix of traditional wooden furnishings and wicker pieces upholstered in soft greens. A full-service spa begs to pamper you with aloe body wraps and *parcha* (passion-fruit juice) massages. Though most room windows are sealed shut to muffle airport noise, many suites open onto terraces. *6961 Av. Los Gobernadores, Isla Verde 00979 787/253–1700 or 800/241–3333 787/253–0700 www.ritzcarlton.com 403 rooms, 11 suites 3 restaurants, room service, in-room data ports, minibars, cable TV, 2 tennis courts, pool, aerobics, gym, hair salon, hot tub, massage, sauna, spa, 3 bars, casino, nightclub, babysitting, children's programs (ages 4–12), dry cleaning, laundry service, concierge, concierge floor, business services, meeting rooms, parking (fee), no-smoking floor AE, D, DC, MC, V EP.*

$$–$$$$ **Wyndham Condado Plaza Hotel & Casino.** The Atlantic and the Laguna del Condado border this high-rise, whose two wings—fittingly named Ocean and Lagoon—are connected by an enclosed, elevated walkway. Standard rooms have walk-in closets and dressing areas. There's a variety of suites, including some with oversize hot tubs. A stay on the Plaza Club floor entitles you to 24-hour concierge service, use of a private lounge, as well as complimentary continental breakfast and refreshments all day. Find your own place in the sun on the beach or beside one of four pools. Dining options include the poolside Tony Roma's as well as Max's Grill, which is open 24 hours. *999 Av. Ashford, Condado 00902 787/721–1000 or 800/468–8588, 800/624–0420 direct to hotel 787/722–7955 www.condadoplaza.com 570 rooms, 62 suites 7 restaurants, room service, in-room data ports, in-room safes, some in-room hot tubs, minibars, cable TV, in-room VCRs, 2 tennis courts, 3 pools, wading pool, health club, 3 hot tubs, beach, dock, boating, 2 bars, 2 lounges, casino, children's programs (ages 4–12), dry cleaning,*

laundry service, concierge, concierge floor, business services, airport shuttle, parking (fee), no-smoking rooms ▭ *AE, D, DC, MC, V* 🍽 *EP.*

★ 🖐 $$$ **Embassy Suites San Juan Hotel & Casino.** As the name implies, the guest quarters here are suites, and all have such amenities as irons and two-line phones with voice mail and call waiting. Hallways and glass elevators face a plant-filled atrium with a pond an waterfall, which help to buffer the sounds from the casino. Thanks to a location near Isla Verde Beach—and just 1 mi from the airport—the hotel is popular with people traveling for either business or pleasure. There's no business center, but the front desk allows guests to use a copier and a computer that has free Internet access; WiFi is available throughout the hotel for a fee. ✉ *8000 Calle Tartak, Isla Verde 00979* ☎ *787/791–0505 or 800/362–2779* 📠 *787/791–7776* 🌐 *www.embassysuitessanjuan.com* *300 suites* *2 restaurants, room service, in-room data ports, in-room safes, minibars, microwaves, refrigerators, cable TV with video games, pool, health club, hot tub, bar, shop, dry cleaning, laundry facilities, laundry service, meeting rooms, travel services, parking (fee), no-smoking floors* ▭ *AE, D, DC, MC, V* 🍽 *BP.*

🖐 $$$ **San Juan Marriott Resort & Stellaris Casino.** The red-neon sign atop the Marriott seems like a beacon, beckoning you to beautiful Condado beach. The hotel's soundproof rooms have soothing pastel carpets, floral spreads, and attractive tropical art; balconies overlook the ocean, the pool, or both. Restaurants include the Tuscany, for northern Italian cuisine, and the casual La Vista, which is open 24 hours. On weekends, there's live entertainment in the enormous lobby, which, combined with the ringing of slot machines from the adjoining casino, makes the area noisy. A large pool area and a gorgeous beach are right outside. ✉ *1309 Av. Ashford, Condado 00907* ☎ *787/722–7000 or 800/228–9290* 📠 *787/722–6800* 🌐 *www.marriott.com* *512 rooms, 17 suites* *3 restaurants, room service, in-room data ports, in-room safes, minibars, cable TV, 2 tennis courts, pool, health club, hair salon, hot tub, beach, 2 lounges, casino, children's programs (ages 4–12), dry cleaning, laundry service, concierge floor, business services, meeting rooms, travel services, parking (fee), no-smoking rooms* ▭ *AE, D, DC, MC, V* 🍽 *EP.*

$$$ **The Water Club.** Every inch of this trendy and modern boutique hotel will soothe you. Aromatherapy scents waft through corridors, candles light your way, and water runs inside the glass walls of elevators that glow with blue neon. They seem the proper ride for trips to the rooftop pool or to the rooms, all of which have ocean views and such contemporary amenities as CD players. Four suites are equipped with telescopes for star-gazing or people watching along Isla Verde beach. The Tangerine Restaurant is sensuous; and water is again a literal and a decorative element in the lobby's Liquid lounge and the rooftop's Wet bar. ✉ *2 Calle Tartak, Isla Verde 00979* ☎ *787/728–3666 or 888/265–6699* 📠 *787/728–3610* 🌐 *www.waterclubsanjuan.com* *84 rooms* *Restaurant, room service, in-room data ports, in-room safes, minibars, cable TV, in-room VCRs, pool, gym, hot tub, massage, beach, 2 bars, dry cleaning, laundry service, concierge, Internet, parking (fee), no-smoking floors* ▭ *AE, D, DC, MC, V* 🍽 *EP.*

$$–$$$ **Courtyard Isla Verde Beach Resort.** This 12-story hotel (formerly a Holiday Inn Crowne Plaza) has been nicely refurbished and reopened in 2003. It's undoubtedly one of the better values in San Juan. Though the lobby can be busy and noisy, cares melt away with attentive service and ocean views from most of the standard-issue rooms, which have thoughtful extras like voice mail and DVD players. Although it caters to the business traveler with free high-speed wireless-Internet access, the hotel nevertheless draws a large quotient of families, drawn by the reasonable prices, beautiful oceanfront pool, and ideal location on San Juan's best beach. ✉ *7012 Boca de Cangrejos Av., Isla Verde 00979* ☎ *787/791–0404 or 800/791–2553* 📠 *787/791–1460* 🌐 *www.sjcourtyard.com* *260 rooms, 33 suites* *2 restaurants, grill, ice-cream parlor, in-room data ports, in-room safes, refrigerators, cable TV, in-room VCRs, pool, gym, hot tub, beach, casino, lounge, shop, dry cleaning, laundry service, Internet, business services, meeting rooms, parking (fee)* *AE, D, DC, MC, V* *BP.*

$$–$$$ **Radisson Ambassador Plaza Hotel & Casino.** A prime location in the busiest part of Condado is the draw here, even though the hotel isn't directly on the beach. Rooms and suites have such amenities as hair dryers and coffeemakers; some suites have microwaves. Business travelers often stay on the Ambassador Club floor, where the Continental breakfasts are free, and there's access to a rooftop lounge with a TV, a pool table, and complimentary snacks. The casino's energy seems to spill out into—if not overrun—the lobby. The second-floor restaurants, Café Mezzanine and La Scala, offer respite from the casino noise. ✉ *1369 Av. Ashford, Condado 00907* ☎ *787/721–7300 or 800/468–8512* 📠 *787/723–6151* 🌐 *www.radisson.com* *148 rooms, 88 suites* *2 restaurants, room service, in-room data ports, in-room safes, some minibars, cable TV with movies, in-room VCRs, pool, gym, hair salon, hot tubs, 2 bars, casino, dry cleaning, laundry facilities, laundry service, concierge, business services, meeting rooms, travel services, parking (fee), no-smoking floors* *AE, MC, V* *EP.*

$–$$ **Hampton Inn & Suites San Juan Resort.** The Hampton Inn offers the benefit of business amenities only at the expense of not being directly on the beach—with rooms at almost half the price of those at luxury establishments. The hotel is across the street from the Isla Verde beach and about 1 mi from the airport. Rooms count coffeemakers and irons among their amenities. The business center is open 24 hours, and free coffee and tea are available in the lobby around the clock as well. The Guacamayo Pool Bar & Grill has a basic menu of hamburgers, fries, and the like. ✉ *6530 Av. Isla Verde, Isla Verde 00979* ☎ *787/791–8777 or 800/426–7866* 📠 *787/791–8757* 🌐 *www.hamptoninn.com* *147 rooms, 54 suites* *Restaurant, in-room data ports, in-room safes, some microwaves, refrigerators, cable TV, pool, gym, bar, laundry facilities, business services, meeting rooms, car rental, parking (fee), no-smoking floors* *AE, MC, V* *CP.*

$–$$ **Howard Johnson Hotel.** Directly across the road from Isla Verde beach, this Howard Johnson has more of a boutique-hotel feel than the typical chain hotel. Though rooms are hotel-standard, they are a step above the typical inexpensive motel. Natural light fills the lobby, reflecting off the polished wood and marble and highlighting the colorful, Mexican-print upholstery. The on-site restaurant not only serves that super-premium ice cream you remember from when you were a kid but also a surprising variety of international and Puerto Rican specialties. For finer dining accompanied by a panoramic view head to the rooftop Fontana Di Roma restaurant. ✉ *4820 Isla Verde Av., Isla Verde 00979* ☎ *787/728–1300* 📠 *787/727–7150* 🌐 *www.hojo.com* *115 rooms* *2 restaurants, in-room data ports, some microwaves, cable TV, pool, gym, beach, bar, no-smoking floor* 💳 *AE, MC, V* 🍽 *EP.*

$–$$ **Numero Uno.** Former New Yorker Esther Feliciano bought this three-story, red-roof guesthouse, spruced it up, and made it a very pleasant place to stay. It's in a quiet residential area, and its rooms are simple and clean; three have ocean views. Two apartments come with kitchenettes. A walled-in patio provides privacy for sunning or hanging out by the small pool, the bar, and Pamela's restaurant. Beyond the wall, the wide, sandy beach beckons; guests are provided with beach chairs and towels. ✉ *1 Calle Santa Ana, Ocean Park 00911* ☎ *787/726–5010* 📠 *787/727–5482* 🌐 *www.numero1guesthouse.com* *11 rooms, 2 apartments* *Restaurant, fans, cable TV, pool, beach, bar* 💳 *AE, MC, V* 🍽 *CP.*

$$ **Park Plaza Normandie.** One of the Caribbean's finest examples of art-deco architecture, this white-and-blue hotel hosted high-society types back in the 1930s. The couple who owned it was both glamorous and eccentric: the wife had a penchant for diving from the second floor into a central pool (now gone). Although the hotel doesn't have quite the same aura today, its French windows and doors, columns with Egyptian motifs, and other period details have been meticulously restored. Guest rooms have mahogany beds; a stay in a room on the corporate floor gets you access to business services and a private lounge. ✉ *Av. Muñoz Rivera at Parque de Tercer Milenio, Puerta de Tierra 00902* ☎ *787/729–2929, 877/987–2929, or 800/448–8355* 📠 *787/729–3083* 🌐 *www.normandiepr.com* *65 rooms, 118 suites* *Restaurant, in-room data ports, in-room safes, cable TV, pool, gym, hair salon, beach, 2 bars, shop, babysitting, laundry facilities, laundry service, business services, meeting rooms, no-smoking floor* 💳 *AE, MC, V* 🍽 *CP.*

$–$$ **Tu Casa Boutique Hotel.** *"Mi casa es su casa"* ("My house is your house") is the motto at this white-adobe lodging in a residential area just steps from Ocean Park beach. Proprietor Nancy Hernández has tastefully combined two houses to create rooms with kitchenettes and suites with full kitchens, living rooms, and dining areas. White-wicker furniture lends serenity, and gingham fabrics add touches of cheer. Common spaces, including a pool and bar area and plant-shaded patios, make it easy to unwind. ✉ *2071 Calle Cacique, Ocean Park 00911* ☎ *787/727–5100* 📠 *787/982–3349* 🌐 *www.tucasaguest.com* *25 rooms, 2 suites* *Restaurant, some kitchens, some kitchenettes, cable TV, pool, beach, bar, no-smoking rooms* 💳 *AE, MC, V* 🍽 *CP.*

$ **At Wind Chimes Inn.** So much about this villa invites you to relax: the spacious guest rooms, the patios shaded by bougainvillea and royal palms, the terra-cotta sundecks, the open terrace that's the perfect place to read, and the small pool with a built-in whirlpool spa. And there's the soft, ever-present jingling of wind chimes, reminding you that Condado beach and its sea breezes are just a block away. The Boat Bar, which is open only to guests, serves a light menu from 7 AM to 11 PM, and the staff is friendly and knowledgeable. ✉ *1750 Av. McLeary, Condado 00911* ☎ *787/727–4153 or 800/946–3244* 🖷 *787/728–0671* 🌐 *www.atwindchimesinn.com* *17 rooms, 5 suites* *Some kitchenettes, cable TV, pool, bar, Internet, parking (fee), no-smoking rooms* 💳 *AE, D, MC, V* 🍽 *EP.*

$ **El Canario by the Sea.** On the same block as the Marriot, this three-story, hunter-green hotel, wedged between blocky condo complexes, is near the beach, which is its main attraction. That said, the water fronting the property is too dangerous for swimming, but a swath of sand with calmer waves is about 200 feet away. Rooms are comfortable (most of the furniture even matches) and have either two twin beds or one double. A simple Continental breakfast of fruit punch, coffee, and pastries is served in a small, enclosed patio. ✉ *4 Av. Condado, Condado 00907* ☎ *787/722–8640 or 800/742–4276* 🖷 *787/725–4921* 🌐 *www.canariohotels.com* *25 rooms* *In-room safes, cable TV, no-smoking rooms* 💳 *AE, DC, MC, V* 🍽 *CP.*

$ **El Consulado.** On Condado's main drag, a couple of blocks from the sea, is this white, colonial-style building with a terra-cotta roof. Once the Spanish consulate, today it's a sedate, no-frills hotel, whose clean, comfortable guest quarters have dark-wood furnishings, paneling, and trim. Some rooms have small refrigerators; all have one queen or two double beds. Continental breakfast is served on a small brick patio beside the hotel, and numerous eateries are within walking distance. ✉ *1110 Av. Ashford, Condado 00907* ☎ *787/289–9191 or 888/300–8002* 🖷 *787/723–8665* 🌐 *www.ihppr.com* *29 rooms* *Some refrigerators, cable TV* 💳 *AE, D, DC, MC, V* 🍽 *CP.*

¢–$ **Casa del Caribe.** Tucked discreetly off Ashford Avenue, just steps from the beach behind the Condado Marriott, this quiet guesthouse attracts sun-seekers—though restaurants, casinos, and shops are all nearby as well. The wraparound veranda is the perfect place for a siesta, accompanied by the singing of birds and the trickling of a fountain. Sarongs and beachwear are for sale at the front desk, and the hospitable staff will help you arrange island tours. Monthly rates are available. ✉ *57 Calle Caribe, Condado 00907* ☎ *787/722–7139 or 877/722–7139* 🖷 *787/723–2575* *12 rooms, 1 suite* *Some kitchenettes, cable TV, parking (fee), some pets allowed (fee), no-smoking rooms* 💳 *AE, D, MC, V* 🍽 *CP.*

¢–$ **Hotel La Playa.** Small, unassuming, and almost hidden, Hotel La Playa sits over the glistening green waters of Isla Verde beach. It bills itself as a quiet, gentle retreat and lives up to this claim. Throughout floors are tiled and clean. Rooms are simple, each with one double bed or a single plus a double bed; those on the upper floors have water views. A plant-filled courtyard leads to a small bar; the restaurant, which is on a deck over the water, is famous for its burgers. ✉ *6 Calle Amapola, Isla Verde 00979* ☎ *787/791–1115 or 800/791–9626* 🖷 *787/791–4650* 🌐 *www.hotellaplaya.com* *15 rooms* *Restaurant, cable TV, beach, bar, free parking* 💳 *AE, MC, V* 🍽 *CP.*

¢–$ **L'Habitation Beach Guest House.** In 2000, Michel Parrabes acquired this guesthouse and has maintained its relaxed and oh-so-French ambience, which draws a primarily gay clientele. Rooms are simple and comfortable; numbers 8 and 9 are the largest and have ocean views. A combined bar–snack bar sits in the corner of a palm-shaded patio between the guesthouse and the sands of Ocean Park. Beach chairs and towels are provided: get your gear together before having a frozen drink or a margarita, which will knock your sandals off. ✉ *1957 Calle Italia, Ocean Park 00911* ☎ *787/727–2499* 📠 *787/727–2599* 🌐 *www.habitationbeach.com* *10 rooms* *Snack bar, fans, cable TV, beach, bar, laundry service, free parking* 💳 *AE, D, MC, V* 🍽 *CP.*

★ ¢–$ **Hostería del Mar.** Condado's high-rises are far to the west of this small, white inn on the beach in Ocean Park. Rooms are attractive and simple, with tropical prints and rattan furniture. Many rooms have ocean views, and four apartments have kitchenettes. The staff is courteous and helpful, and the ground-floor restaurant, which serves many vegetarian dishes as well as seafood and steaks, faces the trade winds and has fabulous beach views. ✉ *1 Calle Tapia, Ocean Park 00911* ☎ *787/727–3302 or 800/742–4276* 📠 *787/268–0772* 🌐 *www.prhtasmallhotels.com* *8 rooms, 4 apartments, 1 suite* *Restaurant, some kitchenettes, cable TV, beach, free parking; no smoking* 💳 *AE, D, DC, MC, V* 🍽 *EP.*

¢ **Hotel Olimpo Court.** Personal attention is key at this quiet, family run hotel. It's something that owner Alexandra Rodríguez learned from her grandmother, and it has rewarded her with many repeat guests. Daily, weekly, and monthly rates are available for the single and double rooms, all of which are impeccably neat. Some have kitchenettes and small private balconies. You can take in ocean views from the sundeck, catch a flick at the nearby fine-arts movie theater, or wander over to the Laguna del Condado. The on-site restaurant, Chayote, is one of the city's best and most creative. ✉ *603 Miramar Av., Miramar 00907* ☎ *787/724–0600* 📠 *787/977–0655* *45 rooms* *Restaurant, kitchenettes, cable TV, free parking, no-smoking floors* 💳 *AE, MC, V* 🍽 *EP.*

NIGHTLIFE & THE ARTS

Several publications will tell you what's happening in San Juan. *Qué Pasa,* the official visitor's guide, has current listings of events in the city and out on the island. For more up-to-the-minute information, pick up a copy of the English-language the *San Juan Star,* the island's oldest daily; the weekend section, which appears each Thursday, is especially useful. *Bienvenidos* and *Places,* both published by the Puerto Rico Hotel & Tourism Association, are also helpful. The English-language *San Juan City Magazine* has extensive calendars as well as restaurant reviews and cultural articles. The English-language radio station WOSO 1040 AM also provides valuable information for visitors.

There are also publications for Spanish-speaking visitors, including the "Wikén" section of the Spanish-language newspaper *El Nuevo Dia*; the paper also gives a weekly rundown of events on its Web site: www.endi.com. *Noctámbulo* is a Spanish-language pocket-size music and nightlife guide aimed at island youth that has extensive listings and is distributed in area clubs, bars, and restaurants.

Nightlife

From Thursday through Sunday, it's as if there's a celebration going on nearly everywhere in San Juan. Be sure you dress to party, particularly on Friday and Saturday nights; Puerto Ricans have flair, and both men and women love getting dressed up to go out. Bars are usually casual, but if you have on jeans, sneakers, and a T-shirt, you may be refused entry at nightclubs and discos.

Well-dressed visitors and locals alike often mingle in the lobby bars of large hotels, many of which have bands in the evening. Some hotels also have clubs with shows and/or dancing; admission starts at $10. Casino rules have been relaxed in recent years, injecting life into what was once a conservative hotel gaming scene. There are more games as well as such gambling perks as free drinks and live music.

In Old San Juan, Calle San Sebastián is lined with bars and restaurants. Salsa music blaring from jukeboxes in cut-rate pool halls competes with mellow Latin jazz in top-flight night spots. The young and the beautiful often socialize in Plaza San José. Late January sees the Fiestas de la Calle San Sebastián, one of the Caribbean's best street parties.

Young professionals as well as a slightly older bohemian crowd fill Santurce, San Juan's historical downtown area, until the wee hours. The revitalized Plaza del Mercado (off Calle Canals, between Ponce de León and Baldorioty de Castro) has structures—many painted in bright colors—dating from the 1930s or earlier. On weekend nights, the area's streets are closed to vehicular traffic. You can wander around with drinks, which are served in plastic cups, and sway to music that pours from countless open-air establishments and the marketplace's front plaza.

Bars

Andale. There's always a soccer match on the television at this authentic-looking Mexican tavern, which also has Mexican classics on the jukebox. At night, mariachis and musical trios perform; sometimes a DJ takes over. You can even get tasy south of the border fare. This place should have a bright future if it survives the years-long redevelopment of the area; it's right across from the large oceanfront plaza being developed by the Commonwealth government and between private renovations of the old Vanderbilt Condado Beach and La Concha hotels. ✉ *1024 Av. Ashford, Isla Verde* ☎ *787/724–4594 or 787/724–4595.*

El Batey. This wildly popular hole-in-the-wall bar, run by crusty New Yorker Davydd Gwilym Jones III, is like a military bunker. Pick up a pool cue for a game, or grab a marker to add your own message to the graffiti-covered walls. The ceiling may leak, but the jukebox has the best selection of oldies in town. ✉ *101 Calle Cristo, Old San Juan* ☎ *787/725–1787.*

Borinquen Brewing Company. Behind glass at the back, sleek metal vats hold this microbrewery's lagers and stouts. The taps sprouting from the wooden bar are a rarity in Puerto Rico, where draft beer is virtually nonexistent. The music is good, and there's often sports on TV. The island art on the walls reaffirms that you're in the Caribbean and not a mainland suburb. ✉ *4800 Av. Isla Verde, Isla Verde* ☎ *787/268–1900* ⊙ *Closed Mon.*

Buddhabar. Like the original in Paris, this restaurant-lounge is all burgundy and red, with gold and lots of floral prints. Handcarved wooden statues, a hypnotic mix of Middle Eastern and Asian music, and a similar culinary blend running through the menu complete the scene. The place attracts young and beautiful *sanjuaneros,* who can be seen cavorting through the glass-front dining room from crowded Condado Avenue. Food choices include three kinds of chop suey as well as tasty sautéed-pork medallions; sides of warm, spicy noodles and fried rice are fresh and flavorful. ✉ *60 Av. Condado, Condado* ☎ *787/724–6630.*

Cigar Bar. The lobby bar of the Wyndham El San Juan Hotel & Casino, with its dark-wood interior and huge chandelier, is both lively and classy. Power brokers often indulge in fine smokes while mingling with local starlets and smartly attired visitors. ✉ *6063 Av. Isla Verde, Isla Verde* ☎ *787/791–1000.*

Coaches. This typical sports pub is well outfitted with televisions if your travel plans coincide with that game you just can't miss. Local Ivy League graduates often congregate here to watch big sporting events showcasing their alma maters. The annual Harvard–Yale football game can get ugly. The restaurant-bar also becomes a venue for live rock, Latin pop, and reggae bands at night, especially on the weekends. Food offerings include U.S.-style burgers, chicken, steaks, and salads, as well as some Mexican food and local goodies. ✉ *137 Av. Roosevelt, Hato Rey* ☎ *787/758–3598.*

Karma. Music of all kinds, from *Rock en Español* to hip-hop to Latin rhythms, is played this popular, spacious bar-lounge in the heart of Santurce, and there's often a lively crowd. A menu of Spanish and Puerto Rican tapas is available when hunger strikes. ✉ *1402 Av. Ponce De León, Santurce* ☎ *787/721–5925.*

Liquid. In the lobby lounge of the Water Club hotel, glass walls filled with undulating water surround fashionable patrons seated on stools that seem carved from gigantic, pale seashells. If the wild drinks and pounding music are too much, head up to Wet, a less frenetic, romantic space on the penthouse floor, where you can relax at the bar or on a plush sitting-area chair, listen to R&B, and enjoy sushi under the stars. ✉ *Water Club, 2 Calle Tartak, Isla Verde* ☎ *787/725–4664 or 787/725–4675.*

Spybar. This sleek, modern James Bond–inspired martini lounge is a hit with San Juan's upwardly mobile youth. Top local DJs spin discs, and a menu of Puerto Rican–Asian fusion cuisine is available into the wee hours. The posters of Bond-ish babes and Mediterranean locales will have you expecting to bump into Sean Connery any second. It's closed Sunday. ✉ *1104 Av. Ashford, Condado* ☎ *787/724–2705.*

Casinos

By law, all casinos are in hotels, and the government keeps a close eye on them. They're allowed to operate from noon to 4 AM, but within those parameters individual casinos set their own hours. In addition to slot machines, typical games include blackjack, roulette, craps, Caribbean stud poker (a five-card stud game), and *pai gow* poker (a combination of American poker and the ancient Chinese game of pai gow, which employs cards and dice). Dress for the larger casinos tends to be on the formal side, and the atmosphere is refined. That said, an easing of gaming regulations has set a more relaxed tone and made such perks as free drinks and live music more common. The range of available games has also greatly expanded. The minimum age is 18.

Inter-Continental San Juan Resort & Casino. You may feel as if you're in Las Vegas here, perhaps because this property was once a Sands. A torch singer warms up the crowd at a lounge-bar just outside the gaming room. Inside, a garish chandelier, dripping with strands of orange lights, runs the length of a mirrored ceiling. ✉ *187 Av. Isla Verde, Isla Verde* ☎ *787/791–6100.*

Ritz-Carlton San Juan Hotel, Spa & Casino. With its golden columns, turquoise and bronze walls, and muted lighting, the Ritz casino is refined by day or night. There's lots of activity, yet everything is hushed. ✉ *Av. Las Gobernadores, Isla Verde* ☎ *787/253–1700.*

San Juan Marriott Resort & Stellaris Casino. The crowd is casual, and the decor is tropical and bubbly at this spacious gaming room. A huge bar, where Latin musicians usually perform, and an adjacent café are right outside. ✉ *1309 Av. Ashford, Condado* ☎ *787/722–7000.*

Wyndham Condado Plaza Hotel & Casino. With its tentlike chandeliers and whirring slots, the Condado is popular with locals. A band performs at one on-site bar, and the TV is tuned into sports at another. ✉ *999 Av. Ashford, Condado* ☎ *787/721–1000.*

Wyndham El San Juan Hotel & Casino. Slow-turning ceiling fans hang from a carved-wood ceiling, and neither the clangs of the slots nor the sounds of the salsa band disrupt the semblance of old world. The polish continues in the adjacent lobby, with its huge chandelier, dark woods, and fine-cigar bar. ✉ *6063 Av. Isla Verde, Isla Verde* ☎ *787/791–1000.*

Wyndham Old San Juan Hotel & Casino. It's hard to escape this ground-floor casino, the only place to gamble in Old San Juan. You can see it from the hotel's main stairway, from the balcony above, and from the lobby lounge. Light bounces off the Bahía de San Juan and pours through its many windows; passengers bound off their cruise ships and pour through its many glass doors. ✉ *101 Calle Brumbaugh, Old San Juan* ☎ *787/721–5100.*

Dance Clubs

Teatro Puerto Rico. This cavernous club, with an upstairs lounge, hosts a variety of DJs spinning trance-like rhythms. There's also often live music and other performances. A popular local drag queen performs Sunday nights. It's closed on Monday and Tuesday. ✉ *1420 Av. Ponce de León, Santurce* ☎ *787/723–3416.*

Babylon. A long line of well-heeled patrons usually runs out the door of the club at the Wyndham El San Juan Hotel & Casino. Those with the staying power to make it inside step into a pop-art style disco with pulsating music and beautiful people. Those who tire of waiting often head to El Chico Lounge, a small room with live entertainment right off the hotel lobby. ✉ *6063 Av. Isla Verde, Isla Verde* ☎ *787/791–1000.*

Candela. This lounge-art gallery housed in an historic building hosts some of the most innovative local DJs on the island and often invites star spinners from New York or London. This is the island's best showcase for experimental dance music. The festive, late-night haunt is open Tuesday through Saturday from 8 PM onward, and the conversation can be as stimulating as the dance floor. ✉ *110 San Sebastián, Old San Juan* ☎ *787/977–4305.*

Club Lazer. This multilevel club has spots for quiet conversation, spaces for dancing to loud music, and a landscaped roof deck overlooking San Juan. The crowd is different every night; Saturday is ladies' night. ✉ *251 Calle Cruz, Old San Juan* ☎ *787/725–7581.*

Martini's. An older, dressy crowd frequents this dance club—a one-time conference room—in the Inter-Continental hotel. It's known for its Las Vegas–style reviews; acts have included celebrity impersonators and flamenco music and dance troupes. Record parties and fashion shows are also held here from time to time. ✉ *Inter-Continental San Juan Resort & Casino, 187 Av. Isla Verde, Isla Verde* ☎ *787/791–6100 Ext. 356.*

The Noise. A young crowd frequents this Old San Juan dance club to listen to hip-hop, reggae, and underground music. There are often long lines out the door from Thursday through Saturday nights, which are the only nights it operates. ✉ *203 Calle Tanca, Old San Juan* ☎ *787/724–3426.*

Rebar. The Pier 10 nightclub is a venue for some of the top acts in tropical and jazz music, but on Friday and Saturday nights from 10 PM onwards, it becomes Rebar, a South Beach–inspired disco, complete with a beautiful crowd, danceable disco music, and lots of colorful drinks. ✉ *Pier 10, Av. Fernández Juncos, Puerta de Tierra* ☎ *787/729–9722.*

The Stargate. This club is an established spot for dancing to either DJ selections or live music despite several name and theme changes. Right now, it's a space-age place. On Wednesday casual attire is the norm, but you better dress up to dance here Thursday through Saturday. There's a cigar bar upstairs. ✉ *1 Av. Robert Todd, Santurce* ☎ *787/725–4664 or 787/725–4675.*

Gay & Lesbian Bars & Clubs

San Juan has a thriving gay and lesbian community, and it has become a popular Caribbean destination for gay and lesbian tourists. The city's nightlife scene has responded. Most discos have specific gay nights. The Condado, perhaps the heart of gay San Juan, hosts an annual gay- and lesbian-pride march each June, full of flamboyant dress and dancing, that rivals Greenwhich Village's Halloween Parade in enthusiasm, if on a much smaller scale. Sure it brings a smattering of protesters, but it also brings cheers from crowds of onlookers. There are also a few bars and clubs that cater specifically—or at least primarily—to a gay and lesbian crowd.

Puerto Rico Breeze (🌐 www.go-breeze.com) is a monthly newspaper covering Puerto Rico's gay and lesbian community. It's chock full of listings, articles, and advertisements on dining options, entertainment, and lodging alternatives.

Atlantic Beach. The oceanfront-deck bar of this hotel is famed in the gay community for its early evening happy hours. But the pulsating tropical music, the wide selection of exotic drinks, and the ever-pleasant ocean breeze make it a hit regardless of sexual orientation. Good food is also served on deck. ✉ *1 Calle Vendig, Condado* ☎ *787/721–6100.*

Cups. This women-oriented bar in downtown Santurce has been a mainstay of San Juan's nightlife for the past 10 years. Karaoke Night on Saturday is especially popular. ✉ *1708 Calle San Mateo, Santurce* ☎ *787/268–3570.*

Eros. The lighting is dim, the dance floor is large, the music is hot, and the balcony bar overlooks all the drama at this popular club. Most of the time DJs entertain, but bands have been known to perform here. It's open Wednesday through Saturday nights. ✉ *1257 Av. Ponce de León, Santurce* ☎ *787/722–1390.*

Kouros. The music is terrific at the newest gay dance club in the San Juan metro area, which opened in 2003. The disco is within walking distance of other gay bars in downtown Santurce, which is fast rivaling Condado as the newest trendy area catering to the gay community. ✉ *1515 Av. Ponce de León, Santurce* ☎ *787/640–1129.*

Nuestro Ambiente. This bar openly markets itself to the lesbian and gay community, offering a wide variety of entertainment—from live music to theatrical performances from Wednesday through Sunday nights. ✉ *1412 Av. Ponce de León, Santurce* ☎ *787/724–9083.*

Latin Music

Café Bohemio. El Convento Hotel's streetside Latin restaurant turns into a club at 11 each night, when the kitchen closes. The music lasts until 2 AM; Thursday is the best night, with Latin jazz and crowds of pretty people who spill out onto a terrace. ✉ *El Convento Hotel, 100 Calle Cristo, Old San Juan* ☎ *787/723–9200.*

El Balcón del Zumbador. A little off the beaten path, this venue has the city's best Afro-Caribbean music. Performers have included salsa great Roberto Roena, master percussionist Cachete Maldonado, and the legendary Cuban group Los Van Van. ✉ *768 Av. Barbosa, Santurce* ☎ *787/726–3082.*

La Fiesta Lounge. The lounge in the Wyndham Condado Plaza sizzles with steamy Latin shows. An older crowd, many of them locals, frequently fills the long room, which has a wall of windows that open onto a handsome terrace overlooking the Atlantic. ✉ *Wyndham Condado Plaza Hotel & Casino, 999 Av. Ashford, Condado* ☎ *787/721–1000.*

Hijos de Borinquen. Famed artist Rafael Tufiño, who stops in once in a while and has a stool with his name on it, immortalized this beloved bar in one of his paintings. The audience often sings along with the Puerto Rican ballads; some people even play maracas, cow bells, or bongos. The pitch is fevered during Andrés Jiménez's revolutionary anthem "Despierta Borinquen." The club is closed on Monday. ✉ *151 Calle San José, at Calle San Sebastián, Old San Juan* ☎ *787/723–8126.*

Nuyorican Café. There's something interesting happening here nearly every night, be it an early evening play, poetry reading, or talent show or a band playing Latin jazz, Cuban son, or Puerto Rican salsa later on. During breaks between performances the youthful, creative set converses in an alley outside the front door. It's closed on Monday. ✉ *312 Callejón de la Capellia, Old San Juan* ☎ *787/977–1276.*

Rumba. The air-conditioning blasts, works by local artists adorn the walls, and the crowd is hip. With a large dance and stage area and smokin' Afro-Cuban bands, it's one of the best parties in town. ✉ *152 Calle San Sebastián, Old San Juan* ☎ *787/725–4407.*

Night Bites

San Juan is a cosmopolitan city by Caribbean standards, welcoming to all kinds of visitors, with many places open late—if not all night, at least for a good portion of it. The establishments listed here are generally open until at least midnight during the week and 2 AM on weekends. But many are open much later. Old San Juan's Brick House, for example, proudly proclaims that its kitchen never closes until 4 AM.

The Brick House Bar & Grill. This friendly bar and sidewalk café on Old San Juan's bustling Plaza Somohano is adjacent to the Teatro Tapia. You can get tasty wraps, burgers, and salads here until 3 AM, as well as plenty of good conversation. If you eat elsewhere, chances are you will see your server here, once his or her shift ends. ✉ *359 Calle Tetuán, Old San Juan* ☎ *787/724–3359.*

Buren. A funky, tropical-color bistro with a charming interior patio, this place across the street from El Convento Hotel serves good pizza and pasta, as well as Caribbean- and Mediterranean-inspired dishes. The house wines by the glass are all good, and there's often a jazz or flamenco musician performing live. ✉ *103 Calle Cristo, Old San Juan* ☎ *787/977–5023.*

Carniceriáa Restaurant Díaz. Come here if you need a snack between dances. The *morcilla* sausage and roast pork go well with a drink. ✉ *319 Calle Orbeta, Santurce* ☎ *787/723–1903.*

Dunbar's. The crowd may be full of young professionals, but everyone is casual at this beachside bar. There's good food, sports on TV, a pool room, and live music Thursday through Saturday. ✉ *1954 Calle McCleary, Ocean Park* ☎ *787/728–2920.*

El Hamburger. This no-frills barbecue shack serves up the best burger in San Juan with sides of crunchy french fries and onion rings. The wood and zinc structure sits on a bluff overlooking the Atlantic. Usually open until midnight, it's open until 3 AM on Friday and Saturday nights. ✉ *402 Av. Muñoz Rivera, Puerta de Tierra* ☎ *787/721–4269.*

Hard Rock Café. Are you really surprised to find that there is a Hard Rock in Old San Juan? These days, they're almost as common as McDonald's. ✉ *253 Recinto Sur, Old San Juan* ☎ *787/724–7625.*

Krugger's. Old San Juan bar hoppers head to this fried-food emporium and adjacent bar when the late-night munchies hit. Codfish fritters, beef turnovers, crab and plantain rolls, and more are served until the wee hours. ✉ *52 Calle San José, Old San Juan* ☎ *787/723–2474* ⏲ *Closed Mon.*

Makarios. Italy meets the Middle East, brick-oven pizza meets hummus, and crostinis meet falafel on a big outdoor-seating area that spills onto a plaza. The first indoor level is a sleek modern bar with a small dining area, where there's a pizza and snack menu and Western music. Upstairs is more serious Middle Eastern cuisine, hypnotic rhythms, and a skillful bellydancer. ✉ *356 Calle Tetuán, Old San Juan* ☎ *787/723–8653.*

Mango's Café. This Caribbean-style bar-restaurant near the beach has live jazz, Spanish pop, and reggae music every night that it's open. The menu has light, down-island fare. ✉ *2421 Calle Laurel, Punta Las Marías* ☎ *787/727–9328* ⏲ *Closed Sun. and Mon.*

El Patio de Sam. The clientele swears that this Old San Juan institution serves the island's best burgers. Potted plants and strategically placed canopies make the outdoor patio a fine place to eat in any weather. ✉ *102 Calle San Sebastián, Old San Juan* ☎ *787/723–1149.*

Restaurant Don Telfo. Photos of famous and not-so famous diners line the walls of this well-kept restaurant. You can head to the dining room for a sit-down meal or feast on the barbecued chicken, *pinchos* (pork kabobs), and *bacalaítos* (salt-cod fritters) that are served curbside. ✉ *180 Calle Dos Hernmanos, Santurce* ☎ *787/724–5752.*

The Arts

San Juan is the epicenter of Puerto Rico's lively arts scene, and on most nights there's likely to be a ballet, a play, or an art opening somewhere in town. If you're in town on the first Tuesday of the month (from September through December and February through May), take advantage of Old San Juan's **Gallery Night** (☎ 787/723–6286). Galleries and select museums open their doors after-hours for viewings that are accompanied by refreshments and music. Afterward, people head to bars and music clubs, and the area remains festive until well past midnight. The event is so popular that finding a parking space is difficult; it's best to take a cab.

Island Culture

LeLoLai. This year-round festival celebrates Puerto Rico's Indian, Spanish, and African heritage. Performances showcasing island music and folklore take place each week in different hotels. Because it's sponsored by the Puerto Rico Tourism Company and major San Juan hotels, passes to the festivities are included in some lodging packages. You can also purchase tickets to a weekly series of events for $15. ☎ *787/723–3135 weekdays, 787/791–1014 weekends and evenings.*

Patron Saint Festivals. Each of Puerto Rico's 78 municipalities has a patron saint associated with it, and almost every one celebrates an annual festival near the saint's birthday, sometimes lasting all week through two consecutive weekends. These festivals are a great opportunity to hear live music; some of the top names in Puerto Rican music perform free during these celebrations. There's also lots of food and drink and the opportunity to buy local arts and crafts. Somewhere in Puerto Rico, it seems, a patron-saint festival is going on nearly every weekend. These festivals are usually advertised in local newspapers, and the Puerto Rico Tourism Company has a complete listing, which is published in its official magazine *Que Pasa*. San Juan celebrates its patron-saint feast in the *noche de San Juan* on June 23, when the entire city takes to the beach on the eve of San Juan's birth. There's a night-long picnic, live music, and lots of dancing. The event culminates at midnight, when crowds plunge into the Atlantic to flip over backwards three times, a cleansing ritual expected to bring good fortune.

Performing Arts

San Juan arguably is one of the most important cultural centers of the Caribbean, both for home-grown culture and the healthy influx of visiting artists that the local population supports. The city hosts the Puerto Rico Symphony Orchestra, the world-renowned Pablo Casals classical-music festival in winter, and an annual series of opera concerts. Many hit plays in New York and other large markets get produced locally, and there are often three or four other local theatrical productions taking place on any given weekend, many of them downright adventurous.

MAJOR EVENTS **The Casals Festival** (Box 41227, San Juan 00940–1227 ☎ 787/721–7727 🌐 www.festcasalspr.gobierno.pr) has been bringing some of the most important figures in classical music San Juan ever since Pablo Casals, the famous cellist, conductor, and composer, started the festival in 1957. After establishing the festival in 1971, Casals went on to direct it until his death in 1973. It has continued to serve as a vibrant stage for top-notch classical performers since then. Most of the shows take place at the Centro de Bellas Artes Luis A Ferré, but there are also performances at the University of Puerto Rico and other venues. The festival, originally held in the summer, now takes place from mid-February through mid-March. Tickets are available at the Ticket Center kiosk outside Borders at Plaza Las Améicas or through the box office of the Centro de Bellas Artes Luis A Ferré.

San Juan is a great place to hear jazz, particularly Latin jazz, and the annual **Puerto Rico Heineken Jazzfest** (🌐 www.prheinekenjazz.com), which takes place in late May and early June, is one of the best opportunities for it. Each year's festival is dedicated to a particular musician. Honorees have included Chick Corea, Mongo Santamaria, and Tito Puente. Although the festival was born at the Tito Puente Amphiteatro, it has since moved to the Puerta de Tierra oceanside park and sports facility right outside Old San Juan. With the Atlantic surf crashing outside the park, and the stars overhead, it's a stimulating atmosphere in which to soak up fine jazz music.

TICKETS Two major outlets sell tickets for events throughout Puerto Rico. **Ticket Center** (✉ Plaza Las Américas, top level adjacent to the food court, Hato Rey ☎ 787/759–5000 ✉ Coliseo Roberto Clemente, Av. Roosevelt, across from Plaza las Américas, Hato Rey ☎ 787/783–8929) has two locations in San Juan. **Ticketpop** (✉ Banco Popular Bldg., Stop 22, 1500 Poncé de León Ave., Santurce ☎ 787/294–0001 or 866/994–0001 🌐 www.ticketpop.com), which is owned by Banco Popular, also sells tickets via the Internet or at Casa de Los Tapes music store locations across the island.

PERFORMANCE VENUES **Amphiteatro Tito Puente.** Surrounded by lagoons and trees, the open-air theater is a great spot to hear hot Latin jazz, reggae, and Spanish pop music. It's named after the late, great musician who many credit with bringing salsa to the rest of the world. Shows usually take place Thursday through Sunday nights. ✉ *Luis Muñoz Marín Park, Hato Rey* ☎ *787/751–3353.*

Centro de Bellas Artes Luis A. Ferré (Luis A. Ferré Center for the Performing Arts). This is the largest venue of its kind in the Caribbean, and there's something going on nearly every night, from pop or jazz concerts to plays, operas, and ballets. It's also the home of the San Juan Symphony Orchestra. Luciano Pavoratti held his annual Operalia competition here in 1999, and Cuban musicians reunited as the Buena Vista Social Club played sold-out shows in 2000. ✉ *Av. José de Diego and Av. Ponce de León, Santurce* ☎ *787/725–7334.*

Coliseo Roberto Clemente. The arena has become an important island venue for concerts in addition to its status as a sports facility. Rap, reggae, salsa, jazz, and pop musicians all play this venue, which holds 10,000 for concerts. ✉ *Av. Roosevelt at Plaza las Américas, Hato Rey* ☎ *787/725–2110.*

Hiram Bithorn Stadium. Particularly big acts often use this outdoor stadium adjacent to the Roberto Clemente Coliseum, which hosts baseball games and large concerts. There's seating capacity for 18,000, more when the infield is used for fans. ✉ *Av. Roosevelt at Plaza las Américas, Hato Rey* ☎ *787/765–5000.*

Teatro Tapia. Named for Puerto Rican playwright Alejandro Tapia, the theater hosts traveling and locally produced theatrical and musical productions. Matinee performances with family entertainment are also held here, especially around the holidays. ✉ *La Fortaleza at Plaza Colón, Old San Juan* ☎ *787/722–0247.*

GROUPS **Puerto Rico Symphony Orchestra** (Orquesta Sinfónica de Puerto Rico). The island's orchestra is one of the most prominent in the Americas. Its 76 members perform a full 48-week season that includes classical music concerts, operas, ballets, and popular-music performances. The orchestra plays most shows at Centro de Bellas Artes Luis A Ferré, but it also gives outdoor concerts at museums and university campuses around the island and has an educational outreach program in island schools. Pablo Casals served as the impetus to this group, helping to create it in 1956. 📫 *Box 41227, San Juan 00940–1227* ☎ *787/721–7727* 🌐 *www.sinfonicapr.gobierno.pr.*

SPORTS & THE OUTDOORS

Many of San Juan's most enjoyable outdoor activities take place in and around the water. With miles of beach stretching across Isla Verde, Ocean Park, and Condado, there's a full range of water sports, including sailing, kayaking, windsurfing, kiteboarding, Jet Skiing, deep-sea fishing, scuba diving, and snorkeling.

Options for land-based activities include tennis and walking or jogging at local parks. With a bit of effort—meaning a short drive out of the city—you'll find a world of championship golf courses and rain-forest trails. Baseball is big in Puerto Rico, and the players are world-class; many are recruited from local teams to play in the U.S. major leagues. The season runs from October through February. Games are played in San Juan as well as other venues around the island.

Beaches

Balneario de Carolina. A government-maintained, gated beach, Balneario de Carolina is about 10 km (6 mi) east of Isla Verde on Avenida Los Gobernadores (Route 187) and so close to the airport that the leaves rustle when planes take off. Its long stretch of sand is shaded by palms and almond trees and edged by surf that's often rough. There's plenty of room to spread out, though, and lots of amenities: lifeguards, bathhouses, picnic gazebos with tables and barbecue grills. The gates are open daily from 8 to 4:30, and although there's plenty of parking ($2), city buses—including the B-40, which travels from Isla Verde and Río Piedras—stop here.

Balneario Escambrón. Just off Avenida Muñoz Rivera on the Puerta de Tierra stretch at the entrance to Old San Juan is the Parque de Tercer Milenio. In it you'll find the Balneario Escambrón, a patch of honey-color beach with shade provided by coconut palms and surf that's generally gentle. There are also lifeguards, showers, bathrooms, and restaurants. The park is open daily from 7 to 7, and parking is $3. City buses A-9 and B-8 will drop you relatively close to this beach.

★ **Playa del Condado.** West of Old San Juan and east of Ocean Park and Isla Verde, this long, wide beach is often full of guests from the hotels and resorts that tower over it. Beach bars, water-sports outfitters, and chair-rental places abound, but there are no lifeguards. You can access the beach from several roads off Avenida Ashford, including calles Vendin, Earl, and Court; if you're driving, on-street parking is your only option. Adjacent to the Wyndham Condado Plaza Hotel and just off Avenida Ashford is **Playita Condado** (its sign says CONDADO PUBLIC BEACH). Rocks in the waters off this tiny beach temper the waves, making it a great place for families with young children. There are also a few shade trees and, despite the gentle surf, lifeguards.

need a break?

★ Of Condado's many beach bars, one of the best is the terrace at **Piu Bello Gelato** (✉ 1302 Av. Ashford, Condado ☎ 787/977–2121), across the street from the Marriott hotel. It serves wraps, foccaccia-bread sandwiches, salads, and—best of all—homemade gelato.

Fodor's Choice ★ **Playa de Isla Verde.** There aren't any lifeguards, but the sands are white, and the snorkeling is good at this beach east of Ocean Park. Like Condado, Isla Verde is bordered by high-rise hotels and has plenty of places to rent beach chairs and water-sports equipment or grab a bite to eat. The best entrance is from the dead-end Calle José M. Tartak off Avenida Isla Verde. Some street parking is available.

★ **Playa de Ocean Park.** A residential neighborhood just east of Condado and west of Isla Verde is home to this wide, 1½-km-long (1-mi-long) stretch of golden sand. The waters are often choppy but still swimmable—take care, however, as there aren't any lifeguards are on duty. It's popular with college students, particularly on weekends, and it's also one of the two city beaches preferred by the gay community. (The other is in front of the Atlantic Beach Hotel.) There are public rest rooms, a playground, and a small police station at Parque Barbosa on the south side of Calle Park Boulevard. To get here by car, take Calle McLeary to Calle Soldado Serrano and Calle Park Boulevard. Parking spots line the roads.

need a break?

★ Surfer Alex García owns **Pinky's** (✉ 51 Calle María Moczo, Ocean Park ☎ 787/727–3347), a lively Ocean Park beach stand that serves fresh, delicious fruit shakes as well as sandwiches and salads. If you're really lazy, this place takes phone orders and will send a scooter-driving delivery guy right to your patch of sand. Note that Pinky's is closed on Monday, the day Alex prays that the waves will be high.

Baseball

Does the name Roberto Clemente ring a bell? The late, great star of the Pittsburgh Pirates, who died in a 1972 plane crash delivering supplies to Nicaraguan earthquake victims, was born near San Juan and got his start in the Puerto Rican pro leagues. Many other Puerto Rican stars have played in the U.S. major leagues, including the brothers Roberto Alomar and Sandy Alomar Jr.; their father, Sandy Alomar; and Hall of Fame inductees Tony Perez and Orlando Cepeda. The island's season runs from October through February. Stadiums are in San Juan (Estadio Hiram Bithorn), Santurce, Ponce, Caguas, Arecibo, and Mayagüez; the teams also play once or twice a season in Aguadilla. General-admission seats run about $15; the most expensive box seats cost $30. You can buy tickets to baseball games at Ticketpop outlets in all branches of **Casa de los Tapes** (✉ 233 Roosevelt Ave., Hato Rey ☎ 787/764–4061 ✉ 62 Condado Ave., Condado ☎ 787/721–0277). Baseball games in the San Juan area are played at **Estadio Hiram Bithorn** (✉ Hato Rey ☎ 787/294–0001 or 787/725–2110) **Montreal Expos** (🌐 montreal.expos.mlb.com) play an exhibition season each year in San Juan.

Biking

Most streets don't have bike lanes, and auto traffic makes bike travel somewhat risky; further, all the fumes can be hard to take. That said, recreational bikers are increasingly donning their safety gear and wheeling through the streets, albeit with great care.

As a visitor, your best bet is to look into a bike tour offered by an outfitter. One popular 45-minute trip travels from Old San Juan's cobblestone streets to Condado. It passes El Capitolio and runs through either Parque del Tercer Milenio (ocean side) or Parque Luis Muñoz Rivera, taking you past the Caribe Hilton Hotel and over Puente Dos Hermanos (Dos Hermanos Bridge) onto Avenida Ashford. The truly ambitious can continue east to Ocean Park, Isla Verde, and right on out of town to the eastern community of Piñones and its beachside bike path.

Adrenalina (✉ 4770 Av. Isla Verde, Isla Verde ☎ 787/727–1233) rents bikes and helmets by the hour ($10), half-day ($15), and full day ($25). **Hot Dog Cycling** (✉ 5916 Av. Isla Verde, Isla Verde ☎ 787/982–5344 🌐 www.hotdogcycling.com) rents Fuji mountain bikes for $30 a day and organizes group excursions to El Yunque and other places out on the island.

Diving & Snorkeling

The waters off San Juan aren't the best places to scuba dive, but several outfitters conduct short excursions to where tropical fish, coral, and sea horses are visible at depths of 30 feet to 60 feet. Escorted half-day dives range from $45 to $95 for one or two tanks, including all equipment; in general, double those prices for night dives. Packages that include lunch and other extras start at $100; those that include accommodations are also available.

Snorkeling excursions, which include transportation, equipment rental, and sometimes lunch, start at $50. Equipment rents at beaches for about $5 to $7. (Caution: Coral-reef waters and mangrove areas can be dangerous. Unless you're an expert or have an experienced guide, stay near the water-sports centers of hotels and avoid unsupervised areas.)

Mundo Submarino (✉ Laguna Garden Shopping Center, Av. Baldorioty de Castro, Carolina ☎ 787/791–5764 🌐 www.mundosubmarino.net) sells and rents snorkeling and diving equipment. **Ocean Sports** (✉ 1035 Av. Ashford, Condado ☎ 787/723–8513 🌐 www.osdivers.com) offers certified scuba dives; airtank fill-ups; and equipment repairs, sales and rentals. It also rents surfboards by the day.

Fishing

Puerto Rico's waters are home to large game fish such as marlin, snook, wahoo, dorado, tuna, and barracuda; as many as 30 world records for catches have been set off the island's shores. Prices for fishing expeditions vary, but they tend to include all your bait and tackle, as well as refreshments, and start at $450 (for a boat with as many as six people) for a half-day trip to $750 for a full day. Other boats charge by the person, starting at $150 for a full day.

Half-day, full-day, split-charter, and big- and small-game fishing can be arranged through **Benitez Deep-Sea Fishing** (✉ Club Náutico de San Juan, Miramar ☎ 787/723–2292 🌐 www.mikebenitezfishing.com).

Golf

Puerto Rico is the birthplace of golf legend and raconteur Chi Chi Rodriguez—and he had to hone his craft somewhere. The island has more than a dozen courses, including some of championship caliber. Several make good day trips from San Juan. Be sure to call ahead for details on reserving tee times; hours vary and several hotel courses allow only guests to play or give preference to them. Greens fees start at $25 and go as high as $115. *See the* Northwestern Puerto Rico *and* Eastern Puerto Rico chapters for more information on golf courses within easy striking distance of San Juan.

★ There are four attractive Robert Trent Jones–designed 18-hole courses shared by the **Hyatt Dorado Beach Resort & Country Club** (✉ Rte. 693, Km 10.8 and Km 11.8, Dorado ☎ 787/796–1234 Ext. 3238 or 3016 🌐 www.doradobeach.hyatt.com) 27 km (17 mi) west of town.

Developed on what was once a coconut plantation, the public, 18-hole course at the **Bahía Beach Plantation** (✉ Rte. 187, Km 4.2, Río Grande ☎ 787/256–5600 🌐 www.golfbahia.com) is an old-time favorite that skirts the coast 35 km (21 mi) east of San Juan. Nonmembers can play golf at **Berwind Country Club** (✉ Rte. 187, Km 4.7, Río Grande ☎ 787/876–3056) on weekdays. The 18-hole course, which is 35 km (21 mi) east of San Juan, is known for its tight fairways. With El Yunque rain ★ forest as a backdrop, the two courses at the **Westin Río Mar Beach Resort & Country Club** (✉ 6000 Río Mar Blvd., Río Grande ☎ 787/888–6000 🌐 www.westinriomar.com), 35 mi (21 km) east of San Juan, are truly inspirational. You'll need to reserve your tee time in advance.

Hiking

Thirteen hiking trails loop past giant ferns, exotic orchids, sibilant streams and waterfalls, and broad trees reaching for the sun at **El Yunque** (✉ Centro de Información El Portal, Rte. 191, Km 4.3, off Rte. 3 ☎ 787/888–1880 🌐 www.southernregion.fs.fed.us/caribbean), about an hour's drive east of San Juan. The park, which is officially known as the Bosque Nacional del Caribe (Caribbean National Forest), has several information centers, but the best one is the Centro de Información El Portal. It's open daily from 9 to 5; admission to the rain-forest center is $3.

Eco-Action Tours (✉ Wyndham Condado Plaza Hotel & Casino, 999 Av. Ashford, Laguna Wing, Condado ☎ 787/791–7509 or 787/640–7385) organizes a variety of hikes and excursions throughout the island.

Horse Racing

Thoroughbred races are run year-round at **Hípodromo El Comandante** (✉ Av. 65th Infantry [Rte. 3], Km 15.3, Canóvanas ☎ 787/724–6060 🌐 www.comandantepr.com) a racetrack about 20 minutes east of San Juan. On race days the dining rooms open at 12:30 PM. Post time is 2:15 or 2:45 (depending on the season) Wednesday and Friday through Monday. Races end around 7 PM.

Kayaking

The Laguna del Condado is popular for kayaking, especially on weekends. You can simply paddle around it or head out under the Puente Dos Hermanos to the San Gerónimo fort right behind the Caribe Hilton and across from the Wyndham Condado Plaza. Kayaks rent for $25 to $35 an hour.

Las Tortugas Adventures (✉ Cond. La Puntilla, 4 Calle La Puntilla, Apt. D1-12, Old San Juan ☎ 787/725–5169 🌐 www.kayak-pr.com) organizes group-kayaking trips to the Reserva Natural Las Cabezas de San Juan and the Bahía Mosquito in eastern Puerto Rico.

Surfing

★ Although the west-coast beaches around Rincón are considered *the* places to surf in Puerto Rico, San Juan was actually the place where the sport got its start on the island. In 1958 legendary surfers Gary Hoyt and José Rodríguez Reyes began surfing at the beach in front of Bus Stop 2½, facing El Capitolio. Although this spot is known for its big waves, the conditions must be nearly perfect to surf here. Today, many surfers head to Puerta de Tierra and a spot known as La Ocho (in front of Bus Stop 8 behind the Dumas Restaurant). Another, called the Pressure Point, is behind the Caribe Hilton Hotel.

In Condado, you can surf La Punta, a reef break behind the Presbyterian Hospital, or the Sheraton, a break named after the hotel (which is now a Marriott) with either surf or boogie boards. In Isla Verde, white water on the horizon means that the waves are good at the beach break near the Ritz-Carlton known as Pine Grove. East of the city, in Piñones, the Caballo has deep-to-shallow-water shelf waves that require a big-wave board known as a "gun." The surf culture frowns upon aficionados who divulge the best spots to outsiders. If you're lucky, though, maybe you'll make a few friends who'll let you in on where to find the best waves.

At Ocean Park beach, famous surfer Carlos Cabrero, proprietor of **Tres Palmas Surf Shop** (✉ 1911 Av. McLeary, Ocean Park ☎ 787/728–3377), rents boards (daily rates are $25 for boogey, $30 short boards, $35 for foam boards and $40 for long boards), repairs equipment, and sells all sorts of hip beach and surfing gear.

Tennis

If you'd like to use the tennis courts at a property where you aren't a guest, call in advance for information about reservations and fees. There are two tennis courts at the **Wyndham Condado Plaza Hotel & Casino** (✉ 999 Av. Ashford, Condado ☎ 787/721–1000). Fees for nonguests range from $10 to $20 per hour. The four lighted courts of the **Isla Verde Tennis Club** (✉ Calles Ema and Delta Rodriguez, Isla Verde ☎ 787/727–6490) are open for nonmember use at $4 per hour, daily from 8 AM to 10 PM. The **Parque Central Municipo de San Juan** (✉ Calle Cerra, exit on Rte. 2, Santurce ☎ 787/722–1646) has 17 lighted courts. Fees are $3 per hour from 8 AM to 6 PM and $4 per hour from 6 PM to 10 PM.

Water Sports

Many of the resort hotels on the Condado and Isla Verde strips either have their own water-sports centers or can refer you to reputable, freestanding outfitters on the beach. These establishments often rent gear, give lessons, and arrange trips for several water sports, including boating, sailing, fishing, scuba diving, and snorkeling.

★ The Normandie Hotel's **Caribe Aquatic Adventures** (✉ Normandie Hotel, Av. Muñoz Rivera at Parque del Tercer Milenio, Puerta de Tierra ☎ 787/724–1882 or 787/281–8858 🌐 www.caribeaquaticadventure.com) has fishing, boating, and sailing trips of all kinds. It also rents snorkeling equipment and organizes group-snorkeling excursions. **Castillo Watersports** (✉ San Juan Marriott Resort & Stellaris Casino, 1309 Av. Ashford, Condado ☎ 787/728–2297 or 787/725–7970) rents gear and arranges fishing, boating, and sailing excursions. **Eco-Action Tours** (✉ Wyndham Condado Plaza Hotel, 999 Av. Ashford, Laguna Wing, Condado ☎ 787/791–7509 or 787/640–7385) rents kayaks, Sunfish, hydrobikes, and Jet Skis; gives windsurfing lessons; and offers kayaking trips to other parts of the island. Its dive master, Peter Zervigón, arranges beginning and advanced beach or boat dives. A good bet for a variety of water sports is the Wyndham El San Juan's **San Juan Water Fun** (✉ Wyndham El San Juan Hotel & Casino, 6063 Av. Isla Verde, Isla Verde ☎ 787/643–4510). **Sun Riders Watersports** (✉ Wyndham Condado Plaza Hotel & Casino, 999 Av. Ashford, Condado ☎ 787/721–1000 Ext. 2699) rents gear for several types of water sports.

Windsurfing & Kite Surfing

★ The waves can be strong and the surf choppy, but the constant wind makes for good sailing, windsurfing, or kiteboarding (maneuvering a surfboard using a parachutelike kite), particularly in Ocean Park and Punta Las Marías (between Ocean Park and Isla Verde). In general, you can rent a Windsurfer for about $25 an hour (including a lesson).

In the same location as the Velauno windsurfing center, **Real Kiteboarding** (✉ 2430 Calle Loíza, Punta Las Marías ☎ 787/728–8716 🌐 www.realkiteboarding.com) is a full-service kiteboarding center that offers lessons. You'll get the best windsurfing advice and equipment from Jaime Torres at **Velauno** (✉ 2430 Calle Loíza, Punta Las Marías ☎ 787/728–8716 🌐 www.velauno.com), the second-largest, full-service windsurfing center in U.S. territory. It has rentals, repair services, and classes. It also sells new and used gear and serves as clearinghouse for information on windsurfing events throughout the island.

SHOPPING

In Old San Juan—especially on calles Fortaleza and San Francisco—you'll find everything from T-shirt emporiums to selective crafts stores, bookshops, art galleries, jewelry boutiques, and even shops that specialize in made-to-order Panama hats. Calle Cristo is lined with factory-outlet stores, including those for Coach, Dooney & Bourke, Polo–Ralph Lauren, Guess, and Tommy Hilfiger.

All the old city's stores are within walking distance of each other, and trolleys are at your beck and call. On weekends, artisans sell their wares at stalls around El Paseo de la Princesa. Caveat emptor: Bargains (and, often, peace) are hard to find in Old San Juan, which is one of the Caribbean's most popular cruise-ship stops.

With many stores selling luxury items and designer fashions, the shopping spirit in Condado is reminiscent of that in Miami. Avenida Condado is a good bet for souvenirs and curios as well as art and upscale jewelry or togs. Avenida Ashford is considered the heart of San Juan's fashion district. There's also a growing fashion scene in the business district of Hato Rey. Thanks to Puerto Rico's vibrant art scene, more and more galleries and studios are opening, and many are doing so in neighborhoods outside the old city walls. If you prefer shopping in air-conditioned comfort, there are plenty of malls in and just outside San Juan.

Markets & Malls

Look for vendors selling crafts from kiosks at the **Artesanía Puertorriqueña** (☎ 787/722–1709) in the tourism company's La Casita at Plaza Dársenas near Pier 1 in Old San Juan. Several vendors also set up shop to sell items such as belts, handbags, and toys along Calle San Justo in front of Plaza Dársenas.

In the suburb of Carolina, a few minutes east of San Juan on Route 3, you'll find a **Mercado Artesanal** (Artisans Market) and cultural fair every Sunday from 1 to 5 at the Parque Julia de Burgos on Avenida Roberto Clemente (corner of Paseo de los Gigantes). In addition to craft and food booths, bands perform, and there's often entertainment for the children.

For a mundane albeit complete shopping experience, head to **Plaza Las Américas** (✉ 525 Av. Franklin Delano Roosevelt, Hato Rey ☎ 787/767–1525), which has 200 shops, including the world's largest JCPenney store, the Gap, Sears Roebuck, Macy's, Godiva, and Armani Exchange, as well as restaurants and movie theaters.

Off Route 26 about 10 minutes east of San Juan you'll find **Plaza Carolina** (✉ Av. Fragosa, Carolina ☎ 787/768–0514). About 30 minutes west of San Juan on Route 167 (off Route 22 and past the Buchanan toll), **Plaza del Sol** (✉ 725 West Main Av., Bayamón ☎ 787/778–8724) includes Old Navy and Banana Republic, restaurants, and a multiscreen cinema. Off Avenida John F. Kennedy, about 15 minutes south of San Juan, **San Patricio Plaza** (✉ Av. San Patricio Av. at Av. Franklin Delano Roosevelt, Guaynabo ☎ 787/792–1255) has a Boston Shoe and a Footaction USA, as well as restaurants and movie theaters.

Specialty Shops

Art

★ Many galleries and a few museums stay open late during Old San Juan's **Gallery Night** (☎ 787/723–6286). It's held from 6 to 9 on the first Tuesday of the month September to December and February to May.

Atlas Art (✉ 208 Calle Cristo, Old San Juan ☎ 787/723–9987) carries contemporary paintings and prints as well as sculptures in glass and bronze.

★ Among those who have displayed their works at **Galería Petrus** (✉ 726 Hoare St., Miramar ☎ 787/289–0505 🌐 www.petrusgallery.com) are Dafne Elvira, whose surreal oils and acrylics tease and seduce (witness a woman emerging from a banana peel); Marta Pérez, another surrealist, whose bewitching paintings examine such themes as how life on a coffee plantation might have been; and Elizam Escobar, a former political prisoner whose oil paintings convey the often-intense realities of human experience. Petrus also sells the architectonic designs of Imel Sierra (who created the sculpture "Paloma" in Condado), which combine wood and metal elements.

★ Half a block from the Museo de Arte de Puerto Rico, **Galería Raíces** (✉ 314 Av. José de Diego, Santurce ☎ 787/723–8909) is dedicated to showing work by such emerging Puerto Rican artists as Nayda Collazo Llorens, whose cerebral and sensitive multimedia installations examine connections and patterns in games, codes, and human memory. Raíces also displays the work of sculptors Annex Burgos and Julio Suárez. **Galería San Juan** (✉ Gallery Inn, 204–206 Calle Norzagaray, Old San Juan ☎ 787/722–1808) shows sensuous sculptures of faces and bodies and watercolors of Old San Juan architecture by artist and innkeeper Jan D'Esopo.

Galería Tamara (✉ 210 Av. Chardón, Suite 104-A, Hato Rey ☎ 787/764–6465) has abstract oil studies of the arc form by Wilfredo Chiesa (whose works also appear at the Peter Findlay Gallery in New York City) and oil paintings of placid home scenes by Carmelo Sobrino. **Galería Viota** (✉ 739 Av. San Patricio, Las Lomas ☎ 787/782–1752 or 787/783–7230) features paintings and silkscreens by master Augusto Marín and large-format abstract expressionist works by the Paris-based Ricardo Ramírez.

José Alegría, who began amassing artworks at age 14 with a Dalí drawing, is as passionate about his gallery as he is about his personal collection. **OBRA** (✉ 301 Calle Tetuán, Old San Juan ☎ 787/723–3206) is a visually pleasing space with museum-quality paintings, drawings, and sculptures by such Puerto Rican masters as Augusto Marín, Myrna Baez, and Rafael Tufiño as well as works by up-and-coming Cuban artists. Look also for the sea forms of world-famous glass artist Chihuly.

Books

A Condado classic, **Bell, Book & Candle** (✉ 102 Av. José de Diego, Condado ☎ 787/728–5000) caters to the local English-speaking community. **The Book Shop** (✉ 203 Calle Cruz, Old San Juan ☎ 787/721–0617) sells books in English and Spanish. Its small, on-site café—with a large window facing Plaza de Armas—is a great place to read or people watch. **Borders** (✉ Plaza Las Américas, 525 Av. Franklin Delano Roosevelt, Hato Rey ☎ 787/777–0916), part of the U.S. superstore chain, fills 28,000 square feet in San Juan's biggest mall.

★ Among the city's finest bookshops is **Cronopios** (✉ 255 Calle San José, Old San Juan ☎ 787/724–1815), which carries a full range of fiction and nonfiction in both English and Spanish, as well as music CDs. There are many small bookstores near the Universidad de Puerto Rico campus in Río Piedras. A local favorite is **Librería La Tertulia** (✉ Calle Amalia Marín and Calle González, Río Piedras ☎ 787/765–1148). Although it specializes in books printed in Spanish, it also has English-language titles.

If you forgot to bring a book with you to Condado Beach, pick up a paperback at **Scriptum Books & Gallery** (✉ 1129 Av. Ashford, Condado ☎ 787/724–1123), which is about midway between the Wyndham Condado Plaza hotel and the Marriott. **Thekes** (✉ Plaza Las Américas, 525 Av. Franklin Delano Roosevelt, Hato Rey ☎ 787/765–1539) sells contemporary fiction, magazines, and travel books in English and Spanish.

Cigars

The **Cigar House** (✉ 255 Calle Fortaleza, Old San Juan ☎ 787/723–5223) has a small, eclectic selection of local and imported cigars. **Club Jibarito** (✉ 202 Calle Cristo, Old San Juan ☎ 787/724–7797), with its large walk-in humidor, is *the* place for Puerto Rican and imported cigars, as well as such smoking paraphernalia as designer lighters, personal humidors, pipes, and pipe tobacco. Also on hand are silk ties, cuff links, and designer pens from Alfred Dunhill.

Clothing

ACCESSORIES **Louis Vuitton** (✉ 1054 Av. Ashford, Condado ☎ 787/722–2543) carries designer luggage and leather items, as well as scarves and business accessories. Aficionados of the famous, lightweight Panama hat, made from delicately hand-woven straw, should stop at **Olé** (✉ 105 Calle Fortaleza, Old San Juan ☎ 787/724–2445). The shop sells top-of-the-line hats for as much as $1,000, as well as antiques, santos, sandals, and delicately crafted marionettes.

MEN'S CLOTHING After many years of catering to a primarily local clientele, **Clubman** (✉ 1351 Av. Ashford, Condado ☎ 787/722–1867) is the classic choice for gentlemen's clothing. **Monsieur** (✉ 1126 Av. Ashford, Condado ☎ 787/722–0918) has casual, contemporary designs for men.

MEN'S & WOMEN'S CLOTHING Prolific designer **David Antonio** (✉ 69 Av. Condado, Condado ☎ 787/725–0600) inaugurated his Condado boutique in April 2001. It may be small, but it's full of surprises. His joyful creations range from updated ★ versions of the men's classic *guayabera* shirt to fluid chiffon and silk tunics and dresses for women. For discounted clothing and home accessories, **Marshall's** (✉ Plaza de Armas, Old San Juan ☎ 787/722–0874) is charmingly integrated into the everyday life of many locals, some of whom consider it "The Temple." **Matahari** (✉ 202 Calle San Justo, Old San Juan ☎ 787/724–5869) sells unusual clothes for men and women as well as accessories, jewelry, and trinkets that proprietor Fernando Sosa ★ collects during his trips around the world. **Nono Maldonado** (✉ 1051 Av. Ashford, Condado ☎ 787/721–0456) is well-known for his high-end, elegant linen designs for men and women.

WOMEN'S CLOTHING **E'Leonor** (✉ 1310 Av. Ashford, Condado ☎ 787/725–3208) is a well-established store for bridal apparel, evening gowns, and cocktail dresses as well as more casual (yet still elegant) attire. Look for designs by Vera Wang and St. John. **Harry Robles** (✉ 1752 Calle Loíza, Ocean Park ☎ 787/727–3885 🌐 www.harryrobles.com) sells his elegant gowns in this shop. **Kation Boutique** (✉ 1016 Av. Franklin Delano Roosevelt, Hato Rey ☎ 787/749–0235) has designs by Fendi, Moschino, Gianni Versace, and Dolce and Gabbana. **La Femme** (✉ 320 Av. Franklin Delano Roosevelt, Hato Rey ☎ 787/753–0915) also sells ★ attractive (and sexy) clothes and accessories. **Lisa Cappalli** (✉ 151 Av. José de Diego, Condado ☎📠 787/724–6575) sells her lacey and sensous designs in this boutique, which she opened in 2000. She has custom-made and ready-to-wear collections and has also developed a line of children's clothing.

Mademoiselle Boutique (✉ 1504 Av. Ashford, Condado ☎ 787/728–7440) sells only European apparel, including NewMan, Gerard Darel, and Ungaro Fever. The window displays at **Nativa Boutique** (✉ 55 Calel Cervantes, Condado ☎ 787/724–1396) are almost as daring as the clothes its sells. **Oui Boutique** (✉ 348 Av. Franklin Delano Roosevelt, Hato Rey ☎ 787/765–2424) sells local and international designer clothes and accessories.

Pasarela (✉ 1302 Av. Ashford, Condado ☎ 787/724–5444), which means "cat walk" in Spanish, seems a fitting name for a boutique offering designs by the likes of Nicole Miller, Luca Luca, La Perla, and Renato Nucci on sale. **Roma** (✉ 241 Av. Eleanor Roosevelt, Hato Rey ☎ 787/764–2120) is among the larger stores that sell designer items in the area. **Serenity** (✉ 200 Calle San Justo, Old San Juan ☎ 787/977–5744) imports attire from India and Morocco.

Furniture & Antiques

★ For almost two decades, Robert and Sharon Bartos of **El Alcázar** (✉ 103 Calle San José, Old San Juan ☎ 787/723–1229) have been selling antiques and objets d'art from all over the world.

At **DMR Gallery** (✉ 204 Calle Luna, Old San Juan ☎ 787/722–4181) artist Nick Quijano sells classic Spanish-colonial furniture and his own designs in a variety of Latin American woods. Near the Museo de Arte de Puerto Rico, **Trapiche** (✉ 316 Av. José de Diego, Condado ☎ 787/724–1469) purveys a fine selection of furniture and home accessories from Puerto Rico and the Dominican Republic.

Gifts

Exotic butterflies mounted in clear cases line the walls of **Butterfly People** (✉ 152 Calle Fortaleza, Old San Juan ☎ 787/732–2432); there's also a café and a gift shop featuring books on butterfly collecting. **Plastic Jungle Toystore** (✉ 101 Calle Fortaleza, Old San Juan ☎ 787/723–1076) sells creative toys, games, puzzles, and masks for children. You can find a world of unique spices and sauces from around the Caribbean, kitchen items, and cookbooks at **Spicy Caribbee** (✉ 154 Calle Cristo, Old San Juan ☎ 787/625–4690).

Handicrafts

At the **Convento de los Dominicos** (✉ 98 Calle Norzagaray, Old San Juan ☎ 787/721–6866)—the Dominican Convent on the north side of the old city that houses the offices of the Instituto de Cultura Puertorriqueña—you'll find baskets, masks, the famous four-string, cuatro guitars, santos, books and tapes, and reproductions of Taíno artifacts. The **Haitian Gallery** (✉ 367 Calle Fortaleza, Old San Juan ☎ 787/725–0986) carries Puerto Rican crafts as well as folksy, often inexpensive, paintings from around the Caribbean. The small shop at the **Museo de las Américas** (✉ Cuartel de Ballajá, Old San Juan ☎ 787/724–5052) sells authentic folk crafts from throughout Latin America. For one-of-a-kind santos, art, and festival masks, head for **Puerto Rican Arts & Crafts** (✉ 204 Calle Fortaleza, Old San Juan ☎ 787/725–5596).

DESIGN LIONS

PUERTO RICO'S YOUNG *fashion designers have opened many a boutique and atélier in metropolitan San Juan during the last few years. Their styles may differ, but these young lions all share an island heritage—complete with a tradition of true craftsmanship—and a level of sophistication acquired after studying and traveling abroad. The result is a fascinating assortment of original, exclusive, high-quality designs, often sold at reasonable prices.*

With all the warmth and sun, it goes without saying that Puerto Rico's designers are most inspired when it comes to creations for the spring and summer seasons. Lacy, flowing creations and lightweight, if not sheer, fabrics dominate her designs for women. For men, the trend is toward updated linen classics in tropical whites and creams. Whatever you find will be one of a kind, with stylish—if not playful or downright sexy—lines. Some of these designers have their own shops in San Juan.

Lisa Cappalli, a graduate of New York City's Parsons School of Design, opened her own boutique in late 2000. She favors laces (lace-making is a family tradition) and soft, sensuous fabrics to enhance the female form. She also has a line of children's clothing.

David Antonio uses upbeat colors—bold reds and vibrant oranges, which he sees as a symbol of freedom—in his updated Caribbean classics. He opened a small shop in 2001.

Harry Robles is a bit more established than his peers. He specializes in gowns for women, and his draping designs are often dramatic but always elegant. He favors red or black-and-white creations in crêpes, chiffon, or Dutchess satin.

Other young designers to watch include Gustavo Arango, who graduated from the Fashion Institute of Technology in New York; he returned to Puerto Rico after September 11, 2001, and has rediscovered his design inspiration in his homeland. His dresses combine the tropical beauty of home (in the choice of bold, bright colors) and the urban femininity of New York City (in almost architectural lines). Lisa Thon's designs tend to be high-waisted clothing for women, mildly softened by the more feminine elements of the dandy look. Her designs are minimal, with simple silhouettes, but also romantic and bohemian. Stella Nolasco, who has been described as an extreme avant-garde designer, also goes for the girly look, with simple, feminine but modern designs.

The Miss Universe events that have taken place on the island in recent years have provided a showcase for Puerto Rican fashion design, giving many of these young designers the opportunity to have their collections exhibited on an international runway.

To learn about all the design lions—and see their collections—consider visiting during ***San Juan Fashion Week*** *(contact Nono Maldonado ☎ 787/721–0456), which takes place twice a year, in March and September. The weeks are full of shows and cocktail parties, all organized by the Puerto Rico Fashion Designers Group under the leadership of island-fashion icons Nono Maldonado and Mirtha Rubio. For more information contact individual designers or Nono Maldonado.*

— Isabel Abislaimán

Jewelry

In the Banco Popular building, the family-run **Abislaimán Joyeros** (✉ Plaza Don Rafael, 206 Calle Tetuán, Old San Juan, ☎ 787/724–3890) sells fine jewelry designs by Sal Prashnik and Jose Hess, as well as watches by Baume & Mercier. **Aetna Gold** (✉ 111 Calle Gilberto Concepción de Gracia, Old San Juan ☎ 787/721–4756), adjacent to the Wyndham Old San Juan Hotel, sells exquisite gold jewelry designed in Greece. For a wide array of watches and jewelry, visit the two floors of **Bared** (✉ Calle Fortaleza and Calle San Justo, Old San Juan ☎ 787/724–4811).

Diamonds and gold galore are found at **Joseph Manchini** (✉ 101 Calle Fortaleza, Old San Juan ☎ 787/722–7698). **Joyería Cátala** (✉ Plaza de Armas, Old San Juan ☎ 787/722–3231) is distinguished for its large selection of pearls. **Joyería Riviera** (✉ 257 Fortaleza St., Old San Juan ☎ 787/725–4000) sells fine jewelry by David Yurman and Rolex watches.

N. Barquet Joyeros (✉ 201 Calle Fortaleza, Old San Juan ☎ 787/721–3366), one of the bigger stores in Old San Juan, has Fabergé jewelry, pearls, and gold as well as crystal and watches. **Rheinhold Jewelers** (✉ Plaza Las Américas, 525 Av. Franklin Delano Roosevelt, Hato Rey ☎ 787/767–7837 ✉ Wyndham El San Juan Hotel, 6063 Av. Isla Verde, Isla Verde ☎ 787/791–2521) sells exclusive designs by Stephen Dueck and Tiffany's.

SAN JUAN A TO Z

To research prices, get advice from other travelers, and book travel arrangements, visit www.fodors.com.

ADDRESSES

Letters addressed to San Juan should carry the recipient's name, the street number and name or post-office box, and "San Juan, PR," plus the five-digit U.S. Postal Service Zip Code. San Juan consists of various neighborhoods, which aren't important to include on an envelope, but which may help you get around. From east to west, roughly, these include Old San Juan, Puerto da Tierra, Condado, Miramar, Ocean Park, Isla Verde, Santurce, and Hato Rey. The metropolitan area includes such suburbs as Cataño, Carolina, Guaynabo, and Bayamón.

AIR TRAVEL

San Juan is the Caribbean hub of American Airlines, which flies non-stop from New York–JFK, Newark, Boston, Miami, and other major cities. Other major U.S. carriers serving San Juan include Continental (which also flies to Aguadilla from Newark), Delta, JetBlue (which also flies to Aguadilla), Northwest, Song (which flies from Orlando), Spirit Air, United, and US Airways.

International carriers serving San Juan include Air Canada, Air France, and British Airways.

Puerto Rico is also a good spot from which to hop to other Caribbean islands. American Eagle serves many islands in the Caribbean; Cape Air connects San Juan to St. Thomas and St. Croix, not to mention Ponce; LIAT, based in Antigua, flies to nearly all the Lesser Antilles islands. Vieques Air-Link connects San Juan with Vieques and Culebra.

Airlines **Air Canada** ☎ 888/247-2262. **Air France** ☎ 800/237-2747. **American Airlines/American Eagle** ☎ 800/433-7300, 787/791-5050 in San Juan. **British Airways** ☎ 800/247-9297. **Cape Air** ☎ 800/352-0714. **Continental** ☎ 800/231-0856. **Delta** ☎ 800/221-1212. **JetBlue** ☎ 800/538-2583, 787/253-3300 in San Juan **LIAT** ☎ 888/844-5428. **Song** ☎ 800/359-7664. **Spirit Air** ☎ 800/772-7117. **United Airlines** ☎ 800/864-8331. **US Airways** ☎ 800/428-4322. **Vieques Air Link** ☎ 787/722-3736 or 888/901-9247 🌐 www.vieques-island.com/val.

AIRPORTS & TRANSFERS

The Aeropuerto Internacional Luis Muñoz Marín is in Isla Verde, 18 km (11 mi) east of downtown. San Juan's other airport, the small Aeropuerto Fernando L. Ribas Dominici (also known as the Isla Grande Airport) near the city's Miramar neighborhood, serves flights to and from destinations on Puerto Rico and throughout the Caribbean. (Note that although the Dominici airport was still operating at this writing, its future was uncertain.)

Aeropuerto Fernando L. Rinas Dominici ☎ 787/729-8711. **Aeropuerto Internacional Luis Muñoz Marín** ☎ 787/791-4670.

AIRPORT TRANSFERS Before arriving, check with your hotel about transfers: many area establishments provide transport from the airport, free or for a fee, to their guests. Otherwise, your best bets are *taxi turísticos* (tourist taxis) or an Airport Limousine Service minibus. Uniformed tourism company information officers at the airport can help you make arrangements.

Rates for both types of vehicles are based on your destination, though minibus prices vary depending on the time of day and the number of passengers. A taxi turiístico to Isla Verde costs $8, a minibus about $2.50. To Condado the rates are $12 and $3, to Old San Juan, they're $16 and $3.50. For taxi turísticos, the officials will give you a slip with your zone written on it to hand to the driver. For minibuses, note that the driver may wait until he has a full load of passengers before leaving.

The Baldorioty de Castro Expressway (Route 26) runs from the airport into the city. Exits are clearly marked along the way, though you should check with your hotel to determine which one is best for you to take. With regular traffic, the drive from the airport all the way west to Old San Juan takes about 20 minutes, but you should plan on 40 minutes.

Airport Limousine Service ☎ 787/791-4745.

BOAT & FERRY TRAVEL

Cruise ships pull into the city piers on Calle Gilberto Concepción de Gracia in Old San Juan. The city bus terminal is next to Plaza de Colón in Old San Juan, and taxis line the street next to Pier 2. The ferry between the old city (Pier 2 on Calle Marina) and Cataño is operated by the Autoridad de los Puertos (Port Authority). It costs a mere 50¢ one-way and runs daily every 15 or 30 minutes from 5:45 AM until 10 PM. This is the ferry you take if you wish to visit the Bacardí Rum Factory.

The **Autoridad de los Puertos** ☎ 787/788-1155.

BUS TRAVEL

Guaguas (buses) run by the Autoridad Metropolitana de Autobuses (AMA, or Metropolitan Bus Authority) operate between 5 AM or 6 AM and 9 PM or 10 PM. They link Old San Juan with the business district, the beach neighborhoods, and the southern and western suburbs. Fares are 25¢ or 50¢, depending on the route, and *paradas* (bus stops) are clearly marked. Buses are comfortable—most are air-conditioned—but schedules are not always adhered to: plan to wait 15 to 30 minutes; longer on Sunday and holidays.

Covadonga and Plaza de Colón are the main Old San Juan stops. Destinations are indicated above the windshield. Bus B-21 runs through Condado all the way to Plaza Las Américas in Hato Rey. Bus A-5 runs from San Juan through Santurce and the beach area of Isla Verde. The A-3 covers Río Piedras and Hato Rey. To reach Santurce, hop the M-1. For more information on routes, contact the tourism company.

Island-wide bus service is less than comprehensive, so it's best to travel by *públicos* (public cars). These 17-passenger vans have yellow license plates ending in "P" or "PD." They stop in the main plazas of communities throughout the island and operate primarily during the day. Routes and fares are fixed, but schedules aren't. Call ahead for details. Línea Caborrojeña provides service to Cabo Rojo, Línea de Choferes Unidos de Ponce to Ponce, and Línea Sultana to Mayagüez.

AMA ☎ 787/767-7979. **Línea Caborrojeña** ✉ 956 Av. Las Palmas, Santurce ☎ 787/723-9155. **Línea de Choferes Unidos de Ponce** ✉ Plaza Degetau, Plaza 18, Santurce ☎ 787/722-3275. **Línea Sultana** ✉ 898 E. Calle González, Río Piedras ☎ 787/767-5205 or 787/767-9377.

CAR RENTAL

Rates can start as low as $30 a day (plus insurance), most often with unlimited mileage. All the major U.S. agencies are represented in San Juan. Local companies, sometimes less expensive, include Charlie Car Rental, L&M Car Rental, and Target.

Major Agencies **Avis** ☎ 787/721-4499. **Hertz** ☎ 787/791-0840. **National** ☎ 787/791-1805. **Thrifty** ☎ 787/253-2525.

Local Agencies **Charlie Car Rental** ☎ 787/791-1101 or 800/289-1227 🌐 www.charliecars.com. **L&M Car Rental** ☎ 787/791-1160 or 800/666-0807. **Target** ☎ 787/728-1447 or 800/934-6457.

CAR TRAVEL

The main highways into San Juan are Route 26 from the east (it becomes the Baldorioty de Castro Expressway after passing the airport), Route 22 (José de Diego Expressway) from the west, and Route 52 (Luis A. Ferré Expressway) from the south.

Avenidas Ashford and McLeary run along the coastal neighborhoods of Condado and Ocean Park. The main inland thoroughfares are avenidas Fernández Juncos, Ponce de León, and Luis Muñoz Rivera, which travel from Old San Juan, through Puerta de Tierra and Santurce, and on to Hato Rey. Running north–south are avenidas Franklin Delano Roosevelt and Central (also known as Piñeiro), which intersect Muñoz

Rivera and Ponce de León. Avenida Kennedy runs mostly north–south and leads to the suburbs of Bayamón and Guaynabo.

EMERGENCY SERVICES Central Towing provides island-wide 24-hour towing, lockout, flat-tire-change, and battery-booster services.

Central Towing ✉ Calle Santa Cecilia A-4, Caguas ☎ 800/981-0087, 800/981-5050, or 787/744-5444.

GASOLINE There aren't any stations in Old San Juan, but they're abundant elsewhere in the city. Some close at 11 PM or so; others are open 24 hours.

PARKING There's some on-street parking, but meters are often broken. No-parking zones are indicated with yellow paint or signs, though rarely both. Just because a spot on the street is painted white (or not at all), doesn't mean it's a parking space. Fines for parking illegally range from $15 to $250.

In Old San Juan, park at La Puntilla, at the head of Paseo de la Princesa. It's an outdoor lot with the old city's cheapest rates (they start at 50¢ an hour). You could also try the Felisa Rincón de Gautier lot, also called Parking de Doña Fela, on Calle Gilberto Concepción de Gracia (also called Calle la Marina) or the Frank Santaella lot, also called the Covadonga lot, between Paseo de Covadonga and Calle Gilberto Concepción de Gracia, across from cruise-ship Pier 4. This is also the main bus terminus in Old San Juan, and the spot where the Old San Juan trolleys originate. Parking starts at $1.25 for the first hour. The lots open at 7 AM and close at 10 PM weekdays and as late as 2 AM on weekends.

ROAD CONDITIONS City streets (the occasional pothole aside) and some highways are in great condition, but several of the older, heavily trafficked routes aren't well maintained. People tend to ignore the law prohibiting jaywalking; watch out for pedestrians when driving in town.

RULES OF THE ROAD Speed limits are posted in miles, distances in kilometers. In general city speed limits are 35 mph; on the highways they're 55 to 65 mph. Right turns on red lights are permitted. Seat belts are required; the fine for not using them is $50.

TRAFFIC Traffic jams are common—particularly at rush hours (7 AM to 9 AM and 3 PM to 6 PM)—throughout the metropolitan area. Several areas along main highways are undergoing repairs; be prepared for sudden slowdowns.

EMERGENCIES

General Emergencies **Ambulance, police, and fire** ☎ 911.

Hospitals **Ashford Presbyterian Memorial Community Hospital** ✉ 1451 Av. Ashford, Condado ☎ 787/721-2160. **Clínica Las Américas** ✉ 400 Av. Franklin Delano Roosevelt, Hato Rey ☎ 787/765-1919. **San Juan Health Centre** ✉ 200 Av. José de Diego, Condado ☎ 787/725-0202.

Police **Tourist Zone Police** ☎ 787/726-7020, 787/726-7015 for Condado, 787/728-4770, 787/726-2981 for Isla Verde.

Pharmacies **Puerto Rico Drug Company** ✉ 157 Calle San Francisco, Old San Juan ☎ 787/725-2202. **Walgreens** ✉ 1130 Av. Ashford, Condado ☎ 787/725-1510.

ENGLISH-LANGUAGE MEDIA

The English-language daily, the *San Juan Star,* covers local and international news and local events. Radio Oso, WOSO 1030 on the AM dial, provides the local English-speaking community with up-to-the minute news.

GAY & LESBIAN TRAVELERS

San Juan is a cosmopolitan and sophisticated city in which gays and lesbians will feel at home. There are many gay-friendly hotels and clubs, and the beach at Condado and Ocean Park tends to attract a gay crowd. Normal precautions regarding overt behavior stand, however; Puerto Ricans are often conservative about matters of sexuality and dress.

Frank Fournier of Connections Travel—which is a member of the International Gay & Lesbian Travel Association—is a reliable contact for gay and lesbian travelers. To find out about events, pick up a copy of the *Puerto Rico Breeze,* the island's gay and lesbian newspaper.

Connections Travel ✉ 257 Calle Tetuán, Old San Juan ☎ 787/721-5550 or 787/721-7090.

HEALTH

Tap water is generally fine; just avoid drinking it after storms. Be sure to thoroughly wash or peel produce you buy in markets and grocery stores before eating it.

MAIL & SHIPPING

San Juan post offices offer Express Mail next-day service to the U.S. mainland and to Puerto Rican destinations. Post offices are open weekdays from 7:30 to 4:30 and Saturday from 8 to noon.

Post Offices **Old San Juan Branch** ✉ 153 Calle Fortaleza, Old San Juan ☎ 787/723-1277. **San Juan Branch** ✉ 163 Av. Fernandez Juncos, Puerta de Tierra ☎ 787/722-4134.

OVERNIGHT SERVICES

Most major courier services—Federal Express, UPS, Airborne Express—do business in Puerto Rico. Your best bet is to let the staff at a store like Mail Boxes Etc. or its sister company, the UPS Store, help you with your shipping. The company has several branches in the metropolitan area.

Mail Boxes Etc. ✉ 202A Calle San Justo, Old San Juan ☎ 787/722-0040 ✉ 2434 Calle Loíza, Punta Las Marías, Carolina ☎ 787/268-1270 or 787/268-1090.

UPS Store ✉ 1357 Av. Ashford, Condado ☎ 787/724-8678 ✉ 1507 Av. Ponce de León, Santurce ☎ 787/723-0613.

MONEY MATTERS

Banks are generally open weekdays from 8 to 4. The island's largest bank is Banco Popular de Puerto Rico, which has currency-exchange services and branches and ATMs all over the island. Other banks include Banco Santander, Banco Bilbao Vizcaya, and Citibank.

Banco Popular de Puerto Rico ✉ 206 Calle Tetuán, Old San Juan ☎ 787/725-2636 ✉ 1060 Av. Ashford, Condado ☎ 787/725-4197 ✉ Plaza Las Américas, 525 Av. Franklin Delano Roosevelt, Hato Rey ☎ 787/753-4590 or 787/753-4511.

SAFETY

As you would in any other major city, use common sense. Guard your wallet or purse at all times, and avoid pulling out large wads of cash to make transactions. Don't wander along the beaches at night or leave anything unattended on the beach during the day. Lock all valuables in the hotel safe, and don't leave things out on the seat of your car.

WOMEN IN SAN JUAN Carry only a handbag that closes completely and wear it bandolier style (across one shoulder and your chest). Open-style bags and those allowed to simply dangle from one shoulder are prime targets for pickpockets and purse snatchers. Avoid walking anywhere alone at night, and don't wear clothing that's skin tight or overly revealing.

TAXIS

The Puerto Rico Tourism Company oversees a well-organized taxi program. Taxi turísticos, which are painted white and have the *garita* (sentry box) logo, charge set rates based on zones; they run from the airport and the cruise-ship piers to Isla Verde, Condado, Ocean Park, and Old San Juan, with rates ranging $6 to $16 per car. They also can be hailed in the same manner as metered cabs. City tours start at $30 per hour.

Metered cabs authorized by the Public Service Commission start at $1 and charge 10¢ for every additional 1/13 mi, 50¢ for every suitcase. Waiting time is 10¢ for each 45 seconds. The minimum charge is $3. Be sure the driver starts the meter.

Although you can hail cabs on the street, virtually every San Juan hotel has taxis waiting outside to transport guests; if there's none available, you or a hotel staffer can call one. Atlantic City Taxi and Major Taxicabs are reliable companies. Note that these radio taxis might charge an extra $1 for the pickup.

Atlantic City Taxi ☎ 787/268-5050. **Major Taxicabs** ☎ 787/723-2460. **Public Service Commission** ☎ 787/751-5050.

TELEPHONES

Puerto Rico's area codes are 787 and 939. Toll-free numbers that work in the U.S. (800, 888, or 877) are also toll-free in Puerto Rico. For North Americans, dialing Puerto Rico is the same as dialing another U.S. state or a Canadian province. Public phones are plentiful. Many use prepaid phone cards as well as coins.

TOURS

In Old San Juan, free trolleys can take you around, and the tourist board can provide you with a copy of *Qué Pasa,* which contains a self-guided walking tour. The Caribbean Carriage Company gives old city tours in horse-drawn carriages. It's a bit hokey, but it gets you off your feet. Look for these buggies at Plaza Dársenas near Pier 1; the cost is $30 to $60 per couple.

Wheelchair Getaway offers city sightseeing trips as well as wheelchair transport from airports and cruise-ship docks to San Juan hotels. Cordero Caribbean Tours runs tours in air-conditioned limousines for an hourly rate. The city has several reliable companies, including Cordero Caribbean Tours, Normandie Tours, and Rico Suntours, that can help you arrange tours in the city or out on the island, and most San Juan hotels also have tour desks.

Caribbean Carriage Company ☎ 787/797-8063. **Cordero Caribbean Tours** ☎ 787/786-9114, 787/780-2442 evenings. **Normandie Tours, Inc.** ☎ 787/722-6308. **Rico Suntours** ☎ 787/722-2080 or 787/722-6090 ⊕ www.ricosuntours.com. **Wheelchair Getaway** ☎ 787/883-0131.

TRAIN TRAVEL

At this writing, San Juan is still building a $1.6-billion elevated train system that will link it with its suburbs. The first phase is expected to connect Bayamón, Guaynabo, and Santurce. The second phase will connect Río Pedras to Carolina, and, later, to Luis Muñoz Marín International Airport. The system will eventually have 16 city stops.

VISITOR INFORMATION

You'll find Puerto Rico Tourism Company information officers (identified by their caps and shirts with the tourism company patch) near the baggage-claim areas at Luis Muñoz Marín International Airport. There are also tourism offices at the American Airlines terminal and at terminals B and C. These are open daily from 9 AM to 10 PM in high season and daily from 9 AM to 8 PM in low season.

In San Juan, the tourism company's main office is at the old city jail, La Princesa, in Old San Juan. It operates a branch in a pretty pink colonial building called La Casita at Plaza Dársenas near Pier 1 in Old San Juan; it's open Monday through Wednesday from 8:30 to 8, Thursday and Friday from 8:30 to 5:30, and weekends from 9 to 8. Be sure to pick up a free copy of *Qué Pasa,* the official visitor guide. Information officers are posted around Old San Juan (look for them at the cruise-ship piers and at the Catedral de San Juan) during the day.

La Oficina de Turismo del Municipio de San Juan is affiliated with the city and has offices at the city hall, Alcaldía, in Old San Juan's Plaza de Armas, and at Playita Condado (in front of the Wyndham Condado Plaza Hotel on Avenida Ashford). Both offices are open weekdays from 8 to 4.

Oficina de Turismo del Municipio de San Juan ✉ Alcaldía, Plaza de Armas, Old San Juan ☎ 787/724-7171 Ext. 2391 ✉ Av. Ashford, Condado ☎ 787/740-9270. **Puerto Rico Tourism Company** Box 902-3960, Old San Juan Station, San Juan 00902-3960 ☎ 787/721-2400 ⊕ www.gotopuertorico.com ✉ Plaza Dársenas, near Pier 1, Old San Juan ☎ 787/722-1709 ✉ Luis Muñoz Marín International Airport ☎ 787/791-1014 or 787/791-2551.

EASTERN PUERTO RICO

2

CRUISE A BIOLUMINESCENT BAY
Bahía Mosquito in Vieques ⇨ *p.103*

HIKE IN AN ANCIENT TROPICAL FOREST
El Yunque, the only rain forest in the U.S. National Forest system ⇨ *p.90*

SLEEP IN A LUXURIOUS SMALL HOTEL
Inn on the Blue Horizon ⇨ *p.105*

SAMPLE ECLECTIC TREATS
at Café Media Luna ⇨ *p.104*

STROLL THE DAZZLING WHITE SAND
of Culebra's Playa Flamenco ⇨ *p.109*

THERE'S SOMETHING FOR EVERYONE
at the Wyndham El Conquistador, Puerto Rico's loveliest large resort ⇨ *p.97*

Revised and Updated by John Marino

TREE FROGS, RARE PARROTS, AND WILD HORSES only start the list of eastern Puerto Rico's offerings. The backdrops for encounters with an array of flora and fauna include the 28,000-acre El Yunque, the only tropical rain forest in the U.S. National Forest system; the seven ecosystems in the Reserva Natural Las Cabezas de San Juan; and Bahía Mosquito off Vieques, where tiny sea creatures appear to light up the waters.

The natural beauty and varied terrain continue in the area's towns as well. Loíza, with its strong African heritage, is tucked among coconut groves. Río Grande—which once attracted immigrants from Austria, Spain, and Italy—sits on the island's only navigable river. Naguabo overlooks what were once immense cane fields as well as Cayo Santiago, where the only residents are monkeys.

You can golf, ride horses, hike marked trails, and plunge into water sports throughout the region. In many places along the coast, green hills cascade down to the ocean. On the edge of the Atlantic, Fajardo serves as a jumping-off point for diving, fishing, and catamaran excursions. Luquillo is the site of a family beach so well equipped that there are even facilities enabling wheelchair users to enter the sea. Culebra's stunning beaches are isolated havens—for people and horses—rivaled only by those of nearby Vieques.

If you wish to get away from it all with a neatly packaged trip, eastern Puerto Rico has some of the island's top resorts: the Wyndham El Conquistador, Westin Río Mar, and the vacation development at Palmas del Mar, with others in the planning stages. You'll also find the island's only all-inclusive resort, new in 2004, the Paradisus Puerto Rico. The extensive facilities and luxury services at these large, self-contained complexes make the list of regional offerings more than complete.

Exploring Eastern Puerto Rico

As the ocean bends around the northeastern coast, it laps onto beaches of soft sand and palm trees, crashes against high bluffs, and almost magically creates an amazing roster of ecosystems. Beautiful beaches at Luquillo and the outer islands of Culebra and Vieques are complemented by more rugged southeastern shores. Inland, green hills roll down toward plains that once held expanses of coconut trees, such as those still surrounding the town of Loíza, or sugarcane, as evidenced by the surviving plantations near Naguabo and Humacao. Most notable, however, is the precipitation-fed landscape: green is the dominant color here.

About the Restaurants

Some restaurants carry the tourist board's *meson gastronómico* designation. Such establishments specialize in typical island food. The eastern region has both formal restaurants, where reservations are very necessary, and casual beach-side eateries, where you can walk in unannounced in beach attire and have a fine meal of fresh fish. Bills generally don't include service charges, so a 15 percent tip is customary and expected. Most restaurants are open for dinner from late afternoon until at least 10 PM.

If you have 3 days

It's easier to explore eastern Puerto Rico if you base yourself in a single place. The most central would be **Fajardo** ⑩. Combine a trip to **El Yunque** ⑤–⑧ with a swim at the beach in nearby **Luquillo** ⑨ on your first day. Don't leave without a snack from one of the seafood kiosks near the beach. On your second day, head to Reserva Natural Las Cabezas de San Juan, finally stopping to check out the sands at Balneario Seven Seas outside of Fajardo before stopping for a late-afternoon nap. If there's no moon, sign up for a late-night excursion from Fajardo to the glow-in-the-dark **Bahía Mosquito** ⑬ at the outer island of **Vieques** ⑪–⑮. Use your third day for a snorkeling trip by catamaran to some coral reefs.

If you have 5 days

Spend your first day hiking and picnicking in **El Yunque** ⑤–⑧; bring binoculars and watch for the rare Puerto Rican green parrot. On your second day, hit the sand and seas at **Luquillo** ⑨, if you have children in tow, or Balneario Seven Seas near **Fajardo** ⑩. On the third day, hop a ferry to **Vieques** ⑪–⑮, lounge on a nearly deserted beach, and drink rum cocktails at sunset. Be sure to visit **Bahía Mosquito** ⑬ for a swim with the sparkling dinoflagellates. On the fourth day, rent a bike and pedal around to the old Spanish fort, the shops, or the lighthouse. Then head to Bananas for a cold beer. Take the ferry back to Fajardo on your fifth day.

If you have 7 days

Head straight to **Fajardo** ⑩, from which you can begin to explore the outer islands. On the first day, take the ferry to **Vieques** ⑪–⑮ for an afternoon on the beach and an evening at **Bahía Mosquito** ⑬, with its glittery sea creatures. Use your second day to explore more of the island. On the third day, catch the ferry to **Culebra** ⑯ and visit stunning Playa Flamenco. On the fourth day, go snorkeling or scuba diving. Head back to **Fajardo** ⑩ the next day, and consider staying at the wonderful Wyndham El Conquistador resort; if there's time, visit the Reserva Natural Las Cabezas de San Juan. Use your sixth day to make an early trip to **El Yunque** ⑤–⑧, then drive farther south along the coast to **Naguabo** ⑰ and take the boat trip to Cayo Santiago—also known as Monkey Island. Afterward, grab a fresh-from-the-ocean snack facing Playa Húcares. You can finish your trip at Palmas del Mar but you'll have to find a condo to rent until the posh Candelero Resort reopens after a renovation. Or spend the afternoon at Palmas del Mar outside **Humacao** ⑱, enjoy the beach and lunch at the resort, then opt to spend the night at one of the guesthouses, dotting the region from Ceiba to Manaubo.

WHAT IT COSTS In U.S. dollars

	$$$$	$$$	$$	$	¢
AT DINNER	over $30	$20–$30	$12–$20	$8–$12	under $8

Prices are per person for a main course at dinner.

About the Hotels

The east coast has a couple of government-approved paradores; several large, lavish resorts; and a few "theme" properties, including an ecolodge. The hotel and casino at the Palmas del Mar Resort were not open at this writing, as both were undergoing a major renovation in 2004; they were expected to reopen by the end of 2004 or beginning of 2005. But the sprawling complex of luxury homes, condos and time-shares remains a draw for its large beachfront, as well as the golf, tennis, horseback riding, and other activities taking place within its confines. Sol Melía just opened the island's first full-scale all-inclusive property in spring 2004, a sprawling, posh, oceanfront resort. Four Seasons and Marriott are also developing properties in eastern Puerto Rico, and Palmas del Mar has more hotel projects on the drawing board. Like all of the Caribbean, Puerto Rico was slammed by the drop-off in tourism in late 2001. Several hotels closed—some for the off-season, some completely. To entice visitors back, establishments began offering discounts; in some cases, rates were reduced by as much as 50%. At this writing, tourism was rebounding, although there were still deals to be found.

WHAT IT COSTS In U.S. dollars

	$$$$	$$$	$$	$	¢
FOR 2 PEOPLE	over $350	$250–$350	$150–$250	$80–$150	under $80

Prices are for a double room in high season, excluding 9% tax (11% for hotels with casinos, 7% for paradores) and 5%–12% service charge.

Timing

High season runs from December 15 through April 15, but the east coast—preferred by those seeking abandoned beaches and nature reserves over casinos and urban glitz—tends to be less in demand than San Juan. The exception is Easter time, when Vieques, Culebra, and Luquillo become crowded with local sun lovers, merrymakers, and campers. Island festivals also draw crowds, but planning a trip around one of them will give you a true sense of the region's culture. Just be sure to make reservations well in advance if you're visiting during Easter or a fête. Although prices go down somewhat after high season, hurricanes are most likely to hit from mid-August through early October.

Numbers in the text correspond to numbers in the margin and on the Eastern Puerto Rico and El Yunque maps.

THE NORTHEAST & EL YUNQUE

Just east of San Juan, at the community of Piñones, urban chaos is replaced with the peace of winding palm-lined roads that are interrupted at intervals by barefoot eateries and dramatic ocean views. The first major town you'll encounter is Loíza, where residents proudly claim their African heritage and where renowned mask-makers live. Farther southeast and inland is Río Grande, a community that grew by virtue of its location beside the island's only navigable river. The river rises within El Yunque, the local name for the Caribbean National Forest, a sprawling

Beaches The Atlantic east coast is edged with sandy, palm-lined shores that are occasionally cut by rugged stretches. Some of these beaches are quiet, isolated escapes. Others—such as Luquillo and Seven Seas near Fajardo—are jammed with water-loving families, especially on weekends and during the Easter holidays. Many of Puerto Rico's most attractive strands are on Culebra and Vieques islands.

Dining Puerto Ricans love sybaritic pleasures, and that includes fine dining—whether it be on Continental, Nueva Latina, or authentically native cuisine. In the east you'll find fine fare of all types. On the traditional side, look for the deep-fried snacks (often stuffed with meat or fish) known as *frituras* as well as numerous dishes laced with coconut. Plantains appear as the starring ingredient in the hearty *mofongo,* a seafood-stuffed dish, or as *tostones* (fried plantain chips). Fresh fish is commonly prepared with tomatoes, onions, garlic, or some combination of the three. Desserts explode with fruit flavors, including passion fruit, mango, guava, and tamarind.

Golf There's something to be said for facing a rolling, palm-tree-lined fairway with the distant ocean at your back. And then there are the ducks, iguanas, and pelicans that congregate in the mangroves near some holes. That's what golf in eastern Puerto Rico is all about. The Arthur Hills–designed course at El Conquistador Resort and Country Club is one of the island's best. The Flamboyán course, a Rees-Jones creation at Palmas del Mar Resort, consistently gets raves, as do the courses at the Westin Río Mar. An old-time favorite is the Bahía Beach Plantation course, which was developed on a former coconut plantation.

---

blanket of green covering a mountainous region south of Río Grande. Back on the coast, Balneario de Luquillo (Luquillo Beach) has snack kiosks, dressing rooms, showers, and facilities that enable wheelchair users to play in the ocean.

Southeast of Luquillo sits the Reserva Natural Las Cabezas de San Juan, with its restored lighthouse and variety of ecosystems. Anchoring the island's east coast is Fajardo, a lively port city with a large marina, ferry service to the outer islands, and a string of offshore cays. Catamarans based here sail to and from great snorkeling spots, yachts stop by to refuel or stock up on supplies, and local fishing craft chug in and out as part of a day's work.

Piñones

❶ *16 km (10 mi) east of San Juan.*

Funky Piñones is little more than a collection of open-air, seaside eateries. Sand floors, barefoot patrons, and tantalizing seafood—traditionally washed down with icy beer—have made it popular with locals, especially on weekend evenings. Chilled *agua de coco* is served right from the co-

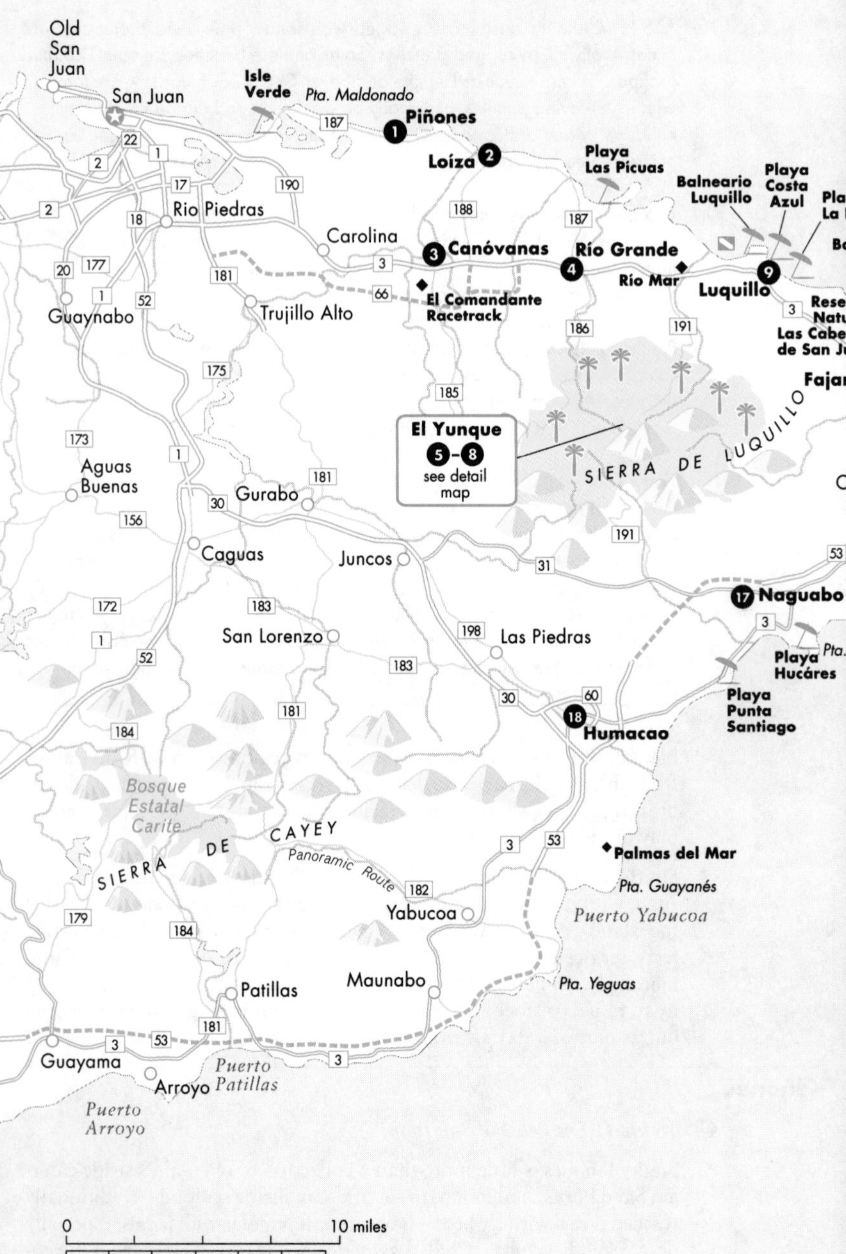

Old San Juan
San Juan
Isle Verde
Pta. Maldonado
Piñones
Loíza
Playa Las Picuas
Balneario Luquillo
Playa Costa Azul
Río Piedras
Carolina
Canóvanas
Río Grande
Río Mar
Luquillo
El Comandante Racetrack
Guaynabo
Trujillo Alto
Las Cabez
de San Ju
El Yunque
5–8
see detail map
SIERRA DE LUQUILLO
Aguas Buenas
Gurabo
Caguas
Juncos
Naguabo
San Lorenzo
Las Piedras
Playa Hucáres
Pta.
Playa Punta Santiago
Humacao
Bosque Estatal Carite
SIERRA DE CAYEY
Panoramic Route
Palmas del Mar
Pta. Guayanés
Puerto Yabucoa
Yabucoa
Patillas
Maunabo
Pta. Yeguas
Guayama
Arroyo
Puerto Patillas
Puerto Arroyo
0
10 miles
0
15 km

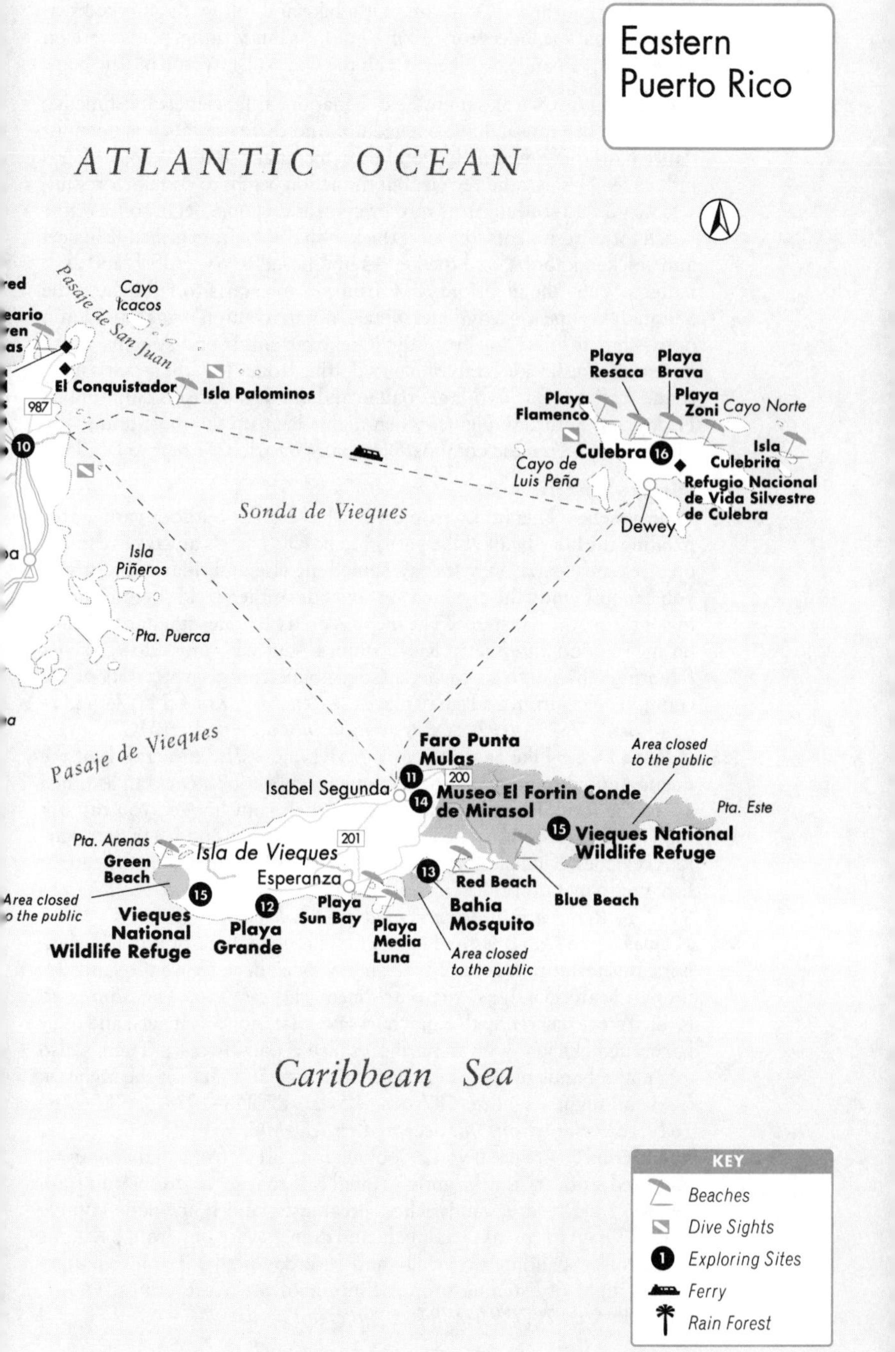
Eastern Puerto Rico
ATLANTIC OCEAN
Pasaje de San Juan
Cayo Icacos
El Conquistador
Isla Palominos
987
10
Sonda de Vieques
Isla Piñeros
Pta. Puerca
Playa Resaca
Playa Brava
Playa Flamenco
Playa Zoni
Cayo Norte
Culebra
16
Isla Culebrita
Cayo de Luis Peña
Refugio Nacional de Vida Silvestre de Culebra
Dewey
Pasaje de Vieques
Faro Punta Mulas
11
200
Isabel Segunda
14
Museo El Fortin Conde de Mirasol
Area closed to the public
Pta. Este
15
Vieques National Wildlife Refuge
Pta. Arenas
Green Beach
Isla de Vieques
201
Esperanza
13
Red Beach
Blue Beach
Area closed to the public
15
Vieques National Wildlife Refuge
12
Playa Grande
Playa Sun Bay
Playa Media Luna
Bahía Mosquito
Area closed to the public
Caribbean Sea
KEY
Beaches
Dive Sights
Exploring Sites
Ferry
Rain Forest

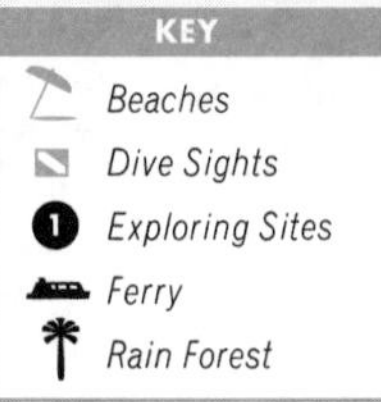

conut. During the day, you can rent a bike and follow the marked seaside trail that meanders for 11 km (7 mi). At this writing, plans were on the table to expand the bike path all the way to Isla Verde in San Juan.

The area has grown as a nightlife designation, as fancier establishments, some with live music, have opened up. And there are raucous open-air dance halls, playing mostly Dominican merengue or local rap, which is influenced by salsa and reggae. But the action begins to cook before sunset. As mid-afternoon turns into evening and people begin to leave the beach for refreshments, the air is thick with smoke from grilled fish, beef and chicken kabobs, and the kettles of oil used to fry codfish and crab fritters. When the giant orange Caribbean sun starts to fall behind the San Juan skyline salsa and merengue—not to mention reggae and Latin pop—start to blare out from the jukeboxes and sound systems of the dozens of ramshackle establishments dotting Route 187, the sector's main road. Traffic on the two-lane road in and out of the area is daunting on Friday and Saturday nights, when nights heat up the most and many places have merengue combos, Brazilian-jazz trios, or reggae bands.

Where to Eat

$–$$$ ✕ **bamboobei.** This funky tropical bar has a great outdoor-eating area fronting the boardwalk, bike path, and beach. There's always live music on weekends—jazz on Saturday, something else on Friday. Other times you can just enjoy the crashing surf outside or the world rhythms floating out from the bar stereo. The menu is pretty Piñones standard—heavy on the seafood and Puerto Rican staples—but with more down-island flavorings thanks to its owner's Guadeloupe roots. Expect lots of coconut, tropical fruit, and curry sauces. ✉ *Rte. 187, Km 4.5* ☎ *787/253–0948 or 787/627–1192* ✍ *Reservations not accepted* ▭ *MC, V.*

$–$$$ ✕ **Pulpo Loco by the Sea.** Octopus, oysters, mussels, and crab lead the lineup here, though many locals come for a beer or a cocktail as much as for the food. If your thirst is greater than your hunger, you can opt for a lighter seafood snack. The menu includes fried codfish fritters, various ceviches, fried plantain fritters stuffed with shellfish, locally caught fish, not to mention chicken and beef. ✉ *Rte. 187, Km 4.5* ☎ *787/791–8382* ✍ *Reservations not accepted* ▭ *AE, MC, V.*

$–$$$ ✕ **Soleil Beach Club & Bistro.** Slightly more refined than some of its neighbors, this restaurant actually sits on a wooden deck *above* the sand. Although seafood reigns, there are meat choices, too. The *churassco* (grilled steak) served with chimchuri sauce is as good as it gets, and juicy barbecued chicken with tamarindo sauce is equally tasty. There's also a bar, and bands playing Brazilian music or Latin jazz set the scene on weekend nights. ✉ *Rte. 187, Km 4.5* ☎ *787/253–1033 or 787/726–7614* ✍ *Reservations not accepted* ▭ *AE, MC, V.*

$–$$$ ✕ **Tutti Frutti En Areyto.** If you're looking for a break from all that seafood and fried stuff, try this brightly painted café that serves fresh-fruit frappés, vegetarian fare, sandwiches, breakfasts, and homemade comida criolla. Open for breakfast, lunch, and dinner every day from 8 AM, the café is also open late on Friday and Saturday nights if you're hungry after a night of listening to music in one of the nearby cafés. ✉ *Rte. 187, Km 5* ☎ *787/791–2787* ▭ *No credit cards.*

$–$$$ ✕ **The Waterfont.** One of the nicest eateries in town is in a modern wooden building and deck perched above a secluded beach. A good sound system, comfortable indoor bar with a satellite TV, and live music weekends keep the place busy. A sampler platter has a little bit of everything, including fresh oysters, crab fritters, and fried chicken and cheese. The main menu is dominated by various kinds of paella as well as such standards as red snapper, mahimahi, lobster, and a grilled strip steak. Everything seems to tastes better where you can hear the waves and smell the salty air. ✉ *Rte. 187, Km 5* ☎ *787/791–5859* *Reservations not accepted* *AE, MC, V* *Closed Mon.*

2

Nightlife

Nearly all the restaurants and cafés in Piñones have live music on weekends, mostly fine jazz and island rhythms, and many locals go as much for the drinks and live entertainment as the food. Many of these beachfront dance halls are frequented by largely Dominican clientele, and you're likely to see some smoking merengue dancing. Couples also twirl to salsa or the grittier beats of local rap. In the immediate vicinity of Pulpo Loco By the Sea and Soleil Beach Club & Bistro, you'll easily find several open-air establishments drawing weekend crowds for their steaming dance floors inside and smoking barbecue pits outside. These places, all on the same turnoff, have live music, cold beer, and barbecued kebabs. Small musical groups play Dominican country music and love ballads on weekend afternoons, which stretch well into evening here. These are all fine places to have a beer, nibble on a snack, and enjoy the sea breezes and music. Some names to look out for are La Terraza, Puerto del Mar, and the Reef.

The Reef (✉ off Rte. 187, Km 1 ☎ 787/791–1973) has one of the most dazzling views of San Juan, including the Old City off in the distance. Perched atop a coastal bluff, it's at the first left once you cross the bridge over Boca de Congrejos and enter Piñones proper. At night, the distant lights of gleaming beachfront condominiums illuminate the water. You can eat fritters and seafood, and there's a jukebox and pool tables; many nights, you can hear live music.

Sports & the Outdoors

Piñones is bordered by a 10-mi strip of beaches along the coast, which winds to a bluff called Vacia Talega, a once infamous lovers' lane with a wonderful view of the coast, which is lined with dense palm groves and towering sea grapes. The area has some fine surf, and several spots have become favorites of local and visiting surfers. You'll also find good fishing, snorkeling, and scuba opportunities. Away from the coast is Torrecilla Baja, one of the largest mangrove swamps on the island.

Environmental concerns and a lack of infrastructure have so far held up large residential and tourism projects that are still planned for the area, but the pressure to build continues. For the moment, Piñones is the largest undeveloped coastal area near San Juan and just a 10-minute drive from Isla Verde. Visitors are well advised to visit it, even if it's the farthest east their time allows them to travel.

BEACHES If you want to find solitary coastline near Piñones, you can. The water is fine; however, the surf is strong, and swimming—especially in winter—can be dangerous at some beaches. You'll find a protected swimming area around Route 187, Km 8, right in front of the cluster of food kiosks built by the government for resident cooks. A large barrier reef blocks the strong currents and serves as the foundation for the large bathing pools in front of a sandy beach. At the end of Piñones, about 2 km before the bridge over the Loíza River, you'll find another protected cove that is a favorite of bathers.

BICYCLING The area's big outdoor attraction is a bike path that follows the swaying coconut palms on a quiet, breezy stretch, sometimes crossing over the main roadway, but mostly running parallel to it. Along most of its 7 mi, it's a wooden boardwalk for bicycles. On weekends and holidays, you can rent bikes from several places along Route 187 and explore the path on your own. The going rate is $5 per hour. Many are clustered at the start of the bike trail, at the first left once you cross the bridge into Piñones. If you want to reserve a bicycle, call **Wheels Unlimited** (✉ Rte. 187, Km 5 ☎ 787/617–1244), which is beside Pulpo Loco By the Sea.

DIVING & FISHING TRIPS Locals go fishing and crabbing right off the coast, and its likely that the crab fritters you eat in any beachfront shack are local as well. Boating, deep-sea fishing, and scuba-diving trips are run out of the Marina right below the bridge from Isla Verde. **Boca de Cangrejos Yacht Club** (✉ Rte. 187, Km 1 ☎ 787/791–1015) is open Monday through Saturday from 8 to 5, on Sunday from 10 to 3.

Capt. José Campos (☎ 787/724–2079) runs offshore deep-sea fishing trips for up to six people, with prices ranging from $475 to $685, depending on the length of the trip, which can run from four to eight hours. He also runs fishing trips through the area's lagoon system. **Nico Guzmán** (☎ 787/383–1502) conducts four-hour deep-sea or lagoon fishing trips on small boats for two people. Trips cost $275.

KAYAKING You can rent kayaks and paddle through the mangrove swamp that runs along the interior of Piñones; the swamp is rich in flora and fauna—both marine and bird life. **Las Tortugas Adventures** (✉ Cond. La Puntilla, 4 Calle La Puntilla, Apt. D1–12, Old San Juan ☎ 787/725–5169 or 787/889–7734 🌐 www.kayak-pr.com) is a reputable outfitter based in Old San Juan that leads organized kayak trips into the mangrove waterway, which is a nature reserve under the jurisdiction of the commonwealth's Department of Natural & Environmental Resources. Trip lengths vary from two to four hours, and prices range from $45 to $65 per person, depending on group size and the extent of the excursion.

Loíza

❷ *15 km (9 mi) east of Piñones.*

The drive from Piñones to Loíza, a coastal town of 30,000 steeped in African heritage, is along a curving road banked by palms and other foliage. The ocean pops into view from time to time, as do pastel wooden houses—sometimes elevated on stilts—and kiosks serving coconut drinks and fried snacks. Locals stroll along the road's shoulder carrying clusters of coconuts, a nod to the area's many groves.

Loíza is known for its colorful festivals and its respect for tradition. Early on the region in which its set was largely undeveloped because the marshy land-bred mosquitoes. It later became a haven for the descendants of slaves. Today the community is a center for the *bomba,* a dance traced to the Kongo people of West Africa. Sometimes wearing a flouncy white dress, the woman of a dancing couple moves in a relatively fixed pattern of steps while her partner improvises to the drumbeat. A lead singer and a choir perform a call-and-response song—recounting a local story or event—while percussionists play maracas, two *fuas* (wooden sticks that are smacked against a hard surface), two *buleadores* (low-timbre, barrel-shape drums), and a *subidor* (higher-pitch drum).

Bomba is key to the revelries at the annual Festival de Santiago Apóstol (St. James the Apostle Festival). During the celebration, which lasts for 10 days late in July, masked and costumed Loízanos combine religious processions—to a spot where a statue of the Virgin Mary is said to have been found under a tree many generations ago—with fireworks and other secular merrymaking. Each year, the family elected to "host" the festival erects an elaborate altar for the Mary statue and provides refreshments for the townspeople. Despite the festivities, St. James isn't Loíza's patron saint. St. Patrick holds that distinction, and the church is dedicated to him. Lively St. Patrick's Day festivities occur if the holiday falls on a weekend. Otherwise, residents save their energy for the bigger Santiago Apóstol fiesta.

Loíza's small downtown has been renovated and is pleasant; its citizens are proud of their town and welcome visitors. When it's not festival time, the area is worth a stop for the scenery and to see the crafts, including museum-quality festival masks made from coconut shells.

Some portions of the **Iglésia de San Patricio** (St. Patrick's Church) date from 1645, making it one of the island's oldest churches. It's home to a statue of the Virgin Mary that is worshiped during the Santiago Apóstol festivities. A side altar holds a statue of St. Patrick, the city's patron saint. If you'd like to see the interior without attending services, you can walk through the church just before or after Sunday mass. ✉ *10 Calle Espíritu Santo, El Centro* ☎ *787/876–2229* 🎟 *Free* ⏲ *Sun. mass 10 AM.*

The Arts

Bomba's renaissance dates from 1961, when a TV producer showed up in Loíza searching for residents who remembered the dance. In response, mask-maker Castor Ayala put together the **Ballet Folklórico Hermanos Ayala** (✉ Artesanías Castor Ayala, Rte. 187, Km 6.6 ☎ 787/876–1130), a folk-music and dance troupe that performs around the island and elsewhere in Latin America. The group has no headquarters, but you can get its schedule at the mask-making shop, Artesanías Castor Ayala.

Shopping

Among the offerings at **Artesanías Castor Ayala** (✉ Rte. 187, Km 6.6 ☎ 787/876–1130) are coconut-shell festival masks dubbed "Mona

Lisas" because of their elongated smiles. Craftsman Raul Ayala Carrasquillo has been making these museum-quality pieces for more than 40 years, following in the footsteps of his late father, the esteemed craftsman for whom the store is named. Many of the masks, priced from $50 to $350, are used in Loíza's festivals. Others are snapped up by collectors. (Buyer beware: these masks have been much-copied by other craftspeople of late.)

At **Estúdio de Arte Samuel Lind** (✉ Rte. 187, Km 6.6 ☎ 787/876–1494), down a short, dusty lane across the street from the Artesanías Castor Ayala, artist Samuel Lind sculpts, paints, and silk-screens images that are quintessentially Loízano. Lind's work is displayed in the two floors of his latticework studio. Of special note are his colorful folk-art posters.

Canóvanas

❸ *8 km (5 mi) southwest of Loíza; 22 km (14 mi) east of San Juan.*

Most people pass right through this town, but it has two superlative draws. Canóvanas is home to the Caribbean's largest thoroughbred horse-racing track and Puerto Rico's biggest factory-outlet mall.

Where to Eat

$–$$ ✕ **Brass Cactus Bar & Grill.** The success of the original branch of this restaurant—which is in Luquillo—has prompted an expansion to this second location. The ribs and burgers with generous helpings of crispy fries are the thing to get here, as there. But you can also get Buffalo wings, poppers (stuffed hot peppers), chicken, and steak. This is a place worth slowing down for. ✉ *Plaza Noreste, Rte. 3* ☎ *787/256–0265* ▭ *AE, MC, V.*

Sports & the Outdoors

HORSE RACING Try your luck with the exactas and quinielas at **Hípodromo El Comandante** (✉ Rte. 3, Km 15.3 ☎ 787/724–6060 🌐 www.comandantepr.com), Canóvanas's large thoroughbred race track. Post time is at 2:15 or 2:45 (depending on the season) on Wednesday and also Friday through Monday. There's a restaurant here as well as an air-conditioned clubhouse, and after Friday's first race, there's dancing to the music of a Latin band in the Winners Sports Bar. Parking and admission to the grandstand are free; clubhouse admission is $3.

Shopping

Right off the highway in Canóvanas, the **Belz Factory Outlet World** (✉ Rte. 3, Km 18.4 ☎ 787/256–7040 🌐 www.belz.com) has more than 75 stores, including Nike, Guess, Mikasa, Gap, Levi's, Liz Claiborne, and Tommy Hilfiger. There's also a large food court and multiplex movie theater showing first-run Hollywood movies—many in English.

Río Grande

❹ *5 km (3 mi) east of Canóvanas; 13 km (8 mi) southeast of Loíza; 35 km (21 mi) southeast of San Juan.*

This urban cluster of about 50,000 residents proudly calls itself "The City of El Yunque," as it's the closest community to the rain forest, and most of the reserve falls within its district borders. Two images of the rare green parrot, which makes its home in El Yunque, are found on the city's coat of arms; another parrot peeks out at you from the town's flag. The city is also near the posh Westin Río Mar resort, known for its seaside golf courses, lovely beach, and first-class restaurants.

Río Espíritu Santo, which runs through Río Grande, begins in El Yunque's highest elevations and is the island's only navigable river. Thus, it was once used to transport lumber, sugar, and coffee from plantations. Immigrants flocked to the region to take advantage of the employment opportunities; many of today's residents can trace their families to Spain, Austria, and Italy.

El Museo del Cartel is devoted to posters, a tradition on the island, and the artists who design them. The collection dates from the 1950s and includes many posters created for island festivals and art exhibits. The facility also offers classes in such arts as silk-screening. ✉ *37 Calle Pimentel, El Centro* ☎ *787/889–5820 or 787/887–2133* 🎫 *Free* ⏲ *Tues.–Sun. 9–5.*

Sports & the Outdoors

BEACH **Playa Las Picúas** is northeast of Río Grande on a bay close to where Río Espíritu Santo meets the Atlantic. There are no facilities, but the water is fine.

HORSEBACK RIDING **Hacienda Carabali** (✉ Rte. 992, Km 4, at Mameyes River Bridge, Barrio Mameyes ☎ 787/889–5820 or 787/889–4954), a family-run operation, is a good place to jump in the saddle and ride one of Puerto Rico's Paso Fino horses. Riding excursions ($45 an hour) include a one-hour jaunt along Río Mameyes and the edge of El Yunque and a two-hour ride along Balneario de Luquillo. Outdoor concerts are sometimes held at the ranch, and staffers can also help you arrange shuttle transportation to and from San Juan. The hacienda is open daily from 9:30 to 5.

Where to Stay & Eat

$$–$$$$ ✕ **Chef Wayne.** For his own establishment, Wayne Michaelson, a veteran of the island's top kitchens, has devised a wide-ranging and eclectic menu with such entrées as Cajun-style chicken breast, grilled Caribbean lobster, and filet mignon. In a large white house in the rain forest, the main dining room has a Western theme. You can also eat on the front balcony, with its ocean views, or on the back balcony, facing the forest. Since the restaurant is well off the main route, on a winding, unmarked road, you should call ahead for directions. ✉ *Off Rte. 992* ☎ *787/889–1962 or 787/889–2911* 💳 *MC, V* ⏲ *Closed Tues. No lunch Fri.*

$$–$$$$ ✕ **Palio.** Executive chef Marcus Rodriguez enlivens his northern Italian dishes with aromatic spices at this beautifully decorated restaurant, with its black-and-white checkerboard floor and its shiny, dark-wood accents. The seafood selections are particularly noteworthy. ✉ *Westin Río Mar, 6000 Bul. Río Mar, Rte. 968, Km 1.4, Barrio Palmer* ☎ *787/888–6000 Ext. 4808* 💳 *AE, MC, V* ⏲ *No lunch.*

$–$$$ ✕ **Shimas.** "Asian" is the word at this casual bistro. The sushi bar is a big draw, and Thai curries join Szechuan dishes and Japanese teriyaki on the tempting cross-cultural menu. ✉ *Westin Río Mar, 6000 Bul. Río*

Mar, Rte. 968, Km 1.4, Barrio Palmer ☎ *787/888–6000 Ext. 4821* ▭ *AE, MC, V.*

$–$$ ✕ **Las Vegas.** At this meson gastronómico the chicken is marinated in local spices and served with rice and *gandules* (pigeon peas). There's also a selection of delicious seafood dishes. The atmosphere is casual thanks to the many hikers that drop in on their way to or from El Yunque rain forest. ✉ *Rte. 191, Km 1.3* ☎ *787/887–2526* ▭ *AE, MC, V.*

$–$$ ✕ **Villa Pesquera.** The view of Río Espíritu may initially draw you into this restaurant, but it's the savory seafood that will keep you coming back. Try the catch of the day—whatever it is, it's always a winner. This is also a sweet spot for a sunset cocktail. ✉ *Rte. 877, Km 6.6* ☎ *787/887–0140* ▭ *MC, V.*

$$$$ **Westin Río Mar Beach Resort.** Golf, biking, tennis, and playing in the waters off a mile-long beach are just some of the attractions at this top-notch resort. Every room in the seven-story hotel, which anchors the complex, has a balcony that faces the sea or the golf courses and mountains. One- and two-bedroom villas are an option for guests who want more space and privacy. Tropical color schemes are used throughout as are such luxurious touches as natural woods, Italian tile, and marble accents. ✉ *6000 Bul. Río Mar, Rte. 968, Km 1.4, Barrio Palmer* *Box 2006, 00721* ☎ *787/888–6000* *787/888–6204* *www.westinriomar.com* *600 rooms, 72 suites, 59 villas* *7 restaurants, in-room data ports, in-room safes, cable TV with movies and video games, in-room VCRs, 2 18-hole golf courses, 13 tennis courts, 3 pools, health club, spa, beach, dive shop, windsurfing, boating, fishing, bicycles, 4 lounges, casino, dance club, shop, children's programs (ages 4–12), dry cleaning, laundry service, concierge, business services, meeting rooms, airport shuttle, car rental, no-smoking rooms* ▭ *AE, MC, V* *EP.*

$$–$$$$ **Paradisus Puerto Rico Sol Meliá All-Inclusive Resort.** Puerto Rico's first all-inclusive resort is on an enviable stretch of pristine coastline. The lobby flows effortlessly between African-inspired, Medieval-looking wood carvings, Taino, and contemporary art; Japanese-style garden pools are lined with teak and wicker Spanish-colonial furniture. Suites are spread among two-story bungalows. At this writing, construction equipment is evident, but resort shows no sign of being a work in progress. Despite occasional service mishaps, the staff are friendly and accommodating. The place is so large that there is no shortage of pool or beach chairs. Restaurants are varied, and the food—particularly at the French restaurant, Romantico—is good. ✉ *Rte. 968, Km 5.8, Coco Beach* ☎ *787/809–1770 or 800/336–3542* *787/809–1785* *www.paradisus-puerto-rico.com* *500 suites, 20 bungalows, 5 villas* *6 restaurants, fans, some in-room hot tubs, minibars, in-room safes, cable TV with movies, golf privileges, 3 tennis courts, pool, wading pool, health club, spa, beach, dive shop, snorkeling, windsurfing, boating, waterskiing, fishing, casino, dance club, showroom, 4 bars, shops, children's programs (ages 4–12), dry cleaning, laundry service, concierge, Internet, business services, meeting room, car rental, travel services* ▭ *AE, D, MC, V* *AI.*

$–$$$ **Río Grande Plantation Eco Resort.** Walking paths pass flowers and wind around fruit trees at this peaceful resort in the foothills of El Yunque. It's on a portion of what was, in the late 1700s, a 200-acre sugarcane plantation and is often used for corporate retreats. Accommodations are primarily two-story villas, which have such amenities as Jacuzzis and kitchenettes. The staff members pride themselves on being attentive to their guests. There's no on-site restaurant, and the closest eatery is a 15-minute drive, so a car is a necessity here. ✉ *Rte. 956, Km 4, Barrio Guzman Abajo* 📫 *Box 6526, Loíza Station, Santurce, San Juan 00914* ☎ *787/887–2779* 🖷 *787/888–3239* 🌐 *www.riograndeplantation.com* ⇨ *19 villas, 4 rooms, 1 cottage* 👍 *Kitchenettes, microwaves, cable TV, in-room VCRs, pool, hot tub, basketball, meeting rooms* 💳 *AE, MC, V* 🍽 *EP.*

Nightlife

Pick a game—Caribbean stud poker, blackjack, slot machines—and then head to the Las Vegas–style **Westin Río Mar Resort Casino** (✉ 6000 Bul. Río Mar, Rte. 968, Km 1.4, Barrio Palmer ☎ 787/888–6000). If all that betting gives you a thirst, step into the Players Bar, which is connected to the gaming room.

Sports & the Outdoors

Activities in Río Grande region are mostly oriented around the two big resorts, the Westin Río Mar and the new Paradisus Puerto Rico, but only guests can use the facilities at Paradisus.

DIVING & SNORKELING The **Westin Dive Center** (✉ Westin Río Mar, 6000 Bul. Río Mar, Rte. 968, Km 1.4, Barrio Palmer ☎ 787/888–6000) offers scuba and snorkeling rentals and lessons. Large catamaran snorkeling trips leave from the resort for the calm seas and deserted islands off the cost of northeastern Puerto Rico. The cost is $45 to $60 per person. Lunch is included, and the trips offer awesome sunbathing and snorkeling opportunities.

GOLF The 18-hole **Bahía Beach Plantation Course** (✉ Rte. 187, Km 4.2 ☎ 787/256–5600 🌐 www.golfbahia.com) skirts the north-coast beaches. A public course, it was carved out of a long-abandoned coconut grove, and coconut palms and other native trees and tropical vegetation dominate the scene. Giant iguanas roam the premises, as hawks, water fowl, and tropical birds fly overhead. The course also offers views of El Yunque, and most greens run either along lakes or the untamed Río Grande coastline. Greens fees range from $65 to $85, depending on day of the week and the time of day. The Bahía Cantina, an on-site bar-restaurant, offers refreshments and sustenance.

The **Berwind Country Club** (✉ Rte. 187, Km 4.7 ☎ 787/876–3056) has an 18-hole course known for its tight fairways and demanding greens. It's open for nonmembers from Tuesday through Friday, with greens fees of $65, which includes a cart and bucket of balls. On Sunday afternoons, nonmembers can play if they make arrangements in advance.

Coco Beach Golf & Country Club (✉ Paradisus Puerto Rico Sol Melía All-Inclusive Resort, 100 Clubhouse Dr. ☎ 787/657–2000) has two 18-hole course designed by Tom Kite and Bruce Besse. The courses are both beautiful, bordered by the coastline and a view of El Yunque, not to mention challenging. At this writing, the courses boasted bargain basement introductory green fees of $45 to $50 for guests and

$60 to $65 for non-guests. Prices were expected to increase to market rates—between $85 and $195—in 2005.

★ Part of the Westin Río Mar Beach Resort, the **Westin Río Mar Country Club** (✉ 6000 Bul. Río Mar, Rte. 968, Km 1.4, Barrio Palmer ☎ 787/888–1401 for golf information 🌐 www.westinriomar.com) has two 18-hole courses offering vistas of El Yunque and the Atlantic. The River Course, designed by Greg Norman, has challenging fairways and bunkers. The Ocean Course has slightly wider fairways than its sister; ducks, iguanas, and pelicans congregate in the mangroves near its fourth hole. If you're not a resort guest, be sure to reserve tee times at least 24 hours in advance. Greens fees range from $105 to $165 for hotel guests and $130 to $190 for nonguests, depending on tee time.

WATER SPORTS You can rent windsurfing equipment ($30 an hour, three hours for $70), sea kayaks ($25 an hour for single-person kayaks, $35 for two-person kayaks, and $45 for three-person kayaks) from **Iguana Watersports** (✉ Westin Río Mar, 6000 Bul. Río Mar, Rte. 968, Km 1.4, Barrio Palmer ☎ 787/888–6000). The helpful staff also rents Jet Skis ($60 per half-hour, $100 per hour) and hobby cats ($45 per hour, plus $20 for instruction). Boogie boards and other beach rentals are available.

Shopping

Puerto Rican pottery, with some designs inspired by the Taíno Indians, fill the shelves of **Cerámicas Los Bohíos** (✉ Av. 65th Infantry, Km 21.7 ☎ 787/887–2620). The picturesque **Treehouse Studio** (✉ Unmarked road off Rte. 3 ☎ 787/888–8062), not far from the rain forest, sells vibrant watercolors by Monica Laird, who also gives workshops. Call for an appointment and directions.

El Yunque

Fodor'sChoice ★ *11 km (7 mi) southeast of Río Grande; 43 km (26 mi) southeast of San Juan.*

Between Río Grande and Luquillo, on Route 191, are the 28,000 acres of verdant foliage and often rare wildlife that make up El Yunque, the only rain forest within the U.S. National Forest system. Formally known as the Bosque Nacional del Caribe (Caribbean National Forest), El Yunque's colloquial name is believed to be derived from the Taíno word, *yukiyu* (good spirit), although some people say it comes directly from *yunque,* the Spanish word for "anvil," because some of the forest's peaks have snub shapes.

Rising to 3,500 feet above sea level, this protected area didn't gain its "rain forest" designation for nothing: more than 100 billion gallons of precipitation fall over it annually, spawning rushing streams and cascades, 240 tree species, and oversized impatiens and ferns. In the evening, millions of inch-long *coquís* (tree frogs) begin their calls. El Yunque is also home to the *cotorra,* Puerto Rico's endangered green parrot, as well as 67 other types of birds.

The forest's 13 hiking trails are well maintained; many of them are easy to walk and less than 1 mi long. If you prefer to see the sights from a car, follow Route 191. Several trailheads, observation points, and other highlights are along this touring road, which is the park's main thoroughfare. Las Cabezas observation point is at Km 7.8; La Coca Falls, one of two waterfalls where you can take a refreshing dip (the other, La Mina Falls, is to the south), lies just past Km 8.1; and the Torre Yokahu observation point sits at Km 8.9. When hurricanes and mud slides haven't caused portions of the road to be closed, you can drive straight from the entrance to Km 13, the base of El Yunque Peak.

Arrive early and plan to stay the entire day. You'll be charged an admission fee for El Portal Information Center, which has interactive exhibits, but entrance to the rest of the park and the other information centers is free. Although camping isn't permitted, there are picnic areas with sheltered tables and bathrooms. (The recreation areas are open from 7:30 AM to 6 PM daily.) Bring binoculars, a camera, water, and sunscreen; wear a hat or visor, good walking shoes, and comfortable clothes. Although daytime temperatures rise as high as 80°F (27°C), wear pants as some plants can cause skin irritations. There are no poisonous snakes in the forest (or on the island as a whole), but bugs can be ferocious, so repellent is a must. And remember: this is a rain forest, so be prepared for showers.

★ 5 A lizard's tongue darts across three video screens, a forest erupts in flames, a tiny seedling pushes up from the ground and flourishes. Before you begin exploring El Yunque, check out the high-tech, interactive displays—explaining forests in general and El Yunque in particular—at **Centro de Información El Portal,** the information center near the northern entrance. Test your sense of smell at an exhibit on forest products, listen to actor Jimmy Smits (who is part Puerto Rican) narrate a movie on El Yunque, and inquire about the day's ranger-led activities. This is also a good place to pick up trail maps, souvenirs, film, water, and snacks. All exhibits and publications are in English and Spanish. ✉ *Rte. 191, Km 4.3, off Rte. 3* ☎ *787/888–1880* 🌐 *www.southernregion.fs.fed.us/caribbean* 🎟 *$3* 🕒 *Daily 9–5.*

6 The **Torre Yokahu** (Yokahu Observation Tower), which resembles a castle turret, rises from a little roadside hill. A peek through the windows of its circular stairway gives you a hint of the vistas awaiting you at the top: 1,000-year-old trees, exotic flowers in brilliant hues, birds in flight. Postcards and books on El Yunque are sold in the small kiosk at the tower's base. The parking lot beside the tower has restrooms. ✉ *Rte. 191, Km 8.9* ☎ *No phone* 🎟 *Free* 🕒 *Daily 7:30–6.*

7 Just beyond the forest's halfway point along Route 191, the **Centro de Información Sierra Palm** is a great place to stop for trail updates. El Yunque's steep slopes, unstable wet soil, heavy rainfall, and exuberant plant life result in the need for intensive trail maintenance; some trails must be cleared and cleaned at least twice a year. Rangers at the office here have information on closures, conditions of open trails, what flora and fauna to look for, and any activities planned that day. There are rest rooms and water fountains by the parking lot. ✉ *Rte. 191, Km 11.6* ☎ *No phone* 🌐 *www.southernregion.fs.fed.us/caribbean* 🎟 *Free* 🕒 *Daily 7:30–6.*

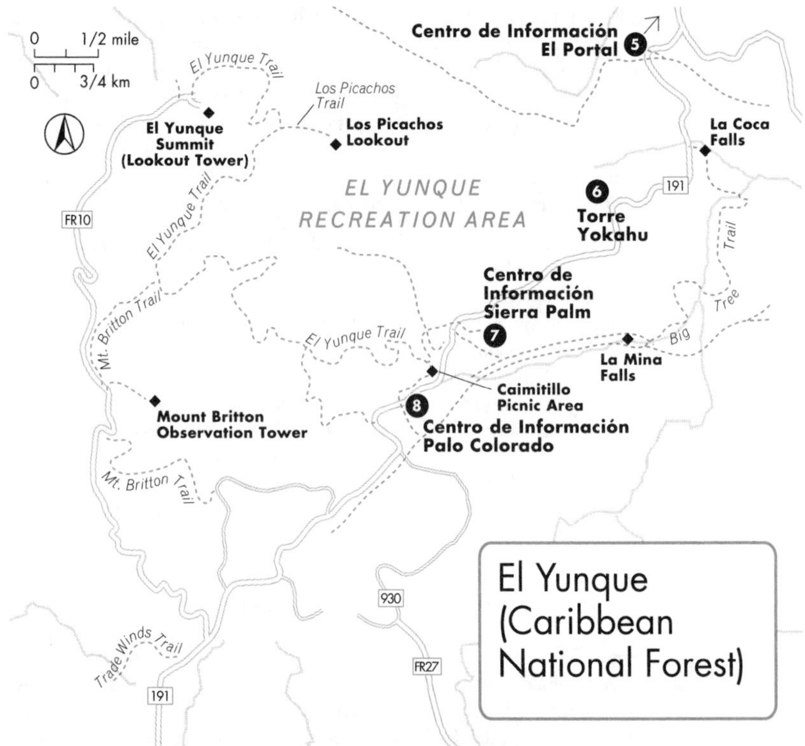

8 Palo Colorado, the red-bark tree in which the endangered cotorra nests, dominates the forest surrounding the **Centro de Información Palo Colorado.** The center—which is home to Forest Adventure Tours and its two-hour, ranger-led hikes (reservations are required)—is the gateway for several walks. The easy Baño del Oro Trail starts at a concrete pool built in the 1930s (swimming isn't permitted) and loops 2 km (1 mi) through an area dubbed the Palm Forest. The even shorter El Caimitillo Trail starts at the same place and runs for about 1 km (½ mi). Although it begins as asphalt, the challenging El Yunque–Mt. Britton Trail turns to gravel as it climbs El Yunque Peak. Just beyond the trailhead is the Palo Colorado Stream, followed by the detour to the Baño del Oro and Caimitillo trails. At a higher elevation you can follow the Mt. Britton spur to an observation tower built in the 1930s. Without detours onto any of the side trails, El Yunque Trail takes about three hours round-trip and includes some mild ascents. Signs clearly mark each turnoff, so it's hard to get lost if you stay on the path. All the trails here are edged by giant ferns, bamboo, and oversized impatiens. There are restrooms and parking at the center and a picnic area nearby. ✉ *Rte. 191, Km 11.9* ☎ *787/888–5646* 🌐 *www.southernregion.fs.fed.us/caribbean* 🎫 *Free, guided hikes $5* 🕒 *Daily 8–5.*

144 PARROTS & COUNTING

THE TAÍNO INDIANS CALLED IT *the* iguaca, *Spanish speakers refer to it as the* cotorra, *and scientists know it as* Amazona vittata. *Whatever moniker it takes, the Puerto Rican green parrot—the only one native to the island—is one of the world's 10 rarest birds. It nests primarily in the upper levels of El Yunque and in the nearby Sierra de Luquillo. The bird is almost entirely green, though there are touches of blue on its wings, white rings around its eyes, and a red band just above its beak. It's only about 12 inches long, and its raucous squawk doesn't match its delicate appearance. The parrots mate for life. In February (the rain forest's driest season), they build nests within tree hollows and lay three to four eggs. Both parents feed the young.*

When the Spanish arrived, the parrot population was an estimated 1 million on the main island, Vieques, and Culebra. But deforestation, hurricanes, and parasites have reduced the population (parrot hunting was common until being outlawed in 1940). By 1967, there were only 19 birds; in a 1975 count, the total was only 13.

In late May 2001, 16 parrots bred in rain forest aviaries were successfully released into El Yunque; such releases are now annual events. Released parrots are given radio tracking beacons. At this writing, there were an estimated 44 green parrots in the wild and another 100 in captivity, and officials are optimistic that their numbers will continue to grow. If you're very observant (and very lucky), you might just spot one.

Shopping

While in El Yunque, buy a recording of the tree frog's song or a video about the endangered green parrot, pick up a coffee-table book about the rain forest, try on El Yunque T-shirts, and check out the books for ecominded children at the large **Caribbean National Forest Gift Shop** (⊠ Centro de Información El Portal, Rte. 191, Km 4.3 ☎ 787/888–1880). Tucked among the rain-forest gifts are other Puerto Rican items, including note cards, maps, soaps, jams, and coffee.

en route

All along Route 3, from Canóvanas to Fajardo, roadside stands and kiosks sell fruit and sugar cane beverages, fried snacks, and fresh seafood. There are also artisans selling their wares, handmade hammocks, even tropical birds for sale. For locals driving from El Yunque or Río Grande to Luquillo, the trip would be unthinkable without a stop at the ***friquitines*** (seafood kiosks) that line Route 3 west of the beach turnoff. They're busy all day, serving passing truckers, area businesspeople, and sand-covered families en route to or from the beach in Luquillo. Although some kiosks have larger seating areas than others, they all offer much the same fare, including cold drinks, plates of fried fish (head and tail still attached), conch salad, and fritters (usually codfish or corn).

Luquillo

9 *13 km (8 mi) northeast of Río Grande; 45 km (28 mi) east of San Juan.*

Known as the "Sun Capital" of Puerto Rico, Luquillo has one of the island's best-equipped family beaches. It's also a community where fishing traditions are respected. On the east end of Balneario de Luquillo, past the guarded swimming area, fishermen launch small boats and drop nets in open stretches between coral reefs.

Like many other Puerto Rican towns, Luquillo has its signature festival, in this case the Festival de Platos Típicos (Festival of Typical Dishes), a late-November culinary event that revolves around one ingredient: coconut. During the festivities, many of the community's 18,000 residents gather at the main square to sample treats rich with coconut or coconut milk. There's also plenty of free entertainment, including folk shows, troubadour contests, and salsa bands.

Beaches

Fodor'sChoice ★ Just off Route 3, gentle, shallow waters lap the edges of palm-lined **Balneario de Luquillo,** which is a magnet for families. It's well-equipped with dressing rooms and restrooms, lifeguards, guarded parking, food stands, picnic areas, and even cocktail kiosks. It's most distinctive facility, though, is the Mar Sin Barreras (Sea Without Barriers), a low-sloped ramp leading into the water that allows wheelchair users to take a dip. The beach is open every day but Monday from 9 to 5. Admission is $2 per car.

Waving palm trees and fishing boats add charm to the small **Playa Costa Azul,** although the ugly residential buildings along the water make an unattractive backdrop. The water here is good for swimming, and the crowds are thinner than elsewhere, but there are no facilities.

Playa La Pared, literally "The Wall Beach," is a surfer haunt. Numerous local competitions are held here throughout the year, and several surfing shops are close by just in case you need a wet suit or a wax for your board. The waves here are medium-range.

Where to Stay & Eat

$–$$ ✕ **Brass Cactus Bar & Grill.** The ribs and burgers melt in your mouth, and the helpings of crispy fries are generous. Buffalo wings, poppers (stuffed hot peppers), chicken, and steak are also mainstays. Nearly every dish—Southwestern or otherwise—is washed down with beer. Televisions broadcast the latest sporting events, and on the weekend bands often replace the jukebox. ✉ *Rte. 3, Complejo Turistico Condominio* ☎ *787/889–5735* 💳 *AE, MC, V.*

$–$$ ✕ **Lolita's.** Burritos—washed down with oversized margaritas, of course—are the specialties of this casual Mexican restaurant. Combo plates let you taste a bit of everything, from tacos to enchiladas. Those who eschew tequila can try the yummy house sangria. ✉ *Rte. 3, Km. 41.3, Barrio Juan Martín* ☎ *787/889–5770 or 787/889–0250* ✍ *Reservations not accepted* 💳 *AE, MC, V.*

$–$$ ✕ **Victor's Place.** In a small blue building on downtown's main plaza, this local institution has been serving up Puerto Rican specialties since the 1940s. Traditionally prepared seafood and steaks come with large servings of beans, rice, and tostones. The atmosphere is casual. ✉ *2 Calle Jesús T. Piñero* ☎ *787/889–5705* ✍ *Reservations not accepted* ▭ *MC, V* ⊗ *Closed Mon.*

$ **Luquillo Beach Inn.** This five-story, white-and-pink hotel is within walking distance of the public beach and caters to families—children stay free with their parents. The modest one- or two-bedroom suites have sofa beds, kitchenettes, and living rooms equipped with TVs and stereos; the largest sleep up to six people. It's a good jumping off point for visits to El Yunque. Transportation (about $45) can be arranged from San Juan if you don't wish to rent a car. ✉ *701 Ocean Dr., 00773* ☎ *787/889–1063 or 787/889–3333* 📠 *787/889–1966* *36 suites* *Fans, kitchenettes, cable TV with movies, in-room VCRs, pool, outdoor hot tub, bar, dry cleaning, laundry service, business services, free parking* ▭ *AE, MC, V* *EP.*

Sports & the Outdoors

DIVING **Divers' Outlet** (✉ 38 Calle Fernández Garcia ☎ 787/889–5721 or 888/746–3483) is a full-service dive shop. It offers PADI certification, rents equipment, and can arrange scuba outings.

SURFING **La Selva Surf** (✉ 250 Calle Fernández Garcia ☎ 787/889–6205 🌐 www.rainforestsafari.com/selva.html), near Playa La Pared, has anything a surfer could need, including news about current conditions. It also sells sunglasses, T-shirts, skateboards, sandals, watches, bathing suits, and other beach necessities.

Fajardo

❿ *11 km (7 mi) southeast of Luquillo; 55 km (34 mi) southeast of San Juan.*

Fajardo, founded in 1772, has historical notoriety as a port where pirates stocked up on supplies. It later developed into a fishing community and an area where sugarcane flourished. (There are still cane fields on the city's fringes.) Today it's a hub for the yachts that use its marinas; the divers who head to its good offshore sites; and for the day-trippers who travel by catamaran, ferry, or plane to the off-islands of Culebra and Vieques. With the most significant docking facilities on the island's eastern side, Fajardo is a bustling city of 37,000—so bustling, in fact, that its unremarkable downtown is often congested and difficult to navigate.

Puerto del Rey Marina, home to 1,100 boats, is one of the Caribbean's largest marinas. It's the place to hook up with a scuba-diving group, arrange an excursion to Vieques's bioluminescent bay, or charter a fishing boat. The marina also has several restaurants and boating-supply stores. ✉ *Rte. 3, Km 51.2* ☎ *787/860–1000.*

Villa Marina is the second-largest marina in Fajardo and is home to charter fishing boats as well as several catamaran operators who give day tours for swimming and snorkeling to the deserted islands right off Puerto Rico's northeast coast. ✉ *Rte. 987, Km. 1.3* ☎ *787/728–2450, 787/863–5131, or 787/863–5061* 🌐 *www.villamarinapr.com.*

The 316-acre **Reserva Natural Las Cabezas de San Juan,** on a headland north of Fajardo, is owned by the nonprofit Conservation Trust of Puerto Rico. You ride in open-air trolleys and wander down boardwalks through seven ecosystems, including lagoons, mangrove swamps, and dry-forest areas. Green iguanas skitter across paths, and guides identify other endangered species. A half-hour hike down a wooden walkway brings you to the mangrove-lined Laguna Grande, where bioluminescent microorganisms glow at night. The restored Fajardo lighthouse is the final stop on the tour; its Spanish-colonial tower has been in operation since 1882, making it Puerto Rico's second-oldest lighthouse. The first floor houses ecological displays; a winding staircase leads to an observation deck. A few miles past the reserve is the fishing area known as Las Croabas, where seafood snacks are sold along the waterfront. Only groups are allowed Wednesday and Thursday. The only way to see the reserve is on a mandatory guided tour; reservations are required. ✉ *Rte. 987 near Las Croabas* ☎ *787/722–5882 or 787/860–2560* 🎫 *$5* ⏲ *Tours Fri.–Sun. at 2, by appointment only.*

Beach

Balneario Seven Seas, on Route 987 near the Reserva Natural Las Cabezas de San Juan, is a long stretch of powdery sand with a smattering of shade. Puerto Rico's National Parks Company undertook a $1.2-million renovation in 2003 to the facilities, which include a few refreshment kiosks, picnic and camping areas, changing rooms, bathrooms, and showers. On weekends, the beach attracts crowds keen on its calm, clear waters—perfect for swimming and other water sports. It's closed on Monday.

Where to Stay & Eat

$$$–$$$$ ✕ **Blossom's.** Teppanyaki creations join Hunan and Szechuan specialties at this restaurant. The sushi bar gets rave reviews. Note that diners tend to dress up here, and there's an overall sense of romance. ✉ *Rte. 987, Km 3.4* ☎ *787/863–1000 Ext. 7048* ✍ *Reservations essential* 💳 *AE, MC, V* ⏲ *No lunch Mon.–Sat.*

$$$ ✕ **Ristorante Otello.** You can dine inside, enveloped in soft, romantic light, or slide outside to the terrace for a breezy meal under the stars at this northern Italian restaurant, one of the many at the Wyndham El Conquistador Resort & Country Club. Start with the minestrone—it's a guaranteed winner—and follow it with one of the pasta or risotto dishes. ✉ *Wyndham El Conquistador Resort & Country Club, Rte. 987, Km 3.4* ☎ *787/860–0555* 💳 *AE, MC, V* ⏲ *No lunch.*

$$–$$$ ✕ **A La Banda.** At this friendly waterside eatery you can sit in a dining room with nautical details or on a terrace overlooking the marina. Steaks and poultry figure on the menu, but the kitchen truly excels at Puerto Rican and seafood dishes, including fresh lobster. ✉ *Puerto del Rey Marina, Rte. 3, Km 51.2* ☎ *787/860–9162* 💳 *MC, V.*

$–$$$ ✕ **Anchor's Inn.** Seafood is the specialty at this meson gastronómico. Clever maritime decor and superb cooking have made it a local favorite; the convenient location down the road from El Conquistador Resort lures resort guests. Try the *chillo entero* (fried whole red snapper) or the paella. ✉ *Rte. 987, Km 2.7, Villas Las Croabas* ☎ *787/863–7200* ✍ *Reservations not accepted* 💳 *AE, MC, V* ⏲ *Closed Tues.*

$–$$ ✕ **Rosa's Sea Food.** Despite its name, this is a good spot for steak and chicken as well as seafood. As this is meson gastronómico, the preparations for many dishes are authentically Puerto Rican. There's a wide selection of Puerto Rican seafood stews and stuffed plantain casseroles. The specialty is grilled and sautéed fresh fish, from tuna to dolphinfish to red snapper. ✉ *Rte. 195, Tablazo 536, Playa Punta Real* ☎ *787/863–0213* ✍ *Reservations not accepted* ▭ *AE, MC, V* ⊙ *Closed Wed.*

¢–$ ✕ **Sardinera Seven Seas.** If you've worked up a hunger at Seven Seas Beach, walk across the sand and over a grassy hill to this no-frills, down-home landmark. You know the seafood here is fresh: fishermen fillet their catches on tables outside the restaurant. Choices include crab stew, grilled red snapper, and a rich selection of *pastelitos* (deep-fried turnovers stuffed with crab, shrimp, or lobster). The place closes at around 7 PM daily, so dinner here must be an early affair. ✉ *Calle Croabas, Km 5.5, Las Croabas* ☎ *787/863–0320* ✍ *Reservations not accepted* ▭ *No credit cards.*

$$$$ **Wyndham El Conquistador Resort & Golden Door Spa.** Many consider this resort on a bluff high above the ocean Puerto Rico's loveliest. The colossal hotel and the villas arranged in five "villages," are Moorish and Spanish colonial in style. Cobblestone streets and fountain-filled plazas convey a sense of cohesiveness. The resort's beach is on Palomino Island, just offshore; a free shuttle boat takes you there and back. The staff prides itself on its attentive service. A branch of the Japanese-influenced Golden Door Spa is widely considered among the Caribbean's best spas. If the place seems familiar, it may be because the James Bond movie *Goldfinger* was filmed here. ✉ *1000 Av. El Conquistador* *Box 70001, 00738* ☎ *787/863–1000, 800/996–3426, or 800/468–5228* *787/253–0178* *www.wyndham.com* *900 rooms, 16 suites* *11 restaurants, in-room data ports, minibars, in-room safes, cable TV with movies and video games, in-room VCRs, 18-hole golf course, 8 tennis courts, 5 pools, health club, spa, beach, dive shop, snorkeling, windsurfing, boating, jet skiing, marina, 4 bars, casino, nightclub, shop, children's programs (ages 4–12), dry cleaning, laundry service, Internet, meeting rooms, airport shuttle, parking (fee)* ▭ *AE, MC, V* *EP.*

Fodor'sChoice ★

$ **Fajardo Inn.** This 4-acre hilltop resort includes the original "scenic" hotel plus a larger hotel building. Suites have kitchenettes, and there are also some larger family rooms with three beds. All have basic furnishings and white-tile floors. The views—of the Atlantic and El Yunque against a backdrop of gardens—are lovely from either. The closest beach is the public Balneario Seven Seas, about a five-minute drive away, but the inn is also convenient to the public ferries to Culebra and Vieques. It's a breezy, comfortable inn with reasonable prices. ✉ *Rte. 195, 52 Parcelas, Beltran Sector, 00740* ☎ *787/860–6000* *787/860–5063* *www.fajardoinn.com* *54 rooms* *2 restaurants, some kitchenettes, some refrigerators, cable TV, pool, sports bar, meeting room, free parking; no smoking* ▭ *AE, MC, V* *EP.*

¢–$ **Parador La Familia.** From the white wooden guesthouse—the property's centerpiece—the view is right out to the ocean. It's a convenient spot to land for the night, close to the Wyndham El Conquistador resort as well as Seven Seas public beach and several seafront seafood restaurants. On the list of government-approved paradores, it's the best place in town to stay if you're not at the Wyndham. The restaurant serves decent breakfasts and light lunches. ✉ *Rte. 987, Km 4.1, Las Croabas, 00648* ☎ *787/863–1193* 🖷 *787/860–5354* *35 rooms* *Restaurant, cable TV, pool, bar, shop, meeting rooms, free parking* 💳 *AE, DC, MC, V* *EP.*

Nightlife

Although most of the evening action takes place in the El Conquistador's lounges, there are a few neighborhood bars where locals drink beer. You can play slots, blackjack, roulette, and video poker at **El Conquistador Casino** (✉ Wyndham El Conquistador Resort & Golden Door Spa, 1000 Av. El Conquistador ☎ 787/863–1000), a typical hotel gambling facility within the resort's lavish grounds.

Sports & the Outdoors

GOLF ★ The 18-hole Arthur Hills–designed course at **Wyndham El Conquistador Resort & Golden Door Spa** (✉ 1000 Av. El Conquistador ☎ 787/863–6784) is famous for its 200-foot changes in elevation. The trade winds make every shot challenging. Greens fees for resort guests range from $100 to $165, whereas for nonguests the price range is from $125 to $190.

DAY SAILS Several reputable catamaran and yacht operators in Fajardo make excursions to the reefs and sparkling blue waters surrounding a handful of small islets just off the coast. Many of the trips include transportation from San Juan and transportation to and from San Juan–metro area hotels. Whether or not you're staying in Fajardo, the day-trips on the water will show you classic Caribbean scenes of coral reefs rife with sealife, breathtakingly clear water, and palm fringed, deserted beaches. The day sails, with stops for snorkeling, include swimming breaks at deserted beaches and picnic lunches. Most of the craft are outfitted for comfort, with quality stereo systems and full-service bars. There are many competent operators offering a nearly identical experience, so your selection will probably be made on price and which operators serve your San Juan hotel, or which operate out of the marina in Fajardo that you are visiting. Prices range from $55 to $95; price is affected by whether you join up with a trip in San Juan or in Fajardo and by what is included in the price. Ask whether extras, such as picnic lunches and a full-service bar, are included. They are quickly becoming standard features.

At **East Winds Excursions** (✉ Puerto del Rey Marina, Rte. 3, Km 51.4 ☎ 787/863–3434 or 877/937–4386 🌐 www.eastwindcats.com) catamarans ranging in size from 45 feet to 65 feet take you offshore for snorkeling. Two of the catamarans are powered, and this cuts down tremendously on the amount of travel time to outlying islands. Trips includes stops at isolated beaches and a lunch buffet. All craft are outfitted with swimming decks, fresh-water showers, and full-service bars. Prices include lunch. These vessels are some of the plushest day sails in the area.

Erin Go Braugh (✉ Puerto del Rey Marina, Rte. 3, Km 51.4 ☎ 787/860–4401 or 787/409–2511 🌐 www.egbc.net) is a sailing yacht based on Fajardo that takes a tour of the glistening waters and islands offshore. Known for its barbecue picnic lunches, snorkel and fishing equipment are also provided. Longer charters are available for groups.

The ***Spread Eagle II*** (✉ Puerto del Rey Marina, Rte. 3, Km 51.4 ☎ 787/887–8821 🌐 www.snorkelpr.com) heads out to isolated beaches on the islands off Fajardo and has an all-you-can-eat sandwich buffet as well as an open bar. There are also sunset and moonlight cruises.

DIVING The waters off eastern Puerto Rico are probably the best-suited for scuba diving and snorkeling and compare favorably to other Caribbean diving destinations. Most operators will take you on dives up to 65 feet down, where visibility averages 40 feet to 60 feet and the water is still warm. The east has bountiful coral reefs, with a good variety of hard and soft corral, as well as a large variety of marine life. Fine snorkeling and diving is available immediately offshore from Fajardo, and there are many small, uninhabited islets from which to dive just off the coast. Experienced divers will find more than enough variety to fufill themselves, and those just starting out will find eastern Puerto Rico a perfect place, with easy dives that offer a taste of the real beauty of life underwater.

La Casa del Mar Dive Center (✉ Wyndham El Conquistador Resort & Golden Door Spa, 1000 Av. El Conquistador ☎ 787/863–1000 Ext. 7919, or 787/860–3483) focuses its scuba and snorkeling activity on the islets of Palominos, Lobos, and Diablo. There are also boating charters and trips to the Vieques Bioluminescent Bay. A two-tank morning dive costs from $99 to $124 depending on your equipment needs; single-tank afternoon dives are $69 to $94. An afternoon of snorkeling costs $50 per person. You can also take a full-day trip to Culebra, which costs $125 to $150 for divers and $85 for snorkelers, including lunch.

At **Sea Ventures Pro Dive Center** (✉ Puerto del Rey Marina, Rte. 3, Km 51.4 ☎ 787/863–3483 or 800/739–3483 🌐 www.divepuertorico.com) you can get PADI certified, arrange dive trips to 20 offshore sites, or organize boating and sailing excursions. A two-tank dive for certified divers, including equipment, is $95; a four-day certification course costs $500.

KAYAKING Several tour operators, including some based in San Juan, offer nighttime kayaking tours in the bioluminescent bay at the Reserva Natural Las Cabezas de San Juan, just north of Fajardo (*see* ⇨ Fajardo, *above*).

Eco Action Tours (✉ Wyndham Condado Plaza Hotel & Casino, 999 Av. Ashford, Laguna Wing, Condado ☎ 787/791–7509 or 787/640–7385) provides transportation and gives tours of the Fajardo shimmering bay by kayak every night, with pickup service in Fajardo area and San Juan hotels. The outfit also offers sailing tours to Culebra, day-long snorkeling trips, and Jet Ski rentals. Prices range from $35 to $95.

Las Tortugas Adventures (✉ Cond. La Puntilla, 4 Calle La Puntilla, Apt. D1–12, Old San Juan ☎ 787/725–5169 or 787/889–7734 🌐 www.kayak-pr.com) provides transportation from San Juan for a one-day kayaking trip in the Reserva Natural Las Cabezas de San Juan. Rates range from $45 to $75 per person, depending on group size and trip length. Rates include transportation from San Juan, but it's possible to join up with the group from Fajardo.

Shopping

Maria Elba Torres runs the **Galería Arrecife** (✉ Wyndham El Conquistador Resort & Golden Door Spa, 1000 Av. El Conquistador ☎ 787/863–3972), which shows only works by artists living in the Caribbean. Look for ceramics by Rafael de Olmo and jewelry made from fish scales. Chocolate-loving Laurie Humphrey had trouble finding a supplier for her sweet tooth, so she opened the **Paradise Store** (✉ Rte. 194, Km 0.4 ☎ 787/863–8182). Lindt and other gourmet chocolates jam the shop, which also sells flowers and such gift items as Puerto Rican–made soaps.

VIEQUES & CULEBRA

A hop west from Fajardo across the water are the two islands where Puerto Ricans go when they want to escape from civilization: Vieques and Culebra. The beauty of both is readily apparent, whether you approach by sea or air. Banana-shape Vieques floats atop azure water; smaller Culebra is edged by white sands and encircled by islets.

These sleepy outposts are—for now, anyway—bereft of traffic lights, casinos, fast-food chains, movie houses, and most other modern trappings. Temperatures hover around 80°, the stunning white beaches are devoid of crowds, and "barefoot" is often part of the dress code. The many open-air restaurants and simple guesthouses rely on overhead fans and trade winds to keep you comfortable.

Both islands—sometimes dubbed the "Spanish Virgin Islands"—are accessible from the main island via 90-minute ferry trips and 10-minute puddle-jumper flights that leave Fajardo daily. There's also air service from San Juan. Note that during the Easter holidays, mainlanders flock here for camping and partying on the beach. If you're planning a trip during Holy Week, make reservations as far in advance as possible and don't expect to find tranquillity.

Vieques

13 km (8 mi) southeast of Fajardo by sea.

Local lore has it that Captain Kidd once visited Vieques when it was a pirate haven. Through the early 1900s, sugarcane dominated the economy. Later in the century, the United States commandeered the island for use as a naval training ground. Through six decades, the military controlled two-thirds of the island, including its eastern and western ends, which contained some of the best beaches. For years, residents complained that their mighty neighbor stifled economic development and harmed the environment, and Puerto Rican political leaders have consistently called on the Navy to return any land it did not need. After an April 1999 bombing accident took the life of a local resident, who was working at the live firing range as a civilian security guard, waves of protests, combined with political pressure, prompted the Navy to reluctantly leave on May 1, 2003.

Some 9,600 civilians call Vieques home, including a strong expatriate community of artists and guesthouse or vacation-villa owners from the mainland United States. Other islanders fish for a living or work in tourism-related fields. All were drawn here by the same thing that lures visitors: quiet days, small-town friendliness, and natural beauty. Only 6 km (4 mi) across at its widest point, the 34-km-long (21-mi-long) island is packed with stunning beaches (so many that some aren't even named) and marvelous scuba and snorkeling opportunities.

Ironically, the Navy's presence has helped to keep the island pristine since there was little land on which to develop megaresorts, and today, most of the military's holdings have been turned into nature preserves. The west end of the island has the most public access; only small areas thought to have been exposed to industrial waste or military munitions remain closed to the public as well as some naval communications facilities that are still in operation.

You can tour the acres of cement military bunkers—blasted out of hillsides to store weapons, lined up along well paved roads—as well as the coastal area around Green Beach and a surrounding nature reserve with boardwalk paths. To get a really good view, drive up as far as you can along the road to Mount Pirata (its summit is closed off), which allows you to peer west to the east coast of Puerto Rico, the El Yunque rain forest beyond it, or to the east, where Cuebra, the U.S. Virgin Islands, and other smaller green swatches of earth break out of emerald waters.

The Vieques town government has development plans in the works. At Mosquito Pier, there are plans to develop a ferry terminal to ply a shorter route to Puerto Rico, directly to the town of Ceiba, where there's a decommissioned naval base that someday might host cruise ships. A new retail area and tram system to bring passengers to the ferry landing on Vieques are also in the works.

Just because Vieques is sleepy doesn't mean there's nothing to do besides hit the beach. There are two communities—Isabel Segunda, where the ferries dock, and the smaller Esperanza. The commercial districts, strings of guesthouses and restaurants, clustered near the ferry in Isabel Segunda, and along the bayfront promenade on Esperanza, get crowded for a few hours every night, longer on weekends. It's also home to the astonishing Bahía Mosquito, a fort built by the early Spanish governors, and several fine eateries and lodging options.

12 The community of **Playa Grande,** built around a sugar mill and surrounding plantation, now covered in thick tropical vegetation, was once the largest community on the island. It's just inland from a south coast beach lined with palm groves. You can still find the ruins of the old sugar mill if you're adventurous and patient enough. It's off a wide dirt road running through the area, once the community's main street, lined with the finest wooden, plantation style homes.

11 **Faro Punta Mulas,** a Spanish-built lighthouse beside a ferry dock, dates from the late 1800s. In 1992 it was carefully restored and now houses a maritime museum that traces much of the island's history, including the visit by South American liberation leader Simón Bolívar. ✉ *At end of Rte. 200* ☎ *787/741–0060* 🎟 *Free* ⏲ *Wed.–Sun. 10–4.*

VIEQUES LIBRE

F **OR NEARLY SIX DECADES,** *the U.S. Navy had set the course of development in Vieques, controlling the island's eastern and western ends and exerting enormous influence over the destiny of the civilian area sandwiched in between. Though long-protested, the bombing continued. When an off-target bomb killed a civilian on Navy land in April 1999, opposition began to transform the island's placid beaches into political hotbeds. As a result of the protests that followed, the Navy finally withdrew from its Atlantic Fleet training grounds in May 2002.*

Protesters camping out on the bombing range kept it shut down from 1999 to 2000. Hundreds of Puerto Rican residents were arrested for trespassing on Navy land during war games. They were joined by celebrity protesters from the United States, including environmental lawyer Robert F. Kennedy Jr. (who gave his baby daughter the middle name "Vieques"), the wife of Reverend Jesse Jackson, and Reverend Al Sharpton, all of whom were arrested for trespassing on the bombing range. For much of 2000 and 2001, protests were so commonplace that there were semi-permanent encampments of opponents. Songs with such titles as "Paz Pa' Vieques" ("Peace for Vieques") began to surface, as did bumper-stickers and T-shirts with protest slogans. Latin pop celebrities such as singer–songwriter Robie Draco Rosa (who wrote Ricky Martin hits like "Livin' la Vida Loca"), actor Edward James Olmos, singer Millie Corejter, Puerto Rican rock band Fiel a la Vega, protest singer Zoraida Santiago, local actors, painters, doctors, and lawyers, added to the fanfare when they joined the activities.

In late 1999, Puerto Rican governor Pedro Rosselló and President Bill Clinton agreed that residents could vote on whether the Navy should stay or go by 2003. A nonbinding referendum in July 2001, which was called by Governor Sila Calderón, found that 68% of Vieques's voters wanted the Navy to leave immediately. Although Congress voted not to hold the referendum promised by Clinton, President George W. Bush said he would abide by the May 1, 2003, exit date called for in the 2001 nonbinding vote. Although some members of Congress pushed to allow the Navy to stay on—increasing their pressure tremendously after September 11, 2001, when even local protesters called for a moratorium on civil disobedience—the Bush administration pursued an exit strategy.

President Clinton had also promised that the Navy would spend $40 million on Vieques, as a way to make up for its past indifference over the small island's economic situation. That promise is also being kept. The most visible examples of spending are airport improvements and plans for a new ferry terminal on former Navy land on the western end of the island.

The Navy's departure will undoubtedly spur increased development on tiny Vieques, which will improve the economy (a full-service resort has already opened), and services to local residents and visitors. But development must be carefully limited if the essential character of Vieques, which doesn't have a single fast-food chain, is to be maintained. Federal and local authorities are now working out cleanup plans for the former naval military-reservation and ammunition facility. The faster those plans proceed, the greater the public access will be on the 18,000 acres comprising the new Vieques National Wildlife Refuge. The hope is that much of the former military lands will be preserved in their natural state and that other land is developed with ecotourism and low-impact development in mind.

13 **Bahía Mosquito** (Mosquito Bay) is also known as Bioluminescent Bay or Phosphorescent Bay. It's one of the world's best spots to have a glow-in-the-dark experience with undersea dinoflagellates. Tour operators offer kayak trips or excursions on nonpolluting boats to see the bay's tiny microorganisms that appear to light up when their water is agitated. Dive into the bay and you'll emerge covered in sparkling water. Look behind your boat, and you'll see a twinkling wake. Even the fish that jump from the water will bear an eerie glow. The high concentration of dinoflagellates sets the bay apart from the other spots (including others in Puerto Rico) that are home to these tiny organisms. The bay is at its best when there's little or no moonlight; rainy nights are beautiful, too, because the raindrops splashing in the water produce ricochet sparkles. Some of the best excursions to the bay are offered by Sharon Grasso of Island Adventures. ✉ *South central side of island, on unpaved roads off Rte. 997* ☎ *No phone* 🎟 *Free* ⏲ *Daily.*

Fodor's Choice ★

14 The **Museo El Fortin Conde de Mirasol** (Count of Mirasol Fort Museum) is housed in what was the last military structure begun by the Spaniards in the New World. It was erected on Vieques's northern coast in 1840 at the order of Count Mirasol, then governor of Puerto Rico. The museum has changing exhibits of local art and displays of items that chronicle Vieques's past: Taíno Indian relics, flags of the European powers that hoped to lay claim to the island, a collection of early maps, and a bust of Simón Bolívar. ✉ *471 Calle Magnolia, Isabel Segunda* ☎ *787/741–1717* 🌐 *www.enchanted-isle.com/elfortin* 🎟 *$1* ⏲ *Wed.–Sun. 10–4.*

15 A portion of the west and the entire eastern end of the island is being administered as the **Vieques National Wildlife Refuge,** comprising 18,000 acres—about 14,900 acres on the eastern end and 3,100 acres on the west—making it the biggest protected natural reserve in Puerto Rico and the U.S. Virgin Islands. Most of eastern Vieques is being administered by the U.S. Fish & Wildlife Service as a nature reserve, except for the 900-acre bombing range on the far eastern end, which will be permanently closed off, a consequence of its contamination by the ordnance shot over its 60-year existence. But most of the rest of eastern Vieques is pristine nature, astonishingly beautiful and well-forested, with a hilly center region overlooking powder-white sandy beaches and a coral-ringed coastline; it served mainly as a buffer zone between the military maneuvers and civilian population. The vast majority of this acreage remains off-limits to visitors, as a search for unexploded munitions and contaminants is carried out. Cleanup plans, which the Puerto Rico government hopes will allow much more public access to the island, were still being drawn up at this writing. 📫 *Box 1527, 00765* ☎ *787/741–2138* 🌐 *southeast.fws.gov/vieques.*

Beaches

★ Of Vieques's more than three dozen beaches, **Playa Sun Bay** on Route 997 is one of the most popular. Its white sands skirt 1 mi-long, crescent-shape bay. You'll find food kiosks, picnic tables, camping areas, and a bathhouse; on weekdays, when the crowds are thin, you might also find wild horses grazing among the palm trees in the shady area facing the sea. Parking is $3, which serves as the admission fee.

★ An unpaved road east of Playa Sun Bay and off Route 997 leads to **Playa Media Luna**, a pretty little beach that's ideal for families because the water is calm and below your knees for yards out. This is a good spot to try your hand at snorkeling. Take note, though, that there are no facilities.

Located on former Navy land on the eastern end of Vieques, **Red Beach** and **Blue Beach** are now open to the public everyday during daylight hours. The adjacent beaches are both primo sunbathing, swimming, and snorkeling spots. The water is crystal clear. There can be strong surf in some spots, making swimming here difficult at times. There are no facilities, so bring snacks and plenty of drinking water. You get here only after traveling a series of unpaved, unnamed roads, so ask one of the park ranger's as you enter for direction.

Where to Stay & Eat

$$$ ✕ **The Blue Macaw.** The island's most elegant restaurant is at Inn on the Blue Horizon, on a bluff above the town of Esperanza overlooking the Caribbean. Start with a drink at the circular bar, with its unforgettable views of the south coast, then move to a table for an unforgettable meal. The menu changes often, but it always lives up to its attempt to deliver "intriguing cuisine." The menu has included everything from herb-crusted Australian rack of lamb, to a traditional beef Wellington, to salmon prepared in a Thai garlic sauce, to broiled sea bass in a mango sauce. ✉ *Inn on the Blue Horizon, Rte. 966, Km. 4.2* ☎ *787/741–3318* ▭ *AE, MC, V* ⏲ *Closed Mon.–Wed. No lunch.*

$$$ Fodor'sChoice ★ ✕ **Café Media Luna.** Tucked into an old building in Isabel Segunda, this eatery is a local favorite. You'll have a hard time figuring out what type of food it specializes in, though; the menu runs the gamut from Vietnamese spring rolls to tandoori chicken to seafood cooked in wine. All of the options are good. ✉ *351 Calle Antonio G. Mellado, Isabel Segunda* ☎ *787/741–2594* ⚠ *Reservations essential* ▭ *AE, MC, V* ⏲ *Closed Mon. and Tues. No lunch.*

$$–$$$ ✕ **Chez Shack.** This rustic open-air restaurant in the hills serves up delicious cuisine in a friendly atmosphere. Chicken, beef, shrimp, or fish are grilled to tender perfection and served with sides and an all-you-can-eat salad bar featuring expertly prepared pasta, bean, and potato salads and sumptuous platters of mixed greens and raw vegetables. It's justifiably famous for its weekly barbecue night with a steel band, but there's usually some good jazz or island rhythms on the sound system and a small but lively bar. ✉ *Rte. 995, Km. 1.8, Barrio Pilón* ☎ *787/741–2175* ⚠ *Reservations essential* ▭ *AE, MC, V.*

$–$$$ ✕ **Taverna Española.** In downtown Isabel Segunda right off the town square, this family-run restaurant has a bar and a separate dining room. The menu is basic Spanish cuisine, heavy on the seafood. You can get a good paella, sautéed clams, and even a dash of comida criollo. The fresh fish served here is often grilled whole with spices, or filleted, then sautéed in tomato, garlic, and olive oil. Reasonable prices and friendly service keep people coming back to this clean, quiet restaurant. ✉ *At Calle Santa Rosa and Calle Carlos Lebrón, off the main plaza, Isabel Segunda* ☎ *787/741–1175* ▭ *AE, MC, V.*

$$ ✕ **La Campesina.** Fine food served in a laid-back, charming setting has made this a Vieques mainstay since the early 1980s. Off the beaten path between Esperanza and the central hills, the restaurant specializes in fresh seafood, served in sauces made from local fruits and herbs. Red snapper comes poached or wrapped and baked to perfection, and homemade lobster raviolis come in a Puerto Rican pepper sauce. The papaya cole slaw also tasty. ✉ *Rte. 201, Km 5* ☎ *787/741–1239* ▭ *AE, MC, V* ⊗ *Closed Mon. and Tues. No lunch.*

$–$$ ✕ **Island Steak House.** This restaurant at the Crow's Nest guesthouse is popular for its happy hour (5 to 7 PM) and the fact that it's built like a treehouse. The menu has several varieties of steak, a fair sampling of seafood, and basics like burgers and French onion soup. The whole Vieques lobster served with spiced rum is recommended. ✉ *Crow's Nest, Rte. 201, Km 1.6, Barrio Florida* ☎ *787/741–0011* ✍ *Reservations essential* ▭ *AE, MC, V.*

$–$$ ✕ **Posada Vistamar.** This nice, family-run restaurant serves up delicious seafood and Puerto Rican cuisine at reasonable prices. Behind the oceanside strip in Ensenada, it's on a secluded street. You can have a cigar on the front porch after dinner and watch the stars twinkling ahead while listening to the song of the coquis. ✉ *Calle Almendro, Esperanza* ☎ *787/741–8716* ▭ *AE, MC, V.*

★ $$$–$$$$ **Wyndham Martineau Bay Resort & Spa.** The first full-scale resort on Vieques has guest rooms with a tropical plantation feel. They are spread out in villas among lushly landscaped grounds, and the location on the north coast is enviable, though the beach isn't as nice as others on the island. Rooms are large—at least 600 square feet—and many have spectacular views. The restaurants are adequate, but you should also go off-property to dine. The resort has its own fleet of jeeps for rent, the cost of which is often included in a room package. Service kinks are still being worked out. ✉ *Rte 200, Km 3.4, between Isabel Segunda and the Airport, along the north coastal roadway* 📫 *Box 9368, 00765* ☎ *787/741–4100 or 877/999–3223* 🖷 *787/741–4171* 🌐 *www.wyndham.com* *156 rooms, 20 suites* *2 restaurants, in-room data ports, fans, some in-room hot tubs, cable TV, pool, 2 tennis courts, gym, spa, boating, snorkeling, bar, Internet, business services, meeting rooms, car rental* ▭ *AE, MC, V* 🍽 *BP.*

★ $$–$$$ **Hix Island House.** On 13 secluded acres in the central hills of Vieques, this unique resort has won raves for its architectural design, ecosensitivity, and gorgeous views. A minimalist aesthetic runs through the 13 loft units, which are clustered in three separate buildings. With private outdoor terraces, outdoor private showers, and huge windows and open spaces, the rooms blend in with the natural beauty outside. You'll be uninterrupted by television and telephones as there are none in the rooms. And the resort's embrace of the environment goes beyond feeling into function, with the use of recycled water and even solar power systems. ✉ *Rte 995, Km. 1.5* 📫 *Box 1556, 00765* ☎ *787/741–3318* 🌐 *www.hixislandhouse.com* *13 rooms* *Kitchens, refrigerators, pool, fitness classes, massage, shop; no room phones, no room TVs* ▭ *AE, MC, V* 🍽 *CP.*

$$–$$$ Fodor's Choice ★ **Inn on the Blue Horizon.** This inn, consisting of six Mediterranean-style villas and a main house near the sea on what used to be a plantation, was the island's first luxury hotel. You truly feel away from it all at this

gorgeous 20-acre complex. None of the elegant rooms has a phone, and even air-conditioning is rare (only two rooms have it), but with the breezy location you won't notice the absence. This isn't a full-scale resort like the Martineau Bay, so guests appreciate the proximity to Esperanza, but the feel is quite in tune with the intimacy of Vieques. ✉ *Rte. 996, Km 4.2, outside Esperanza* 📭 *Box 1556, 00765* ☎ *787/741-3318* 📠 *787/741-0522* 🌐 *www.innonthebluehorizon.com* *9 rooms* *Restaurant, fans, pool, massage, beach, bicycles, bar, library; no a/c in some rooms, no room TVs, no kids under 14* 💳 *AE, MC, V* 🍽 *BP.*

$$ **Casa Cielo.** The fact that it has no physical address is an indication of just how much of a getaway this sprawling great house—atop a windswept hill 13 km (8 mi) from Vieques's east coast—really is. Seven of its rooms face the ocean (some the Atlantic, some the Caribbean) and have private balconies; two face the garden patio. The inn prides itself on providing such sumptuous extras as all-cotton sheets and massages. 📭 *Box 310, 00765* ☎📠 *787/741-2403* 🌐 *www.casacielo.net* *9 rooms* *Fans, cable TV, pool, massage, meeting rooms; no a/c in some rooms, no kids, no smoking* 💳 *MC, V* 🍽 *BP.*

$–$$ **Crow's Nest.** This quiet guesthouse has 5 acres and an outdoor deck with a marvelous view. Although it's not on the water, it's just a few minutes' drive from Esperanza and its restaurants and is an easy jumping-off point for visits to beaches on either coast. Large rooms have tile floors. Though not on the beach, the guesthouse does have a wonderful pool in a country setting. ✉ *Rte. 201, Km 1.6, Barrio Florida, 00765* ☎ *787/741-8525* 📠 *787/741-1294* 🌐 *www.crowsnestvieques.com* *15 rooms* *Restaurant, fans, kitchenettes, cable TV, pool* 💳 *AE, MC, V* 🍽 *BP.*

$–$$ Fodor'sChoice ★ **Hacienda Tamarindo.** Interior designer Linda Vail and her husband Burr are the charming hosts at this hilltop guesthouse, which is named after the venerable tamarind tree that rises three stories in the lobby. The panoramic views include grounds landscaped with coconut palms and mahogany trees as well as tropical flowers. Half the guest rooms—which have terra-cotta floors, light pastel color schemes, and antiques—are air-conditioned. The rest are cooled by overhead fans and trade winds. A full breakfast is served on the second-floor terrace. ✉ *Rte. 996, Km 4.5, outside Esperanza* 📭 *Box 1569, 00765* ☎ *787/741-8525* 📠 *787/741-3215* 🌐 *www.enchanted-isle.com/tamarindo* *16 rooms* *Fans, cable TV, pool; no a/c in some rooms, no kids under 15* 💳 *AE, MC, V* 🍽 *BP.*

★ ¢–$ **Banana's.** This is one of a string of inexpensive guesthouses along the main road in Esperanza. Most rooms are large; all are clean but more functional than aesthetic. Some have private screened porches. Some are air-conditioned, others not. The restaurant here serves tasty casual American fare for lunch and dinner: burgers, chicken wings, potato skins, and the like. ✉ *142 Calle Flamboyán, Esperanza* 📭 *Box 1300, 00765* ☎ *787/741-8700* 📠 *787/741-0709* 🌐 *www.bananasguesthouse.com* *Fans, some refrigerators; no a/c in some rooms, no room TVs* 💳 *AE, MC, V* 🍽 *EP.*

VILLA RENTALS One good way to visit Vieques is to rent one of the beautiful vacation homes that have been built in the hilly interior or along the coasts. These are concentrated in three major areas: Bravos de Boston, Esperanza, and Pilón. Several local real-estate agents deal in short-term rentals of at least a week. A list of properties rented by owner with links to the individual properties is available at www.enchanted-isle.com. **Connections** (☎ 787/741–0023 or 787/741–2012). **Crow's Nest Realty** (☎ 787/741–3298). **Guayacan** Realty (☎ 787/741–4883). **Rainbow Realty** (☎ 787/741–4312). **Vieques Island Realty** (☎ 787/741–0330).

Nightlife

Al's Mar Azul (✉ Calle Plinio Peterson, at the ferry terminal on the harbor, Isabela Segunda ☎ 787/741–3400) is a lively bar right next to the ferry terminal with good sunset specials from 5 to 7. Its main draw is an outdoor deck that overlooks the channel between Vieques and Puerto Rico. You'll find dart boards, pool tables, slots, a juke box, and cable TV. It's also a good information center for residents and visitors alike. Tasty sandwiches and fried clams are served irregularly; more regular is the gregarious owner, who often buys shots of tequila for whomever is at the bar. **Amapola Tavern** (✉ 144 Calle Flamboyán, Esperanza ☎ 787/741–1382) has salsa music coming from its sound system, the island's biggest TV screen (making this *the* place to be on sports nights), and a bartender who turns out exquisite tropical concoctions. **Bananas** (✉ 142 Calle Flamboyán, Esperanza ☎ 787/741–8700) equals burgers and booze—not to mention enthusiastic crowds. There's sometimes live music and dancing. **La Nasa** (✉ Calle Flamboyán, Esperanza ☎ no phone) is the only establishment on the waterfront side of the street in Esperanza. This simple wooden shack serves up cheap and very cold beer and rum drinks. Tourists and locals congregate on plastic chairs out front or stare off into the placid Caribbean from an open-air back room.

Sports & the Outdoors

BOATING **Aqua Frenzy Kayaks** (✉ At dock area below Calle Flamboyán, Esperanza ☎ 787/741–0913) rents kayaks and arranges kayak tours of Bahía Mosquito and other areas. Reservations for the bio-bay excursions, which cost $25, must be made at least 24 hours in advance. There's also a daily two-hour mangrove kayak tour. The best trip is the $85 barbecue, which runs from around 2 to 8 and includes snorkeling, a beach bonfire barbecue with music and drinks, and a bay tour. You can also get custom tours from the accommodating staff. **Blue Caribe Kayaks** (✉ 149 Calle Flamboyán, Esperanza ☎ 787/741–2522 🌐 www.enchanted-isle.com/bluecaribe) offers kayak trips to the Bahía Mosquito, as well as kayak fishing and snorkeling trips off Vieques and to nearby islets. Tours range in price from $23 to $50, and hourly kayak and other rentals are available. Former schoolteacher Sharon Grasso's **Island Adventures** (✉ Rte. 996, Esperanza ☎ 787/741–0720 🌐 www.biobay.com) will take you to the glowing Bahía Mosquito aboard nonpolluting, electrically powered pontoon boats. The cost is about $20 per person.

DIVING & SNORKELING ***Marauder* Sailing Charters** (☎ 787/435–4858 🌐 www.enchanted-isle.com/marauder) operates the *Marauder,* a 34-foot sailing yacht anchored off Esperanza, which takes groups on day sails around the south coast, allowing a close-up look of the pristine nature across much of the island, as well as the surrounding water filled with reefs and sealife.

There's a midday stop at a secluded spot for swimming, snorkeling, and sun bathing followed by a gourmet lunch, then a ride back to Esperanza. The yacht has a good sound system and open bar. A minimum of two people and a maximum of six people can book a trip, which runs from 10 AM to 3 PM. The cost is $95 per person. A two-hour sunset sail is also offered for $45 per person.

Shopping

Atlantic Caribbean Sports Shop (✉ 200 Calle Antonio Mellado, Isabel Segunda ☎ 787/741–2999) is a local sports shop where you can pick up beach supplies, swimsuits, and water-sports gear. Try **Kim's Cabin** (✉ 136 Calle Flamboyán, Esperanza ☎ 787/741–0520) for jewelry, swimsuits, summer dresses, and other attire. Artists show and sell their work at **Casa Vieja Gallery** (✉ Rte. 996, outside Esperanza ☎ 787/741–3078), in a Caribbean-style building at the entrance to the grounds of Inn on the Blue Horizon. **18 Degrees North** (✉ Calle Flamboyán ☎ 787/741–8600) has swimsuits and beach supplies, as well as souvenirs. Artist **Sandra Reyes** (☎ 787/741–1494) shows handmade mosaics by appointment only during the afternoons. The framed mosaic designs, made to be hung like paintings, draw inspiration from Taíno images as well as nature scenes of the island. **Siddhia Hutchinson Fine Art Studio & Gallery** (✉ 15 Calle 3 ☎ 787/741–8780) is up the road toward Bravos de Boston from the ferry dock, between the ferry and the lighthouse. The artist has lived on Vieques since the early 1990s, creating pastel watercolor prints of Caribbean scenes, as well as limited-edition ceramic dinnerware. The gallery is open Monday through Saturday, 10 AM to 4 PM. **Taína Pottery Workshop** (☎ 787/741–1556), a local female artisans collective, makes beautiful ceramics, pottery, and other artwork. Visits to the studio are by appointment only.

Culebra

28 km (17 mi) east of Fajardo by sea.

There's archaeological evidence that small groups of pre-Columbian people lived on Culebra, and certainly pirates landed here from time to time. But Puerto Rico's Spanish rulers didn't bother laying claim to it until 1886; its dearth of freshwater made it unattractive for settlement. Although it now has modern conveniences, its pace seems little changed from a century ago.

Twelve kilometers (7 mi) long, 5 km (3 mi) wide, and mostly unspoiled, Culebra is actually more of an islet than an island. At one point it was controlled, like its neighbor Vieques, by the U.S. Navy. When the military withdrew, it turned much of the land into a wildlife reserve. There's only one town, Dewey, named after U.S. Admiral George Dewey.

The whole island operates like a small town: people know each other, people respect each other, and no one wants noise or drama. When the sun goes down, Culebra winds down as well. But during the day it's a delightful place to stake out a spot on the beach and read, swim, or search for shells. So what causes stress on the island? Nothing.

Commissioned by President Theodore Roosevelt in 1909, **Refugio Nacional de Vida Silvestre de Culebra** is one of the nation's oldest wildlife refuges. Some 1,500 acres of the island make up a protected area. It's a lure for hikers and bird-watchers: Culebra teems with seabirds, from laughing gulls and roseate terns to red-billed tropic birds and sooty terns. Maps and trails of the refuge are hard to come by, but you can stop by the U.S. Fish and Wildlife Service office near the airport (and close to the cemetery) to find out about trail conditions and determine whether you're headed to an area that requires a permit. The office also can tell you whether the leatherback turtles are nesting. From mid-April to mid-July, volunteers help to monitor and tag these creatures, which nest on Culebra's beaches, especially Playa Resaca and Playa Brava. If you'd like to volunteer, you must agree to help out for at least three nights. ✉ *Between Rte. 250 and Rte. 251, near Monte Resaca, north of Dewey* ☎ *787/742–0115, 787/254–3456 for information about leatherback monitoring* 🌐 *southeast.fws.gov* 🎫 *Free* ⏲ *Daily.*

Beaches

Playa Culebrita. Take a dive boat or water taxi to Culebra's offshore islet, Culebrita, where you'll find this beach and a fabulous coral reef. The beach is gorgeous, and there's a series of rocks that form natural pools. Snuggling into one of them is like taking a warm bath. This is a superb spot for snorkeling right from the shore. You can also visit an old lighthouse.

Fodor'sChoice ★ **Playa Flamenco.** Off Route 250 on Culebra's north coast is an amazingly long stretch of white sand. During the week it's pleasantly uncrowded; on the weekend, though, it fills up. As you stroll along it, don't be surprised if you come upon a rusting tank or two—they're left over from when the area was used by the U.S. Navy. (To get here, you should ask for directions from a local; the nearest roads are unnamed and unnumbered.)

Playa Zoni. Once only accessible by rugged roads at the end of Route 250, a paved road now makes the trip to this breathtakingly beautiful beach all the more easy to reach. On the island's northeastern end, about 11 km (7 mi) northeast of Dewey, this beach is far more isolated than Playa Flamenco, and it's just as beautiful. It's also a good spot for snorkeling. The beach is still uncrowded by U.S. standards, but without the once tortuous journey to get here, it's less so than it once was.

Where to Stay & Eat

$$ ✕ **Dinghy Dock.** Dinghy Dock is a pulse point for Dewey. Culebra's version of heavy traffic—including the arrival and departure of the thatch-cover water taxi takes place around the dock where this restaurant sits. The long menu includes everything from vegetarian specialties to T-bone steaks. Daily specials often concentrate on the restaurant's forte: creole-style seafood, including grilled native grouper and yellowtail. ✉ *Carretera Fulladoza, Dewey* ☎ *787/742–0581* ▭ *MC, V.*

$ ✕🏨 **Mamacitas.** On a breezy dock overlooking the canal, the restaurant ($–$$) here is the kind of place where you start up a conversation with the folks at the plastic table next to yours and end up making lasting friendships. Begin with a tropical drink and then move on to well-made pasta dishes or seafood fresh from the ocean. The restaurant now has a bar, and the adjoining guesthouse was expanded between 1998 and 2002 and is now renting rooms and suites. The suites are charming, with balconies and a view over the canal. The penthouse has a kitchenette. The owners were expecting to install satellite TV in summer 2004 at this writing. ✉ *66 Calle Castelar, Dewey 00775* ☎ *787/742–0090* 🌐 *www.mamacitaspr.com* *10 rooms* *Restaurant, fans, some kitchenettes, dock; no room TVs* *AE, MC, V* *EP.*

$$–$$$ **Tamarindo Estates.** Sixteen beach cottages are on this 60-acre estate with its own coastline, including a long, sandy beach. There's also a common beach house with showers and sitting areas and a pool with an oceanside deck. Most of the cottages are a bit farther inland, in the hilly vegetated interior, affording great views of the coastline and natural surroundings. Each cottage has its own outdoor deck to enjoy the view. The waters off the shore here are perfect for swimming and snorkeling, and it's about a 10-minute drive from town on the road to Flamenco Beach. ✉ *Off Rd. 251 to Flamenco Beach, look for a sign for Tamarindo Estates right before beach, Box 313, Culebra 00775* ☎ *787/742–3343* *787/742–3342* 🌐 *www.tamarindoestates.com* *16 cottages* *Fans, kitchens, cable TV, in-room VCRs, pool, beach, car rental* *MC, V* *EP.*

¢–$$ **Harbor View Villas.** Wooden beach villas in the hills overlook Culebra's beautiful coastline. French doors open up to large decks with splendid views. Each villa has a large living area, private bath, kitchen, and master bedroom; some have two bedrooms. Smaller suites are also available. On the road from Dewey to Melones Beach, the villas are on 6 acres of tropical countryside. A restaurant on premises, Juanita Bananas, was scheduled to open in December 2004 at this writing. ✉ *Melones Rd., Km. 1, 00775* ☎ *787/742–3855 or 800/440–0070* *787/742–3171 or 787/742–3855* 🌐 *www.harbourviewvillas.com* *3 villas, 3 suites* *Fans, kitchens, deck; no a/c in some rooms, no room TVs* *No credit cards* *EP.*

$ **Club Seaborne.** Overlooking Fulladoza Bay and a 10-minute drive from Dewey, this pretty pink complex consists of a main house with communal rooms and two guest rooms, eight villas, a two-bedroom cottage, and a small efficiency apartment dubbed the Crow's Nest. The cottage has kitchen facilities and is popular with families. Gardens form the backdrop. ✉ *Carretera Fulladoza, Km 1.5* *Box 357, 00775* ☎ *787/742–3169* *787/742–3176* *3 rooms, 8 villas, 1 cottage with kitchen* *Restaurant, some kitchens, cable TV, pool, bar, library* *AE, MC, V* *BP.*

¢–$ **Posada La Hamaca.** Functional rather than cozy, this little guesthouse is in a concrete building at the edge of Dewey. It's within walking distance of restaurants, shops, and grocery stores. Ice, coolers, and towels for the beach are provided for free. You can hang out at the back dock, which is on a canal that separates Culebra's harbor from the Caribbean. ✉ *68 Calle Castelar (Box 388), Dewey 00775* ☎ *787/742–3516* *787/742–0181* 🌐 *www.posada.com* *8 rooms, 3 apartments* *Fans, some kitchenettes, dock; no a/c in some rooms, no room TVs* *MC, V* *EP.*

Sports & the Outdoors

BIKING Biking is a good way to explore the island on your own. You can rent bikes for $20 a day at **Culebra Bike Shop** (✉ 138 Calle Escudero, Dewey ☎ 787/742–2209).

BOATING **Culebra Boat Rentals** (✉ 142 Calle Escudero, Dewey ☎ 787/742–3559) rents small motor and sail boats. Rates range from $100 to $200 per day, depending on the vessel. Longer range rentals are also available. At **Flamenco Resort & Fishing Club** (✉ 10 Pedro Nárquez, Playa Flamenco ☎ 787/742–3144) you can charter sailboats for offshore exploring.

DIVING & SNORKELING Travelers have recounted that dives with **Culebra Dive Shop** (✉ 317 Calle Escudero, Dewey ☎ 787/742–0566 🌐 www.culebradiveshop.com) are spectacular. A one-tank dive runs about $45. For about the same price, the shop also offers day-long snorkeling trips. **Culebra Divers** (✉ 4 Pedro Marquez, Dewey ☎ 787/742–0803) caters to beginners and specializes in coral reefs near Culebra. Day and weekly packages are available, as are snorkeling trips.

Shopping

Paradise Gift Shop (✉ 6 Calle Salisbury, Dewey ☎ 787/742–3565) is a good spot for T-shirts, jewelry, island photographs and watercolors, and other souvenirs. The tiny gift shop at **Mamacitas** (✉ 66 Calle Castelar, Dewey ☎ 787/742–0090) guesthouse has exceptional hand-painted T-shirts and other original-design gifts.

THE SOUTHEASTERN COAST

From Fajardo, a good way to explore the southeast is to travel along the old coastal road, Route 3, as it weaves on and off the shoreline and passes through small towns. The route takes a while to travel but offers terrific beach and mountain scenery.

Naguabo

 *18 km (11 mi) southwest of Fajardo.*

In this fast-growing municipality's downtown, pastel buildings give the main plaza the look of a child's nursery: a golden-yellow church on one side faces a bright-yellow city hall, and a pink-and-blue amphitheater anchors one corner. It's a good spot for people watching until the heat drives you to the beach.

Offshore, Cayo Santiago—also known as Monkey Island—is the site of some of the world's most important rhesus monkey research. A small colony of monkeys was introduced to the island in the late 1930s, and since then scientists have been studying their habits and health, especially as they pertain to the study of diabetes and arthritis. You can't land at Cayo Santiago, but Captain Frank Lopez sails a small tour boat—*La Paseadora Naguabeña*—around it.

Beach

Off Route 3 just outside Naguabo, **Playa Húcares** is *the* place to be. Casual outdoor eateries and funky shops vie with the water for your attention. Two Victorian-style houses anchor one end of the waterfront promenade; a dock with excursion boats anchors the other.

Where to Stay & Eat

¢–$$ ✕ **Chumar.** As at the other food kiosks on Playa Húcares, you order at the counter and then grab a seat at one of the plastic tables that line the sidewalk. Paper plates and plastic cutlery accompany the yummy, down-home seafood. ✉ *Rte. 3, Km 66.5* ☎ *No phone* ▭ *MC, V.*

¢–$ ✕ **El Bobby.** This outdoor eatery is one of many in a cluster—the local version of a food court—on Playa Húcares. The fare is unpretentious: fish dishes, deep-fried meat- or seafood-stuffed snacks, and well-chilled beer. On weekends, this place is packed. ✉ *Rte. 3, Km 66.5* ☎ *No phone* ▭ *MC, V.*

$ **Casa Cubuy Ecolodge.** El Yunque's southern edge is the setting for this hotel. If you're up for a hike, trails from the lodge lead to a waterfall. If you'd rather relax, hammocks await you on the tiled verandah. Guest rooms are simple—no phones or TVs—but comfortable, with tile floors, rattan furniture, white bedspreads, plenty of windows and balconies. You must climb many stairs to reach the upper rooms; if this a problem request a room on the lower level. The proprietor, who believes that healthful eating translates into healthful living, serves breakfasts that are both tasty and wholesome. Light picnic lunches can also be ordered in the morning to take with you on hikes. ✉ *Rte. 191, Km 22, Barrio Río Blanco, 00744* ☎ *787/874–6221* 🌐 *www.casacubuy.com* *8 rooms* *Fans, hiking; no a/c, no room TVs, no smoking* ▭ *AE, MC, V* *BP.*

Sports & the Outdoors

Captain Frank Lopez will sail you around Cayo Santiago aboard ***La Paseadora Naguabeña*** (✉ Playa Húcares dock, Rte. 3, Km 66.6 ☎ 787/850–7881). Lopez, a charming, well-informed guide, gears the outings to the group. In an hour or 90 minutes, you can motor around the island and watch the monkeys. You can also make arrangements in advance for snorkeling stops or for the captain to drop you off at another islet and pick you up later.

Humacao

18 *15 km (9 mi) southwest of Naguabo; 55 km (34 mi) southeast of San Juan.*

Humacao, a city of 52,000, is a southeastern powerhouse. It's an educational center and has a growing industrial sector that's slowly replacing the agriculture-based economy. Although it's not considered a tourist destination, it's the city associated with the sprawling Palmas del Mar resort, which is outside town. At this writing, the resort and its casino were closed but expected to reopen sometime in late 2004 or early 2005. However, the two exceptional golf courses are still open. Downtown Humacao, with its narrow, heavily trafficked streets, contains some interesting neocolonial architecture.

Museo Casa Roig, the former residence of sugarcane plantation owner and banker Antonio Roig Torruellas, was built in 1919. Czech architect Antonio Nechodoma designed the facade, unusual for its wide eaves, mosaic work, and stained-glass windows with geometric patterns. This was Puerto Rico's first 20th-century building to go on the register of National Historic Places. The Roig family lived in the home until 1956, and it was then abandoned before being turned over to the University of Puerto Rico in 1977. It's currently a museum and cultural center, with historical photos, furniture, and rotating exhibits of works by contemporary island artists. ✉ *66 Calle Antonio López* ☎ *787/852–8380* 🌐 *www.uprh.edu/~museocr* 🎫 *Free* ⏲ *Wed.–Fri. and Sun. 10–4.*

Plaza de Humacao, downtown's broad square, is anchored by the pale pink Catedral Dulce Nombre de Jesús (Sweet Name of Jesus Cathedral), which dates from 1869. It has a castlelike facade, and even when its grille door is locked, you can peek through to see the sleek altar, polished floors, and stained-glass windows dominated by blues. Across the plaza, four fountains splash under the shade of old trees. People pass through feeding the pigeons, children race down the promenade, and retirees congregate on benches to chat. Look for the little monument with the globe on top; it's a tribute to city sons who died in wars. ✉ *Av. Font Martel at Calle Ulises Martinez.*

As you travel from Naguabo to Humacao, there are stretches of beach and swaths of undeveloped land, including the swamps, lagoons, and forested areas of the **Refugio de Vida Silvestre de Humacao.** This nature reserve has recreational areas, an information office, restrooms, children's activities, and camping sites. Fishing and hiking are allowed in some parts, but you should check to see what permits are required. ✉ *Rte. 3, Km 74.3* ☎ *787/852–6088 or 787/724–2500* 🎫 *Free* ⏲ *Weekdays 7:30–4, weekends 7:30–5:30.*

Beach

Right beside the Refugio de Vida Silvestre de Humacao, north of the city on Route 3, is **Playa Punta Santiago,** a long strand with closely planted palm trees that are perfect for stringing up hammocks. The beach, one of 12 government-operated public beaches, has changing facilities with showers and and restrooms, food kiosks, and lifeguard stations. Parking is $3.

Where to Stay & Eat

$$$–$$$$ ✕ **Bamboo.** A distinctive menu—heavy on seafood and classic European preparations—reigns at this elegant restaurant in the Palmas del Mar Country Club. Start off with a grilled sushi salad or roasted quail on a bed of onion medallions. The sautéed salmon is served with a bath of herbs and white-truffle mashed potatoes, the grilled dorado with a mango chutney. Grilled Colorado lamb chops in a pommery mustard crust come with garlic oven-baked potatoes, while lobster comes in a classic French *beurre blanc* sauce. ✉ *Palmas del Mar Country Club, Rte. 906, Km 86.4* ☎ *787/285–2277 or 787/285–2266* ✍ *Reservations essential* 💳 *AE, MC, V* ⏲ *No lunch. No dinner Sun. and Mon.*

$$–$$$ ✕ **Chez Daniel.** The dockside setting and casual atmosphere belie the elegance of Chef Daniel Vasse's meals. His French country–style dishes are noteworthy, and the Catalan-style *bouillinade,* full of fresh fish and bursting with the flavor of a white garlic sauce, is exceptional. When the stars are out and the candles are lit, this spot is 100% romantic. ✉ *Palmas del Mar Marina, Rte. 906, Km 86.4* ☎ *787/852–6000* ✍ *Reservations essential* 💳 *AE, MC, V* ⏲ *Closed Tues.*

$–$$ ✕ **Otoki Bar & Grill.** This friendly, casual bar and restaurant at the Palmas del Mar Country Club has a surprisingly lively menu. In addition to wraps, basic salads, and pizzas, there are also fried coconut shrimp and grilled dorado salad, and entrées like sautéed pork medallions in a wild-mushroom sauce. It's a good place for a drink or light snack if you come to play golf or tennis, even if you are not banking on dining out. ✉ *Palmas del Mar Country Club, Rte. 906, Km 86.4* ☎ *787/285–2277 or 787/285–2266* *Reservations essential* *AE, MC, V* *No dinner Mon.*

$–$$ ✕ **La Pesqueria.** It's difficult to find this rustic waterside restaurant. There's no sign, so be on the lookout for a busy parking lot and picnic tables. The day's fresh catch comes from the kitchen whole; if it's available, the red snapper is especially good as are any of the menu's snacks. ✉ *Off Rte. 906, near Palmas del Mar Marina* ☎ *No phone* *No credit cards.*

LODGING ALTERNATIVES Although El Candelario, the hotel, is closed through the end of 2004, there's a 106-unit time-share complex and more than 100 villas at **Palmas del Mar** (✉ Rte. 906 ☎ 787/852–6000 787/852–6320 www.palmasdelmar.com). These luxury villas are expensive but in a highly prized area, and there's no shortage of activities here, despite the absence of the hotel and casino.

Punta Santiago, north of Humacao, is one of five vacation centers run by the government. Cabins cost $65.40 per night and larger villas $109 nightly. There's a two-night minimum, and renters must supply linens and cooking utensils. For more information call **Punta Santiago Vacation Center** (☎ 787/852–1660 or 787/850–6628).

Sports & the Outdoors

FISHING **Shiraz Charters** (✉ Rte. 906, Palmas del Mar Resort, Site 6 ☎ 787/285–5718 www.charternet.com/fishers/shiraz) specializes in deep-sea fishing charters in search of tuna. Eight-hour trips start about $150 per person, including equipment and snacks.

GOLF **Palmas del Mar Resort** (✉ Rte. 906 ☎ 787/285–2256) has two good golf courses: the Rees Jones–designed Flamboyán course is named for the nearly six dozen flamboyant trees that pepper its fairway. The course winds around a lake, over a river, and to the sea before turning toward sand dunes and wetlands. The older, Gary Player–designed Palmas course has a challenging par 5 that scoots around wetlands. Greens fees are $70 to $100.

EASTERN PUERTO RICO A TO Z

To research prices, get advice from other travelers, and book travel arrangements, visit www.fodors.com.

AIR TRAVEL

In peak season, Isla Nena Air Service, M & N Aviation, and Vieques Air Link offer several daily flights from San Juan and Fajardo to Vieques and Culebra; trips last about 30 minutes from San Juan and 10 minutes from Fajardo; the cost ranges from $75 to $120 round-trip from

San Juan and from $25 to $38 round-trip from Fajardo. There are also daily flights (about 15 minutes) between San Juan and Fajardo.

Carriers **Isla Nena Air Service** ☎ 787/741-6362 🌐 www.islanena.8m.com. **M & N Aviation** ☎ 787/722-5980. **Vieques Air Link** ☎ 888/901-9247 or 787/722-3736.

AIRPORTS

Travelers from outside Puerto Rico generally fly into San Juan's Aeropuerto Internacional Luis Muñoz Marín and then transfer to Aeropuerto Fernando L. Rivas Dominici (also known as the Isla Grande Airport) for flights elsewhere on the island. Fajardo is served by the small Aeropuerto Diego Jiménez Torres, which is just southwest of the city on Route 976. The tiny Aeropuerto Antonio Rivera Rodríguez is on Vieques's northwest coast, less than a 15-minute cab ride from Isabel Segunda. Culebra's Aeropuerto Benjamin Rivera Noriega is at the north end of Calle Escudero, which runs right into downtown Dewey. The landing field at Aeropuerto Regional de Humacao is used mostly by private planes.

Aeropuerto Antonio Rivera Rodríguez ☎ 787/741-8358. **Aeropuerto Benjamin Rivera Noriega** ☎ 787/742-0022. **Aeropuerto Diego Jiménez Torres** ☎ 787/860-3110. **Aeropuerto Fernando L. Rivas Dominici** ☎ 787/729-8790. **Aeropuerto Internacional Luis Muñoz Marín** ☎ 787/791-4670. **Aeropuerto Regional de Humacao** ☎ 787/852-8188.

BUS TRAVEL

Puerto Rico's bus system is inefficient and difficult to use if you don't know the island well and/or don't speak Spanish fluently. There are two basic services: the *públicos* (minivans run by transportation cooperatives) and local, city buses. Públicos travel between San Juan and Fajardo (with a stop at the ferry terminal) Monday through Saturday from 4 AM to 6 PM. The full journey can take up to two hours; fares run up to $5, depending on where you board and where you are dropped off, and you pay the driver directly (it's not necessary to tip). There are no central terminals and no information numbers: you simply flag públicos down anywhere along the route (most of which is Route 3).

Within cities and towns, local buses pick up and discharge at marked stops and cost 35¢ to 50¢. You enter and pay (the exact fair is required) at the front of the bus and exit at the front or the back. Vieques and Culebra are served by their own inexpensive públicos, whose drivers often speak English. Just flag them down. Rates vary depending on your destination, but are usually under $1.

CAR RENTAL

If you rent a car at the San Juan airport, you'll have a choice of major car-rental agencies. On Vieques and Culebra, by contrast, you'll find primarily local agencies, including several that specialize in SUVs. Rates generally start about $25 a day, but it's sometimes possible to rent directly from your lodging, so ask about packages that include lodging and a car or SUV rental.

Agencies **Acevedo's Car Rental** ✉ Rte. 201, Km 1.0, Vieques ☎ 787/741-4380. **Carlos Jeep Rental Rental** ✉ Culebra ☎ 787/742-3514. **Culebra Car Rental** ✉ Benjamin Rivera Noriega Airport, Culebra ☎ 787/742-3277. **L & M** ✉ Rte. 3 Marginal, Km 43.8, Fajardo ☎ 787/860-6868 🌐 www.lmcarrental.com. **Leaseway of Puerto Rico** ✉ Rte. 3, Km 44.4, Fajardo ☎ 787/860-5000. **Martineau Car Rental** ✉ Rte. 200, Km 3.4, Vieques

☎ 787/636-7071 🌐 www.enchanted-isle.com/martineaucar. **Prestige Car Rental** ✉ Benjamin Rivera Noriega Airport, Culebra ☎ 787/742-3242.

CAR TRAVEL

From San Juan, the east coast is accessible via Route 3 or Route 187 if you want to visit Loíza. At Fajardo, the road intersects with Route 53, a fast toll road that continues down the coast. Route 3, however, also continues along the coast and provides a more scenic, if slower, trip. Although Puerto Ricans are good about giving directions, be sure to get good maps before you set out.

EMERGENCY SERVICES Rental-car agencies usually give customers emergency road-service numbers to call. There's no AAA service on Puerto Rico.

GASOLINE Gas stations are found along major roads and within cities and towns. Gasoline is sold in liters, not gallons. Although few eastern stations have round-the-clock hours, many are open until midnight and most are open seven days a week. Note that gas is rarely self-service; an attendant usually pumps it.

PARKING Although parking can be a nightmare (a pricey one at that) in San Juan, it's no problem out on the island except during festivals. Some mid-size cities have metered on-street parking as well as lots; in smaller communities street parking is the norm, and it's generally free. You should be aware that some of the bigger resorts—the El Conquistador is a notable example—charge for parking.

ROAD CONDITIONS The main roads are in good shape, but many highway exit and other signs have been blown down by hurricanes and may or may not have been replaced. When it rains, be alert for flash flooding, even on the major highways.

EMERGENCIES

Emergency Numbers **General** ☎ 911. **Medical Clinics** ☎ 787/876-2042, 787/876-2429 in Loíza, 787/823-2550, 787/887-2020 in Río Grande, 787/889-2620, 787/889-2020 in Luquillo, 787/863-2550, 787/863-2020 in Fajardo, 787/874-7440, 787/874-2020 in Naguabo.

Hospitals **Hospital Dr. Dominguez** ✉ 300 Font Martello, Humacao ☎ 787/852-0505. **Hospital Gubern** ✉ 110 Antonio R. Barcelo, Fajardo ☎ 787/863-0294. **Hospital San Pablo del Este** ✉ General Valero, Km 2.4, Fajardo ☎ 787/863-0505. **Ryder Memorial Hospital** ✉ Salida Humacao-Las Piedras, Humacao ☎ 787/852-0768.

Pharmacies **Farmacia Mediania** ✉ Rte. 187, Km 7.0, Loíza ☎ 787/876-1927. **Walgreens** ✉ Fajardo Plaza, Fajardo ☎ 787/860-1060 ✉ Oriental Plaza, Humacao ☎ 787/852-1868.

ENGLISH-LANGUAGE MEDIA

Puerto Rico has one English-language daily newspaper, the *San Juan Star,* which is circulated all over the island and on the off-islands. English-language magazines and books are readily available in shopping malls and in hotel shops on the island's eastern side, although proper bookstores are in short supply outside of metropolitan San Juan.

FERRY TRAVEL

The Puerto Rico Ports Authority runs passenger ferries from Fajardo to Culebra and Vieques. Service is from a terminal in the Fajardo port zone at the end of Route 195, about a 90-minute drive from San Juan. The terminal office is open daily from 8 to 11 and 1 to 3; a municipal parking lot next to the ferry costs $5 a day, handy if you are going to one of the islands just for the day. On Culebra, the ferry pulls right into downtown Dewey. The Vieques ferry dock is within walking distance of downtown Isabel Segunda.

FARES & SCHEDULES The ferry from Fajardo to Vieques runs three times a day, seven days a week; the one from Fajardo to Culebra operates twice a day, seven days a week. Although there's a published schedule, it's always best to phone and confirm the departure times. The Vieques trip costs $2 one way; for Culebra it's $2.25. The ferry takes about 45 minutes to Vieques, just under 90 minutes to Culebra.

Culebra ferry terminal ☎ 787/742-3161. **Fajardo ferry terminal** (Fajardo Port Authority) ☎ 787/863-4560. **Vieques ferry terminal** ☎ 787/741-4761.

MAIL & SHIPPING

Puerto Rico is part of the U.S. postal system, and most communities of any size have multiple branches of the post office. Some aren't open on Saturday, however. Big hotels and resorts also have postal drop boxes.

Post Offices **Fajardo main post office** ✉ 102 Calle Garrido Morales E, Fajardo ☎ 787/863-0802. **Naguabo main post office** ✉ 100 Rte. 31, Naguabo ☎ 787/874-3115. **Vieques main post office** ✉ 97 Calle Muñoz Rivera, Suite 103, Isabel Segunda, Vieques ☎ 787/741-3891.

OVERNIGHT SERVICES Puerto Rico has express overnight mail delivery through the U.S. Postal Service as well as Federal Express, which usually operates through office supply stores or other commercial outlets. (Note that FedEx doesn't offer Saturday pickup on the island.)

Office Max ✉ Rte. 3, Fajardo ☎ 800/463-3339. **Post Net** ✉ Rte. 3, Río Grande ☎ 800/463-3339 ✉ 118 Av. Ortiz Estela, Humacao ☎ 800/463-3339.

MONEY MATTERS

Banks and ATMs (or ATHs, as they're known here) are plentiful. Banks are usually open weekdays from 9 to 5; very few have hours on Saturday, and those that do are open only until noon.

Banco Popular ✉ 115 Muñoz Rivera, Isabel Segunda, Vieques ☎ 787/741-2071 ✉ Rte. 3, Km 42.4, Fajardo ☎ 787/860-1570. **Banco Roig** ✉ 55 Calle Antonio Lopez, Humacao ☎ 787/852-8601. **Citibank** ✉ 15 Calle Pedro Marquez, Dewey, Culebra ☎ 787/742-0220. **Westernbank** ✉ Calderón Mujica at L. M. Rivera, Canóvanas ☎ 787/876-3745.

SAFETY

Although crime isn't as high in the island's eastern areas as it is in San Juan, use prudence. Avoid bringing valuables with you to the beach; if you must do so, be sure not to leave them in view in your car. It's best to keep your car locked while driving, and avoid out-of-the way beaches after sunset.

LOCAL SCAMS If in doubt about another motorist's behavior (or you suspect a fender bender is part of a scam), drive to a populated area, a gas station, or highway toll booth rather than stopping. Such scams aren't common, but they happen from time to time.

TAXIS

You can flag cabs down on the street, but it's faster and safer to have your hotel call one for you. Either way, make sure the driver is clear on whether he or she will charge a flat rate or use a meter to determine the fare. In most places, the cabs are metered.

Fajardo Taxi Service ☎ 787/860-1112. **Humacao Taxi** ☎ 787/852-6880. **Lolo Felix Tours** ✉ Vieques ☎ 787/485-5447. **Ruben's Taxi** ✉ Culebra ☎ 787/405-1209.

TELEPHONES

The area codes in Puerto Rico are 787 and 939. Public phones are abundant throughout the island. They operate with phone cards, credit cards, and coins (25¢ for a local call). You need to dial the area code, even for local calls, but not the "1" prefix unless it's a long-distance number.

TOURS

Captain James Smith's Blackbeard West Indies Charter offers fishing and dive-boat excursions out of Fajardo; prices start at about $45 for half-day dive trips. East Wind has sailing, snorkeling, and beachcombing excursions aboard a 62-foot catamaran; a packaged half-day trip costs about $55. Culebra Divers is one of that island's best-known operators for diving and snorkeling trips; prices vary depending on whether classes are involved and the duration of the trip. A three-hour snorkeling excursion, for example, starts at about $30. Vieques Nature Tours arranges educational snorkeling trips on glass-bottom boats; these trips are popular with children, and rates depend on group size. (Note that Vieques Nature Tours has no office; you must call to arrange tours.)

Blackbeard West Indies Charter HC-01 Box 13025, Río Grande 00745 ☎ 787/887-4818. **Culebra Divers** ✉ 4 Calle Pedro Marquez, Dewey, Culebra ☎ 787/742-0803 www.culebradivers.com. **East Wind** ✉ Puerto del Rey Marina, Rte. 3, Km 51.4, Fajardo ☎ 787/860-3434 www.eastwindcats.com. **Vieques Nature Tours** ☎ 787/741-1980.

VISITOR INFORMATION

The island's tourism offices are hit and miss when it comes to helpful material. The cities usually offer information through offices connected to city hall, and most are open only during business hours on weekdays. The tourism desk in Isabel Segunda's city hall has information on bike rental, maps and brochures, and details on how to reach all the beaches on Vieques. The *Vieques Times* and *Vieques Events,* both monthly newsletters, are useful, as is the bimonthly tabloid *El Nuevo Vieques.*

Culebra Tourism Office ✉ 250 Calle Pedro Marquez, Dewey, Culebra ☎ 787/742-3521. **Fajardo Tourism Office** ✉ 6 Av. Muñz Rivera, Fajardo ☎ 787/863-4013 Ext. 274. **Luquillo Tourism Office** ✉ 154 Calle 14 de Julio St., Luquillo ☎ 787/889-2225. **Naguabo Tourism Office** ✉ Rte. 3, Km 66.6, Playa Húcares, Naguabo ☎ 787/874-0389. **Río Grande Office of Tourism and Culture** ✉ Calle San José, Plaza de Recreo, Río Grande ☎ 787/887-2370. **Vieques Tourism Office** ✉ 449 Calle Carlos Lebrón, Isabel Segunda, Vieques ☎ 787/741-5000 Ext. 26.

WEB SITES

The Enchanted Isles www.enchanted-isle.com

SOUTHERN PUERTO RICO

3

SEE 500 YEARS OF HISTORY
in San Germán ⇨ *p.147*

IT'S WORTH DRIVING FROM SAN JUAN
to dine at Mark's at the Meliá ⇨ *p.140*

CABO ROJO'S BEST BEACH
is Balneario Boquerón ⇨ *p.152*

TRANQUILLITY REIGNS
at Mary Lee's by the Sea ⇨ *p.145*

FEEL THE GENTLE BREEZE AS YOU DINE
at Sand and the Sea ⇨ *p.126*

VIEW THE WIDE-RANGING COLLECTION
at the Museo de Arte de Ponce ⇨ *p.139*

Updated by Martin Delfin

FROM LUSH TROPICAL MOUNTAINS to arid seacoast plains, Puerto Rico's southern region lets you sample the island from a local's perspective. The south is where San Juan families escape the hustle and bustle of the city for weekends on the beach. Though rich in history, the area also provides ample opportunities for golf, swimming, hiking, and cave exploration. Snaking roads between major highways reveal a glimpse of how rural Puerto Ricans enjoy life. Every mile or so, you'll see a café or bar, which is the social center of activity for neighbors. The only traffic jams you'll likely incur will be caused by slow-moving farmers taking their goods to the local market.

Agriculture is very important to the economy of southern Puerto Rico. Coffee, pineapples, bananas, and plantains are grown throughout the region. The island's largest beef producer has a sprawling ranch near Salinas. But heavy industry—including the largest cement factory in the Caribbean—can be found in Ponce.

Called the "Pearl of the South," Ponce was founded in 1692 by farmers attracted to the rich soil, which was perfect for growing sugar cane. Evidence found at the Tibes Indian ceremonial site, just north of Ponce, suggests that people have been living here as far back as 400 BC. Many residents still carry the last names of the dozens of European pioneer families who settled here during the 19th century. The region's largest city, Ponce is home to one of the island's most important art museums and a pre-Lenten festival. Nearby San Germán, the second-oldest city in Puerto Rico, is known for its two historic main squares and well-preserved in a wide variety of architectural styles. High in the mountains, such towns as Aibonito and Barranquitas have steep streets and spectacular views.

On the coast, Guayama, Arroyo, and Patillas show off their splendors as little-known destinations for beachgoers. But the real beach party takes off during the long Easter weekend in Cabo Rojo, where two resort areas, Boquerón and Combate, attract a young but noisy crowd. Nowhere is underwater life so visual during the night than in La Parguera, whose bioluminescent bay draws people from all over.

If you're willing to explore beyond the casinos, high-rises, and daily traffic congestion of the island's capital, the south is a wise escape from the island's usual tourist fare. Don't be surprised by the help many of its residents will offer whether you ask for it or not. Southern *puertorriqueños* are known for their friendliness as well as their hospitality.

Exploring Southern Puerto Rico

Less than an hour's drive south from San Juan on the Luis A. Ferré Expressway (Route 52) brings you to an elevation of almost 3,000 feet as you cross the Cordillera Central (central mountain range) into southern Puerto Rico. Towns such as Cayey, Aibonito, and Barranquitas are cooler than those on the coastal plain; in winter, overnight temperatures can drop into the 40s when it's in the 60s or 70s on the coast. Elsewhere, southern Puerto Rico is drier and hotter than the north or east. Although

If you have
3 days

Head south from San Juan to **Ponce** 9–21 via Route 52, stopping for a seafood lunch in **Salinas** 7 before touring Ponce's historical center. On the following day, visit some of the other attractions in and around the city, perhaps the Museo de Arte de Ponce, the Castillo Serrallés, or the Centro Ceremonial Indígena de Tibes. Dedicate your final day to **Guánica** 22, where you'll find wonderful beaches and the Bosque Estatal de Guánica.

If you have
5 days

Make a leisurely trip south from San Juan on Route 52, spending a night in one of the mountain towns. You can take the thermal waters of **Coamo** 8, thought by some to be Ponce de León's Fountain of Youth. If you're a serious hiker, seek out El Cañon de San Cristóbal. Continue to **Ponce** 9–21 for two days of exploring. Travel west along the coast and settle at a waterfront hotel near either **Guánica** 22 or **Cabo Rojo** 36. For your last two days, stretch out an a beach or hike the Bosque Estatal de Guánica.

If you have
7 days

Travel to **Cabo Rojo** 36, making it your base for four days of sunbathing, snorkeling the reefs, hiking in the Bosque Estatal de Guánica, and exploring colonial **San Germán** 25–35. Set aside a night for dinner at one of the many fine seafood restaurants in nearby Joyuda. If your trip falls during a new moon, take a nighttime excursion to the Bahía Fosforescente to see the shining dinoflagellates. Finish up with three days of sightseeing in **Ponce** 9–21.

El Yunque in the east gets an average of 200 inches of rain yearly, the southwestern town of Guánica averages 30 inches.

The southeastern part of the island—which includes a section of the scenic Ruta Panorámica (Panoramic Route)—has a rugged shoreline, where cliffs drop right into the water. Covered with dry vegetation, the southwest's ragged coast has wonderful inlets and bays and jagged peninsulas that make for breathtaking views.

Numbers in the text correspond to numbers in the margin and on the Southern Puerto Rico, Ponce Centro, Greater Ponce, and San Germán maps.

About the Restaurants

Open-air dining and traditional Puerto Rican cuisine are the norm south of the cordillera. Some of more ambitious restaurants are experimenting, which means you might find chicken or pork with tamarind or guava sauce or fish in a plantain crust. The southern coast—especially the city of Salinas and the Joyuda area in Cabo Rojo—is known for seafood. Along Route 184, near Cayey, look for *lechoneras,* restaurants serving slow-roasted *lechón* (pork), a local delicacy cooked outdoors over coals. Reservations are usually optional, but you might want to make them on weekends in the more touristy areas. A 15% to 20% tip is customary; most restaurants won't include it in the bill, but it's wise to check.

WHAT IT COSTS In U.S. dollars					
	$$$$	$$$	$$	$	¢
AT DINNER	over $30	$20–$30	$12–$20	$8–$12	under $8

Prices are per person for a main course at dinner.

About the Hotels

Modest, family-oriented establishments near beaches or in small towns are the most typical accommodations. Because the southeast is so popular with islanders, some hotels consider summer their high season and have lower rates in winter, contrary to the norm in the rest of the island. Southern Puerto Rico doesn't have the abundance of luxury hotels and resorts found to the north and east; however, the Hilton Ponce & Casino and the Copamarina Beach Resort in Guánica are self-contained complexes with the breadth of facilities and services.

WHAT IT COSTS In U.S. dollars					
	$$$$	$$$	$$	$	¢
FOR 2 PEOPLE	over $350	$250–$350	$150–$250	$80–$150	under $80

Prices are for a double room in high season, excluding 9% tax (11% for hotels with casinos, 7% for paradores) and 5%–12% service charge.

Timing

The temperate climate of the mountainous central zone makes it a pleasure to visit year-round. Locals especially like to head up to this area in summer, when Aibonito holds its Flower Festival (late June or July), and Barranquitas hosts its Artisans Fair (July). The resort towns of Cabo Rojo, Guánica, and La Parguera are also popular with residents over Easter weekend and in summer, when children are out of school. Ponce's spirited pre-Lenten Carnival, held the week before Ash Wednesday, draws many visitors. Note that during busy times, some *paradores* and hotels require a minimum two- or three-night stay on weekends.

CENTRAL SOUTHERN PUERTO RICO

In this mountainous region on the southern side of the Cordillera Central, church steeples rise above villages, trees arch over winding roads that also serve as cattle crossings. In spring, *flamboyáns* (flamboyant trees) transform green hills into a vermilion conflagration. By the time the Luis A. Ferré Expressway (Route 52) hits the city of Cayey, known for the views from its hillside restaurants, you truly feel "*en la isla*" ("out on the island"). At about 2,000 feet above sea level, Aibonito is the island's highest town. It's called "The Queen of Flowers" because of the abundant flora that thrive there. Barranquitas is more remote, nevertheless history claims it as a cradle of intellectuals. This quaint town is revered as the home of patriot Luis Muñoz Rivera.

Leaving the Cordillera Central, the scenery becomes drier and more rugged. The Caribbean sparkles in the distance, and the plain between

Beaches You'll find surfing beaches, like Inches near Patillas, and calm bays for swimming, such as Boquerón Beach in Cabo Rojo. Ballena Bay, near Guánica, has oft-deserted sandy stretches. Boat operators make trips to such uninhabited cays as Gilligan's Island off the coast of Guánica and Caja de Muertos off Ponce.

Diving & Snorkeling Southern Puerto Rico is an undiscovered dive destination, which means unspoiled reefs and lots of fish. You can arrange for dive boats at Caribe Playa Beach Resort in the southeast, Ponce's La Guancha, and the Hotel Copamarina in the southwest. Shore diving and snorkeling are best around islands or cays or along the western coast between Ponce and Cabo Rojo.

Hiking Vegetation in the region's two reserves is dramatically different: the Bosque Estatal Carite between Cayey and Patillas is a tropical rain forest; outside Guánica is a rare dry tropical forest. Both provide excellent bird-watching. Guides take you on tours through Cañon de San Cristóbal near Aibonito, the island's deepest gorge. The walk to the Cabo Rojo Lighthouse along the rugged cliffs at the southwesternmost tip of the island is beautiful, especially at sunset. There are good trails throughout the area, but printed guides to routes outside the reserves are rare. Ask locals for directions to their favorite paths.

---

the sea and the mountains, once the heart of the sugarcane industry, is now the domain of cattle. Tucked into the foothills, Coamo, an important center in Spanish times and a popular thermal springs resort since the early 1900s, has many historical buildings. The strip malls and shopping centers lining the route into Ponce, "The Pearl of the South," belie its charming colonial center.

Cayey

❶ *50 km (30 mi) south of San Juan.*

Since it was founded in 1773, Cayey has attracted both visitors and settlers. Early on, the Spanish realized that the valley surrounding it was perfect for growing coffee and tobacco. Later, people were simply drawn by the refreshing breezes. Today its population of some 56,000 swells—particularly on weekends—with *sanjuaneros* (residents of San Juan) who shop in the strip malls on its outskirts, dine in its hillside restaurants, or picnic in the nearby Bosque Estatal Carite.

In the 7,000-acre **Bosque Estatal Carite,** 40 km (25 mi) of trails run through stands of palms, Honduras mahogany, and Spanish cedars—many of which host orchids. One trail leads to Charco Azul (Blue Pond), whose cool waters appeal to overheated hikers. Before setting out, get hiking information at the park manager's office near the entrance on Route 184. If you'd like a space in one of the two campgrounds, be

Southern Puerto Rico

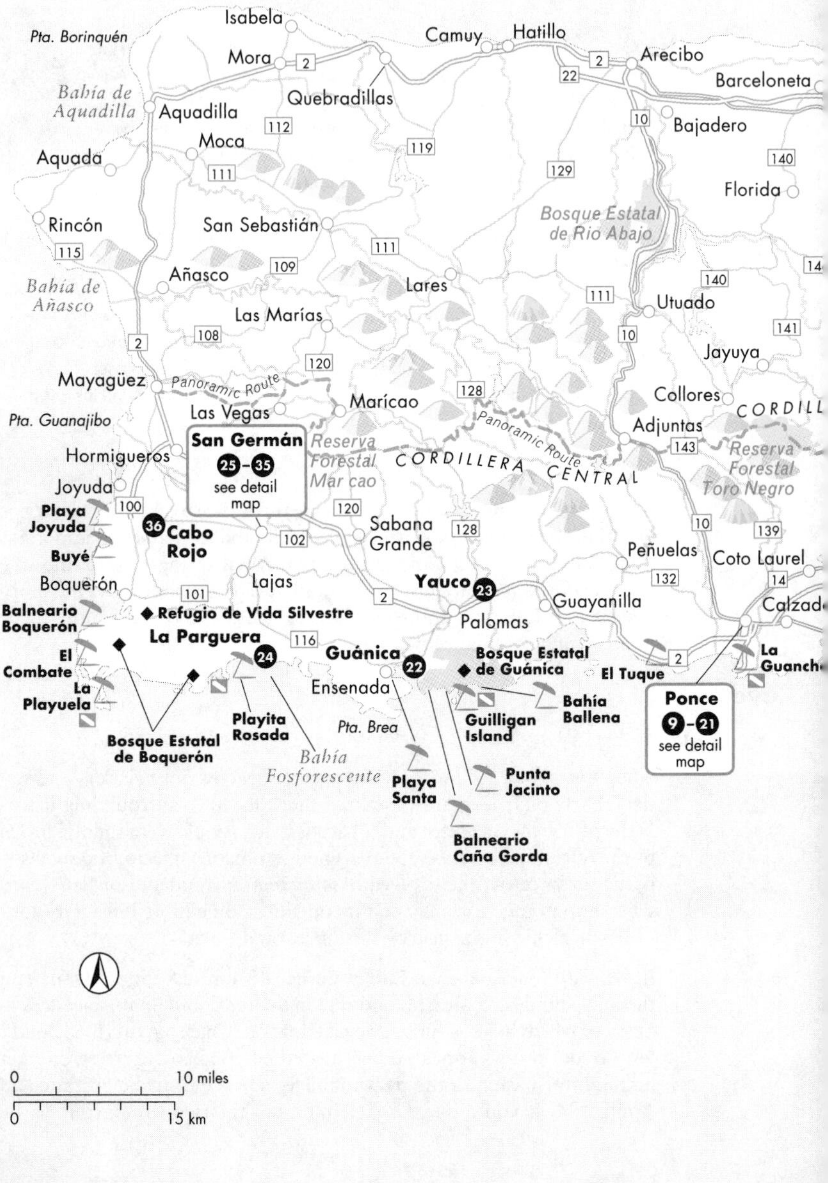

Pta. Borinquén
Isabela
Mora
Camuy
Hatillo
Arecibo
Barceloneta
Bahía de Aquadilla
Aquadilla
Quebradillas
Bajadero
Moca
Aquada
Florida
Rincón
San Sebastián
Bosque Estatal de Rio Abajo
Bahía de Añasco
Añasco
Lares
Utuado
Las Marías
Jayuya
Mayagüez
Panoramic Route
Las Vegas
Marícao
Collores
Pta. Guanajibo
Adjuntas
CORDILL
Hormigueros
San Germán
25–35
see detail map
Reserva Forestal Mar cao
CORDILLERA CENTRAL
Reserva Forestal Toro Negro
Joyuda
Playa Joyuda
36 Cabo Rojo
Buyé
Sabana Grande
Peñuelas
Coto Laurel
Boquerón
Lajas
Yauco 23
Guayanilla
Calzad
Balneario Boquerón
◆ Refugio de Vida Silvestre
Palomas
La Parguera
24
Guánica 22
Bosque Estatal
◆ de Guánica
El Tuque
La Guanch
El Combate
La Playuela
Ensenada
Bahía Ballena
Guilligan Island
Ponce
9–21
see detail map
Pta. Brea
Playita Rosada
Bosque Estatal de Boquerón
Bahía Fosforescente
Playa Santa
Punta Jacinto
Balneario Caña Gorda

2, 22, 10, 112, 119, 111, 129, 140, 115, 109, 14, 108, 141, 120, 128, 143, 100, 139, 102, 132, 101, 116

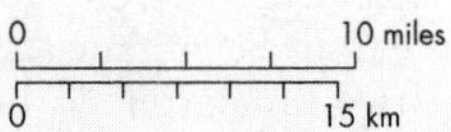

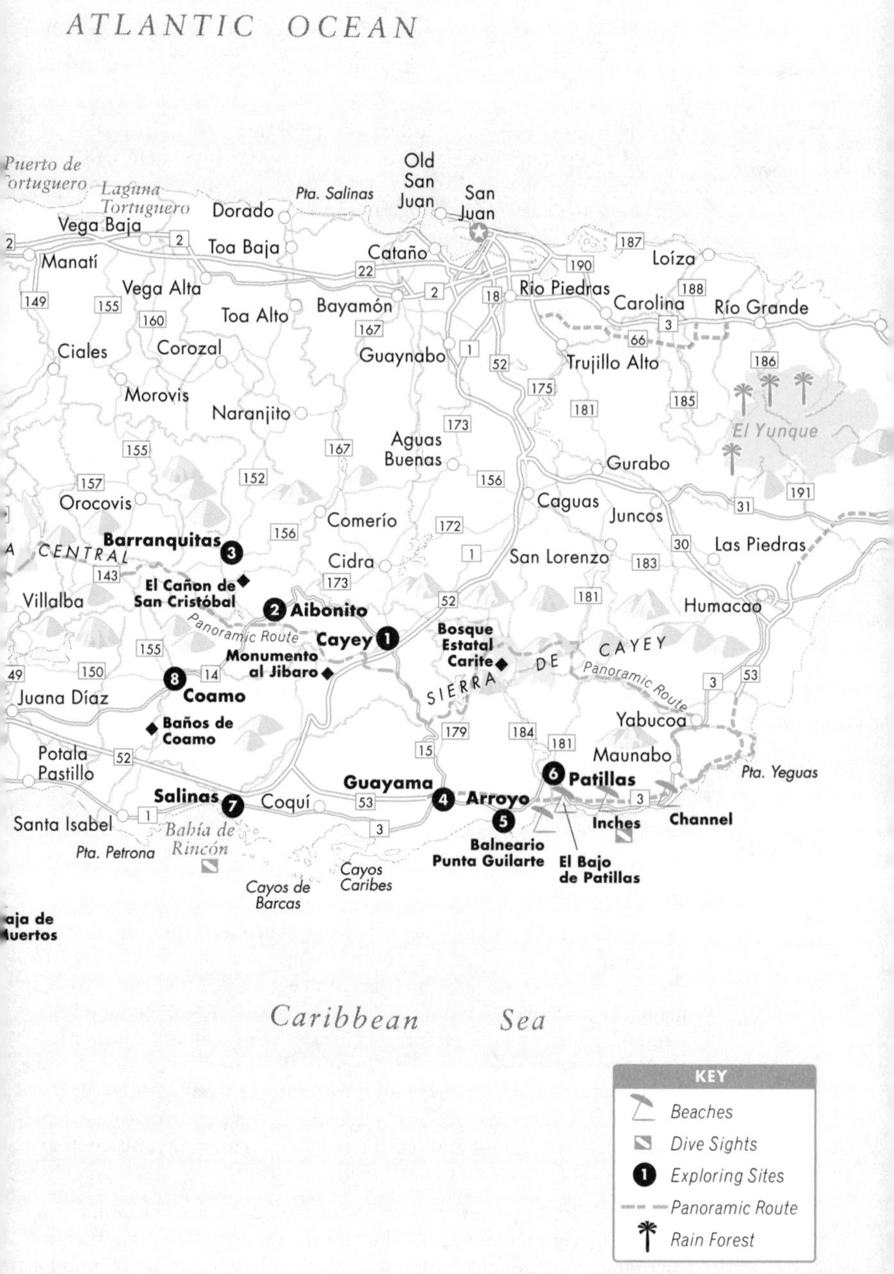

ATLANTIC OCEAN

Puerto de Tortuguero
Laguna Tortuguero
Pta. Salinas
Old San Juan
San Juan
Vega Baja
Dorado
Toa Baja
Manatí
Cataño
Loíza
Vega Alta
Bayamón
Rio Piedras
Carolina
Río Grande
Toa Alto
Ciales
Corozal
Guaynabo
Trujillo Alto
Morovis
Naranjito
El Yunque
Aguas Buenas
Gurabo
Orocovis
Comerío
Caguas
Juncos
Barranquitas 3
CENTRAL
Cidra
San Lorenzo
Las Piedras
El Cañon de San Cristóbal
Villalba
2 Aibonito
Humacao
Panoramic Route
Cayey 1
Bosque Estatal Carite
Monumento al Jibaro
SIERRA DE CAYEY
Panoramic Route
8 Coamo
Juana Díaz
Yabucoa
Baños de Coamo
Maunabo
Potala Pastillo
6 Patillas
Pta. Yeguas
Guayama
Salinas 7
Coquí
4 Arroyo
Santa Isabel
5
Inches
Channel
Bahía de Rincón
Balneario Punta Guilarte
El Bajo de Patillas
Pta. Petrona
Cayos de Barcas
Cayos Caribes
Caja de Muertos

2, 22, 149, 155, 160, 167, 1, 18, 52, 187, 190, 188, 3, 66, 186, 175, 181, 185, 173, 156, 152, 157, 172, 191, 31, 30, 183, 143, 14, 150, 49, 179, 184, 15, 53

Caribbean Sea

sure to get a permit in advance from the Puerto Rico Department of Natural Resources in San Juan. Picnic tables are scattered throughout the forest, and bathroom facilities are available near the campgrounds. ✉ *Rte. 184, Km 20, Guavate Sector* ☎ *787/747–4545 or 787/724–3724, 787/724–3724 for camping permits* 🎟 *Free* ⏲ *Manager's office open weekdays 9–5.*

need a break?

Mouthwatering marinated lechón, slow-roasted over open pits, is offered at a string of **lechoneras** along Route 184 just before the entrance to the Bosque Estatal Carite. They also serve slow-roasted chicken and a variety of compatible side dishes. Traffic jams are legendary on Sunday, when locals gather here along the strip to spend the day eating and listening to local bands.

Where to Eat

$$–$$$ Fodor'sChoice ★ ✕ **Sand and the Sea.** In the open-air dining room, the south-coast views are breathtaking, and the evening breezes are cool enough that you might find the fireplace ablaze. Nightly piano performances of show tunes and Puerto Rican ballads take away any remaining chill, especially when they become sing-alongs. Grilled steak, known as churrasco, and seafood dominate the menu, which changes so often that it's posted on a blackboard. Try the Russian tostones (with sour cream and caviar). For overnight stays, four rooms (¢)—decorated like those in a New England bed-and-breakfast—are available, but be sure to make room reservations at least a week in advance. ✉ *Rte. 714, Km 5.2, Cercadillo Sector, 00736* ☎ *787/738–9086* 💳 *AE, D, MC, V* ⏲ *Closed Mon.–Thurs.*

¢–$ ✕ **Martin's BBQ.** Locals come to this restaurant, part of an island-wide chain, for a quick fix of traditional slow-roasted chicken with all the trimmings—rice and beans, *tostones* (fried plaintains), and yucca. You order your food at the counter, choosing precisely how much chicken and which side dishes you want. There are picnic tables outside, tables inside, and take-out service. ✉ *Rte. 1 at Cayey exit off Rte. 52* ☎ *787/738–1144* 💳 *MC, V.*

Aibonito

❷ *20 km (12 mi) northwest of Cayey.*

Legend has it that Aibonito got its name when a Spaniard exclaimed "*¡Ay, que bonito!*" ("Oh, how pretty!") upon seeing the valley where the town now stands. At 1,896 feet above sea level, it's Puerto Rico's highest city. Aibonito is known as "The Queen of Flowers" because flowering plants thrive in its temperate climate. The city hosts a flower festival every year, usually in late June or July, and gives awards for blossoms and garden design. Live music and craft stalls add to the festivities. A double-steeple cathedral graces the charming town square, which is surrounded by shops and restaurants. Local guides organize outings to nearby El Cañon de San Cristóbal.

Mirador Piedra Degetau (Degetau Lookout Rock) is a scenic point near Aibonito. From the tower, use the telescope to get a closer look at the surrounding mountains. You'll find picnic tables under gazebos and a playground nearby. ✉ *Rte. 7718, Km 0.7* ☎ *787/735–3880* 🎫 *Free* ⏲ *Wed.–Sun. 9–6.*

★ **El Cañon de San Cristóbal** is difficult to find without local help, but it's well worth the effort. Trails of tropical, but somewhat dry, vegetation lead to a breathtaking waterfall. Félix Rivera, a local guide, heads expeditions to the island's deepest gorge, starting from La Piedra restaurant. ☎ *787/735–5188, 787/644–5122 to contact Felix Rivera directly, 787/735–8721 to reserve a trip with Felix Rivera* 🎫 *Canyon free, guided hike about $20 per person depending on number of people guided* ⏲ *Canyon daily, hikes by appointment only.*

Where to Eat

$–$$$ ✕ **La Piedra.** Ingredients straight from the garden liven up the menu at this restaurant on the outskirts of Aibonito. If you're in the area on Sunday, try the excellent buffet of Puerto Rican food—*arroz con pollo* (rice with chicken), lechón, tostones, yucca, and rice and *gandules* (pigeon peas). ✉ *Rte. 7718, Km 0.8* ☎ *787/735–1034* 💳 *D, MC, V* ⏲ *No dinner Mon. and Tues.*

Barranquitas

❸ *15 km (9 mi) northwest of Aibonito.*

Founded in 1804, the small mountain town of Barranquitas appears to have changed little over the years. Its steep streets and quaint plaza seem light-years away from the frenetic energy of Puerto Rico's larger cities. Its tranquillity has made Barranquitas a popular location for summer homes. One of the most beautiful, **El Cortijo** (on Route 162 at Km 9.9), was built in 1938 and is said to be haunted by a former servant. Although it's closed to the public, consider stopping to admire the sprawling white structure from the road. You *can* visit the former home and the mausoleum of two of Barranquitas' most famous residents: Luis Muñoz Rivera, a politician and newspaperman, and his son, Luis Muñoz Marín, the island's first elected governor. In July, craftspeople gather in Barranquitas for the annual Feria Nacional de Artesanías (National Artisans Fair), one of the most popular such events on the island.

Museo Luis Muñoz Rivera, one block west of the main square, occupies the house where Luis Muñoz Rivera—a politician, poet, and journalist famous for his support of Puerto Rican autonomy—was born in 1859. Many personal belongings and the manuscripts of his political writings and poems are housed here. There's also a friend's car—a 1912 Pierce Arrow—which transported Muñoz to political events. The small wooden house is considered a superb example of 19th-century rural architecture. It's wise to call in advance; the museum doesn't always stick to its posted hours. ✉ *10 Calle Muñoz Rivera* ☎ *787/857–0230* 🎫 *Free* ⏲ *Mon.–Sat. 8:30–5.*

Steps away from Luis Muñoz Rivera's birthplace you'll find the **Mausoleo de la Familia Muñoz** (✉ Calle Padre Berríos, 2 blocks west of main plaza), where Muñoz Rivera and his son, Luis Muñoz Marín, are buried with other members of their family. There's a small, parklike area and a memorial to the two island politicians.

Where to Stay & Eat

¢–$$ ✕ **Casa Bavaria.** Enjoy a bit of Germany at this out-of-the-way eatery outside the town of Orocovis, about 16 km (10 mi) northwest of Barranquitas. Owned by Mike López, whose mother is German, and Mike's German-born wife, Martina Bolik, Casa Bavaria is a kitschy blend of biergarten and casual country restaurant. Choose bratwurst and sauerkraut or chicken with rice and beans. On weekends, patrons spend a good part of the day enjoying the view from the terrace, singing along with the jukebox, and joking with the waiters, many of whom speak German as well as English and Spanish. ✉ *Rte. 155, Km 38.3* ☎ *787/862–7818* 💳 *AE, MC, V* ⏲ *Closed Mon.–Wed.*

¢ ✕🏨 **Hacienda Margarita.** This secluded hotel just north of Barranquitas is known for its sweeping mountain views. Seventeen modern rooms—each with a balcony—are in a concrete building. Smaller wooden buildings house 10 other more rustic rooms that can accommodate up to four people bunkhouse-style. Smaller wooden buildings house 10 more rustic rooms that have two beds and can accommodate up to four people. Watch the sun go down from the outdoor terrace or dine in the restaurant ($–$$$), well known for its Puerto Rican cuisine. It's open Friday for dinner and Saturday and Sunday for lunch and dinner. ✉ *Rte. 152, Km 1.7* 📫 *Box 100, PMB 583, 00794* ☎ *787/857–0414* 📠 *787/857–1265* 🛏 *27 rooms* ♨ *Restaurant, cable TV, pool, meeting rooms* 💳 *MC, V* 🍽 *EP.*

Guayama

❹ *28 km (17 mi) southeast of Cayey; 49 km (31 mi) southeast of Barranquitas.*

Guayama was founded in 1736, but was destroyed by fire in the early 1800s. In the 19th century it recovered when the sugarcane industry grew and construction exploded. Examples of colonial and creole buildings can be seen throughout the city. One of the finest 19th-century creole homes is the Casa Cautiño on the main plaza, now a museum.

Guayama's 44,000 residents are proud of the claim that their city is the cleanest on the island. On Sunday, trolley tours of town start at the Casa Cautiño museum, often with the mayor at the wheel. The nearby countryside is home to Paso Fino horses. Each March at the Marcelino Blondet Stadium you can watch these high-stepping show horses strut their stuff during the Feria Dulce Sueño, a fair named after one of the island's most famous Paso Finos. Folk music and crafts are part of the festivities. At this writing, the much publicized El Legado Golf Resort, built by golf legend Chi Chi Rodríguez, was expected to open to the public by late 2004. On Route 53 between Salinas and Guayama, the 7,213-yard course will include 12 lakes and one green built on a small island in one of the lakes.

★ **Casa Cautiño** is an elegant home built in 1887 for sugar, cattle, and coffee baron Genaro Cautiño Vázquez and his wife, Genoveva Insúa. A balcony with ornate grillwork graces the exterior. You'll be swept back in time walking through the home's rooms, which are filled with Victorian and art-deco furniture. Don't miss the modern-for-its-time bathroom, complete with a standing shower. ✉ *1 Calle Palmer, at Calle Vicente Palé Matos* ☎ *787/864–9083* 🎟 *$1* ⏲ *Tues.–Sat. 9–4, Sun. 10–5.*

Where to Stay & Eat

¢–$ ✕ **El Suarito.** You're surrounded by history at this restaurant in a building that dates from 1862. The site has seen life as a repair shop for horse-drawn buggies, a gas station, and—since the mid-1950s—a restaurant. The place is always hopping with townspeople who stop by at all hours for a meal or a drink. You can get eggs and toast for breakfast, sandwiches throughout the day, and roasted chicken or pork chops for dinner. ✉ *6 Calle Derkes, at Calle Hostos* ☎ *787/864–1820* 💳 *MC, V* ⏲ *Closed Sun.*

¢ ✕ **Rex Cream.** The natural, tropical-fruit-flavor ice cream at this small shop in the center of town is hard to pass up. Flavors vary, depending on what's in season, but often include lime, pineapple, tamarind, and *guanábana* (soursop). You can also get milk shakes—the mango shake is outstanding. ✉ *24 Calle Derkes* ☎ *No phone* 💳 *No credit cards.*

$$ ✕🏨 **Molino Inn.** This tidy hotel is on the outskirts of Guayama, near the ruins of a Spanish *molino* (sugar mill). Nine acres of grounds—including flower beds and a large pool—surround its two buildings. Although the grounds are attractive and lush, the rooms are plain and provide only the basics. Join the local business crowd for the international and Caribbean cuisines at the Molinito restaurant ($–$$). There's often live music on weekends. ✉ *Av. Albizu Campos at Rte. 54* 📮 *Box 2393, 00785–2393* ☎ *787/866–1515* 📠 *787/866–1510* 🛏 *20 rooms* 👍 *Restaurant, cable TV, tennis court, pool, basketball, lounge, laundry service* 💳 *AE, MC, V* 🍽 *EP.*

Sports & the Outdoors

GOLF For $22, golfers can get in nine holes at the **Aguirre Golf Club** (✉ Rte. 705, Km 3, Aguirre ☎ 787/853–4025), built in 1925 for the executives of a local sugar mill. Open daily, it's known as a short but tough course. At this writing, the **El Legado Golf Resort** (✉ Rte. 153 at intersection 713 ☎ 787/648–1818 🌐 www.ellegadogolfresort.com) by golf legend and native son Chi Chi Rodríguez was scheduled to open in late 2004. The 7,213-yard 18-hole course has 12 lakes.

Arroyo

❺ *6 km (4 mi) east of Guayama.*

Arroyo is popular for its nearby beaches, especially Punta Guilarte, and its many fiestas. Its festival honoring the Virgin of Carmen, patron saint of fishermen, is held every July, and its fish festival is in October. Most of the events take place on the boardwalk along the *malecón* (sea wall), officially known as Paseo de Las Américas.

In 1855 Arroyo was a small but bustling port surrounded by cane fields. Today, remnants of its past are scattered throughout the town. The old customs house is now a museum, and a refurbished sugarcane train, which runs on weekends and holidays, is one of the main attractions. Arroyo also contributed to the development of modern communications. Samuel

F. B. Morse installed a telegraph machine in his son-in-law's farm on the outskirts of town in 1858 and connected it to another in the center of town, creating what is believed to be the Caribbean's first telegraph line. The main street is named after Morse, and there's a monument to the inventor in the main plaza. A trolley makes a scenic tour of the town with stops along the way.

An ornate pink building next to the city hall, the **Museo Antigua Aduana de Arroyo** (Museum of the Old Customs House of Arroyo) traces the history of the town and some of its well-known inhabitants, including Samuel F. B. Morse. It also has a small display of Indian artifacts and revolving exhibits of contemporary works by local artists. ✉ *65 Calle Morse* ☎ *787/839–8096* 🎫 *Free* ⏲ *Wed.–Fri. 9–noon and 1–4:30, weekends 9–4:30.*

El Tren del Sur (The Train of the South) takes passengers for one-hour trips along an old rail line between Arroyo and Guayama. The train carried cane from the fields to the mills from 1915 to 1958; today it's one of the island's few working trains. Call in advance; service is frequently disrupted. ✉ *Rte. 3, Km 130.9* ☎ *787/271–1574* 🎫 *$3* ⏲ *Trains run hrly on weekends and holidays 9:30–4:30.*

Beach

Balneario Punta Guilarte. East of Arroyo's city center, this is one of the south coast's most popular beaches. There are palm trees for shade, changing facilities, picnic tables, and barbecue grills. In summer it's crowded with locals, especially on weekends and holidays; in winter it's almost deserted.

Where to Stay & Eat

$–$$ ✕ **La Llave del Mar.** This casual air-conditioned restaurant is across from Arroyo's malecón. It's popular with townsfolk for its wide variety of seafood. The menu also includes grilled steaks. ✉ *Paseo de Las Américas* ☎ *787/839–6395* 💳 *AE, MC, V* ⏲ *Closed Mon. and Tues.*

¢–$ **Centro Vacacional Punta Guilarte.** Geared primarily to Puerto Rican families, this government-run vacation center is great if you're looking for no-frills beachside accommodations. Cabins and villas have refrigerators and stoves, but you need to bring bed linen and kitchen utensils. (In a pinch you can find inexpensive supplies at the Wal-Mart 15 minutes west on Route 3 at the Guayama exit.) Some pillows and blankets are available, but you should make arrangements for them when you make your reservation. Also state in advance the number of beds you need. ✉ *Balneario Punta Guilarte, Rte. 3, Km 128.5, 00714* ☎ *787/722–1771 or 787/839–3565* 📠 *787/722–0090* *28 cabins, 32 villas* *Some fans, some kitchenettes, some refrigerators, cable TV, 2 pools, beach; no a/c in some rooms* 💳 *MC, V* 🍽 *EP.*

Patillas

❻ *6 km (4 mi) northeast of Arroyo.*

Patillas, the so-called "Emerald of the South," is a tranquil city of about 22,000, with a small plaza and steep, narrow streets. The best sightseeing is along the coast east of town, where Route 3 skirts the Caribbean. This stretch passes rugged cliffs and beautiful beaches, many of which have not yet been discovered by visitors.

Where to Stay & Eat

$–$$$ **El Mar de la Tranquilidad.** Get a table on the deck at the edge of the Caribbean. You'll find good Puerto Rican cuisine and lots of seafood, including lobster, red snapper, and *mofongo* (mashed plantains with seafood). Be sure to sample one of the restaurant's daiquiris—there's a huge list from which to choose. *Rte. 3, Km 118.9* *787/839–6469* *AE, MC, V* *No dinner Mon.–Wed.*

★ $ **Caribe Playa Beach Resort.** The resort is a good base from which to explore the southeast coast. Comfortable rooms have a patio or a balcony and border a crescent-shape beach (it's a little rocky, but it's still good for a refreshing dip). Unwind by the pool, in a hammock tied between coconut trees, or in the informal library. You can arrange for boat trips, fishing and scuba diving excursions, and massages. The Seaview Terrace ($–$$$) is open for breakfast, lunch, cocktails, and dinner; reservations are required for dinner. *Rte. 3, Km 112.1* *HC 764, Box 8490, 00723* *787/839–7719 or 787/839–6339* *787/839–1817* *www.caribeplaya.com* *32 rooms* *Restaurant, BBQs, fans, some in-room data ports, some refrigerators, cable TV in some rooms, pool, wading pool, hot tub, massage, beach, dive shop, boating, fishing, library, playground, some pets allowed; no a/c in some rooms, no phone in some rooms, no TV in some rooms* *AE, MC, V* *EP.*

Beaches

El Bajo de Patillas. On Route 3 south of Patillas, this beach offers tranquil sunning and good swimming.

Channel. The beach in front of the Caribe Playa resort is good for bodysurfing and swimming, although the bottom can be rocky.

Inches. A few miles east of Patillas is this popular surfing beach.

off the beaten path

FARO DE MAUNABO – Route 3 going eastward intersects with Route 901, the eastern portion of the cross-island Ruta Panorámica. Along the way you'll pass animals grazing in fields and cliffs that drop straight down to the ocean. If you turn off on Route 760 and take it to the end, you'll be rewarded by a dramatic view of the Faro de Maunabo (Maunabo Lighthouse, not open to the public) at Punta Tuna.

Salinas

7 *29 km (18 mi) west of Guayama; 35 km (22 mi) west of Patillas.*

Most visitors are familiar with this town only from seeing its name on an exit sign along Route 52. Islanders, however, know that the road from the expressway exit to Salinas leads to some of Puerto Rico's best seafood restaurants. Most of them are along the seafront in the Playa de Salinas area, reached by heading south on Route 701. This is the place where *mojo isleño* (a popular sauce made from tomatos, onions, and spices) was created.

Where to Eat

$–$$$ ✕ **Puerta la Bahía.** The spacious, air-conditioned dining area has huge windows overlooking the water and an extensive seafood menu. For a lighter meal, try one of the fish soups or the croquettes stuffed with crab. Heartier dishes include salmon fillets, grouper, lobster, and mofongo. You can also get chicken or beef dishes. ✉ *End of Calle Principal, Sector Playita Final* ☎ *787/824–7117* ▭ *AE, MC, V.*

Coamo

❽ *33 km (20 mi) southwest of Cayey; 20 km (13 mi) northwest of Salinas.*

Founded by the Spanish in 1579, Coamo was the third city established in Puerto Rico. It dominated the south of the island until the mid-1880s, when political power shifted to Ponce. Coamo town, however, remained an important outpost; several decisive battles were fought here during the Spanish-American War in 1898.

The thermal springs outside Coamo are believed by some to be the Fountain of Youth for which Ponce de León was searching. In the mid-1800s a fashionable resort was built nearby, and people have been coming for a soak in the waters ever since. Coamo is also famous for the San Blas Half-Marathon, which brings competitors and spectators from around the world. The race, held in early February, covers 18 km (13 mi) of the city's hilly streets.

The city's spiritual heart is an 18th-century church on the central plaza. Other buildings dating from the 19th century line Coamo's steep streets, and today you'll find car mechanics, hair salons, and pharmacies operating out of them.

Off the main square, the **Museo Histórico de Coamo** is appropriately housed in the former residence of one of the city's illustrious citizens, Clotilde Santiago, a wealthy farmer and merchant born in 1826. The museum is on the second floor of this sprawling, tangerine-color building that dates from 1863. Several rooms are decorated with colonial-style furnishings, and photographs of the town and the Santiago family line the walls. ✉ *29 Calle José I. Quintón* ☎ *787/825–1150 Ext. 206* 🎟 *Free* ⏲ *Weekdays 8–noon and 1–4:30, weekends by reservation.*

Outside Coamo on Route 546, you can take a dip at the famous **Baños de Coamo,** thermal springs that are said to have curative powers. Parador Baños de Coamo allows day-trippers to bathe in its own warm pool for $5 (parador guests enjoy it on the house). There's also a free public bathing area at the end of a path behind the parador. ✉ *Rte. 546, Km 1* ☎ *787/825–2186 for Parados Baños de Coamo* 🎟 *$5, public bathing area free* ⏲ *Daily 10–5:30.*

Where to Stay & Eat

$–$$ ✕ **Chicken Burger.** Don't let the name fool you. Although it's known for its grilled chicken, this popular restaurant has a much more extensive menu that also includes steaks, hamburgers, fish, mofongo, and more. Eat indoors with air-conditioning or outside on a patio. ✉ *Rte. 153* ☎ *787/825–4761* ▭ *MC, V.*

★ $ **Parador Baños de Coamo.** On weekends musicians play in the interior patio of this rustic country inn, portions of which date from the 19th century. Rooms—in four modern two-story buildings—open onto latticed wooden verandas and have a cozy, lodgelike feel. Thermal water flows from sulfur springs into a swimming pool a few steps away from a cool-water pool, where you can still see walls dating from 1843. In the dining room ($–$$), portions of delicious *churrasco* (barbecued meats) with rice and beans are generous. *Rte. 546, Km 1 Box 540, 99769 787/825–2186 or 787/825–2239 787/825–4739 48 rooms Restaurant, cable TV, 2 pools, bar, video game room AE, D, MC, V EP.*

3

Sports & the Outdoors

GOLF The **Coamo Springs Golf Course** (Rte. 546 just before Baños de Coamo parador 787/825–1370) is popular for its rugged beauty. It's the only 18-hole, par-72 course with Bermuda grass on the island. When it's raining in the capital, sanjuaneros drive down here for a day of play. The 6,647-yard course, designed by Ferdinand Garbin, is open daily; greens fees are $50.

PONCE

34 km (21 mi) southwest of Coamo.

"Ponce is Ponce and the rest is parking space" is the adage used by the residents of Puerto Rico's second-largest city (population 194,000) to express their pride in being a *ponceño*. The rivalry with the island's capital began in the 19th century when European immigrants from England, France, and Spain settled here. Because the city's limits extend from the Caribbean to the foothills of the Cordillera Central, it's a lot hotter in climate than San Juan. Another contrast is the architecture of the elegant homes and public buildings that surround the main square.

Many of the 19th-century buildings in Ponce Centro, the downtown area, have been renovated, and the Museo de Arte de Ponce—endowed by its late native son and former governor Luis A. Ferré—is considered one of the Caribbean's finest art museums. Just as famous is Ponce's pre-Lenten carnival. The colorful costumes and *vejigante* (mischief maker) masks worn during the festivities are famous throughout the world. The best dining in Ponce is just west of town. Seafood restaurants line the highway in an area known as Las Cucharas, named for the spoon-shape bay you'll overlook as you dine.

Exploring Ponce

Las Delicias Plaza (Plaza of Delights) with its trees, benches, and famous l&ion fountain is a perfect people-watching square to spend an hour or two on a Sunday afternoon. The old red-and-black firehouse is right on the plaza and has a fire-fighting museum on its second floor. Ponce is known for its museums and has several dedicated to music, art, history, sports, and architecture. You can catch a free, city-run trolley or "*chu chu*" train from Plaza las Delicias to the major attractions. On weekends there are free horse-and-carriage rides around the plaza. Ponceños are proud of their city, called the "Pearl of the South," and offer all visitors a warm welcome.

Ponce Centro

At the heart of Ponce Centro is the Plaza las Delicias (Plaza of Delights) with trees, benches, and the famous Lion fountain. Several interesting buildings are on this square or the adjacent streets, making the area perfect for a leisurely morning or afternoon stroll.

a good walk

Start on the tree-lined Plaza las Delicias. (You'll find parking nearby on Calle Marina, Calle Isabel, and Calle Reina.) Dominating it is the **Catedral Nuestra Señora de Guadalupe** 9 ⚑, dating from 1835. Across the street is the **Casa Armstrong-Poventud** 10, home of the institute of culture's Ponce branch. Leaving Armstrong-Poventud, cross back to the plaza, circle south by the Alcaldía (City Hall), and continue to the plaza's east side to visit the red-and-black striped fire station, **Parque de Bombas** 11.

From the intersection of Calles Marina and Cristina, take Calle Cristina a block east to one of the city's first restoration projects, **Teatro La Perla** 12, at the corner of Cristina and Mayor. One block north of the theater, at calles Mayor and Isabel, is a former home that's now the **Museo de la Historia de Ponce** 13. A block east, at the corner of Calles Salud and Isabel, is the **Museo de la Música Puertorriqueña** 14. Four blocks west (you will go by Plaza las Delicias again, and Calle Isabel will turn into Calle Reina) is the 1911 architectural masterpiece **Casa Wiechers-Villaronga** 15. For more early-20th-century architecture, continue west on Calle Reina, where you'll see examples of *casas criollas,* wooden homes with the spacious front balconies that were popular in the Caribbean during the early 1900s.

TIMING Although it's possible to see Ponce Centro in one morning or afternoon, it's best to devote a full day and evening to it. Explore the streets and museums during daylight, then head for the plaza at night when the lion fountain and street lamps are lighted and townspeople stroll the plaza.

WHAT TO SEE

10 **Casa Armstrong-Poventud.** Banker and industrialist Carlos Armstrong and his wife, Eulalia Pou, moved into this neoclassical house designed and built for them in 1901 by Manuel V. Domenech. The house is known for its ornate facade, which is chock-full of columns, statues, and intricate moldings. It now houses the Ponce offices of the Institute of Puerto Rican Culture, but you can walk through several rooms decorated with colonial furniture. Note the high, pressed-tin ceilings and the decorative glass doors in the foyer. ✉ *Calle Union at Catedral, Ponce Centro* ☎ *787/844–2540 or 787/840–7667* 🎟 *Free* ⏲ *Weekdays 8–4:30.*

15 **Casa Wiechers-Villaronga.** Alfredo B. Wiechers returned to Ponce after studying architecture in Paris to become one of the city's premier architects. He designed this house, built in 1911, for himself. In 1918 he sold it to the Villaronga-Mercado family. Arches and columns found throughout the interior are typical of Wiechers' designs. The facade has a chamferred corner, common on Ponce's early-20th-century buildings. Check out the stained-glass windows and the rooftop gazebo. Inside you'll

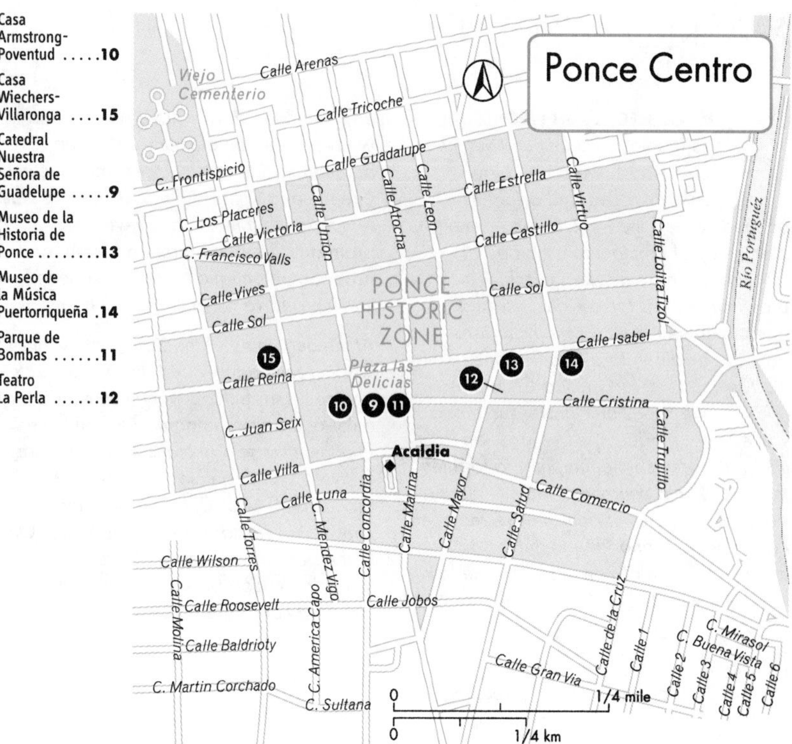

find original furnishings and exhibits on Wiechers and other Ponce architects of his era. ✉ *Calle Reina and Calle Meléndez Vigo, Ponce Centro* ☎ *787/843–3363* 🎫 *$1* ⏲ *Wed.–Sun. 8:30–4:30.*

9 **Catedral Nuestra Señora de Guadalupe.** This cathedral dedicated to the Virgin of Guadalupe is built on the site of a 1670 chapel destroyed by earthquakes. Part of the current structure, where mass is still held, dates from 1835. After another earthquake in 1918, new steeples and a roof were put on and neoclassical embellishments were added to the facade. Inside you'll see stained-glass windows, chandeliers, and two alabaster altars. ✉ *Plaza las Delicias, Ponce Centro* ☎ *787/842–0134* ⏲ *Services daily 6 AM and 11 AM.*

13 **Museo de la Historia de Ponce.** Housed in two adjoining, neoclassical buildings, this museum has 10 exhibition halls covering Ponce's development from the Taíno Indians to the present. Guided tours in English and Spanish last 50 minutes and give an overview of Ponce's past. ✉ *51–53 Calle Isabel, Ponce Centro* ☎ *787/844–7071 or 787/843–4322* 🎫 *$3* ⏲ *Wed.–Mon. 9–5.*

14 **Museo de la Música Puertorriqueña.** At this museum you'll learn how Puerto Rican music has been influenced by African, Spanish, and Native Amer-

MASKED MISCHIEF

A **WEEK BEFORE ASH WEDNESDAY,** *vejigantes (pronounced veh-hee-GAN-tays), wearing long, colorful robes and brightly painted horned masks, turn the normally placid city of Ponce into a hotbed of rowdiness. These masked mischief makers prowl city streets for a week, scaring anyone in their path. Some historians date this tradition to a Spanish one of the 1600s that targeted lapsed Christians. Men in long robes and grotesque masks waved cow bladders, or* vejigas, *on long sticks at passersby, attempting to frighten them back into churches for Lent. Today, balloons and plastic bottles have replaced cow bladders, and the playful masks present the face of Ponce's exquisite folk art to the world.*

Unlike carnival masks from other parts of the island, which are made of coconut shells (Loíza) *or fine metallic screening* (Hatillo), *Ponce masks are made of papier-mâché. Many have African and Native American elements; it's even possible to detect influences from ancient Greece and Rome. All masks have at least two horns, but most have several protruding from the forehead, chin, and nose. Some antique masks have been known to have more than 100 horns.*

At the beginning of the 20th century, masks were usually painted red with yellow dots or vice versa, but today they come in every color and pattern imaginable. You'll also find them for sale at crafts stores and arts festivals. Small, simple masks start at around $20 or $30; larger ones by well-known makers cost as much as $100. One of the best-known mask-making families today is the Caraballo family from the Playa de Ponce area.

ican cultures. On display are instruments, such as the *triple* (a small string instrument resembling a banjo), and memorabilia of local composers and musicians. The small museum takes up several rooms in a neoclassical former residence. ✉ *Calle Isabel and Calle Salud, Ponce Centro* ☎ *787/848–7016* 🎫 *$1* ⊙ *Wed.–Sun. 8:30–4:30.*

11 **Parque de Bombas.** Built in 1882 as a pavilion for an agricultural fair and then used as a firehouse, this distinctive red-and-black striped building is now a fire-fighting museum, complete with antique trucks. Half-hour tours in English and Spanish are given on the half hour. ✉ *Plaza las Delicias, Ponce Centro* ☎ *787/284–4141 Ext. 342* 🎫 *Free* ⊙ *Wed.–Mon. 9:30–6.*

need a break?

An institution for more than 40 years, **King's** (✉ 9223 Calle Marina ☎ 787/843–8520), across from Plaza las Delicias, is *the* place for ice cream in Ponce. It serves 12 varieties, from tamarind and passion-fruit to classic chocolate and vanilla. A bench in the tiny storefront seats three, but most folks take their cups and cones across the street and stake out shady plaza benches. King's is open daily from 8 AM to midnight.

12 **Teatro La Perla.** This theater was restored in 1941 after an earthquake and fire damaged the original 1864 structure. The striking interior contains seats for 1,047 and has excellent acoustics. It's generally open for a quick look on weekdays. ✉ *Calle Mayor and Calle Cristina, Ponce Centro* ☎ *787/843–4322 information, 787/843–4080 ticket office* 🎫 *Free* ⏲ *Weekdays 8–4:30.*

Greater Ponce

The greater Ponce area has some of Puerto Rico's most notable cultural attractions, including one of the island's finest art museums and its most important archaeological site.

a good tour

The **Museo de Arte de Ponce** 16 ⚑ is on Avenida Las Américas, south of Plaza las Delicias and not far from the Luis A. Ferré Expressway (Route 52). Anyone with a taste for art can happily while away many hours in its galleries. East of the museum you can pick up Route 14 south to the Caribbean and **La Guancha** 17, a boardwalk with food kiosks, a playground, and a child-friendly public beach. It's a good place to relax and let the younger generation work off energy. From here, if you retrace your path north past downtown you'll be heading to Calle Bertoly and El Vigía (Vigía Hill), where the **Cruceta El Vigía** 18 towers over the city and the **Castillo Serrallés** 19, a former sugar baron's villa, is a popular attraction.

Farther north on Route 503 is the **Centro Ceremonial Indígena de Tibes** 20, which displays native artifacts dating back more than 1,500 years. You'll have to backtrack to reach Route 10, then head north to **Hacienda Buena Vista** 21, a former coffee plantation that's been restored by the Puerto Rican Conservation Trust. (Call ahead to arrange a tour.)

You can drive to all these sights or hop on the free trolleys or *chu chu* trains that run from Plaza las Delicias to the museum, La Guancha, and El Vigía. You'll need a car or a cab to reach Tibes and Hacienda Buena Vista.

TIMING To visit all the sights mentioned above, you'll need at least 1½ or 2 days. If you don't want to devote that much time, visit only the sights that have the most appeal for you personally.

WHAT TO SEE

★ 19 **Castillo Serrallés.** Now a museum, this lovely Spanish-style villa overlooking the city and the sea was built in the 1930s for Ponce's wealthiest family, the makers of Don Q rum. Guided tours give you a glimpse of the lifestyle of the sugar barons and explain the area's sugar production history. The extensive garden, with sculptured bushes and a shimmering reflection pool, is considered the best kept in the island. ✉ *17 El Vigía, El Vigía* ☎ *787/259–1774* 🌐 *www.castilloserralles.net* 🎫 *$5 for museum and gardens, $2 for gardens only, $6 for museum, gardens, and Cruceta El Vigía* ⏲ *Tues.–Thurs. 9:30–5, Fri.–Sun. 9:30–5:30.*

20 **Centro Ceremonial Indígena de Tibes.** The Tibes Indian Ceremonial Center, discovered after flooding from a tropical storm in 1975, is a very important archaeological site. The pre-Taíno ruins and burial grounds date from AD 300 to AD 700. Be sure to visit the small museum before taking a walking tour of the site, which includes ceremonial playing

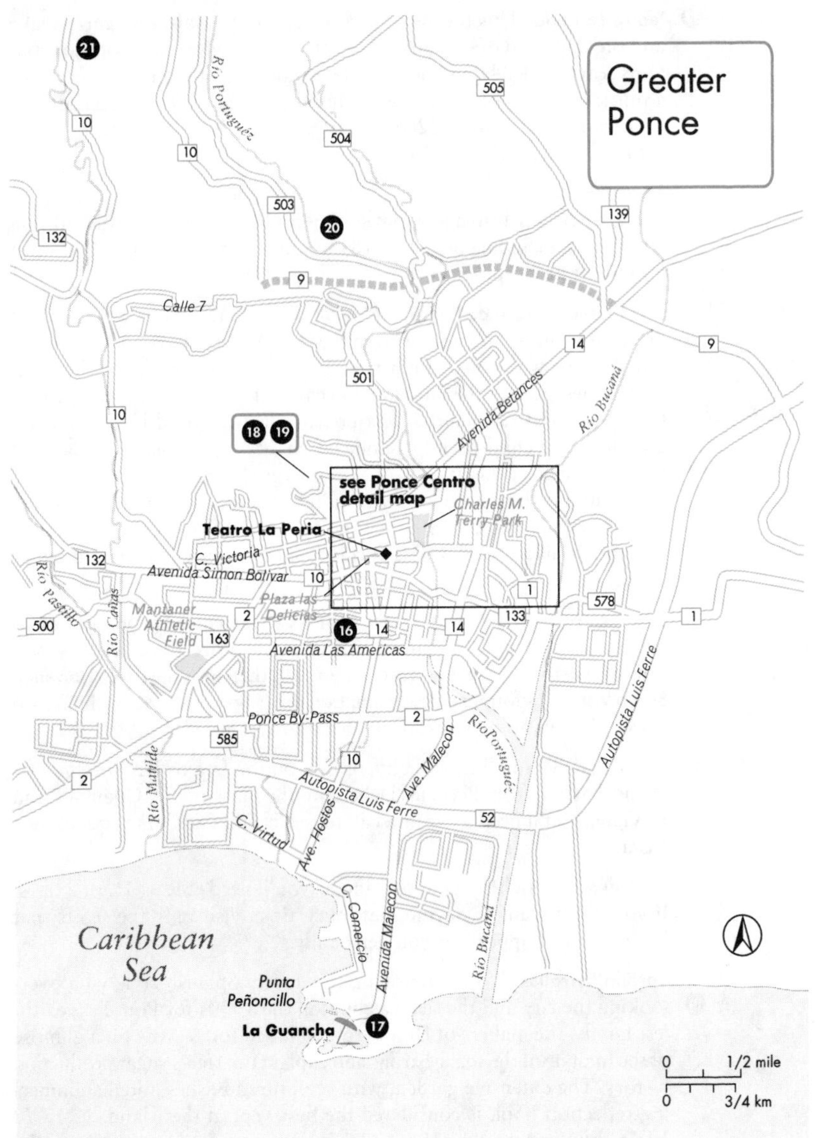

Castillo Serrallés **19**

Centro Ceremonial Indígena de Tibes **20**

Cruceta El Vigía **18**

La Guancha **17**

Hacienda Buena Vista **21**

Museo de Arte de Ponce **16**

fields used for a ritual ball game that some think was similar to soccer. The fields are bordered by smooth stones, some engraved with petroglyphs that researchers believe might have ceremonial or astronomical significance. A village with several thatch huts has been reconstructed in an original setting. ✉ *Rte. 503, Km 2.2, Barrio Tibes* ☎ *787/840–2255 or 787/840–5685* 🌐 *ponce.inter.edu/tibes/tibes.html* 🎫 *$2* ⏲ *Tues.–Sun. 9–4.*

18 **Cruceta El Vigía.** At the top of Vigía Hill is a colossal cross where the Spanish once watched for ships, including those of marauding pirates. You can climb the stairs or take an elevator to the top of the 100-foot cross for a panoramic view of the city and beyond. ✉ *Across from Castillo Serrallés, El Vigía* ☎ *787/259–3816* 🌐 *www.castilloserralles.net* 🎫 *$2; can be visited on combined ticket with Castillo Serrallés* ⏲ *Tues.–Sun. 9:30–5:30.*

17 **La Guancha.** Encircling the cove of a working harbor, the seaside boardwalk features kiosks where vendors sell local food and drink. The adjacent park has a large children's area filled with playground equipment and on weekends, live music. The nearby public beach has rest rooms, changing areas, a medical post, and plenty of free parking. ✉ *End of Rte. 14, La Guancha* ☎ *787/844–3995.*

21 **Hacienda Buena Vista.** Built as a fruit farm in 1838 by Salvador Vives, Hacienda Buena Vista later became a corn-flour mill and finally a coffee plantation. In 1987 the plantation house was restored by the Puerto Rican Conservation Trust, which also preserved the original waterwheel, hydraulic systems, and additional machinery. Inside the two-story house, furniture, documents, and other memorabilia give a sense of what it was like to live on a coffee plantation nearly 150 years ago. The two-hour tour, given four times a day (once in English), is by reservation only. (Allow yourself a half hour to travel the winding Route 10 from Ponce.) Afterward, you can buy coffee beans and souvenirs at the gift shop. ✉ *Rte. 10, Km 16.8, Sector Corral Viejo* ☎ *787/722–5882 weekdays, 787/284–7020 weekends* 🎫 *$2* ⏲ *Fri.–Sun. by reservation only.*

Fodor'sChoice ★

16 **Museo de Arte de Ponce.** The lovely building designed by Edward Durrell Stone, who was also an architect for New York's Museum of Modern Art, contains more than 1,500 paintings, sculptures, and prints. You'll find the work of Puerto Rican artists such as Francisco Oller; Latin American painters such as Bartolome Murillo; and Europeans such as Peter Paul Rubens, Auguste Rodin, and Thomas Gainsborough. The highlight of the European collection is the pre-Raphaelite paintings, particularly *Flaming June,* by Frederick Leighton, which has become the museum's unofficial symbol. Watch for special exhibits and occasional concerts. ✉ *2325 Av. Las Américas, Sector Santa María* ☎ *787/848–0505* 🌐 *www.museoarteponce.org* 🎫 *$4* ⏲ *Daily 10–5.*

Fodor'sChoice ★

Beaches

Caja de Muertos (Coffin Island). This island a few miles off the coast has the best beaches in the Ponce area and is, perhaps, the second-best area in southern Puerto Rico for snorkeling, after La Parguera. Ask one of the many boatsmen at La Guancha to take you out for about $30 round-trip.

La Guancha. Ponce's public beach at the end of Route 14 is small, but the shallow water makes it nice for children. There's some shade under thatched umbrellas, but bring sunscreen.

El Tuque. About 5 km (3 mi) west of Ponce on Route 2, this beach has a swimming area and picnic tables.

Where to Stay & Eat

★ **$$$** ✕ **La Cava.** Dark-wood paneling and low lighting set a romantic tone at this intimate restaurant in the Hilton Ponce & Casino. It's known for an award-winning wine list and a menu that gracefully melds international cuisines. Try the goulash of venison, ostrich medallions on a mango chutney tart, or lamb chops. The appetizer list includes sushi and selections from an oyster bar. ✉ *1150 Av. Caribe, La Guancha* ☎ *787/259–7676* *Reservations essential* ▭ *AE, D, MC, V.*

$$–$$$ FodorsChoice ★ ✕ **Mark's at the Meliá.** One of the island's best restaurants is tucked off the lobby of the Meliá hotel. Chef Mark French has won praise from the Caribbean Chefs Association, and his dishes live up to that honor. The menu here changes often, but you'll always find a long list of appetizers that could include a three-cheese onion soup or a bacon, lettuce, and tomato salad. The restaurant has drawn raves for creations such as plantain-crusted dorado with *congri* (a Cuban dish of black beans and rice), and the chocolate truffle cake draws fans from as far away as San Juan. ✉ *Hotel Meliá, 75 Calle Cristina, La Guancha, Ponce* ☎ *787/284–6275* ▭ *AE, MC, V* ⊗ *Closed Mon. and Tues.*

$–$$$ ✕ **El Ancla.** Families favor this restaurant at the edge of the sea. The kitchen serves generous and affordable plates of fish, crab, and other fresh seafood with tostones, *papas fritas* (french fries), and garlic bread. Try the shrimp in garlic sauce, salmon filet with capers, or the delectable mofongo. The piña coladas—with or without rum—and the flan are exceptional. There are two dining rooms—one for those who smoke and another for those who don't. ✉ *9 Av. Hostos Final, Ponce Playa* ☎ *787/840–2450* ▭ *AE, MC, V.*

$–$$$ ✕ **Lupita's.** Knock-your-socks-off margaritas are the perfect accompaniment to the heaping portions of highly seasoned Mexican-American food at this downtown restaurant. You can eat indoors or in the courtyard. There's live music Tuesday through Saturday after 11 PM. ✉ *60 Calle Isabel, Ponce Centro* ☎ *787/848–8808* ▭ *MC, V.*

$–$$$ ✕ **Pito's.** Dine indoors or on a waterfront balcony at this restaurant in Las Cucharas. In addition to a wide selection of seafood, you can also order chicken and steak dishes. To indulge, try the shrimp wrapped in bacon, a specialty here. There's live music on Friday and Saturday nights. ✉ *Rte. 2, Sector Las Cucharas* ☎ *787/841–4977* ▭ *AE, MC, V.*

¢–$ ✕ **Café Tompy.** The prices are right at this no-frills cafeteria, which draws a big lunch crowd. You can sample such down-home Puerto Rican cuisine as roasted chicken that has been marinated in different local spices such as coriander, garlicky lechón, rice and beans, and yucca. You can also get a sandwich or simply re-energize with a strong cup of coffee.

It's open daily for lunch and dinner; though breakfast is served only Monday through Saturday. ✉ *56 Calle Isabel, Ponce Centro* ☎ *787/840–1965* 💳 *MC, V* ⏲ *No breakfast Sun.*

★ **$$$–$$$$** **Hilton Ponce & Casino.** The south coast's biggest resort—a major conference center—is a cream-and-turquoise complex on 80 acres 6 km (4 mi) outside of Ponce on a black-sand beach. The open-air lobby has an efficient, businesslike feel, but the hotel can also be a welcoming place for families and offers a wide range of outdoor activities as well as an expansive shopping arcade. A large pool is surrounded by palm trees and has a spectacular view of the Caribbean. All of its bright spacious rooms are decorated in a lush, tropical motif and have balconies overlooking the sea. The casino is busy at night. ✉ *1150 Av. Caribe, La Guancha* 📫 *Box 7419, 00732* ☎ *787/259–7676 or 800/445–8667, 800/981–3232 direct to hotel* 📠 *787/259–7674* 🌐 *www.hilton.com* *148 rooms, 5 suites* *2 restaurants, some in-room hot tubs, in-room safes, minibars, cable TV with movies and video games, driving range, 4 tennis courts, pool, gym, hot tub, sauna, spa, beach, bicycles, basketball, Ping-Pong, volleyball, 3 bars, casino, dance club, video game room, shops, babysitting, children's programs (ages 8–12), playground, business services, meeting rooms, parking (fee)* 💳 *AE, DC, MC, V* 🍽 *EP.*

$ **Holiday Inn & El Tropical Casino Ponce.** The *trío* music that fills the lobby bar nightly and the dance beat that pulsates from the disco lend considerable Latin flair to this Holiday Inn on the outskirts of Ponce. Adding to the energy is the sound of slots ringing each evening at the Tropical Casino. The Tanama restaurant serves Spanish, Puerto Rican, and nouvelle cuisine; several seafood restaurants are also in the nearby Las Cucharas area. Rooms are spacious, and each has its own balcony. ✉ *3315 Ponce Bypass, El Tuque 00731* ☎ *787/844–1200 or 800/465–4329* 📠 *787/841–8683* 🌐 *www.ichotelsgroup.com* *116 rooms* *Restaurant, room service, in-room data ports, refrigerators, cable TV, 2 pools, gym, 2 bars, casino, dance club, video game room, Internet, meeting rooms* 💳 *AE, MC, V* 🍽 *EP.*

★ **$** **Hotel Meliá.** In the heart of Ponce, near Plaza las Delicias, this family-owned hotel is a good, low-key base for exploring downtown's landmark buildings and museums. The lobby, with its high ceilings and blue-and-beige tile floors, is well-worn but charming. Rooms, which have high ceilings, tile floors, and stone balconies, have a somewhat dated European feel. The balconies of the six suites have terrific views of Ponce's historic district. The restaurant is one of the city's best. Breakfast is served on the rooftop terrace, which overlooks the city and mountains. ✉ *75 Calle Cristina, Ponce Centro* 📫 *Box 1431, 00733* ☎ *787/842–0260 or 800/742–4276* 📠 *787/841–3602* 🌐 *home.coqui.net/melia* *72 rooms, 6 suites* *Restaurant, cable TV, bar, parking (fee)* 💳 *AE, MC, V* 🍽 *CP.*

¢ **Hotel Bélgica.** Right off Plaza las Delicias, this hotel is both comfortable and economical. A stairway off the large 1940s-era lobby leads to clean rooms with dark-wood furniture and pastel walls. These vary widely in size (Room 3 is one of the largest); many have a table or a desk, and some have a balcony with wooden shutter-style doors. However, some rooms have no windows, and bathroom walls don't always reach the ceiling. Friendly staff and low prices may make up for the lack of amenities. The hotel has no restaurant or bar, but there are plenty of options in the neighborhood. ✉ *122 Calle Villa, Ponce Centro 00731* ☎ *787/844–3255* 📠 *787/844–6149* *20 rooms* *Cable TV, some pets allowed* *MC, V* *EP.*

Nightlife & the Arts

Nightlife

In downtown Ponce, people embrace the Spanish tradition of the *paseo,* an evening stroll with family and friends around Plaza las Delicias, which is spectacular at night when its old-fashioned street lamps glow and the fountain is lit. The boardwalk at La Guancha is also a lively scene with ponceños out for a stroll and a bite to eat, and live bands often play there on weekends.

The **Hilton Ponce & Casino** (✉ Rte. 14, 1150 Av. Caribe, La Guancha ☎ 787/259–7676) has several options for nightlife: the casino stays open nightly until 4 AM; on Thursday, Friday, and Saturday you can dance at the Pavilion disco; and on Friday and Saturday merengue and salsa fill La Bohemia lounge. The **Holiday Inn Ponce** (✉ 3315 Ponce Bypass, El Tuque ☎ 787/844–1200) features live music nightly in its Caribbean Lobby Bar and live dance music Friday and Saturday nights at Holly's disco. The casino is open nightly until 4 AM. **Hollywood Café** (✉ Bul. Miguel Pou, Km 5.5, Ponce Centro ☎ 787/843–6703) has occasional live music and draws a college-age crowd. **Lupita's** (✉ 60 Calle Isabel, Ponce Centro ☎ 787/848–8008) often has live music, ranging from guitar to blues and rock-and-roll, Tuesday through Saturday. **Olé Plena** (✉ 57 Calle Isabel, Ponce Centro ☎ 787/841–6162) schedules live music, often jazz, many weeknights and some Saturdays.

The Arts

Check for Spanish-language theater productions and concerts at the **Teatro La Perla** (✉ Calle Mayor and Calle Cristina, Ponce Centro ☎ 87/843–4322 information, 787/843–4080 ticket office). The **Museo de Arte de Ponce** (✉ 2325 Av. Las Américas, Sector Santa María ☎ 787/848–0505) occasionally sponsors chamber music concerts and recitals by members of the Puerto Rico Symphony Orchestra.

Sports & the Outdoors

Diving & Snorkeling

You'll see many varieties of coral, parrotfish, angelfish, and grouper in the reefs around the island of Caja de Muertos. Snorkeling around La Guancha and the beach area of the Ponce Hilton is also fairly good.

Marine Sports & Dive Shop (✉ 1244 Av. Muñoz Rivera, Villa Grillasca ☎ 787/844–6175) rents equipment and arranges tours to Caja de Muertos. **Rafy Vega's Island Venture** (☎ 787/842–8546) offers two-tank dive excursions as well as snorkeling trips. The company also takes day-trippers from La Guancha to Caja de Muertos—a 45-minute boat ride—for a day of relaxing on the beach. The trips cost $30 per person and include a light lunch.

Shopping

On holidays and during festivals, artisans sell wares from booths in the Plaza las Delicias. Souvenir and gift shops are plentiful in the area around the plaza, and Paseo Atocha, a pedestrian mall with shops geared to residents, runs north of it. Carnival masks, hammocks, Puerto Rican coffee, and rum fill the shelves of **Mi Coquí** (✉ 9227 Calle Marina, Ponce Centro ☎ 787/841–0216). Just outside town, **Plaza del Caribe Mall** (✉ Rte. 2, Km 227.9 ☎ 787/259–8989), one of the island's largest malls, has stores such as Sears Roebuck, JCPenney, and Gap. With more than 25 stores **Ponce Mall** (✉ Rte. 2, Km. 225.8 ☎ 787/844–6170) is an older shopping center with many local clothing and discount stores. **Utopia** (✉ 78 Calle Isabel, Ponce Centro ☎ 787/848–8742) sells carnival masks and crafts.

SOUTHWESTERN PUERTO RICO

With sandy coves and palm-lined beaches tucked in the coastline's curves, southwestern Puerto Rico fulfills everyone's fantasy of a tropical paradise. The area is popular with local vacationers on weekends and holidays, but many beaches are nearly deserted on weekdays. Villages along the coast are picturesque places where oysters and fresh fish are sold at roadside stands. On the southwesternmost peninsula, the rugged stretch leading to the Cabo Rojo Lighthouse has pink-sand beaches.

Guánica

22 *24 mi (38 km) west of Ponce.*

Juan Ponce de León first explored this area in 1508 when he was searching for the elusive Fountain of Youth. Nearly 400 years later, U.S. troops landed first at Guánica during the Spanish-American War in 1898. The event is commemorated with an engraved marker on the city's malecón. Sugarcane dominated the landscape through much of the 1900s, and the ruins of the old Guánica Central sugar mill, closed in 1980, loom over the town's western area, known as Ensenada. Today most of the action takes place at the beaches and in the forests outside of Guánica.

Fodor'sChoice ★ The 9,200-acre **Bosque Estatal de Guánica** (Guánica State Forest), a United Nations Biosphere Reserve, is a great place for hikes and bird-watching expeditions. It's an outstanding example of a tropical dry coastal forest, with some 700 species of plants and more than 100 types of birds. There are 12 major trails through the sun-bleached hills, from which you'll see towering cacti as well as guayacan (soap-bush) and gumbo limbo trees. There are also several caves to explore. You can enter on Route 333, which skirts the forest's southwestern portion, or at the end of Route 334, where there's a parks office. ✉ *Rte. 333 or 334* ☎ *787/821–5706* 🎫 *Free* ⏲ *Daily 9–5.*

Beaches

Bahía Ballena. At the end of Route 333, this U-shape strand combines a beautiful beach with calm water.

Balneario Caña Gorda. The gentle water at this beach on Route 333 washes onto a wide swath of sand fringed with palm trees. There are picnic tables, bathrooms, showers, and changing facilities.

Gilligan's Island. Off the southwest coast near Guánica is a cay surrounded by coral reefs and skirted by gorgeous beaches. There are picnic tables and restrooms but no other signs of civilization. Boats leave the San Jacinto dock, stopping for passengers at nearby hotels, during the week every hour, on the hour, from 10 to 5; on weekends boats leave every half hour from 8:30 to 5. Round-trip passage is $4. (To reach San Jacinto, take the first right after the Copamarina Beach Resort on Route 333 and go less than ¼ mi.) The island is often busy on weekends and around holidays, but during the week it's usually quiet. On Monday it's closed for cleaning.

Playa Santa. You can rent Jet Skis, kayaks, and pedal boats at this beach at the end of Route 325 in the Ensenada district.

Punta Jacinto. Rugged cliffs make a dramatic backdrop for this beach on Route 333, but the water can be rough.

Where to Stay & Eat

$–$$$ ✕ **La Concha.** A tourist board–designated *meson gastronómico* (restaurant that serves traditional island dishes), this family favorite specializes in seafood. Mofongo leaves the kitchen filled with shrimp, lobster, or conch. The hearty *asopao* (a gumbolike soup) is made with seafood or chicken. There's also fried chicken with rice and beans, filet mignon in onion sauce, and churrasco covered with mushrooms. ✉ *C-4 Calle Principal, Playa Santa, Ensenada* ☎ *787/821–5522* 💳 *AE, MC, V.*

$$–$$$ ✕🏨 **Copamarina Beach Resort.** To one side of the Copamarina's 16 acres of flowers and fruit trees is the Caribbean; to the other, is dry tropical forest. If the resort's beach is too crowded with other guests and their children, several equally beautiful stretches are minutes away. Rooms are basic but spacious; all have balconies or patios and at least partial ocean views. The red snapper is a must at the Coastal Cuisine restaurant ($$–$$$), but you'll need to rent a car for outings to other area eateries and nightspots. All-inclusive packages are available. ✉ *Rte. 333, Km 6.5* 📫 *Box 805, 00653* ☎ *787/821–0505 or 800/468–4553* 📠 *787/821–0070* 🌐 *www.copamarina.com* 🛏 *106 rooms, 2 villas* 👍 *Restaurant, refrigerators, in-room safes, cable TV, 2 tennis courts, 2 pools, 2 wading pools, gym, 2 hot tubs, massage, spa, beach, dive shop, snorkeling, windsurfing, boating, volleyball, bar, playground, business services, meeting rooms* 💳 *AE, MC, V* 🍴 *EP.*

$–$$ 🏨 **Paul Julien's Caribbean Vacation Villa.** No need to bring your own sports gear—it's included in the price of a room. The villa consists of three efficiency apartments and a two-bedroom apartment on a small swimming beach. The villa comes with beginner and racing kayaks, windsurfers, mountain bikes, and snorkeling and scuba gear. Windsurfing and kayaking lessons are available for an extra charge. ✉ *Rte. 333, #15, San Jacinto Sector* 📫 *Box 432, 00653* ☎ *787/821–5364* 📠 *787/821–0681* 🌐 *www.caribbeanvacationvilla.com* 🛏 *4 units* 👍 *Kitchens, cable TV, dive shop, windsurfing, boating, bicycles; no room phones* 💳 *No credit cards* 🍴 *EP.*

$ **Mary Lee's by the Sea.** This meandering complex of apartments and suites looks out on the water from quiet grounds full of bright flowers. Most of the units have a sea view; in the others you'll catch a glimpse of the ocean as well as of the Bosque Estatal de Guánica. Each is decorated in bright colors; the larger rooms have ample balconies for a barbeque. Maid service is provided weekly; daily service can be arranged for an additional fee. You can rent kayaks or hop a boat to Gilligan's Island; the nearest mainland beaches are about a 10-minute drive. *Rte. 333, Km 6.7, San Jacinto Sector Box 394, 00635 787/821–3600 787/821–0744 www.maryleesbythesea.com 10 rooms BBQs, some kitchenettes, some kitchens, dock, boating, laundry facilities, some pets allowed; no room phones, no room TVs MC, V EP.*

Fodor's Choice ★

Sports & the Outdoors

DIVING & SNORKELING Dramatic walls created by the continental shelf provide great diving off the Guánica coast. There are also shallow gardens around Gilligan's Island and Cayo de Caña Gorda (off Balneario Caña Gorda) that attract both snorkelers and divers. **Dive Copamarina** (Copamarina Beach Resort, Rte. 333, Km 6.5 787/821–6009 Ext. 771 or 719) offers instruction and trips. **Paul Julien's Caribbean Vacation Villa** (Rte. 333, #15, San Jacinto Sector 787/821–5364) rents scuba gear as well as windsurfing equipment.

HIKING The Bosque Estatal de Guánica has 12 major trails for which the forest office on Route 334 has maps. **Paul Julien's Caribbean Vacation Villa** (Rte. 333, #15, San Jacinto Sector 787/821–5364) arranges guided hikes and rents gear, such as lighted helmets for cave exploration.

Yauco

23 *8 km (5 mi) north of Guánica.*

The picturesque town of Yauco in the southern foothills of the Cordillera Central is known for its coffee and the February festival celebrating the end of the bean harvest. It's rumored to be the birthplace of *chuletas can can* (twice-cooked pork chops), called "can can" because of the resemblance the pork chop's edges have to dancers' skirts.

Where to Eat

$–$$ **La Guardarraya.** In an old-fashioned country-style house, with windows that look out on gardens, you'll find some of the best *chuletas can can* (twice-cooked pork chops) anywhere. Other traditional dishes include stewed rice and pork, steak with onions, and fried chicken. Save room for the vanilla flan. *Rte. 127, Km 6.0 787/856–4222 MC, V Closed Mon.*

Sports & the Outdoors

HORSEBACK RIDING **Campo Allegre** (Rte. 127, Km 5.1 787/856–2609) is a 204-acre horse ranch that conducts ½-hour, 1-hour, and 2-hour rides through the hills surrounding Yauco. There are also pony rides for children. The on-site restaurant serves Yauco's specialty: chuletas can can.

La Parguera

24 *13 km (8 mi) west of Guánica; 24 km (15 mi) southwest of Yauco.*

La Parguera is famous for its bioluminescent bay, which may not be as spectacular as that near Vieques island but which is still a beautiful sight on a moonless night. Glass-bottom boats leave for 45-minute bay trips from a pedestrian walkway that has a Coney Island feeling, with booths selling candy and tropical drinks. The town bursts with Puerto Rican vacationers on long holiday weekends and in summer. From February through April, keep your eyes open for roadside vendors selling the area's famous pineapples. There's good diving and fishing in the area, and swimmers can take boats to cays or head to beaches in nearby Guánica or Cabo Rojo.

At night, small fishing boats line up along the pedestrian mall in La Parguera to take visitors out to view the **Bahía Fosforescente.** Microscopic dinoflagellates glow bright on moonless nights when disturbed by movement. ✉ *On pedestrian mall* *Boat ride $5* ⏲ *Nightly 7:30–midnight.*

Beaches

Cayo Caracoles. You can take a boat to and from this island for $5 per person. There are mangroves to explore as well as plenty of places to swim and snorkel.

Isla Mata de la Gata. For about $5 per person boats will transport you to and from this small island just off the coast for a day of swimming and snorkeling.

Playita Rosada. The small beach at the end of Calle 7 in La Parguera, doesn't compare to some of the longer beaches on the southwestern coast, but it's convenient for a quick swim and a picnic.

Where to Stay & Eat

$$ ✕ **La Casita.** The decor is simple, but generous portions of seafood make this family-run restaurant one of the town's favorites. Try the asopao, which is made with lobster or shrimp here, or one of several surf-and-turf dishes. ✉ *Calle Principal, at western edge of town* ☎ *787/899–1681* ▭ *MC, V* ⏲ *Closed Mon.*

$–$$ ✕ **Parguera Blues Café.** Off La Parguera's main street, this publike restaurant serves its own special "blues burgers" (made with blue cheese); the menu also includes filet mignon, chicken or shrimp with pasta, and the fish of the day. There's live music Friday and Saturday nights. ✉ *Centro Commercial El Muelle, Av. Los Pescadores* ☎ *787/899–4742* ▭ *MC, V.*

$ **Parador Villa del Mar.** "Peaceful" best describes this parador on a hill overlooking La Parguera. Air-conditioned rooms are comfortable and clean, but they don't have spectacular views. You'll find a small lounge by the reception area and a small pool tucked between the administrative building and the guest rooms. An open-air restaurant serves breakfast to guests for an additional $5 per person. ✉ *3 Calle Albizu Campos* *Box 1297, San Germán 00683* ☎ *787/899–4265* *787/899–4832* 🌐 *www.pinacolada.net/villadelmar* *25 rooms* *Cable TV, pool; no room phones* ▭ *AE, MC, V* *EP.*

★ $ **Parador Villa Parguera.** Each large, colorful room in this parador on the Bahía Fosforescente has a balcony or terrace, and throughout the complex you'll see bright tropical flowers. A spacious dining room ($–$$$), overlooking the pool and the bay beyond, serves excellent Puerto Rican and international dishes. On Saturday night there's live music and a floor show in the dance club. *Rte. 304, Km 3.3 Box 273, Lajas 00667 787/899–7777 or 787/899–3975 787/899–6040 www.villaparguera.com 70 rooms Restaurant, cable TV, pool, dock, lounge, dance club, video game room, meeting rooms AE, D, DC, MC, V EP.*

Nightlife & the Arts

Action at the pedestrian mall heats up at sunset, when people stroll near the sea. The live floor show at **Parador Villa Parguera** (Rte. 304, Km 2.3 787/899–7777 or 787/899–3975) starts at 7 on Saturday and includes a buffet. The show changes every three months; performances have included a comedy revue and folkloric dancing. The cost is $35, including the dinner. On Friday and Saturday **Parguera Blues Café** (3 Calle Albizu Campos 787/899–4265) has a rock or blues band starting at 9 or 10 PM.

Sports & the Outdoors

DIVING & SNORKELING Endangered leatherback turtles, eels, and an occasional manatee can be seen from many of the sites that attract divers and snorklers from all parts. There are more than 50 shore-dive sites off La Parguera. **Paradise Scuba** (Rte. 304, Km 1.3 787/899–7611) has classes and trips, including night snorkeling excursions in phosphorescent waters. **Parguera Divers** (Posada Porlamar, Rte. 304, Km 3.3 787/899–4171 www.pargueradivers.com) offers scuba and snorkeling expeditions and basic instruction.

FISHING You can spend a day or half-day fishing for blue marlin, tuna, or reef fish with Captain Mickey Amador at **Parguera Fishing Charters** (Rte. 304, Km 3.8 787/382–4698 or 787/899–4698 members.aol.com/mareja).

Shopping

Outdoor stands near Bahía Fosforescente sell all kinds of souvenirs, from T-shirts to beaded necklaces. In La Parguera's center, there are several small souvenir shops, including **Nautilus** (Rte. 304 787/899–4565), that sell T-shirts, posters, mugs, and trinkets made from shells.

San Germán

10 km (6 mi) north of La Parguera, 166 km (104 mi) southwest of San Juan.

During its early years, San Germán was a city on the move. Although debate rages about the first settlement's exact founding date and location, the town is believed to have been established in 1510 near Guánica. Plagued by mosquitoes, the settlers moved north along the west coast, where they encountered French pirates and smugglers. In the 1570s they fled inland to the current location, but they were still harassed. Determined and creative, they dug tunnels and moved beneath the city (the tunnels are now part of the water system). Today San Germán has a population of 39,000, and its intellectual and political activity is anything but underground. Students and professors from the Inter-American University often fill the town's bars and cafés.

Around San Germán's two main squares—Plazuela Santo Domingo and Plaza Francisco Mariano Quiñones (named for an abolitionist)—are buildings done in every conceivable style of architecture found on the island including mission, Victorian, creole, and Spanish colonial. The city's tourist office offers a free guided trolley tour. Most of the buildings are private homes; two of them—the Capilla de Porta Coeli and the Museo de Arte y Casa de Estudio—are museums. The historical center is surrounded by strip malls, and the town is hemmed to the south and west by busy seaside resorts.

25 The **Museo de Arte y Casa de Estudio,** at the city's southern edge, is a yellow, early-20th-century home with neoclassical influences that has been turned into a museum. Displays include colonial furnishings, religious art, and Taíno artifacts; there are also changing art exhibits by local painters. ✉ *7 Calle Esperanza* ☎ *787/892–8870* 🎟 *Free* ⏲ *Wed.–Sun. 10–noon and 1–3.*

26 The **Casa de Lola Rodríguez de Tió** (circa 1870) is on the National Registry of Historic Places and bears the name of poet and independence activist Lola Rodríguez de Tió. A plaque claims she lived in this light green creole-style house, though town officials say it belonged to her sister. Rodríguez, whose mother was a descendent of Ponce de León, was deported several times by Spanish authorities here for her revolutionary ideas. She lived in Venezuela and then in Cuba, where she died in 1924. The museum, which contains Rodríguez's desk and papers, isn't regularly open to the public; check with the tourist office. ✉ *13 Calle Dr. Santiago Veve* ☎ *787/892–3500 to arrange a visit* 🎟 *Free* ⏲ *By appointment only.*

27 The central Plaza Francisco Mariano Quiñones is dominated by the **Iglesia de San Germán de Auxerre.** This yellow-and-white neoclassical church dates from 1739 and was built atop its predecessor. Be sure to look up at the carved wood ceiling in the nave. The impressive crystal chandelier was added in 1860. ✉ *Plaza Francisco Mariano Quiñones* ☎ *787/892–1027* ⏲ *Mass Mon.–Sat. at 7 AM and 7:30 PM and Sun. at 7, 8:30, and 10 AM and 7:30 PM.*

On the north side of Plaza Francisco Mariano Quiñones, at Calle José
28 Julien Acosta and Calle Cruz, is the two-story, yellow **La Casona.** It was built in 1871 for Tomás Agrait, who made it his home and a center of cultural activities in San Germán. It was later owned by the Bahr family and is also known as La Casona de Bahr. **Casa Vieja** (☎ 787/264–3954), one of the tenants of La Casino, is a small shop that carries Caribbean antiques.

29 The **Casa Alcaldía Antigua** (Old Municipal Building) is at the eastern end of Plaza Francisco Mariano Quiñones. From 1844 to 1950 it served as

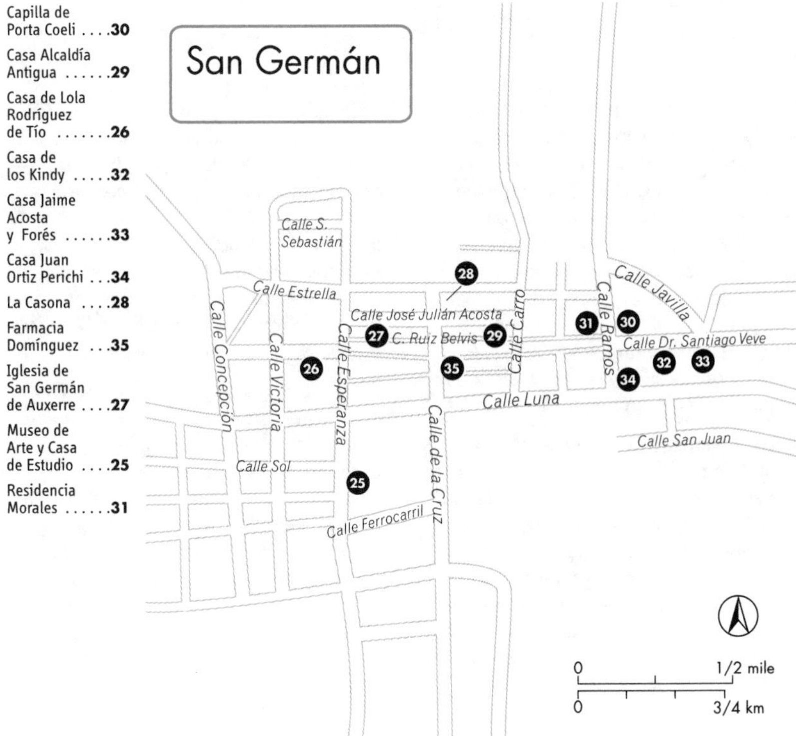

the city hall and municipal prison. At this writing the Spanish-colonial style building was being renovated.

★ 30 One of the oldest Christian religious structures in the Americas, the **Capilla de Porta Coeli** (Heaven's Gate Chapel), overlooks the long rectangular Plazuela de Santo Domingo. The original complex, which included a convent, was built in 1606; much of it was demolished in 1866, leaving only the chapel and a vestige of the convent's front wall. The mission-style chapel was restored and reopened for services in 1878. Now it functions as a museum of religious art, displaying painted wooden statuary by Latin American and Spanish artists. ✉ *Plazuela Santo Domingo* ☎ *787/892–5845* 🎫 *$1* ⏲ *Wed.–Sun. 9–4:45.*

31 The **Residencia Morales** (✉ 38 Calle Ramos), across the street from the Capilla de Porta Coeli on the Plazuela de Santo Domingo, is a private home designed in 1913 by architect Pedro Vivoni for his brother, Tomás Vivoni. The white Victorian building takes up an entire city block and has numerous towers and gables. The current owners have kept it in mint condition.

32 **Casa de los Kindy** (✉ 64 Calle Dr. Santiago Veve), east of the Plazuela de Santo Domingo, is a 19th-century home known for its eclectic ar-

CloseUp

LIVES OF THE SANTOS

WHEN THEY ARRIVED ON PUERTO RICO, *Spanish missionaries spread the word of God and fostered a spirited folk art. Since few people were literate, the missionaries often commissioned local artisans to create pictures and statues depicting Bible stories and saints or* santos. *These figures—fashioned of wood, clay, stone, or even gold—are still given a place of honor in homes throughout the island.*

Early santeros *(carvers) were influenced by the Spanish-baroque style. Later figures are simple and small, averaging about 8 inches tall. The carving of santos is usually a family tradition, and most of today's santeros have no formal art training. San Germán has been associated with santos-making since the origins of the art form, and the Rivera family has been known for its carvings for more than 150 years.*

Each santo has a traditional characteristic. You can spot the Virgin by her blue robes, St. Francis by the accompanying birds and animals, St. Barbara by her tower, and the Holy Spirit by its hovering dove. St. John, the island's patron saint, is an ever-popular subject, as is the Nativity, which might be just the Holy Family, or the family with an entire cast of herald angels, shepherds, and barnyard animals.

Carvings of Los Santos Reyes (The Three Kings) are also popular. Their feast day, January 6, is important on Puerto Rico. Celebrations often continue for days before or after the actual holiday, when it's difficult to find a home without these regal characters. In Puerto Rico, a magi is often strumming the cuatro, an island guitar.

chitecture, which includes neoclassical and creole elements. Note the stained-glass windows and the latticework on the balcony. It's now a private residence and not open to the public.

33 Down the street from Casa de los Kindy is **Casa Jaime Acosta y Forés** (✉ 70 Calle Dr. Santiago Veve), a beautiful yellow-and-white wooden house built in 1918. Inside, the walls are covered floor to ceiling with stenciling, and over the door is attractive fretwork. The house isn't open to the public.

34 You'll find an excellent example of Puerto Rican ornamental architecture in the **Casa Juan Ortiz Perichi** (✉ 94 Calle Luna), a block southeast of the Plazuela de Santo Domingo. This gigantic white home with a wraparound balcony was built in 1920. Note the stained-glass windows and wood trim around the doors. It's not open to the public.

35 Constructed in 1877, the dark-orange, Spanish colonial **Farmacia Domínguez** (✉ Calles Cruz and Dr. Santiago Veve) started out as a pharmacy and then became a restaurant. (At this writing, it was closed to the public.)

Where to Stay & Eat

$–$$$ **Cilantro's.** In a 120-year-old mansion called Casa Real, chef Carlos Rosario serves new Puerto Rican cuisine in an intimate, second-floor dining room (reservations are a good idea). Surrounded by arched walls, stained-glass windows and decorative Spanish tiles, you can try dorado with a black bean sauce or squid stuffed with sausage and lobster. There are also vegetarian dishes, and on Tuesday nights sushi is added to the menu. The restaurant offers changing lunch specials. ✉ *85 Calle Luna* ☎ *787/264–2735* ▭ *D, MC, V* ⊗ *Closed Wed.*

$–$$$ **Del Mar y Algo Mas.** Chef Eric John has made paella the signature dish of his restaurant near the Capilla de Porta Coeli. The menu includes a variety of Puerto Rican dishes, with an emphasis on seafood. ✉ *Plazuela Santo Domingo at Calle Carro* ☎ *787/636–4265* ▭ *MC, V.*

¢ **Parador Oasis.** San Germán's only hotel is in a melon-color, Spanish-colonial mansion near the center of town. It's far from luxurious, but there's a small pool and a helpful staff. Rooms are small and dark; those in a newer annex are better maintained than those in the original mansion. The restaurant ($–$$$) serves generous portions of Puerto Rican food. ✉ *72 Calle Luna* *Box 1063, 00683* ☎ *787/892–1175 or 800-942–8086* *787/892–4546* *52 rooms* *Restaurant, cable TV, pool, bar* ▭ *AE, D, DC, MC V* *EP.*

Cabo Rojo

36 *11 km (7 mi) west of San Germán.*

Named for the pinkish cliffs that surround it, Cabo Rojo was founded in 1771 as a port for merchant vessels—and for the smugglers and pirates who inevitably accompanied ocean-going trade. Today the area is known as a family resort destination, and many small, inexpensive hotels line its shores. There's also a town called Cabo Rojo, which is inland. Seaside settlements such as Puerto Real and Joyuda—the latter has a strip of more than 30 seafood restaurants overlooking the water—are found along the coast. Two others, Boquerón and Combate, are one-road seaside hamlets that are popular weekend and holiday destinations popular with local college students, though local ordinances, first passed in 2003, now curb the rowdiness by prohibiting liquor sales after midnight. Although you can hike in wildlife refuges at the outskirts of town, there aren't any area outfitters, so be sure to bring along water, sunscreen, and all other necessary supplies.

★ The **Bosque Estatal de Boquerón** (Boquerón National Forest) encompasses three tracts of land at the island's southern tip. You can hike along a rugged peninsula to the 1881 Cabo Rojo Lighthouse at the end of Route 301, but the lighthouse itself is not open to the public. **Refugio de Vida Silvestre** (✉ Rte. 301, Km 1.2 ☎ 787/851–7258), a part of the Bosque Estatal de Boquerón, is run by the U.S. Fish and Wildlife Service. An interpretive center has exhibits of live freshwater fish and sea turtles. You see as many as 100 species of birds along the trails, even the elusive yellow-shouldered blackbird. The refuge and its interpretive center are open weekdays from 7 to 3:30, and admission is free. ✉ *Rte. 101, Boquerón*

☎ 787/851–7260 interpretive center 🎫 Free ⏲ Interpretive center weekdays 7–3:30.

Beaches

Fodor'sChoice ★ **Balneario Boquerón.** The long stretch of sand at this beach off Route 101 is a favorite with islanders, especially during the Easter weekend. You'll find changing facilities, cabins, showers, restrooms, and picnic tables; it costs $2 to enter with a car.

Buyé. The white-sand beach at Km 4.8 on Route 307 has palm trees and crystal-clear waters.

Fodor'sChoice ★ **El Combate.** At the end of Route 3301 is this great beach that draws college students to its rustic waterfront eateries. You can rent small boats and kayaks here, and in summer there are often concerts and festivals.

Playa Joyuda. Palms dot this good swimming beach that runs alongside Route 102.

La Playuela. The crescent-shape strand is the most secluded of the area's beaches. It's on Route 301 near the salt flats.

Where to Stay & Eat

★ $$–$$$ ✕ **El Bohío.** Watch tarpon play in the water while you dine on the enclosed deck at this informal restaurant. The long list of seafood is prepared in a variety of ways: shrimp comes breaded, stewed, or in a salad; conch is served as a salad or cooked in a butter and garlic sauce. ✉ *Rte. 102, Km 9.7, Joyuda* ☎ *787/851–2755* 💳 *AE, DC, MC, V.*

$–$$$ ✕ **Annie's.** A dining room with windows facing the ocean is a fitting place to try some of the southwest coast's best seafood. You can snack on *empanadillas* (deep-fried fritters) stuffed with seafood or feast on red snapper with rice and beans. This place is casual and friendly. ✉ *Calle 3, El Combate* ☎ *787/254–0021* 💳 *AE, MC, V* ⏲ *Closed Mon.–Wed.*

$–$$ ✕ **Galloway's.** From a porch overlooking Bahía Boquerón, catch the sunset while enjoying seafood—caught fresh from local waters and often prepared in traditional ways. The menu also has a few international choices, including some Italian dishes. There's a lively happy hour and occasional live music. ✉ *12 Calle José de Diego, Boquerón* ☎ *787/254–3302* 💳 *MC, V* ⏲ *Closed Wed.*

¢–$ ✕ **Cafetería Los Chapines.** This rustic seaside shack sells cold drinks, snacks, and fish and chicken dishes. Be sure to try one of the specialty sandwiches, which are made with deep-fried plantains instead of bread. ✉ *Calle 3, El Combate* ☎ *787/254–4005* 💳 *MC, V.*

★ $ ✕🏨 **Bahía Salinas Beach Hotel.** The Cabo Rojo Lighthouse is this resortlike parador's closest neighbor. You can wander along the boardwalk or the garden paths, bask in the sun on a deck or terrace, or relax in a Jacuzzi that's filled with therapeutic salt crystals from the nearby salt flats. Rooms are spacious and have reproduction Puerto Rican antiques. The Agua al Cuello restaurant ($$–$$$) serves seafood; don't overlook the giant tostones. ✉ *End of Rte. 301, La Playuela* 📫 *HC-01, Box 2356, 00622* ☎ *787/254–1212 or 877/205–7507* 📠 *787/254–1215* 🌐 *www.bahiasalinas.net* 🛏 *24 rooms* 👍 *Restaurant, cable TV, pool, gym, hot tub, bar, lounge, playground; no room phones* 💳 *MC, V* 🍽 *EP.*

¢–$ **Parador Boquemar.** It's 5 to 10 minutes by car to Balneario Boquerón from this parador. Rooms are decorated with tropical prints and rattan furniture; ask for a third-floor room with a balcony overlooking the water. La Cascada restaurant ($$–$$$) offers Puerto Rican cuisine. On weekends the lounge is filled with live music. *Calle Gill Buyé, Boquerón Box 133, 00622 787/851–2158 or 888/634–4343 787/851–7600 www.boquemar.com 75 rooms Restaurant, refrigerators, cable TV, pool, boating, jet skiing, bicycles, lounge, meeting rooms AE, D, DC, MC, V EP.*

¢ **Combate Beach Hotel.** A five-minute walk from El Combate beach, this hotel has large guestrooms as well as six apartments with full kitchens. The Puerto Angelino restaurant ($–$$$) serves seafood and Puerto Rican fare. Other restaurants and night spots are within walking distance along the shore. *Rte. 3301, El Combate Box 1138, 00622 787/254–7053 or 787/254–2358 787/254–2358 20 units Restaurant, refrigerators, cable TV, pool, bar; no room phones MC, V EP.*

★ ¢–$ **Parador Joyuda Beach.** Right on the shore, near Joyuda's restaurant row, this friendly parador has a large lobby and spacious rooms. Ask for one of the sunset suites, which have ocean views. You'll find drinks and a snack bar by the pool. *Rte. 102, Km 11.7, Joyuda HC-01, Box 18410, 00623 787/851–5650 or 800/981–5464 787/255–3750 www.joyudabeach.com 41 rooms Snack bar, cable TV, pool, beach, Internet AE, MC, V EP.*

¢ **El Muelle Guest House.** About a five-minute walk from Boquerón Beach, the somewhat rustic rooms are clean and spacious, suitable for one person or a couple. All rooms have TV, some have kitchen facilities. It's a good choice if you're planning to stay the week. At this writing, nine more rooms are in the works, with plans to open them in 2005. *Calle Jose de Diego, Boquerón 00623 787/ 254–2801 802/609–9105 www.elmuelleguesthouse.com 8 rooms BBQ AE, MC, V.*

Nightlife

The **Bahía Salinas Beach Hotel** (End of Rte. 301, La Playela 787/254–1212) often has live music shows. **Galloway's** (Calle Jose de Diego, Boquerón 787/254–3302) draws an interesting crowd to its bar and has occasional live music. Check in at **Tropicoro Sports Bar** (El Combate 787/254–2466), a lively spot with billiard tables, to see whether there's a band playing.

Sports & the Outdoors

GOLF Get in nine holes at the **Club Deportivo del Oeste** (Rte. 102, Km 15.4, Joyuda 787/254–3748 or 787/851–1880). Jack Bender incorporated the region's hills in his design to provide golfers with panoramic views while they play. The course is open daily; greens fees are $30. At this writing, the course was in the process of an expansion to a full 18 holes.

DIVING & SNORKELING Several reef-bordered cays lie off the Cabo Rojo area near walls that drop to 100 feet. A mile-long reef along Las Coronas, better known as **Cayo Ron,** has a variety of hard and soft coral, reef fish, and lobster. You can arrange snorkeling and scuba trips with **Tour Marine** (Rte. 101,

Km 14.1, Joyuda ☎ 787/851–9259). The company will also take anglers out to waters off Cabo Rojo's coast.

SOUTHERN PUERTO RICO A TO Z

To research prices, get advice from other travelers, and book travel arrangements, visit www.fodors.com.

AIR TRAVEL

Aeropuerto Mercedita is about 8 km (5 mi) east of Ponce's downtown. It accommodates private planes and Cape Air flights from San Juan. Taxis at the airport operate under a meter system; it costs about $6 to get downtown Ponce. Some hotels have shuttles from the airport, but you must make arrangements in advance.

Airport Information **Aeropuerto Mercedita** ✉ Rte. 506 off Rte. 52, Ponce ☎ 787/842-6292.

Carriers **Cape Air** ☎ 787/844-2099 in Ponce, 787/253-1121 in San Juan, 800/352-0714 in U.S. 🌐 www.flycapeair.com.

BUS TRAVEL

There's no easy network of buses linking the towns in southern Puerto Rico with the capital of San Juan or with each other. Some municipalities and private companies operate buses or *públicos* (usually large vans) that make many stops. Call ahead; although reservations aren't usually required, you'll need to check on schedules, which change frequently. The cost of a público from Ponce to San Juan is about $15 to $20; agree on a price before you start your journey.

Choferes Unidos de Ponce ✉ Terminal de Carros Públicos, Calle Vives and Calle Mendéz Vigo, Ponce Centro, Ponce ☎ 787/764-0540. **Línea Caborrojeña** ✉ Rte. 103 in center of town, Cabo Rojo ☎ 787/723-9155. **Línea San Germeña** ✉ Terminal de Carros Públicos, Calle Luna at entrance to town, San Germán ☎ 787/722-3392 or 787/892-1076.

CAR RENTAL

You can rent cars at the Luis Muñoz Marín International Airport and other San Juan locations. There are also car-rental agencies in some of the larger cities along the south coast. Rates run about $35 to $45 a day, depending on the car. You may get a better deal if you rent a car for a week or more. Test your vehicle before heading out to be sure it runs properly.

Avis ✉ Mercedita Airport, Ponce ☎ 787/842-6154. **Budget** ✉ Mercedita Airport, Ponce ☎ 787/848-0907. **Dollar** ✉ Av. Los Caobos and Calle Acacia, Ponce ☎ 787/843-6940. **International Car Rental** ✉ Rte. 100, Km 6.0, Cabo Rojo ☎ 787/254-0384. **Leaseway of Puerto Rico** ✉ Rte. 3, Km 140.1, Guayama ☎ 787/864-8149 🌐 www.leasewaypr.com ✉ Ponce ☎ 787/843-4330.

CAR TRAVEL

A road map is essential in southern Puerto Rico. So is patience: allow extra time for twisting mountain roads and wrong turns. Some roads, especially in rural areas, aren't plainly marked. The fastest route through the region is the Luis Ferré Expressway (Route 52), a toll road that runs from San Juan to Ponce, crossing the island's central mountain range.

EMERGENCY SERVICES There's no AAA service in Puerto Rico, but independent tow trucks regularly scout the Luis A. Ferré Expressway (Route 52) looking for disabled vehicles. Police also patrol the expressway. A number of towing companies will send trucks on request.

Alfredo Towing Service ☎ 787/251-6750. **Dennis Towing** ☎ 787/504-5724.

GASOLINE Gas stations are plentiful, particularly near expressway exits and at town entrances on secondary roads. Some stations are open 24 hours, but many close at around midnight or 1 AM. Prices in Puerto Rico are given in liters.

PARKING You can find free on-street parking in most southern cities; metered parking is rare. Larger communities have lots in their downtown areas. Prices are usually less than $1 an hour.

ROAD CONDITIONS Major highways in southern Puerto Rico are well maintained. You may encounter some construction on Highway 2 between Ponce and Guánica. Watch out for potholes on secondary roads, especially after heavy rains.

EMERGENCIES

Emergency Number **General Emergencies** ☎ 911.

Hospitals **Hospital de Area Alejandro Buitrago** ✉ Av. Central and Calle Principal, Guayama ☎ 787/864-4300 or 787/892-1860. **Hospital de la Concepción** ✉ 41 Calle Luna, San Germán ☎ 787/892-1860. **Hospital Damas** ✉ 2213 Ponce Bypass Rd., Villa Grillasca, Ponce ☎ 787/840-8686.

Pharmacies **El Amal** ✉ Valle Real Shopping Center, Rte. 2 Urbanización Valle Real, Ponce ☎ 787/844-5555. **Walgreens** ✉ 1 Calle Marginal, Guayama ☎ 787/864-5355 ✉ 13 Av. Fagot, Ponce Centro, Ponce ☎ 787/841-2135 ✉ 64 Calle Luna, San Germán ☎ 787/892-1170.

ENGLISH-LANGUAGE MEDIA

Publications in English are harder to find in southern Puerto Rico than in San Juan. Look for the English-language edition of the *San Juan Star* on newsstands and in drug stores and gas stations. Some hotel gift shops have a small selection of English-language books and newspapers. Your best bet is Isabel II Books & Magazine in Ponce, which has a large selection of books, magazines, and mainland papers, although the newspapers are normally delivered a day or two late.

Isabel II Books & Magazine ✉ 66 Calle Isabel, Ponce Centro, Ponce ☎ 787/848-5019.

HEALTH

The island's tap water is generally safe to drink. Fruits should be well washed before being eaten if bought from a roadside stand or in a market. Remember that the sun is strong and shines most of the time on the south coast, so be sure to have sunscreen and drinking water with you.

MAIL & SHIPPING

There are branches of the U.S. Post Office throughout the region. You can buy stamps in Pueblo Supermarkets and in many gift shops.

Post Offices **Cabo Rojo Post Office** ✉ 64 Calle Carbonell, Cabo Rojo ☎ 787/851-1095. **Guayama Post Office** ✉ 151 Calle Ashford, Guyama ☎ 787/864-1150. **Ponce Post Office** ✉ 94 Calle Atocha, Ponce Centro, Ponce ☎ 787/842-2997.

OVERNIGHT SERVICES Express delivery services are available at the U.S. Post Office. Some shops are authorized to handle Federal Express (FedEx) packages, and there are FedEx stations in Ponce and Guayama. Note that there's no Saturday pick-up service in the area. You can drop off packages and U.S. mail at area PostNet stores, which also sell envelopes and boxes.

FedEx ✉ Plaza Guayama, Rte. 3, Km 134.9, Guayama ☎ 877/838-7834 ✉ Mercedita Airport, Ponce ☎ 877/838-7834. **PostNet** ✉ Calle 3, Urbanization Borinquen, Cabo Rojo ☎ 787/254-0384.

MONEY MATTERS

You'll find plenty of banks in the region, and many supermarkets, drug stores, and gas stations have ATMs. Banks are normally open weekdays from 9 AM to 3 PM or 4 PM. Some banks—such as the Scotiabank branch in Ponce—are also open until noon on Saturday. You can exchange foreign currency in Banco Popular branches; Scotiabank exchanges Canadian currency. Western Union service is available at Pueblo Supermarkets.

Banco Popular ✉ Plaza Guayama, Rte. 3, Km 134.9, Guayama ☎ 787/866-0180 ✉ Plaza las Delicias, Ponce Centro, Ponce ☎ 787/843-8000 or 787/848-2410. **Scotiabank** ✉ Plaza las Delicias, Ponce Centro, Ponce ☎ 787/259-8535.

PUBLIC TRANSPORTATION

Ponce offers free transportation to its major attractions on trolleys and tourist trains. They run daily from 8:30 AM to about 7:30 PM, and leave from Plaza las Delicias. On Sunday, Guayama has a free trolley that runs to many sights. Arroyo's free trolley operations on Saturday and Sunday, and a trolley tour of San Germán is available by appointment.

Arroyo Trolley ✉ Acaldía de Arroyo, 64 Calle Morse, Arroyo ☎ 787/721-1574. **Guayama Trolley** ✉ Acaldía de Guayama, Calle Vicente Pales, Guayama ☎ 787/864-7765. **Ponce Trolley & Chu Chu** ✉ Ponce Municipal Tourism Office, Plaza las Delicias, Ponce Centro, Ponce ☎ 787/841-8160. **San Germán Trolley** ✉ Acaldía de San Germán, 136 Calle Luna, San Germán ☎ 787/892-3500.

SAFETY

Crime is on the rise in Puerto Rico and, as in any unfamiliar destination, you need to exercise reasonable caution. Don't leave valuables unattended at the beach or out in plain sight inside your car. Use caution when walking in cities, especially at night.

TAXIS

In Ponce, you can hail taxis in tourist areas and outside hotels. In smaller towns, it's best to call a taxi. You can also hire a car service (make arrangements through your hotel); often you can negotiate a rate that's lower than what you would pay for a taxi.

Borinquen Taxi ☎ 787/843-6000, 787/843-6100 in Ponce. **Ojeda Taxi** ☎ 787/259-7676 in San Germán. **Ponce Limousine Service** ☎ 787/848-0469. **Ponce Taxi Association** ☎ 787/842-3370 in Ponce.

TELEPHONES

Puerto Rico's two area codes are 787 and 939. You must dial the area code and the 7-digit number on any call you make in Puerto Rico. Dial 1 before the area code when calling from one municipality to another. Public phones are readily available throughout the southern part of the island, but you may have to try two or three phones before you find one that works. A local call costs 25¢, and you can pay with credit cards, phone cards, or coins.

TOURS

Call the Museo de la Historia de Ponce to arrange for a tour of Ponce's historical sights. Tours, which vary in length, start at $5 per person. Alelí Tours and Encantos Ecotours Southwest in La Parguera offer ecological tours of the southwestern area, including two- or three-hour kayak trips that cost about $25. Sunshine Tours, based in San Juan, also offer trips to the Bosque Estatal de Guánica, Ponce, and elsewhere. Prices start around $45 per person and include transportation from San Juan hotels.

Alelí Tours ✉ Rte. 304, Km 3.2, La Parguera ☎ 787/899-6086. **Encantos Ecotours Southwest** ✉ El Muelle Shopping Center, Av. Pescadores, La Parguera ☎ 787/808-0005. **Museo de la Historia de Ponce** ✉ 51-53 Calle Isabel, Ponce Centro, Ponce ☎ 787/844-7071. **Sunshine Tours** ✉ Normandie Hotel, Av. Muñoz Rivera at Parque de Tercer Milenio, Puerta de Tierra, San Juan ☎ 787/729-2929 🌐 www.puerto-rico-sunshinetours.com.

VISITOR INFORMATION

In Ponce, the municipal tourist office is open weekdays from 8 to 4:30, and the Puerto Rico Tourism Company has hours weekdays from 8 to 5. The Cabo Rojo branch is open Monday through Saturday from 8 to 4:30. Smaller cities generally have a tourism office in the city hall that's open weekdays from 8 to noon and 1 to 4.

Ponce Municipal Tourist Office ✉ 2nd fl. of Citibank, Plaza las Delicias, Ponce Centro, Ponce ☎ 787/841-8160 or 787/841-8044. **Puerto Rico Tourism Company** ✉ Rte. 101, Km 13.7, Cabo Riojo ☎ 787/851-7070 ✉ 291 Av. Los Caobos, Sector Vallas Torres, Ponce ☎ 787/843-0465.

NORTHWESTERN PUERTO RICO

4

LEARN TO SURF
at Rincón Surf School ⇨ *p.183*

JOIN GOLFERS FROM FAR AND WIDE
at the Hyatt Dorado courses ⇨ *p.163*

WANDER AN UNDERGROUND RIVER
in Parque de las Cavernas del Río Camuy, one of world's largest caves ⇨ *p.166*

RENT A BRIGHTLY COLORED COTTAGE
at Villas del Mar Hau ⇨ *p.170*

PLAY ON ONE OF THE BEST BEACHES
Playa Crashboat ⇨ *p.178*

ESCAPE TO UTTER LUXURY
at Horned Dorset Primavera ⇨ *p.181*

PLAY YOUR OWN GAME OF SURVIVOR
on Mona Island ⇨ *p.185*

Updated by
Kevin Mead

LESS THAN A CENTURY AGO, northwestern Puerto Rico was overwhelmingly rural. Some large fruit plantations dotted the coast, while farther inland coffee was grown on hillside *fincas* (farms). Regardless, a few ports, notably the west-coast city of Mayagüez, took on a somewhat cosmopolitan air and drew immigrants from around the world.

The generally slow pace of the area began to change during the mid-20th century. The government's Operation Bootstrap program drew more manufacturing into the area, new roads brought once-isolated towns into the mainstream, and tourists began to discover the gold sand of the Atlantic coast and the mighty waves near the town of Rincón.

On the Atlantic coast, Dorado was one of the first areas to develop luxury resorts, and it now offers top-notch hotels, golf courses, and almost every kind of water sport imaginable. Inland, the more remote mountain areas still produce coffee; they also lure more adventurous travelers to their narrow, winding roads. Just past Arecibo begin the rolling hills of karst country, terrain built up by limestone deposits in which erosion has produced fissures, sinkholes, underground streams, and caverns. It's here, in several large forest reserves and around the Río Camuy cave network, that Puerto Rico has its greatest ecotourism potential—though you'll still find yourself far from crowds.

On the west coast, the waves around Aguadilla and Rincón are as popular as ever. Visitors of all kinds come here to surf or just enjoy the beaches and sunsets. Many have decided not to return home.

Exploring Northwestern Puerto Rico

Highway 22 heads west from San Juan and swings around the northwestern part of the island, skirting the beaches of the northern coast. A short 45 minutes from the capital is the resort town of Dorado. Farther west, at Arecibo, the island's limestone karst country begins, filled with strangely shaped hills, cliffs, and sinkholes. You can delve into the area by taking Route 10 south, which leads to the Río Abajo Forest Reserve and the mountain town of Utuado, or by taking Route 129, which leads to the karst country's premier attraction, Las Cavernas del Río Camuy.

Numerous small, narrow roads traverse the rugged Cordillera Central, the island's central mountain range. Much of the Ruta Panorámica, a network of small roads running horizontally across the island, passes through this area.

After Arecibo, Highway 22 turns into Highway 2 and continues down the west coast, where the ragged shoreline holds some of the island's best surfing beaches—as well as calmer swimming beaches—and a steady contingent of surfers gives the area a laid-back atmosphere.

Numbers in the text correspond to numbers in the margin and on the Northwestern Puerto Rico map.

About the Restaurants

Throughout northwestern Puerto Rico you'll find wonderful *criollo* cuisine, interspersed with international restaurants ranging from French to Japanese. You can enjoy five-course meals in elegant surroundings at night, then sip coffee on an outdoor balcony the next morning. Tips, normally 15% to 20%, are usually not included in the bill, but it's always wise to double-check.

WHAT IT COSTS In U.S. dollars					
	$$$$	**$$$**	**$$**	**$**	**¢**
AT DINNER	over $30	$20–$30	$12–$20	$8–$12	under $8

Prices are per person for a main course at dinner.

About the Hotels

Lodging in the area runs the gamut from posh resorts offering windsurfing lessons and championship golf courses to rustic cabins in the middle of a forest reserve. The Dorado area has a concentration of sleek resorts; the western part of the island near Rincón has a variety of hotels, from furnished apartments geared toward families to colorful small hotels. In the central mountains, a few old plantation homes have been turned into wonderful country inns that transport you back to slower and quieter times.

WHAT IT COSTS In U.S. dollars					
	$$$$	**$$$**	**$$**	**$**	**¢**
FOR 2 PEOPLE	over $350	$250–$350	$150–$250	$80–$150	under $80

Prices are for a double room in high season, excluding 9% tax (11% for hotels with casinos, 7% for paradores) and 5%–12% service charge.

Timing

In winter the weather is at its best, but you'll have to compete with other visitors for hotel rooms; book well in advance. Winter is also the height of the surfing season on the west coast. In summer, many family-oriented hotels fill up with *sanjuaneros* escaping the city for the weekend—some hotels require a two-night stay. Larger resorts normally drop their rates in summer by at least 10%. The weather gets hot, especially in August and September, but the beaches help keep everyone cool.

THE NORTH COAST

West of San Juan, large tracts of coconut palms silhouette Dorado and its environs, the scenic remnants of large coconut and fruit plantations. Farther west, near Arecibo, the island's limestone karst country is distinguished by haystack-shaped hills (called *mogotes* by locals) and underground rivers and caves. One of the island's most fascinating geological wonders is the Río Camuy cave system, one of the largest such systems in the western hemisphere. Nearby, science takes center stage at the Arecibo Observatory, the largest radar–radio telescope in the world.

If you have 3 days

If you feel like indulging yourself, spend three days at one of the resorts in **Dorado** 1. Set aside a day to visit one of Puerto Rico's greatest natural wonders, Parque de las Cavernas del Río Camuy, and one of its greatest man-made ones, Observatorio de Arecibo, both of which are near **Arecibo** 2.

If you want a more relaxed, secluded environment, try **Isabela** 3, a quiet town with a gorgeous shoreline and get-away-from-it-all inns. Spend your first day on the beach, capping it off with a sunset horseback ride along the shore. On the second day, head to Parque de las Cavernas del Río Camuy and Observatorio de Arecibo, and on Day 3 visit the friendly beachfront town of **Rincón** 10.

If you have 5 days

For the first three days use one of the converted coffee plantations near **Utuado** 4 as your base camp and explore the area's sights, such as Parque Ceremonial Indigena de Caguana and Lago Dos Bocas, both of which are near Utuado; Parque de las Cavernas del Río Camuy or Observatorio de Arecibo near **Arecibo** 2; or Bosque Estatal de Toro Negro near **Jayuya** 5. Then make your way to the west coast and **Rincón** 10 for two days of great waves, beautiful sunsets, and laid-back good times.

If you have 7 days

Start out with two days at a **Dorado** 1 resort, spend three days exploring the inlands and staying at a former coffee plantation in the mountains near **Utuado** 4 or **Jayuya** 5, and finish up with two days in **Rincón** 10 on the west coast. Or . . . forget about variety and dedicate your entire week to one of those three locations—just make sure you don't miss Parque de las Cavernas del Río Camuy near **Arecibo** 2, a highlight of any trip to this region.

Dorado

1 *27 km (17 mi) west of San Juan.*

This small and tidy town has a definite festive air about it, even though more and more it's turning into a suburb for San Juan's workers. It's one of the oldest vacation spots on the island, having gotten a boost in 1955 when Laurance Rockefeller bought the pineapple, coconut, and grapefruit plantation of Dr. Alfred Livingston and his daughter, Clara, and built a resort on the property. Today, the former plantation is the site of the Hyatt Dorado Beach Resort & Country Club, one of Puerto Rico's premier luxury resorts. Although its sister hotel, the Hyatt Regency Cerromar Beach Resort & Casino, no longer accepts guests, its restaurants, casino, and other facilities are open. In addition to the Cerromar's two golf courses, which are still in operation, the Hyatt Dorado Beach has four of the best-known golf courses in Puerto Rico. The town of Dorado itself is fun to visit; its winding road leads across a bridge to a main square, and there are small delis, restaurants, and shops nearby. Most visitors, however, don't stray too far from the beach or their hotel.

Beaches

At the end of Route 697, Dorado's **Playa Sardinera** is suitable for swimming and has shade trees, changing rooms, and restrooms. **Playa Breñas,** where the Hyatt resort is located, is known for its surfing; adventurous swimmers also enjoy the waves. The 2,500-foot-long **Playa Cerro Gordo,** at the end of Route 690, is lined with cliffs. It's very popular and can get crowded on weekends. **Playa Los Tubos,** on Route 687 in Vega Baja, is popular for both swimming and surfing. It holds a summer festival with live music and water-sports competitions, normally the first week of July.

Where to Stay & Eat

$$–$$$ ✕ **El Ladrillo.** This cozy spot with brick floors and walls (*el ladrillo* means "the brick") is known for its grilled steaks, including T-bones and filet mignon. It also has a wide selection of seafood—try the *zarzuela,* a combination of lobster, squid, octopus, clams, and more. ✉ *Calle Méndez Vigo 334* ☎ *787/796–2120* ▭ *AE, MC, V.*

$$ ✕ **Mangére.** You'll find a long menu of Italian cuisine and an impressive wine list at this spacious restaurant decorated in pastel colors. Entrées to be recommended include veal medallions with portobello and porcini mushrooms, smoked Norwegian salmon with capers, and linguine carbonara. ✉ *Rte. 693, Km 8.5* ☎ *787/796–4444* ▭ *AE, D, MC, V.*

$–$$ ✕ **A La Brasa Steakhouse.** The black tables and chairs of this Argentine steak house are offset by red-and-green walls. Meat is served with a *chimichurri* sauce (parsley garlic, vinegar, and oregano). A delicious dessert selection is the *panqueque de dulce de leche,* a caramel crêpe. ✉ *Rte. 693, Km 8.5* ☎ *787/796–4477* ▭ *AE, D, MC, V.*

$$$$ 🏨 **Hyatt Dorado Beach Resort & Country Club.** Sprawling over 1,000 acres on a secluded white-sand beach, the former plantation still utilizes the great facilities at the shuttered Regency Cerromar Beach—including its famous river pool—which are reached by a free trolley. Most rooms have four-poster beds, patios or balconies, and marble baths. The Cerromar's casino and Club Bacchus disco are centers of nightlife. For the requisite romantic dinner, ask for a balcony table at Su Casa, one of the Dorado Beach's five restaurants. Note that MAP is compulsory from December 15 through the end of February. ✉ *Rte. 693, Km 10.8, 00646* ☎ *787/796–1234 or 800/233–1234* 📠 *787/796–2022* 🌐 *www.doradobeach.hyatt.com* *298 rooms* *9 restaurants, room service, minibars, cable TV with movies, 4 18-hole golf courses, miniature golf, 15 tennis courts, 3 pools, spa, health club, hair salon, beach, snorkeling, windsurfing, boating, jet skiing, bicycles, hiking, casino, video game room, bar, shop, baby-sitting, children's programs (ages 3–12), dry cleaning, laundry service, business services, car rental* ▭ *AE, D, DC, MC, V* 🍽 *EP.*

$$–$$$$ 🏨 **Embassy Suites Dorado del Mar Beach & Golf Resort.** All the handsomely appointed suites in this beachfront resort have a living room and separate bedroom; most have ocean views. Golfers can take in the mountains and the sea at the same time while playing the Chi Chi Rodríguez–designed course, then head to the Paradise Cafe for a dinner of crusted sea bass with mango butter and yucca mofongo. ✉ *201*

Ecotourism The concept of ecotourism is catching on in Puerto Rico. Not surprisingly, many outfits are based in Rincón and center around trips to Mona Island. This protected island has world-class diving as well as a series of trails that wind their way along the edge of steep cliffs.

Hiking Northwestern Puerto Rico has a number of forest reserves that rival the better-known El Yunque in beauty. The Bosque Estatal de Río Abajo has trails in the island's "karst country." The cloud-covered Bosque Estatal de Toro Negro has waterfalls, natural pools, and the island's tallest mountain peak, Cerro de Punta, which rises to 4,398 feet. The drier Bosque Estatal de Maricao is known for its numerous species of birds, including many on the endangered list. For the truly adventurous, the uninhabited Mona Island 31 km (50 mi) off the western coast, has hiking, camping, fishing, and diving.

Surfing The waves of northwestern Puerto Rico have long served as siren-song for traveling surfers. Spared the trade winds that can limit surf in other areas, Rincón hosted the World Surfing Championship in 1968, and its beaches have some of the best waves in the world, especially in winter. Other areas on the north coast, such as Aguadilla and Arecibo, have impressive waves as well. The area around Isabela has some well-known breaks but this stretch of coast can reveal some hidden gems to those willing to explore a little.

Dorado del Mar Blvd., 00646 ☎ 787/796–6125 📠 787/796–6145 🌐 www.embassysuitesdorado.com ⇆ 229 suites, 38 villas ♁ 2 restaurants, room service, in-room data ports, kitchenettes, cable TV with in-room movies, 18-hole golf course, pool, gym, hot tub, shop, bar, video game room, dry cleaning, laundry facilities, laundry service, meeting rooms ▭ AE, D, DC, MC, V ⑩ BP.

Sports & the Outdoors

DIVING & SNORKELING The north coast has several good areas for snorkeling and diving, including an underwater "aquarium" full of tropical fish and coral just off Cerro Gordo Beach. For trips, call **Dorado Marine Center** (✉ 271 Calle Méndez Vigo ☎ 787/796–4645).

FISHING **Dorado Marine Center** (✉ 271 Calle Méndez Vigo ☎ 787/796–4645) has equipment and packages for deep-sea and light-tackle fishing.

GOLF ★ The four 18-hole golf courses at Dorado's **Hyatt Dorado Beach Resort & Country Club** (✉ Rte. 693, Km 10.8 and Km 11.8 ☎ 787/796–1234) were all designed by Robert Trent Jones; Sr. Jack Niklaus has said that the 4th hole at the **East Course** is one of the top 10 holes in the world. The **West Course** is buffeted by constant breezes off the Atlantic, making it tough to negotiate. The **South Course** has challenging winds and lagoons. The **North Course** has a links-style design; the beautiful 7th hole is surrounded by flowering plants and has a view of the ocean and the re-

Northwestern Puerto Rico

0 10 miles

0 15 km

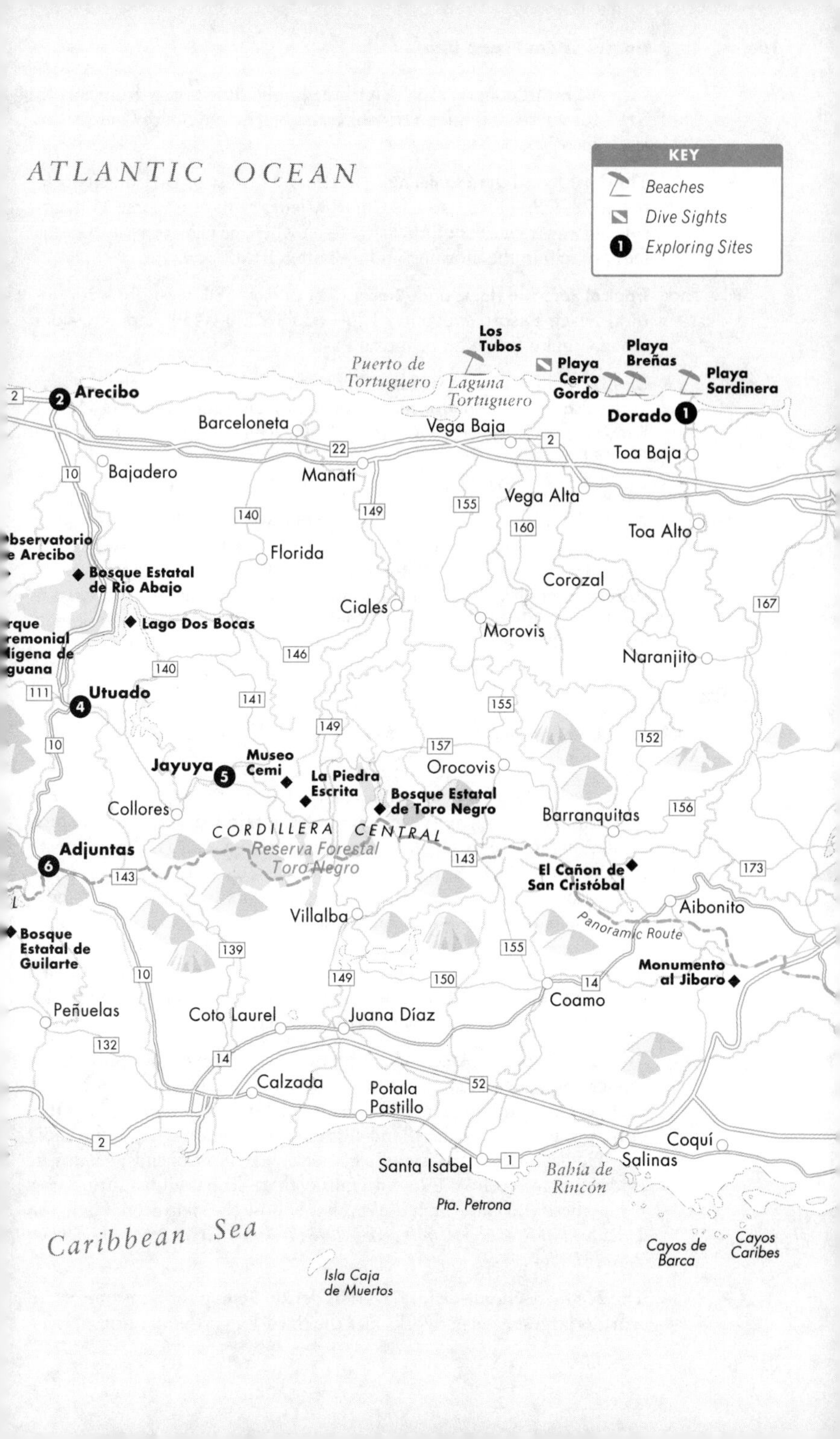

ATLANTIC OCEAN

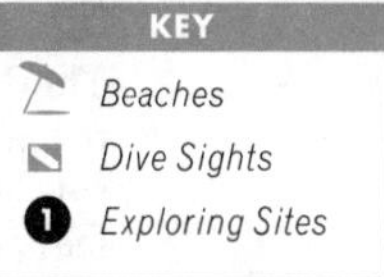

Los Tubos
Puerto de Tortuguero
Laguna Tortuguero
Playa Cerro Gordo
Playa Breñas
Playa Sardinera
2 Arecibo
Dorado 1
Barceloneta
Vega Baja
Toa Baja
Bajadero
Manatí
Vega Alta
Toa Alto
Florida
Corozal
Observatorio de Arecibo
Bosque Estatal de Río Abajo
Ciales
Morovis
Lago Dos Bocas
Parque Ceremonial Indígena de Caguana
Naranjito
4 Utuado
Jayuya 5
Museo Cemí
La Piedra Escrita
Orocovis
Bosque Estatal de Toro Negro
Collores
Barranquitas
CORDILLERA CENTRAL
Reserva Forestal Toro Negro
6 Adjuntas
El Cañon de San Cristóbal
Aibonito
Villalba
Panoramic Route
Bosque Estatal de Guilarte
Monumento al Jíbaro
Coamo
Peñuelas
Coto Laurel
Juana Díaz
Calzada
Potala Pastillo
Coquí
Salinas
Santa Isabel
Bahía de Rincón
Pta. Petrona
Caribbean Sea
Cayos de Barca
Cayos Caribes
Isla Caja de Muertos

2 · 10 · 22 · 2 · 155 · 140 · 149 · 160 · 167 · 146 · 140 · 111 · 141 · 155 · 149 · 10 · 157 · 152 · 156 · 143 · 143 · 173 · 139 · 155 · 10 · 149 · 150 · 14 · 132 · 14 · 52 · 2 · 1

sort. All Hyatt courses are open to the public. Prices vary from $95 to $145 for guests and nonguests alike; the North and South Courses are less expensive.

The 7,100-yard **Dorado del Mar** (✉ Rte. 693, west of Dorado city center ☎ 787/796–3065) is a Chi Chi Rodríguez signature course with narrow fairways that can be a challenge to hit when the wind picks up. Greens fees are $90 in the morning and $40 after 1 PM.

HORSEBACK RIDING **Tropical Paradise Horse Back Riding** (✉ Off Rte. 690, west of Hyatt Dorado Beach Resort& Country Club ☎ 787/720–5454) arranges rides along Cibuko Beach on beautiful Paso Fino horses.

WINDSURFING Lisa Penfield, a former windsurfing competitor, gives beginner lessons at the **Lisa Penfield Windsurfing School and Watersports Center** (✉ Hyatt Dorado Beach Resort & Country Club, Rte. 693, Km 10.8 ☎ 787/796–2188).

Shopping

About 20 minutes from Dorado via Highway 22 at Exit 55 is Puerto Rico's first factory outlet mall. **Prime Outlets Puerto Rico** (✉ Hwy. 2, Km 54.8, Barceloneta ☎ 787/846–9011) is a pastel village of more than 40 stores selling discounted merchandise from such familiar names as Liz Claiborne, Polo, Calvin Klein, Brooks Brothers, the Gap, Reebok, and Tommy Hilfiger.

Arecibo

❷ *60 km (38 mi) west of Dorado.*

As you approach Arecibo on Highway 22, you see its white buildings glistening in the sun against an ocean backdrop. The town was founded in 1515 and is known as the "Villa of Captain Correa" because of a battle fought here by Captain Antonio Correa and a handful of Spanish soldiers to repel a British sea invasion in 1702. Today it's a busy manufacturing center, and serves as a link for visits to two of the island's most fascinating sights—the Parque de las Cavernas del Río Camuy and the Observatorio de Arecibo, both south of the city—and for heading deeper into the central mountain region. For one of the best ocean drives on the island, get off the main road at Barceloneta and take Route 681 into Arecibo's waterfront district.

The **Faro de Arecibo** (Arecibo Lighthouse) has a museum and scaled down replicas of Christopher Columbus's *Niña, Pinta,* and *Santa María* ships that you can explore. There are also model huts and *bateyes,* or gathering places, used by the island's original inhabitants, the Taíno Indians. Guides discuss the island's history, and, on weekends, groups in traditional masks fill the air with music; there's a bar with a sitting area from where you can watch the revelry. Follow the signs from Highway 2. ✉ *End of Rte. 655, Km 0.5* ☎ *787/817–1936* 🎫 *$5* ⏲ *Mon.–Thurs. 9–6, Fri.–Sun. 9–9.*

Fodor's Choice ★ The 268-acre **Parque de las Cavernas del Río Camuy** contains one of the world's largest cave networks and the third-longest underground river in the world. A tram takes you down a mountain covered with bamboo and banana trees to the entrance of Cueva Clara de Empalme. Hour-long guided tours in English and Spanish lead you on foot through the 180-foot-high cave, which has large stalactites and stalagmites and blind fish found only in the region's caves. The visit ends with a tram ride to Tres Pueblos sinkhole, where you can see the river passing from one cave to another, 400 feet below. Tours are first-come, first-served; plan to arrive early on holidays and weekends, when local families join the tourists. There's a picnic area; camping is possible. ✉ *Rte. 129, Km 18.9* ☎ *787/898–3100* 🎫 *$10* ⏲ *Wed.–Sun. 8–4; last tour at 3:45.*

4

★ Hidden among fields and hills is **Observatorio de Arecibo,** the world's largest radar–radio telescope, operated by the National Astronomy and Ionosphere Center of Cornell University. A 20-acre dish, with a 600-ton suspended platform hovering eerily over it, lies in a 563-foot-deep sinkhole in the karst landscape. The observatory has been used to search for extraterrestrial life, and if it looks familiar it may be because scenes from the movie *Contact* were filmed here. You can walk around the platform and view the huge dish, and tour the visitor center, which has two levels of interactive exhibits on planetary systems, meteors, and weather phenomena. ✉ *Rte. 625, Km 3.0* ☎ *787/878–2612* 🌐 *www.naic.edu* 🎫 *$4* ⏲ *Wed.–Fri. noon–4, weekends 9–4.*

off the beaten path

LARES – Follow Route 129 south to Route 111 and you'll arrive at the small town of Lares, known for a national uprising that took place there in 1868. A rebellious group declared a Republic of Puerto Rico, but the insurgency, now known as "El Grito de Lares," was quickly put down by the Spanish. Today, *independentistas* flock to the town's square, Plaza de la Revolución, each September 23 to honor the anniversary of the brief cry for independence. Across from the square, Heladería de Lares has been making a more modest nationalistic statement for more than 30 years by serving up ice cream in such flavors as rice, bean, and plantain.

Where to Stay & Eat

¢–$$ ✕ **El Buen Café.** Between Arecibo and the neighboring town of Hatillo, this diner attached to a parador is a local favorite and is often packed on the weekends. Favorites dishes include *carne mechada* (stuffed pot roast), chicken and rice soup, and seafood. Breakfast is also served starting at 5 AM. ✉ *381 Hwy. 2, Km 84, Hatillo* ☎ *787/898–3495* 💳 *AE, MC, V.*

¢–$$ ✕ **El Nuevo Olímpico.** A convenient stop when heading west from Arecibo on Highway 22, this restaurant offers fast food Puerto Rican–style. You can get snacks such as *empanadillas* (deep-fried turnovers) or full meals such as *mofongo* (mashed plantains filled with meat or seafood). Breakfast consists primarily of egg dishes and sandwiches. There's a small, air-conditioned seating area, or you can join the locals outside at picnic tables on the balcony. The restaurant is open weekdays from 7 AM to midnight and stays open even later on weekends. ✉ *Hwy. 2, Km 93.3, Camuy* ☎ *787/898–4545* 💳 *MC, V.*

¢–$ **Hotel Villa Real.** The Villa Real is at the main entrance to Arecibo, making it a good spot for an overnight stay if you're heading to the cave park or observatory or are en route to the central mountains or the west coast. The rooms are clean and spacious; some have refrigerators, and others have fully equipped kitchens. A separate building has 13 larger apartments. The restaurant serves criollo food. ✉ *Hwy. 2, Km 67.2* *Box 344, 00613* ☎ *787/881–4134* *787/881–1992* *40 rooms, 4 villas, 13 apartments* *Restaurant, some kitchens, some refrigerators, cable TV, pool* *AE, MC, V* *EP.*

Sports & the Outdoors

KAYAKING & RAFTING **Locura Arecibeña/Río Grande de Arecibo Kayak Rentals** (☎ 787/878–1809) offers weekend kayaking, including bird-watching trips that go to Caño Tiburones Channel between Barceloneta and Arecibo, the Río Grande south of Arecibo, and the Río Manatí near Ciales. Weekend rafting trips are also available, mainly in winter when the rapids are at their best, and mainly on Río Manatí. Reservations must be made three days in advance.

Isabela

❸ *36 km (23 mi) west of Arecibo.*

Founded in 1819 and named for Spain's Queen Isabella, this small, whitewashed town on the northwesternmost part of the island skirts tall cliffs that overlook the rocky shoreline. Locals have long known of the area's natural beauty, and lately more and more off-shore tourists have begun coming to this niche, which offers secluded hotels, fantastic beaches, and, just inland, hiking through one of the island's forest reserves.

Explore karst topography and subtropical vegetation at the 2,357-acre **Bosque Estatal Guajataca** (Guajataca State Forest) between the towns of Quebradillas and Isabela. On more than 46 walking trails you can see 186 species of trees, including the royal palm and ironwood, and 45 species of birds—watch for red-tailed hawks and Puerto Rican woodpeckers. Bring a flashlight and descend into the **Cueva del Viento** to find stalagmites, stalactites, and other strange formations. At the Route 446 entrance to the forest there's an information office where you can pick up a hiking map. A little farther down the road is a recreational area with picnic tables and an observation tower. ✉ *Rte. 446, Galateo Alto Sector* ☎ *787/872–1045* *Free* *Information office weekdays 8–5.*

Beaches

Playa Shacks, on Route 4466 at Route 466 is known for its snorkeling and surfing. Along Route 466 **Playa Jobos** is famous for surfing but can have dangerous breaks. Not far from Playa Jobos on Route 466, **Playa Montones** is a beautiful beach for swimming and frolicking in the sand and has a natural protected pool where children can splash. Toward Quebradillas and off Route 113, **Playa Guajataca** stretches by what is called El Tunel, part of an old tunnel used by a passenger and cargo train that ran from San Juan to Ponce from the early to mid-1900s. Today, kiosks selling local snacks and souvenirs surround the area with live music playing on weekends. Just

THE ABOMINABLE CHUPACABRA

THE HIMALAYAS HAVE THEIR YETI, *Britain has its crop circles, New Jersey has its legendary Jersey Devil . . . and Puerto Rico has its Chupacabra. This "goat sucker" (as its name translates) has been credited with strange attacks on goats, sheep, rabbits, horses, and chickens since the mid-1970s. The attacks happen mostly at night, leaving the animals devoid of blood, with oddly vampirelike punctures in their necks.*

Though the first references to these attacks were in the 1970s, the biggest surge of reports dates to the mid-1990s, when the mayor of Canóvanas received international attention and support from local police for his weekly search parties equipped with a caged goat as bait. The police stopped short of fulfilling the mayor's request for a special unit devoted to the creature's capture.

Sightings offer widely differing versions of the Chupacabra; it has gray, scraggly hair and resembles a kangaroo or wolf, or walks upright on three-toed feet. Some swear it hops from tree branch to tree branch, and even flies, leaving behind, in the tradition of old Lucifer, the acrid stench of sulphur. It peers through large, oval, sometimes red eyes, and "smells like a wet dog" as its reptilian tongue flicks the night air. It has, according to some, attacked humans, ripped through screen windows, and jumped family dogs at picnics.

Anthropologists note that legends of blood-sucking creatures permeate history, from the werewolves of France to the vampires of eastern Europe. Even the ancient Mayans included a vampire deity in their pantheon. And legendary blood-lusters are legion throughout the history of South America and the Caribbean. According to a 1995 article in the San Juan Star, island lore abounds with monsters predating the Chupacabra. The comecogollo was a version of bigfoot—but smaller and a vegetarian. It was particularly sweet on cogollo, a baby plantain that springs up near its parent plant. In the early 1970s, the Moca vampire also attacked small animals, but opinion differed on whether it was alien, animal, or really a vampire. The garadiablo, a swamp creature that emerged from the ooze at night to wreak havoc on the populace also struck fear in the early 1970s. This "sea demon" was described as having the face of a bat, the skin of a shark, and a humanlike body.

The Chupacabra has also been active in other spots with large Hispanic communities—Mexico, southern Texas, and Miami—and its scope is pretty wide. The list of reported sightings at www.elchupacabra.com includes such unlikely locales as Maine and Missouri. And the Chupa's coverage on the Web isn't limited to sci-fi fan sites: Princeton University maintains a Web site meant to be a clearinghouse for Chupa information, and the beast's story appears on the Learning Channel's site at tlc.com.

What to make of Chupa? Above the clamor of the fringe elements, one hears the more skeptical voice of reason. Zoologists have suggested that the alleged condition of some Chupacabra victims may actually be the result of exaggerated retelling of the work of less mysterious animals, such as a tropical species of bat known to feed on the blood of small mammals. Even some bird species are known to eat warm-blooded animals. Skeletal remains of an alleged Chupacabra found in Chile were determined to be those of a wild dog. This, however, doesn't explain the sightings of the hairy, ravenous beast. Then again, there's no accounting for the Loch Ness Monster either.

— Karl Luntta

4

before El Tunnel, off Highway 2, is **El Merendero de Guajataca,** a picnic area with cliffside trails for a spectacular view of the coastline.

Where to Stay & Eat

$–$$ ✕ **Happy Belly's on the Beach.** If you're in the mood for a hamburger or fajita, this laid-back restaurant with outdoor seating on the beach is a good stop after a day of fun in the sun. ✉ *Playa Jobos, Rte. 4466, Km 7.5* ☎ *787/872–6566* ▭ *AE, MC, V.*

$$–$$$ ✕ **Villa Montaña.** This secluded cluster of buildings near the border of Isabela and Aguadilla feels like a community unto itself. The airy one-, two-, and three-bedroom suites have mahogany furniture and canopied beds; some have kitchenettes and laundry facilities. The grounds abut Playa Shacks, and the open-air Eclipse restaurant and bar ($$$) serves Caribbean-Asian fusion cuisine highlighting local seafood. ✉ *Rte. 446, Km 1.2, Box 530, 00662* ☎ *787/872–9554 or 888/780–9195* 🖷 *787/872–9553* 🌐 *www.villamontana.com* *26 rooms* *Restaurant, some kitchenettes, cable TV, 2 tennis courts, 2 pools, gym, laundry facilities* ▭ *AE, D, MC, V* *EP.*

$–$$ ✕ **Villas del Mar Hau.** The hub of the Villas del Mar Hau is a fanciful row of pastel one-, two-, and three-bedroom cottages overlooking Playa Montones. The villas aren't luxurious, but if you're looking for comfort and seclusion in an unpretentious atmosphere, you'll have a hard time doing better. There are also 16 suites, some with kitchens. The popular restaurant, Olas y Arena ($–$$$), is known for fish and shellfish; the paella is especially good. The hotel also has a stable of horses for the use of guests only. ✉ *Rte. 4466, Km 8.3* *Box 510, 00662* ☎ *787/872–2045 or 787/872–2627* 🖷 *787/872–0273* 🌐 *www.paradorvillasdelmarhau.com* *40 rooms* *Restaurant, fans, some kitchens, tennis court, pool, basketball, horseback riding, laundry facilities; no a/c in some rooms, no TV in some rooms* ▭ *AE, MC, V* *Restaurant closed Mon.* *EP.*

Fodor's Choice ★

¢–$ **Parador El Guajataca.** Perched on a small bluff overlooking the Atlantic, this small inn between Quebradillas and Isabela makes the most of its fabulous location. Its rooms are modest but have extraordinary ocean views. The palm-lined swimming pool overlooks the ocean as well and paths lead to Guajataca Beach. ✉ *Hwy. 2, Km 103.8, Quebradillas* *Box 1558, 00678* ☎ *787/895–3070* 🖷 *787/895–2204* 🌐 *www.elguajataca.com* *38 rooms* *Restaurant, cable TV, 2 tennis courts, pool, beach, basketball, bar, playground* ▭ *AE, MC, V* *EP.*

Sports & the Outdoors

HORSEBACK RIDING

Tropical Trail Rides (✉ Rte. 4466, Km 1.9 ☎ 787/872–9256 🌐 www.tropicaltrailrides.com) has two-hour morning and afternoon rides along the beach and through a forest of almond trees. Groups leave from Playa Shacks. The **Villas del Mar Hau** (✉ Rte. 466, Km 8.3 ☎ 787/872–2045) will make horseback-riding arrangements for guests only, using horses from its own stable.

DIVING & SNORKELING

Beginning and advanced divers can explore the submerged caves off Playa Shacks through **La Cueva Submarina Dive Shop** (✉ Rte. 466, Km 6.3 ☎ 787/872–1390 🌐 www.lacuevasubmarina.com), which also offers certification courses and snorkeling trips.

off the beaten path

PALACETE LOS MOREAU – In the fields south of Isabela toward the town of Moca, a French family settled on a coffee and sugar plantation in the 1800s. The grand two-story house, trimmed with gables, columns, and stained-glass windows, was immortalized in the novel *La Llamarada,* written in 1935 by Puerto Rican novelist Enrique A. Laguerre. In Laguerre's novel about conditions in the sugarcane industry, the house belonged to his fictional family, the Moreaus. Although it doesn't have many furnishings, you can walk through the house and also visit Laguerre's personal library in the mansion's basement. *Hwy. 2 to Rte. 464, then turn left at Ruben's Supermarket* ☎ *787/830–2540* *Free* *Weekdays 8–11 and 1–3:30.*

4

WEST-CENTRAL INLANDS

Spanning unruly karst terrain and parts of the Puerto Rico's rugged central mountain range, the west-central inlands is a beautiful mixture of limestone cliffs, man-made lakes, and sprawling forest reserves. It's here, in the Bosque Estatal de Toro Negro, that the island's highest peak, Cerro de Punta, rises 4,398 feet above sea level.

Coffee was once a dominant crop along hillsides between Utuado and Maricao, and it can still be seen growing in small plots today. A few of the old plantation homes have been turned into quaint country inns, all of them stocked with plenty of blankets for cool evenings when temperatures—especially in higher elevations—can drop into the 40s.

Sans large resorts, glitzy casinos, and beaches, this area of Puerto Rico is for those who like to get off the well-traveled roads and spend time exploring small towns, rural areas, and unspoiled nature. Driving here takes patience; some of the roads aren't clearly marked, and others twist and turn for what seems an eternity. But the area's natural beauty has attracted people for centuries, including pre-Columbian Indians, who have left behind remnants of earlier civilizations.

Utuado

❹ *32 km (20 mi) south of Arecibo; 104 km (65 mi) from San Juan.*

Utuado was named after a local Taíno chief, Otoao. Surrounded by mountains and dotted with blue lakes, the town of Utuado sits in the middle of lush natural beauty. Just driving on Route 10 between Arecibo and Utuado is an experience—imposing brown limestone cliffs flank the road, and clouds often hover around the tops of the surrounding hills. The town's narrow and sometimes busy streets lead to a double-steepled church on the main plaza. The best sights, however, are outside town along winding side roads.

In the middle of karst country, the **Bosque Estatal de Río Abajo** (Río Abajo State Forest) spans some 5,000 acres and includes huge bamboo stands and native silk-cotton trees. It also has several plantations of Asian teaks, Dominican and Honduran mahogany, and Australian pines, which are part of a government tree management program that supplies wood for the local economy (primarily for artisans and fence building). Walking trails wind through the forest, which is one of the habitats of the rare Puerto Rican parrot. An information office is near the entrance, and a recreation area with picnic tables is farther down the road. ✉ *Rte. 621, Km 4.4* ☎ *787/817–0984* 🎟 *Free* ⏲ *Daily dawn–dusk.*

East of Bosque Estatal de Río Abajo is **Lago Dos Bocas,** one of several man-made lakes near Utuado. Government-operated boats take you around the U-shaped lake from a dock, called El Embarcadero, near the intersection of Routes 123 and 146. Although the boats are used primarily as a means of public transit for residents, the 45-minute ride around the lake is pleasant and scenic, and gets you to four shoreline restaurants known for criollo cuisine and seafood. The boats are free and leave daily at 7 AM, 8:30 AM, and every hour on the hour between 10 and 5. Note: trips after 3 are for residents and returning passengers only. The lake is stocked with sunfish, bass, and catfish; you can also fish from the shore. ✣ *Off Rte. 10, accessed via Rtes. 621, 123, 146, and 612* ☎ *787/879–1838 for El Embarcadero* 🎟 *Free* ⏲ *Boats daily 7–5.*

The 13 acres of **Parque Ceremonial Indígena de Caguana** were used more than 800 years ago by the Taíno tribes for worship and recreation, including a game—thought to have religious significance—that resembled modern-day soccer. Today you can see 10 *bateyes* (courts) of various sizes, large stone monoliths (some with petroglyphs), and recreations of Taíno gardens. ✉ *Rte. 111, Km 12.3* ☎ *787/894–7325* 🎟 *$2* ⏲ *Daily 8:30–4.*

Where to Stay & Eat

$–$$$ ✕ **El Fogón de Abuela.** This rustic restaurant on the edge of Dos Bocas Lake would make any Puerto Rican grandmother envious. The menu features stews, red snapper (whole or filleted), and fricassees, including pork chop, goat, and rabbit. You arrive either by taking the public boat from El Embarcadero on Route 612, by calling the restaurant from the dock and requesting a boat be sent to pick you up (free of charge), or by driving to the south side of the lake. From Utuado, take Route 111 to Route 140 to Route 612 and follow that to its end. ✉ *Lago Dos Bocas* ☎ *787/894–0470* 💳 *MC, V* ⏲ *Closed Mon.–Thurs.*

★ $ ✕🏨 **Hotel La Casa Grande.** It's not hard to imagine Tarzan swinging in for dinner at this quaint inn on a former coffee plantation. The main house contains a restaurant, bar, and reception area; the other five wooden buildings hold 20 guest rooms. There are no TVs, phones, or radios in the rooms, but a chorus of tiny tree frogs provides symphonies at night. Yoga classes are offered every morning. Dining is on an outdoor patio at Jungle Jane's restaurant ($$–$$$); the menu features lemon-garlic chicken breast, and Puerto Rican specialties such as *asopao* (stew) with shrimp. MAP packages are available. ✉ *Rte. 612, Km 0.3* 📫 *Box 1499, 00641* ☎ *787/894–3939 or 800/343–2272* 📠 *787/894–3900* 🌐 *www.hotelcasagrande.com* 🛏 *20 rooms* 👍 *Restaurant, fans, pool, fitness classes, hiking; no a/c, no room phones, no room TVs, no smoking* 💳 *AE, MC, V* 🍽 *EP.*

MODERN DAY TAÍNOS?

*P**UERTO RICO'S FIRST INHABITANTS**— today known as Arcaicos (Archaics)—appear to have traveled on rafts from Florida around AD 500. These hunter-gatherers lived near the shore and subsisted on fish and fruit. By AD 1000, the Arawak, who came from South America by canoe, were replacing the Arcaicos. The agrarian Taíno (a subgroup of the Arawak) established thatched villages on the island, which they called Boriquén.*

In his journal Columbus describes the Taíno as "beautiful and tall, with a gentle, laughing language." Although this language was unwritten, it still echoes in some island place names and in everyday items, such as casabe (a kind of bread). Many Taíno folktales have also survived, as have some art and artifacts. They were adept at wood, shell, and stone carving, and the small figures they made of people and animals had great significance. Known as cemí (or zemí), the diminutive statues were believed to have the power to protect villages and families.

Studies suggest that there are still islanders with Taíno genes. In some isolated communities in the mountains of Maricao, around 70% of subjects with dark skin and straight black hair had traces of Amerindian DNA. A study in Mayagüez found that 50% of the subjects had such traces. Although it's been long thought the Taíno died out after their 1493 encounter with Columbus, it's possible the Taínos survived much longer or were more numerous than previously thought.

— Karen English and John Marino

Sports & the Outdoors

HIKING **Expediciones Tanamá** (✉ Rte 111, Km 14.5, Barrio Angeles ☎ 787/894–7685 🌐 home.coqui.net/albite/albite/index.html) leads half-day ($59) or full-day ($95) excursions into the Río Tanamá underground-cave system. Guides speak limited English, but are friendly and eager. Lunch is included. There's a free camping site adjacent to the office, which provides electricity and bathrooms.

HORSEBACK RIDING **Rancho de Caballos de Utuado** (✉ Rte. 612, across from Hotel La Casa Grande ☎ 787/894–0240) offers three- to four-hour horse rides along a river, lake, and through mountain forests.

KAYAKING Jenaro Colón at **Locura Arecibeña/Río Grande de Arecibo Kayak Rentals** (☎ 787/878–1809) can arrange for rentals and weekend guided tours. Kayaks are available for rent at **Rancho Marina** (✉ Rte. 612, Lago Dos Bocas ☎ 787/894–8035).

Jayuya

5 *24 km (15 mi) southeast of Utuado.*

This small town of 15,000 is in the foothills of the Cordillera Central, Puerto Rico's tallest mountain range. Cerro de Punta, the island's highest peak, looms to the south of the town center. Named after the Indian chief Hauyua, Jayuya is known for preserving its Indian heritage and draws people from all over the island for its yearly Indigenous Festival in November, which features crafts, exhibits, parades, music, and dancing. Coffee is still grown in the area—look for the locally produced Tres Picachos.

★ The main attraction of the 7,000-acre **Bosque Estatal de Toro Negro** (Toro Negro State Forest) is the 4,398-foot Cerro de Punta. It has the island's highest lake, Lago Guineo; natural ponds; waterfalls (including the 200-foot Doña Juana Falls); and gigantic bamboo, royal palms, and oak trees. The Doña Juana Recreational Area off Route 143 has picnic tables and a campground. Take one of the many hiking trails branching out from the recreational area to watch for exotic birds such as the Guadalupe woodpecker, or drive to a trail on the western edge of the forest that leads to the top of Cerro de Punta (a 30- to 45-minute hike). The reserve also contains a huge but often out-of-service swimming pool built into the side of a mountain. If you're going to camp, be sure to bring blankets, as it can get cold here at night. You will need a permit to camp; get it from the Department of Natural & Environmental Resources in San Juan (see the Camping subsection *under* ⇨ Lodging *in* Smart Travel Tips). ✉ *Rte. 143, Km 31.8* ☎ *787/867–3040* 🎫 *Free* ⏲ *Forest daily 7:30–5, Information Center daily 7:30–4.*

The tiny **Museo Cemí** (Cemí Museum) is named for its shape, which is like that of a *cemí,* a Taíno artifact believed to have religious significance. On display is a collection of Taíno pottery and religious and ceremonial objects found on the island. ✉ *Rte. 144, Km 9.3* ☎ *787/828–1241* 🎫 *Free* ⏲ *Weekdays 8–4:30, weekends 10–3:30.*

La Piedra Escrita (Written Rock) is a huge boulder with several highly visible Taíno petroglyphs, located in a stream among several other large rocks. It's somewhat hard to find—watch for a sign along the road, then pull over and look for an old stairway that takes you down to the stream. This is also a nice, secluded spot for a picnic lunch. ✣ *Off Rte. 144, near Museo Cemí* 🎫 *Free.*

Where to Stay & Eat

★ **$$** ✕🏨 **Parador Hacienda Gripiñas.** Built on the grounds of a coffee plantation, this elegant inn is surrounded by gardens and mountain peaks. Rooms have balconies overlooking lush scenery. The restaurant ($$–$$$) serves steaks, lobster, shrimp, and criollo fare such as chicken with rice and beans. For dessert, try the *tembleque*—a custard made from coconut milk and sugar. Across from the house are a bar and a swimming pool filled with cool mountain water. One hiking trail near the property leads to Cerro de Punta, about a 2½-hour climb. ✉ *Rte. 527, Km 2.7* 📫 *Box 387, 00664* ☎ *787/828–1717* 📠 *787/828–1718* 🌐 *www.haciendagripinas.com* 🛏 *19 rooms* 🖒 *Restaurant, cable TV, pool, hiking, bar* 💳 *AE, MC, V* 🍽 *MAP.*

COFFEE—PUERTO RICO'S BLACK GOLD

*W**HEN THE LATE ISLAND POET** Tomás Blanco wrote that coffee should be "black as the devil, hot as hell, and sweet as sin," he may well have had Puerto Rican brews in mind. Cultivated at high altitudes in a swirl of cool, moist air and mineral-rich soil, the island's beans are like gold—the black and aromatic sort.*

Introduced in the mid-18th century from nearby Martinique (after being brought there from France), coffee started its life in Puerto Rico as a minor cash crop, cultivated mainly for consumption. But by the end of the 1700s, Puerto Rico was producing more than a million pounds of coffee a year, and by the late 19th century, the island was the world's seventh largest producer of coffee.

Puerto Rican coffee benefited from the labors and experimentation of immigrants experienced in coffee production, and it was highly respected by connoisseurs in Europe and the Americas. Its status grew, yet Puerto Rican coffee suffered after Spain ceded the island to the United States in 1898, and after several major hurricanes. Today, with chichi coffee bars opening daily in major urban centers worldwide, Puerto Rican beans have once again taken their place next to the Jamaica Blue Mountain and Hawaiian Kona varieties as one of the world's premium coffees.

The secret is in the coffee bean itself (called "cherry"). The island's dominant bean is the arabica; it has a more delicate and lower-yielding cherry and produces half the caffeine of the prolific robusta bean found on the mega-plantations of Central and South America. The arabica cherry, in the proper conditions, is known as the richest and most flavorful among the coffee varieties. Cloud cover, tree shade, soil composition, and the altitude at which the coffee bushes are grown—higher than 3,000 feet above sea level—combine to produce a slow-ripening bean that stays on the bush at least two months longer than at lower elevations. This lengthy ripening process acts as a sort of "pre-brew," imbuing the bean with a rich flavor and a slightly sweet aftertaste.

As the beans ripen, they turn from green to yellow to red and the trees produce a white flower with a pleasant aroma similar to jasmine. Coffee picking season starts in August and continues through February. The process is slow and delicate because workers pick through bushes manually to collect only the cherries that are fully ripe. Small, family-run pulperies are the norm. The ripened beans are pulped (shelled) to remove the outer covering, then fermented to remove a thin layer that covers the bean, called the "mucilago." The beans are then dried, roasted, and packed. The main coffee-growing areas of the island lie in the wet, mountainous regions of Yauco, Lares, and Las Marís, where the limited suitable terrain makes large-scale production impossible, making the coffee all the more precious a commodity.

Throughout Puerto Rico look for local brands: Yauco Selecto, Rioja, Yaucono, Cafe Rico, Crema, Adjuntas, Coqui, and Alto Grande Super Premium. Alto Grande has gained the most fame off the island and is guaranteed to have been grown at high altitudes. It's best consumed straight up as espresso, though many prefer to cut it with hot milk, the traditional café con leche, a local equivalent of café au lait. It also makes a great gift to carry home.

— Karl Luntta

Adjuntas

6 *27 km (17 mi) southwest of Jayuya.*

The coffee-growing town of Adjuntas sits north of Puerto Rico's Ruta Panorámica. Although known for its coffee, it's also the world's leading producer of citron, a fruit whose rind is processed here and then shipped for use in sweets, especially fruitcakes. Few tourists do more than drive through the town itself, but it has a quaint central plaza and a sporadic trolley used mostly by locals and school children.

Hiking trails, surrounded by wild-growing impatiens, lead up to the 3,900-foot Pico Guilarte and into other areas of **Bosque Estatal de Guilarte** (Guilarte State Forest). Bird-watchers have 26 different species to look for, including the carpenter bird. Or if your interest is botany, you can find a variety of trees, including candlewood, trumpet, Honduran mahogany, and Honduran pine. There's a pleasant picnic area near a eucalyptus grove. ✉ *Rte. 518 at Rte. 131* ☎ *787/829–5767* *Free* ⏲ *Information Center weekdays 7–3:30, weekends 9–5:30.*

Where to Stay & Eat

$–$$ **Villas de Sotomayor.** Covering 14⅓ acres, this complex of modern villas has a summer-camp atmosphere. The focus is on horseback riding, and there are stables on the premises. You can also take horse-and-carriage rides around the grounds. Freestanding villas range in size from one bedroom with a refrigerator only to two bedrooms with a kitchenette. The on-site restaurant ($$–$$$) is open daily and serves international and criollo cuisine—it's known for its *mofongo relleno* (stuffed mashed plantains). ✉ *Rte. 123, Km 36.8, Box 28, 00601* ☎ *787/829–1717* *787/829–1774* *www.villassotomayor.com* *35 villas* *Restaurant, some kitchenettes, some refrigerators, cable TV, 2 tennis courts, 2 pools, badminton, basketball, horseback riding, meeting room* *AE, D, MC, V* *EP.*

Maricao

7 *59 km (37 mi) west of Adjuntas; 43 km (27 mi) east of Mayagüez.*

Puerto Rico's smallest municipality (pop. 6,200), Maricao is part of the island's coffee country and hosts a well-known Coffee Harvest Festival each February. Although not far from Mayagüez—the third-largest urban area on the island—Maricao has an isolated feeling; driving in the area is more akin to being deep in the central mountain region.

Drier than other forest reserves found near the central mountains, ★ **Bosque Estatal de Maricao** (Maricao State Forest) is known as one of the island's most important bird-watching destinations. The 60 species found here—29 of which are endangered—include the Puerto Rican vireos and the elfin woods warbler. Part of the reserve is the Maricao Fish Hatchery on Route 410 at Km 1.7, which contains a collection of ponds and tanks where fish are raised to stock island lakes. You'll find an information center and a stone observation tower about ½ mi beyond the forest entrance. The Centro Vacacional Monte de Estado has rustic cabins for rent. ✉ *Rte. 120 at Rte. 366* ☎ *787/838–1040 or 787/838–1045, 787/838–3710 for hatchery tours* 🎫 *Free* ⏲ *Park daily dawn–dusk. Hatchery Wed.–Sun. 8:30–11:30 and 1–3:30.*

Where to Stay & Eat

★ $ **Parador La Hacienda Juanita.** Part of a coffee plantation in the 1800s, the hotel is on a 24-acre farm surrounded by forest and exudes the slower pace of days gone by. Rooms are in four separate buildings, some with four-poster beds and antiques from the coffee industry's heyday. The accommodations are rustic—most have classic wooden shutters instead of glass windows. La Casona de Juanita restaurant ($$–$$$) serves up criollo cuisine, including *sancocho,* a hearty soup made with meat and root vegetables. Meals are served on a sweeping balcony where you can reach up and pull fruit off the trees. ✉ *Rte. 105, Km 23.5* *Box 777, 00606* ☎ *787/838–2550* *787/838–2551* 🌐 *www.haciendajuanita.com* *21 rooms* *Restaurant, fans, cable TV, tennis court, pool, hiking; no a/c, no TV in some rooms* *AE, MC, V* *MAP.*

THE WEST COAST

Adventurers since the time of Christopher Columbus have been drawn to the jagged coastline of northwestern Puerto Rico. Columbus made his first stop here on his second voyage to the Americas in 1493. His exact landing point is the subject of ongoing dispute—both Aguadilla on the northernmost tip of the coast and Aguada, just to Aguadilla's south, claim the historic landing, and both have monuments honoring the explorer.

In the 21st century, people are still discovering the area, lured primarily by the numerous beaches. The town of Rincón, which gained notoriety by hosting the World Surfing Championship in 1968, draws surfers from around the globe, especially in winter when the waves are at their best. Numerous calmer beaches nearby fit the bill if you just want to catch some rays, have a swim, and relax. From December through February, if you keep your eyes on the ocean you may spot humpback whales.

About halfway down the coast is Mayagüez, the island's third-largest urban area, where you'll find an interesting mix of Spanish colonial and eclectic 20th-century architecture. The city makes for an enjoyable day trip, but come nightfall you'll want to make your way back to the shore, where you can view some of the island's most spectacular sunsets.

Aguadilla

8 *20 km (13 mi) southwest of Isabela; 130 km (81 mi) west of San Juan.*

Weathered but lovely, the faded facades of many of Aguadilla's buildings seem indicative of its long and somewhat turbulent past. Officially incorporated as a town in 1775, Aguadilla subsequently suffered a series of catastrophes, including a devastating earthquake in 1918 and strong hurricanes in 1928 and 1932. Determined to survive, the town rebuilt after each disaster, and by World War II it became known for the huge U.S. Air

Force base north of it, originally called Borinquen Field but later renamed Ramey Air Force Base. The base was an important link in the U.S. defense system throughout World War II and the Cold War. Ramey ceased to be an active base in 1973, and today comprises an airport, a golf course, and some small businesses, although many structures stand empty.

Downtown Aguadilla has many small wooden homes and resembles a fishing village. The natural spring where Columbus is said to have gotten water during his stop is now part of the somewhat rundown El Parterre Parque on Avenida Muñoz Rivera. Residents mingle in Parque Colón (Columbus Park) at the end of Calle Comercio, but the biggest attractions are swimming, surfing, snorkeling, and diving off Aguadilla's beaches. Modest hotels near town attract budget-conscious travelers; those looking for more luxurious accommodations usually stay in the nearby towns of Isabela or Rincón.

Along Route 107—an unmarked road crossing through a golf course—you'll find the ruins of **La Ponderosa**, an old Spanish lighthouse, as well as its replacement Punta Borinquen at Puerto Rico's northwest point. The original was built in 1889, and later destroyed by an earthquake in 1918. The U.S. Coast guard rebuilt the structure in 1920.

Las Cascadas Aquatic Park (✉ Hwy. 2, Km 126.5 ☎ 787/819–1030) has a large wave pool, giant slides, and the "Crazy River," a long, free-flowing river pool. Admission is $12.95; the park is closed in October and November.

Beaches

Fodor'sChoice ★ Aguadilla's **Playa Crashboat,** off Route 458, is famous throughout the island for the colorful fishing boats docked on its shores, its long, beautiful stretch of sand, and its clear water, which often looks like glass. Named after rescue boats that used to be docked here when Ramey Air Force Base was in operation, the beach is good for swimming and snorkeling when waters are calm, and has picnic huts, showers, and restrooms. It often hosts music festivals, especially in summer. On Route 107, **Playa Borinquen** is calmer than the surfing beaches to the south. **Playa Wilderness and Playa Gas Chambers,** north of Playa Crashboat via Route 107, are often frequented by surfers. (Wilderness is recommended only for experienced surfers, as it can have dangerous breaks.)

Where to Stay & Eat

$ **Hotel Cielomar.** Almost every room at this beachfront property has an ocean view, and most rooms, which are modern but simple and motel-like, have balconies as well. The specialty of the open-air restaurant El Bohío ($–$$) is seafood. There's often live music on the weekends. ✉ *84 Av. Montemar, 00605* ☎ *787/882–5959 or 787/882–5961* 📠 *787/882–5577* 🌐 *www.cielomar.com* *52 rooms* *Restaurant, refrigerators, cable TV, pool, bar, video game room, playground, business services, meeting rooms* *AE, MC, V* *EP.*

$ **Parador El Faro.** This family-owned resort has modern and roomy but simply decorated rooms. The property isn't exactly beachfront, but Crashboat and other beaches are 2.4 km (1½ mi) away, as is a golf course. Needless to say, a car is a necessity if you stay here. There are two restaurants on the premises, including the popular Three Amigos ($$), which features a combination of Italian, Mexican, and criollo cuisines. ✉ *Rte. 107, Km 2.1, Box 5148, 00605* ☎ *787/882–8000 or 866/321–9191* 🖷 *787/882–1030* 🌐 *www.ihppr.com* 70 *rooms, 5 suites* 2 *restaurants, cable TV, tennis court, pool, basketball, playground, Internet, meeting rooms* 💳 *AE, D, DC, MC, V* 🍽 *EP.*

Sports & the Outdoors

DIVING & SNORKELING **Aquatica Underwater Adventures,** (✉ Rte. 110, Km 10, Gate 5 ☎ 787/890–6071 🌐 www.aquatica.cjb.net), offers scuba-diving certification courses as well as diving and snorkeling trips. You can also rent equipment. It's open Monday through Saturday from 9 to 5, Sunday from 9 to 3.

GOLF The 18-hole **Punta Borinquen Golf Course** (✉ Rte. 107, Km 2 ☎ 787/890–2987 🌐 www.puntaborinquengolfclub.com), on the former Ramey Air Force Base, was built in 1940 for use by the military and is said to have been played by U.S. presidents, including Dwight D. Eisenhower. Now a public course, it's known for its tough sand traps and strong cross winds. Greens fees are approximately $18 to $20 per person, and it's another $26 to rent a cart. The course is open daily.

Aguada

❾ *8 km (5 mi) south of Aguadilla.*

The town of Aguada (pop. 36,000) gleams with modern concrete buildings and has the bustling feel of a large city. It shares with Aguadilla the claim that Christopher Columbus first set foot in Puerto Rico in its vicinity, and it has a statue of the explorer in its main plaza. Regardless of where Columbus actually landed, Aguada seems to be the sentimental favorite; on November 19, crowds descend on the town to celebrate Discovery Day with parades, food, and music. The rest of the year, Puerto Ricans and off-shore visitors find tranquillity on Aguada's beaches.

Beaches

Balneario Pico de Piedra, also called the Aguada Public Beach, is a nice swimming beach frequented by families. It's at the end of Route 441, and it has parking facilities, changing rooms, and restrooms. **Playa Table Rock,** north of Balneario Pico de Piedra on Route 441, is known for its snorkeling and surfing.

Where to Stay & Eat

¢–$$ ✕ **El Plátano Loco.** You'll never think of the plantain as being a simple side dish again. "The Crazy Plantain" finds new uses for plantains, using them as "bread" to surround burgers and sandwiches, turning them into soups and french fries, adding them to mofongo, pizza, and flan. The restaurant, which consists mostly of an open-air pavilion, sits on a bluff and can be hard to find, but the locals will be glad to point you in the right direction. From Aguada's central plaza, take Route 115 to Route 441. Turn right at a bar called Parada 5 and follow the signs. ✉ *Rte. 441, Jagüey Bajío* ☎ *787/868–0241* ⊗ *Closed Mon.–Wed.*

¢–$$ 🏨 **JB Hidden Village.** This whitewashed hotel in a rural area is part of the government's parador program and is known for being family-friendly. The modern rooms and suites all have balconies, some overlook the countryside, others the pool. Two larger suites have Jacuzzis. There's a restaurant on the premises, and fine beaches are close by—Aguada Public Beach is 10 minutes away, and it's a 20-minute drive to Rincón. ✉ *Rte. 416, Km 9.5, Box 937, 00602* ☎ *787/868–8686* 📠 *787/868–8701* ⇄ *45 rooms* ♿ *Restaurant, cable TV, pool, meeting room* 💳 *MC, V* 🍴 *EP.*

Rincón

10 *9.5 km (6 mi) southwest of Aguada.*

Jutting out into the ocean along the rugged western coast, Rincón, meaning "corner" in Spanish, may have gotten its name because of how it's nestled in a corner of the coastline. Some, however, trace the town's name to Gonzalo Rincón, a 16th-century landowner who let poor families live on his land. Whatever the history, the name suits the town, which is like a little world unto itself.

Rincón has long been known for its small hotels and cottages, not to mention the Horned Dorset Primavera—the only Relais & Chateaux property in Puerto Rico and one of only a handful in the Caribbean. But in the last few years, large, concrete condominiums and a couple of larger hotels, including the Rincón of the Seas and Rincón Beach Resort, have been built. Nevertheless, it remains laid-back and unpretentious after having first jumped in the surfing spotlight as the host of the 1968 World Surfing Championship. The town remains a mecca for wave-seekers, particularly those from the east coast of the United States who aren't interested in flying all the way to the Pacific to catch their waves. The town continues to cater to all sorts of travelers, from budget-conscious surfers to families to those looking for a romantic getaway.

The beat picks up from October through April, when the waves are the best, but tourists can be found here year-round, and many American mainlanders have settled here. If you visit between December and February, you might get a glimpse of the humpback whales that winter off the coast.

Because of its unusual setting, Rincón's layout can be a little disconcerting. The main road, Route 413, loops around the coast, and many beaches and sights are on dirt roads intersecting with it. Most hotels and restaurants hand out detailed maps of the area.

Surrounding the Punta Higuera Lighthouse, **Parque Pasivo El Faro** has small kiosks at the water's edge with telescopes you can use to look for whales. (Have patience, though, even during the "season," from December through February; it could take days to spot one.) You can also glimpse the rusting dome of the defunct Bonus Thermonuclear Energy Plant from here; it has been closed since 1974 but is being resurrected as a nuclear-energy museum. The park is a nice place to take in sunsets, and there are also benches, a shop, and a refreshment stand on the grounds. The lighthouse is closed to the public, but it's hard to walk away without taking a photo of the stately white structure. Half a block up the street is a playground and a paintball course. ✉ *Calle El Faro off Rte. 413* 🎟 *Free* ⏲ *Daily 8 AM–midnight.*

Beaches

Dome's (named for the nuclear-power plant's nearby dome), **Maria's,** and **Steps** (named for a concrete set of steps sitting mysteriously at water's edge) are lined up in a row off Route 413 going north toward the lighthouse. Surfers swear by the waves at **Playa Tres Palmas,** where the snorkeling is also good when the water is calm. It's on Route 413. Swimmers can enjoy the tranquil waters of the **Balneario de Rincón,** on Route 115 just before it intersects with Route 413. It has a playground, parking facilities, restrooms and a clubhouse renovated in 2003. The long stretch of yellow sand at **Playa Corcega,** in front of Parador Villa Antonio and Hotel Villa Cofresí, is considered one of the best swimming beaches in Rincón.

Where to Stay & Eat

$$–$$$ ✕ **The Landing.** This spacious restaurant has a large, beautiful wooden bar that's often filled with a mix of people, from surfers to retirees. You can dine on pasta, steaks, and burgers inside or on a back terrace overlooking the ocean. There's also a children's menu with junior burgers and chicken fingers. On weekend nights when live bands play, the place often fills with a younger crowd. ✉ *Rte. 413, Km 4.7* ☎ *787/823–3112* 💳 *AE, MC, V.*

$–$$ ✕ **Rincón Tropical.** Fresh seafood is the name of the game at this low-key eatery. Using fish caught just offshore, the kitchen keeps it simple. Highlights include the mahimahi with onions and peppers, or whole fried red snapper. ✉ *Rte. 115, Km 12* ☎ *787/823–2017* 💳 *AE, MC, V.*

$–$$ ✕ **Sandy Beach.** On top of a hill overlooking the beach with the same name, this restaurant offers rooftop dining for the best view of the coast. Specialties include fresh fish, steaks, pasta, and salads, with signature desserts like the chocolate marquise, a rich chocolate pudding. ✉ *Rte. 413, Km 4.3* ☎ *787/823–1034* 💳 *No credit cards.*

¢–$ ✕ **Cowabunga's Ice Cream & Internet Cafe.** Run by a young married couple, this is Rincón's answer to Baskin-Robbins—only much cooler. After taking on the town's legendary waves, you can sit down to a juicy hamburger or hot dog while surfing though cyberspace or thumbing through a tome from its lending library. The only rush is to eat your ice cream before it melts. ✉ *Rte. 115, Km 11.6* ☎ *787/823–5225* 💳 *AE, MC,V.*

$$$$ Fodor'sChoice ★ ✕🏨 **Horned Dorset Primavera.** Each room at this secluded hotel is uniquely furnished with antiques, including four-poster beds. Some rooms have private plunge pools. A place to really get away, the hotel has no radios, TVs, or phones in the rooms, and no facilities for children. The main house has elegant West Indian plantation–style furniture and glistening chandeliers. Dinner in the Blue Room has tropical touches and a heavy Cordon Bleu influence. The fixed-price menu changes daily but might include crab salad with cilantro and mango, and roasted duck with black cherries. Dress is formal by island standards—no shorts allowed, and reservations are required. Breakfast and lunch are more casual. ✉ *Rte. 429, Km 3, Box 1132, 00677* ☎ *787/823–4030, 787/823–4050, or 800/633–1857* 📠 *787/725–6068* 🌐 *www.horneddorset.com*

55 rooms Restaurant, fans, 2 pools, gym, beach, croquet, library; no room phones, no room TVs AE, MC, V EP.

$–$$ **Beside the Pointe.** This perennial favorite sits right on Sandy Beach, one of Rincón's most popular novice surfing beaches. The tiled, tropical-theme rooms are fine—some are full-size apartments with full kitchens—but it's the action downstairs that keeps many tourists and locals coming year after year. Hanging right over the beach, the Tamboo Tavern is a great place to hang out, have a drink, and catch some live music. It's hard to tell where the tavern ends and the Seaside Grill begins, but no one seems to complain when the fresh fish dishes or juicy cheeseburgers arrive. *Rte. 413, Km 4.7, 00677 787/823–8550 www.besidethepointe.com 4 rooms, 4 apartments Restaurant, bar, fans, some kitchens, refrigerators, cable TV MC, V CP.*

$ **Hotel Villa Cofresí.** With large balconies, an outdoor restaurant, and a beachfront bar, the Hotel Villa Cofresí gives you plenty of ways to enjoy the ocean view. The restaurant's menu ($$–$$$) includes steaks, seafood, and Puerto Rican cuisine. Some rooms have kitchens. There's also a souvenir shop, and the hotel can arrange a host of water sports. *Rte. 115. Km 12.0, 00677 787/823–2450 787/823–1770 www.villacofresi.com 51 rooms Restaurant, refrigerators, some kitchenettes, cable TV, pool, beach, bar, shop, meeting room AE, D, MC, V CP.*

★ **$** **Lazy Parrot.** This fanciful hotel built on a mountainside offers rooms decorated in different tropical themes, such as whale and fish motifs. A honeymoon suite includes a waterbed and private Jacuzzi. The inn's restaurant ($$) is popular with surfers and features conch fritters, chicken wings, snapper breaded with almonds and cornflakes, coconut shrimp, and Thai chicken. *Rte. 413, Km 4.1, 00677 787823–5654 or 800/294–1752 787/823–0224 www.lazyparrot.com 11 rooms Restaurant, refrigerators, cable TV, pool, hot tub, 2 bars AE, D, MC, V CP.*

$$–$$$ **Rincón Beach Resort.** This oceanfront resort is tucked about halfway between downtown Rincón to the north and Mayaguez to the south. It's a bit off the beaten path, and that's part of the allure. West Indian–style interiors are updated by splashes of color that are drawn from the stunning sunsets this part Puerto Rico is known for. The rooms have a classic feel, from the ceiling fans to the dark wood furnishings. Unlike many of the beaches just a few miles north, the waters here are calm—not great for surfing, but perfect for a dip. *Rte. 115, Km. 5.8, Añasco 00610 787/589–9000 787/589–9010 www.rinconbeach.com 112 rooms 3 restaurants, pool, playground, gym, cable TV AE, D, MC, V CP.*

$$–$$$ **Rincón of the Seas.** Keep your eyes open, or you're liable to drive past this hidden gem, tucked at the end of a palm-lined drive. Hand-painted murals decorate the open-air lobby, which was designed to take full advantage of the gardens that surround the unobtrusive, mango-color hotel. The tropical art-deco furnishings are carried into the hotel rooms, each of which has a private balcony. Dine on steaks and seafood alfresco at the casual Royal Palm Cafe, or try some of chef Roberto Ruiz's signature creations at the elegant Deco. *Rte. 115,*

Km. 12.2, 00677 ☎ 787/823–7500 📠 787/823–7503 🌐 www.rinconoftheseas.com 109 rooms 2 restaurants, fans, in-room data ports, in-room safes, cable TV, 2 bars, pool, beach, Internet, meeting room ▭ AE, MC, V EP.

$ **Lemontree Waterfront Cottages.** These large, sparkling-clean apartments sit right on the beach. Each unit is decorated with a bright tropical colors and local artwork and has a deck with a wet bar and grill. Choose from one three-bedroom unit with two baths, one two-bedroom unit, two one-bedroom units, or two newer studios with kitchenettes. Maid service can be arranged. The beach here is small, but larger ones are nearby. ✉ *Rte. 429, Km 4.1* *Box 200, 00677* ☎ *787/823–6452* 📠 *787/823–5821* 🌐 *www.lemontreepr.com* *6 apartments* *BBQs, kitchenettes, cable TV, beach* ▭ *AE, MC, V* *EP.*

4

Nightlife

On weekends **Calypso** (✉ Rte. 413, at Maria's Beach ☎ 787/823–4151) often has Latin or rock-and-roll bands. **The Landing** (✉ Rte. 413, Km 4.7 ☎ 787/823–3112) is a popular spot for live music on weekends. For a romantic drink after dinner, try the second-floor dining room of the **Sandy Beach Surf Club** (✉ Rte. 413, Km 4.3 ☎ 787/823–1146), which has a fantastic view of the town's lights.

Sports & the Outdoors

SURFING With both north- and west-facing beaches, Rincón has some of the most consistent surf in Puerto Rico. Waves run the gamut from gentle, low waves suitable for beginners to expert-only breaks. Dome's and Sandy Beach are good spots for novices, at least on the calmer days. Maria's Beach and Indicators are best for more-experienced surfers. Only seasoned chargers should take on Tres Palmas, an almost mythical big-wave spot that needs truly huge swell to break. When the surf is on here—which may be only a handful of days each year, at best—this epic wave spot is one of the world's best.

Rincón Surf School (✉ Rincón Surf & Board Guest House, Rte. 413 ☎ 787/823–0610) offers full-day lessons for $89, which includes board rental and transportation. You can also arrange two-, three-, and five-day surfing seminars for $169 to $369. Boards can be rented for $20 without lesson. **West Coast Surf Shop** (✉ 2E Calle Muñoz Rivera ☎ 787/823–3935) is a good place to pick up new and used surfboards, body boards, kayaks, and snorkeling equipment, or rent equipment. Surfboards rent for $20 per day, lessons are $35 per hour.

WATER SPORTS Marlin, dorado, wahoo, and kingfish can be hooked in the waters off Rincón. For divers, **Desecheo Island,** about 20 km (13 mi) off the coast of Rincón, has abundant reef and fish life. A rocky bottom sloping to 120 feet rims the island; one formation known as Yellow Reef is distinguished by long tunnels and caverns covered with purple hydrocoral. There are other sites with plentiful fish and coral in the shallower water just off Rincón's shores.

Desecheo Dive Shop (✉ Rte. 413, Km 2.5 ☎ 787/823–0390) rents surfing and snorkeling equipment, and organizes fishing charters and diving trips. Scuba certification courses are available. Along with organizing a fishing charter or whale-watching trip, **Moondog Charters** (✉ Black Eagle Marina off Rte. 413 ☎ 787/823–3059 🌐 www.moondogcharters.com) will take a minimum of four people on a trip to Desecheo Island to snorkel or scuba dive. Prices are from $45 to $95 per person. **Taíno Divers** (✉ Black Eagle Marina off Rte. 413 📫 Box 164, 00677 ☎ 787/823–6429 📠 787/823–7243 🌐 www.tainodivers.com) has daily fishing trips, dive charters to Desecheo Island, excursions to Mona Island, and whale-watching rides. They also have scuba PADI certification courses.

Shopping

Eco-Logic-Co (✉ Parque Pasivo El Faro, Calle El Faro ☎ 787/823–1252) has fun and ecologically oriented souvenirs.

Mayagüez

11 *24 km (15 mi) southeast of Rincón.*

Known as the "Sultan of the West," Mayagüez was founded in 1760 and is said to have gotten its name from a local Taíno chief called Mayagez, whose name means "place of great waters." The city was a busy port under Spanish rule and was rebuilt after several natural disasters, including a fire in 1841 that devastated the downtown area. Evidence of the influence of diverse immigrants and constant rebuilding is seen in the variety of the city's structures, which run the gamut from neoclassical to Victorian to baroque.

With some 100,000 residents, Mayagüez is now the third-largest urban area on the island, after San Juan and Ponce. Small wooden houses dot the landscape, lending a working-class feel to this port city that became known for its tuna-canning industry in the 20th century. Although not a tourist mecca, Mayagüez is nevertheless fun to explore on a morning or afternoon outing. Its pleasant main square, Plaza Colón with lots of shade trees and benches, is dominated by a large statue of Christopher Columbus. One block away on McKinley Street is the city's most noteworthy building, the domed Teatro Yagüez, which dates from 1902. Just outside the city center, the U.S. Department of Agriculture runs a research station with acres of botanical gardens near the University of Puerto Rico's Mayagüez campus.

Puerto Rico's only (and modest) zoo, **Zoológico Dr. Juan A. Rivero,** is about 24 km (15 mi) outside the city. Zebras, rhinoceros, giraffes, tigers, camels, and hippopotami make up an African savannah exhibit. Future plans include an aviary and invertebrate and butterfly exhibits. ✉ *Rte. 108, north of Rte. 65* ☎ *787/834–8110* 🎟 *$3–$6* ⏲ *Wed.–Sun. 8:30–4; Tues.–Sun. 8:30–4 in summer.*

Founded in 1901 on a 235-acre farm on the outskirts of Mayagüez, the **Estación Experimental de Agricultura Tropical** (Tropical Agriculture Research Station) is run by the U.S. Department of Agriculture and contains a tropical plant collection that has been nurtured for more than a half century. More than 2,000 plant species from all over the tropical world are found here, including teak, mahogany, cinnamon, nutmeg, rubber, and numerous exotic flowers. Free maps are available for self-guided tours. ✉ *Hwy. 2 and Rte. 108* ☎ *787/831–3435* 🎟 *Free* ⏲ *Weekdays 7–4.*

The **Teatro Yagüez** is an extravagant beige-and-white theater dating from 1902 that's famed throughout the island for its lavish, columned facade and domed roof. The structure is still the main venue for theater in Mayagüez. If there aren't rehearsals going on, you can step in for a view of the enormous stage. ✉ *Calle McKinley at Calle Dr. Basora* ☎ *787/834–0523* 🎟 *Free* ⏲ *Daily, except when rehearsals are scheduled.*

off the beaten path

MONA ISLAND – Known as the Galapagos of the Caribbean, Mona Island, about 50 mi off the coast of Mayagüez, has long been an adventurers' outpost. It's said to have been settled by the Taíno and visited by both Christopher Columbus and Juan Ponce de León. Pirates were known to use the small island as a hideout, and legend has it that there is still buried treasure to be found here. Today, however, Mona's biggest lures are its natural beauty and distinctive ecosystem. The island has 200-foot cliffs filled with caves and is home to a number of endangered species, such as the Mona iguana and leatherback sea turtle. A number of seabirds, including red-footed boobies, also inhabit the island. Off its coast are reefs filled with tropical fish, black coral, and underwater caverns. The island is uninhabited except for transient campers and personnel from the Department of Natural and Environmental Resources. Travelers must get there by boat—planes aren't permitted to land. Several tour operators offer overnight camping and diving trips to the island (*see* ⇨ Tours *in* Northwestern Puerto Rico A to Z). The best time to visit is between July and October, but reservations must be made well in advance—as in several months.

4

Beaches

Mayagüez isn't famous for its beaches—you'll find better stretches in Rincón, about 25 minutes north—but the **Balneario de Añasco,** also called Tres Hermanos Beach, is 10 minutes north of town via Highway 2 and Routes 115 and 401. The beach, dotted with palm trees, is nice for swimming and has changing facilities and restrooms.

Where to Stay & Eat

$$–$$$$ ✕ **El Estoril.** Splurge in the elegant tiled dining room, or have a more relaxed meal at the wood-and-brick bar area. Seafood is the specialty: order a traditional paella or try the lobster *al Estoril* (wrapped in mozzarella and bacon and flambéed). There are also meat and pasta dishes. ✉ *100 Calle Méndez Vigo* ☎ *787/834–2288* 💳 *AE, MC, V* ⏲ *Closed Sun.*

¢–$$ ✕ **Ricomini Bakery.** This popular bakery is open daily from 6 AM to midnight and is a good spot to try one of Mayagüez's trademark delicacies, a Brazo Gitano (literally "Gypsy Arm")—a gigantic jellyroll filled with anything from guava to lemon to sweet cheese. You can also find another famous local product here, Fido's Sangría, made from the closely guarded secret recipe of Mayagüez resident Wilfredo Aponte Hernández. There are also other pastries, sandwiches, and freshly baked bread. ✉ *202 Calle Méndez Vigo, next to cathedral* ☎ *787/832–0565* 💳 *AE, MC, V.*

$$–$$$ **Mayagüez Resort & Casino.** Despite the presence of the casino, this hotel has an elegant yesteryear air, especially at the Veranda Terrace Bar, a long, sweeping terrace where you can sip a cocktail while watching large plants sway in the breeze and guests frolic in the pool. Outside of downtown, off Highway 2, the resort draws a mix of leisure and business travelers. Some rooms have private balconies. The restaurant, El Castillo ($$–$$$), specializes in seafood. The Añasco Public Beach is 10 minutes away. *Rte. 104, Km 0.3, off Hwy. 2 Box 3781, 00681 787/832–3030 or 888/689–3030 787/265–1430 www.mayaguezresort.com 140 rooms Restaurant, cable TV with movies, 3 tennis courts, pool, wading pool, gym, hot tub, bar, lounge, casino, playground, business services, meeting rooms, parking (fee) AE, D, DC, MC, V EP.*

$–$$$ **Holiday Inn Mayagüez & Tropical Casino.** Here you'll find all the comforts associated with the Holiday Inn name and an easy-to-reach location close to the downtown historic district and 5 minutes from the airport. Golf, beaches, and shopping are nearby. The Holly Cafe ($$–$$$) serves a mixture of Caribbean and international cuisine with a Sunday "South American nights" brunch. The hotel bar and the Holly Disco are packed with locals on weekends. The hotel has salsa lessons as well. *2701 Hwy. 2, Km 149.9, 00681 787/833–1100 787/833–1300 www.ichotelsgroup.com 142 rooms Restaurant, in-room data ports, cable TV, pool, gym, bar, lounge, casino, dance club, shop, dry cleaning, laundry facilities, laundry service, video game room, Internet, business services AE, D, MC, V CP.*

¢–$ **Parador El Sol.** In the heart of downtown Mayagüez, this small inn, part of the government's parador program, offers clean and modern rooms with rattan furnishings. The lobby area feels somewhat cramped, but the rooms are spacious, and the hotel also has a bar, restaurant, and small swimming pool. *9 Calle Santiago Riera Palmer, 00680 787/834–0303 or 866/765–0303 787/265–7567 www.hotelelsol.com 52 rooms Restaurant, refrigerators, cable TV, pool, bar, business services AE, D, MC, V CP.*

Nightlife & the Arts

Dom Pepe Italian Restaurant & Gallery Bar (56 Calle Méndez Vigo 787/834–4941) is a block from Plaza Colón and has live eclectic music upstairs on Thursday night. **Holiday Inn Mayagüez** (Hwy. 2, Km 149.9 787/834–0303) has a busy casino, and its disco is a popular spot for the younger crowd on Friday and Saturday nights. The casino at the **Mayagüez Resort & Casino** (Rte. 104, Km 0.3 787/832–3030) is popular with both residents and tourists. **Teatro Yagüez** (Calle McKinley at Calle Dr. Basora 787/834–0523) often has plays and comedy revues on the bill, mostly in Spanish.

Shopping

Small stores and pharmacies dot downtown Mayagüez. For heavy-duty shopping, the **Mayagüez Mall** (Hwy. 2, Km 159.4 787/834–2760) has local stores, a food court, and stateside chains such as JCPenney.

NORTHWESTERN PUERTO RICO A TO Z

To research prices, get advice from other travelers, and book travel arrangements, visit www.fodors.com.

AIR TRAVEL

Continental Airlines flies several times a week from Newark to Aguadilla. JetBlue has daily service from New York–JFK to Aguadilla. American Eagle has three daily flights between San Juan and Mayagüez. North American Airlines has several flights a week between New York—JFK and Aguadilla.

Airlines **American Eagle** ☎ 787/749-1747 🌐 www.aa.com. **Continental** ☎ 800/433-7300 🌐 www.continental.com. **JetBlue** ☎ 787/253-3300 in San Juan. **North American Airlines** ☎ 718/322-1300 or 800/371-6297 🌐 www.northamair.com.

AIRPORTS & TRANSFERS

Aguadilla's Rafael Hernández Airport (BQN) is on the old Ramey Air Force Base. The Eugenio María de Hostos Airport (MAZ) is just north of Mayagüez on Highway 2. There are no airport shuttles in either Aguadilla or Mayagüez. A taxi from either airport into town is about $6 to $10; a taxi from Aguadilla to Mayagüez is about $20 to $25.

Eugenio María de Hostos Airport ✉ Hwy. 2, Km 148.7, Mayagüez ☎ 787/833-0148 or 787/265-7065. **Rafael Hernández Airport** ☎ 787/891-2286.

BOAT & FERRY TRAVEL

Ferry service by Ferries del Caribe from Mayagüez to Santo Domingo leaves Mayagüez Monday, Wednesday, and Friday and returns Tuesday and Thursday. Trips are overnight leaving at 8 PM and arriving at 8 AM. Small cabins with sleeping accommodations for two, three, and four persons are provided. Tickets are usually available, but reserve well in advance if you're bringing your car. Most of the year, fares are around $149 per person and an additional $146 for cars; fares are higher from December through January. Ships leave from the Zona Portuaria (Ports Zone), past the Holiday Inn on Highway 2.

Ferry Reservations ☎ 787/832-4800 🌐 www.ferriesdelcaribe.com.

BUS & VAN TRAVEL

There's no easy network of buses linking the towns in northwestern Puerto Rico. Some municipalities and private companies operate buses and large vans *(públicos)* from one city to another, but schedules are loose. It's not wise to count on them as your primary means of transportation. That said, if you're adventurous and not easily frustrated, it's possible to arrange cheap transportation from San Juan to Aguadilla, Rincón, Mayagüez, Utuado, among others towns. Prices from terminal to terminal are set, but drivers may go to another destination if arranged beforehand.

Driver Andrio Placeres has a five-passenger van (the van must be full to leave); a trip from San Juan to Rincón costs $10 per person one-way. Choferes Unidos travels from San Juan to Aguadilla ($10 one-way) and will negotiate a price to go to nearby towns. Linea Sultana has vans to

Mayagüez that leave San Juan every two hours, from 7:30 AM to 5:30 PM, and they will also drop off passengers along Highway 2 in Aguada, Quebradillas, and Isabella; the price is $12 per person one-way. Linea Utuado leaves San Juan for Utuado daily at 1 PM; return trips are daily at 6 AM. Prices are $12 per person one-way; you must make reservations; trips to Jayuya and Lares are also possible.

Arecibo has a bus system going in and around the city. The main Terminal del Norte is at Plaza del Mercado. Public vans go to San Juan from Terminal del Sur on Avenida Santiago Iglesias.

Andrio Placeres ☎ 787/730-5725. **Choferes Unidos** ☎ 787/751-7622. **Linea Sultana** ☎ 787/765-9377. **Linea Utuado** ☎ 787/765-1908. **Terminal del Norte** ☎ 787/880-0129. **Terminal del Sur** ☎ 787/879-3425.

CAR RENTAL

If you are not flying in San Juan, you can rent a car in Aguadilla, Arecibo, and Mayagüez. Prices vary from $25 to $65 per day.

Avis ☎ 787/890-3311 in Aguadilla, 787/832-0406 in Mayagüez, 787/796-7243 at the Hyatt Dorado Beach Resort. **Budget** ☎ 787/890-1110 in Aguadilla, 787/823-4570 in Mayagüez. **Hertz** ☎ 787/832-3314 in Mayagüez, 787/890-5650 in Aguadilla, 787/879-1132 in Arecibo. **L & M Rent a Car** ☎ 787/890-3010 in Aguadilla, 787/831-4740 in Mayagüez. **Leaseway of Puerto Rico** ☎ 787/878-1606 in Arecibo. **Thrifty** ☎ 787/834-1590 in Mayagüez.

CAR TRAVEL

You really need a car to see northwestern Puerto Rico, especially the mountain area. The toll road, Highway 22, makes it easy to reach Arecibo from San Juan. Highway 22 turns into Highway 2 just after Arecibo, swings by the northwestern tip of the island, then hleads south to Mayagüez. The well-maintained and scenic Route 10, which can be accessed in Arecibo, is a main link to the central mountain region. The Ruta Panorámica runs east–west across the island and near some of the central mountain towns. It's made up of a number of small roads, many of which can be hilly and curving.

EMERGENCY SERVICES If you rent a car, call your car rental company for assistance.

Arecibo Towing Service ✉ 313 Av. Juan Rosado, Arecibo ☎ 787/879-2902. **Gruas Fernandini** ✉ 25 Rte. 135, Km 75.02, Bo Yahuecas, Adjuntas ☎ 787/829-6102. **Gruas Sanchez** ✉ Hwy. 2, Km 149.7, Bo Algarrobo, Mayagüez ☎ 787/832-6704. **Gruas Warren** ✉ 7-O Calle 11, Urb Villas Los Santos, Arecibo ☎ 787/879-4444. **Junker Nazario** ✉ Rte. 105, Km 1.1, Bo Limón, Mayagüez ☎ 787/833-2755.

GASOLINE Gas stations can be found throughout the region, but are spread out in the mountain towns. When exploring in the mountains, make sure to fill up before you head out. Prices are measured in liters instead of gallons and are not terribly different than those in the United States. The chain gas stations, Esso and Shell, are open 24 hours. Locally owned stations in small towns generally close before 6 PM.

PARKING Parking is usually available on the street, though downtown Arecibo and Mayagüez can become congested especially in the historic districts where streets are narrower. At tourist or commercial sites, parking is normally provided.

ROAD CONDITIONS The major highways throughout the northwest region, Highways 22 and 2, are well maintained. The Ruta Panorámica throughout the central mountains is also in good condition and has amazing vistas, but its twists and turns should be driven with caution. Road signs in the mountains may be missing—some have been blown down by storms or hurricanes and have yet to be replaced.

EMERGENCIES

General emergencies ☎ 911.

Hospitals **Centro de Salud** ✉ Calle Isaac González Martínez, Utuado ☎ 787/894-2875. **General Hospital Dr. Ramón Emeterio Betances** ✉ Hwy. 2, Km 157, Mayagüez ☎ 787/834-8686. **Hospital Bella Vista** ✉ Rte. 349, Km 2.7, Mayagüez ☎ 787/834-2350. **Hospital Regional Dr. C. Coll y Toste** ✉ Rte. 129, Km 0.7, Arecibo ☎ 787/878-7272. **Hospital Subregional Dr. Pedro J. Zamora** ✉ Hwy. 2, Km 141.1, Aguadilla ☎ 787/791-3000.

24-hr Pharmacies **Walgreens** ✉ Hwy. 2, Km 129.7, Aguadilla ☎ 787/882-8035 ✉ 342 Calle Méndez Vigo, Dorado ☎ 787/796-1046 ✉ Calle del Mar 547, Hatillo ☎ 787/880-8290 ✉ Mayagüez Mall, Hwy. 2, Km 159.4, Mayagüez ☎ 787/831-9249 ✉ Plaza Universitaria, Mayagüez ☎ 787/805-4005 ✉ Rte. 123. Bldg. 940, Utuado ☎ 787/894-0100.

ENGLISH-LANGUAGE MEDIA

The *San Juan Star*, the only English daily newspaper published on the island, is sporadically offered in towns outside San Juan. If newspapers aren't available at your hotel, ask the concierge where you might find one. Bookstores in larger towns like Arecibo and Mayagüez have a good selection of English reading materials.

Bookstores **The Bookshop** ✉ Plaza del Norte Mall, Hatillo ☎ 787/817-4459 ✉ Mayagüez Mall, Hwy. 2, Km 159.4, Mayagüez ☎ 787/805-3415.

HEALTH

The water on the island is generally good to drink. Always wash fruit. It's possible to catch dengue fever if bitten by an infected mosquito. Mosquitos exist in all areas of the island (though occasionally cooler mountain temperatures make them less of a problem), so wear repellent.

MAIL & SHIPPING

Larger towns like Arecibo and Mayagüez have a main post office with smaller branches throughout the city. You can often buy stamps in grocery and drug stores. Generally, post offices are open weekdays from 7 or 8 AM until 5 or 6 PM and for a few hours Saturday morning.

Post Offices **Arecibo Main Office** ✉ 10 Av. San Patricio, Arecibo 00612 ☎ 787/878-2775. **Dorado Main Office** ✉ 100 Rte. 698, Dorado 00646 ☎ 787/796-1052. **Mayagüez Main Office** ✉ 60 Calle McKinley W, Mayagüez 00680 ☎ 787/265-3138. **Rincón Main Office** ✉ 100 Rte. 115, Rincón 00677 ☎ 787/823-2625. **Utuado Main Office** ✉ 41 Av. Fernando L. Ribas, Utuado 00641 ☎ 787/894-2940.

OVERNIGHT SERVICES Express Mail, overnight, and two-day service is available at all main post offices. FedEx has offices in Aguadilla at the Borinquen Airport (Hangar 404) and in Arecibo (Rte. 10, Km 83.2). There are drop boxes at the Holiday Inn Mayagüez and the Mayagüez Resort & Casino. UPS has branches in Arecibo at the Domingo Ruiz Airport and in Mayagüez at Airport El Maní. Both locations close at 5 PM.

Major Services FedEx ☎ 877/838-7834. UPS ☎ 800/742-5877 or 787/253-2877.

MONEY MATTERS

Banks are plentiful in larger cities, and smaller towns usually have at least one; banks are sometimes attached to grocery stores. All banks have ATMs (called ATHs), and many businesses accept ATM cards. If you need to change money into U.S. dollars, you can do that in banks in either Aguadilla or Mayagüez.

Banco Popular ✉ 227 Calle Paz, Aguada ☎ 787/868-2380 ✉ Calle Mercedes Moreno, corner of Muñoz Rivera, Aguadilla ☎ 787/891-2085 or 787/891-5987 ✉ Mayagüez Mall, Hwy. 2, Km 159.4, Mayagüez ☎ 787/834-4750 ✉ Calle Zuzuaregui, Maricao ☎ 787/838-3660 ✉ 13 Av. Agustín Ramos Calero, Isabela ☎ 787/872-3100.

SAFETY

Unless you're camping in a recreational area, it's best to go to forest reserves during daylight hours only. Outside metro areas there's little crime, but you should take normal precautions: remember to lock your car and don't leave valuables unattended.

TAXIS

Taxis can be hailed near the main plaza in Mayagüez, but in the smaller towns they may be hard to come by. Check with your hotel or restaurant, and they may be able to call one for you. In Mayagüez, White Taxi is reliable and charges flat rates—no meters—by location. In Arecibo, try Arecibo Taxi Cab, but note that they close at midnight. Fares to or from San Juan are steep: for example, service is $50 from Arecibo and $120 from Mayagüez.

Cab Companies Arecibo Taxi Cab ☎ 787/878-2929. White Taxi ☎ 787/832-1115.

TELEPHONES

There are pay phones throughout the region, but often they're out of order. Puerto Rico's main area code is 787; a new, 939 area code is being introduced gradually. All local calls are prefaced with the area code. Many calls may be long distance, even to a nearby town. Public phones take coins or prepaid phone cards.

TOURS

AdvenTours, Desecheo Divers, Moondog Charters, and Tour Marine offer overnight camping and diving trips to Mona Island. Permits are required, and reservations must be made in advance (AdvenTours requires reservations three months in advance). Trips are subject to weather and water conditions. Day-trips range from $150 to $175 per person, including dive tanks and food. Prices for weekend camping trips range from $425 to $475 per person.

AdvenTours offers bird-watching, biking, and kayaking trips. Desecheo Divers has daily trips to Desecheo Island (minimum of four people) for snorkeling or scuba diving, also whale-watching trips and fishing charters. Prices range from $45 to $95. Tour Marine also goes to Desecheo

Island (minimum of 10 people); you can request a cook or guide for extra. They offer diving, fishing, and whale-watching.

Expediciones Tanamá has guided hiking trips through the Tanamá River cave system. Northwestern Land Tours has trips to the Camuy Caves and the Arecibo Observatory, and will arrange other excursions.

AdvenTours ✉ 17 Calle Uroyán, Mayagüez ☎ 787/831-6447 🌐 www.angelfire.com/fl2/adventours. **Atlantic San Juan Tours** 📫 Box 215, Utuado 00611 ☎ 787/894-7804 or 787/644-9841 🌐 www.puertoricoexcursions.com. **Desecheo Divers** ✉ Rte. 413, Km 2.5, Rincón ☎ 787/823-0390. **Expediciones Tanamá** ✉ Rte. 111, Km 14.5, Barrio Angeles ☎ 787/894-7685 🌐 home.coqui.net/albite/albite/index.html. **Moondog Charters** ✉ Black Eagle Marina, off Rte. 413 before Steps Beach, Rincón ☎ 787/823-3059 🌐 www.moondogcharters.com. **Tour Marine** ✉ Rte. 102, Km 15.4, Cabo Rojo ☎ 787/851-9259.

VISITOR INFORMATION

The Puerto Rico Tourism Company has an office at the Rafael Hernández Airport in Aguadilla. The town of Rincón has a tourism office on Route 115; it's open weekdays from 9 to 4. Mayagüez, Arecibo, Jayuya, and Maricao have tourism offices in their towns or city halls.

Arecibo City Hall ☎ 787/879-2232. **Jayuya Town Hall** ☎ 787/282-5010 Ext. 9704. **Maricao Town Hall** ☎ 787/838-2290. **Mayagüez City Hall** ✉ 8 McKinley St., Mayagüez ☎ 787/834-8585. **Puerto Rico Tourism Company** ✉ Rafael Hernández Airport, Aguadilla ☎ 787/890-3315. **Rincón Tourism Office** ✉ Rte. 115, Rincón ☎ 787/823-5024.

UNDERSTANDING PUERTO RICO

PUERTO RICO AT A GLANCE

COCINA CRIOLLA

THE STATE OF THE ARTS IN PUERTO RICO

CHRONOLOGY

A GAMBLING PRIMER

SPANISH VOCABULARY

PUERTO RICO AT A GLANCE

Fast Facts

Capital: San Juan
National anthem: *La Borinquéña (The Borinquen Anthem)*
Type of government: U.S. commonwealth, with a local governor, bicameral legislature, and a nonvoting commissioner to the U.S. House of Representatives, all elected. Local municipalities each have a mayor and an assembly. Foreign affairs are dealt with by the United States.
Administrative divisions: 78 municipalities
Constitution: July 25, 1952
Legal system: Based on Spanish civil code, but within the U.S. Federal System of Justice
Suffrage: 18 years of age, universal; indigenous inhabitants are U.S. citizens, but residents of Puerto Rico do not vote in U.S. presidential elections
Legislature: Bicameral Legislative Assembly consists of the Senate (28 seats; members are directly elected by popular vote to serve four-year terms) and the House of Representatives (51 seats; members are directly elected by popular vote to serve four-year terms)
Population: 3.9 million
Population density: 698 people per square mi
Median age: female: 34.9, male: 31.6
Life expectancy: female: 81.44, male: 73.27
Infant mortality rate: 9.38 deaths per 1,000 live births
Literacy: 93.8%
Language: Spanish, English (both official languages)
Ethnic groups: White (mostly Spanish origin) 80.5%; other 10.9%; black 8%; Amerindian 0.4%; Asian 0.2%
Religion: Roman Catholic 85%; Protestant and other 15%
Discoveries & Inventions: Cuatro guitar (1800s), coconut cream (1948), piña colada (1954)

Geography & Environment

Land area: 3,459 square mi
Coastline: 311 mi
Terrain: Mountains, with coastal plain belt in north, mountains precipitous to sea on west coast, 28,000-acre Caribbean National Forest (known as El Yunque), sandy beaches along most coastal areas (highest point: Cerro de Punta at 4,390 feet)
Islands: Vieques, Culebra, Desecheo, Mona
Natural resources: Copper, nickel, potential for onshore and offshore oil
Natural hazards: Periodic droughts, hurricanes
Environmental issues: Erosion, occasional drought causing water shortages

Economy

Currency: U.S. dollar
GDP: $43.01 billion
Per capita income: $13,139
Inflation: 5%
Unemployment: 12%
Work force: 1.3 million; services 77%; industry 20%; agriculture 3%
Major industries: Apparel, electronics, food products, pharmaceuticals, tourism
Agricultural products: Bananas, chickens, coffee, livestock products, pineapples, plantains, sugarcane
Exports: $46.9 billion

Major export products: Apparel, beverage concentrates, canned tuna, chemicals, electronics, medical equipment, rum
Export partners: U.S. 88.2%; U.K. 1.5%; Dominican Republic 1.4%
Imports: $29.1 billion
Major import products: Apparel, chemicals, food, fish, machinery and equipment, petroleum products
Import partners: U.S. 53.5%; Ireland 16.3%; Japan 4.5%

Political Climate

The issue of statehood, or independence is perennial in Puerto Rican politics. Nonbinding referendums on the island's independence were held in 1967, 1993, and 1998, but each time a majority favored keeping Puerto Rico as a commonwealth. In 2001, the federal government agreed to halt live ammunition training on the island of Vieques, conceding to local pressures in an enduring battle. Puerto Rico elected its first female governor in 2000, Sila Marìa Calderón.

Did You Know?

- Puerto Ricans have a unique national identity. No resident pays federal taxes, but all natives can be U.S. citizens. They can be called to serve in the military, but cannot vote in U.S. presidential elections as long as they reside in Puerto Rico.

- The average daily temperature in Puerto Rico is 74 degrees.

- The Puerto Rican flag is almost identical to the Cuban flag for a reason. It was created in 1895 by Puerto Rican members of the Cuban Revolutionary Party to bind both nations in the fight against Spanish rule. Before Puerto Rico gained official status as a U.S. commonwealth, anyone displaying the flag could be arrested on charges of insubordination against the United States.

- Puerto Rico produces 75% of all rum sold in the United States. Among the island's largest distillers is the Bacardí company, which produces most of its rum in Puerto Rico. With sales of more than 240 million bottles annually, it's the fourth-largest spirits company in the world, and the world's largest family-owned spirits company.

- The Sierra de Luquillo Mountains northeast of San Juan are the wettest place on the island. More than 1,700 rain showers drop 170 inches of rain a year. The precipitation keeps land in the north part of the island well watered, benefiting Puerto Rico's many farms.

- Plena is some of Puerto Rico's most well-known native music. Drawing on indigenous Taíno traditions, the music was created by a merger with African singing, clapping, and dancing traditions in the city of Ponce and became a "singing newspaper" for the black slaves. Today it's played at Christmas and on other holidays.

COCINA CRIOLLA

PUERTO RICAN *COCINA CRIOLLA*—literally, the creole kitchen—is a relative of other Caribbean cuisines, sharing basic ingredients common to Cuban, Dominican, and to some extent even Brazilian culinary traditions. Still, it has its own distinct flavorings.

The origins of contemporary Puerto Rican cuisine can be traced to the Taíno people, who inhabited the island in the 15th century. Taíno staples still used today include yucca, peppers, and corn. The Taíno used yucca to make *casabe,* a flat bread, and also a variety of vinegar that they used for seasoning instead of salt. Taínos also are believed to have grown guava, pineapple, and soursop.

When the Spaniards arrived on the island, they brought other ingredients, including olives, eggplant, onion, garlic, rice, and cilantro. Wheat would not grow on the island, so yucca remained a staple, as did rice. Regional culinary specialties from Spain, such as paellas, came out of the Spanish-influenced kitchen. These specialties played an important role in the development of Puerto Rican recipes, recognizable today in such dishes as *arroz con pollo.* Lacking olive oil, early Puerto Ricans often used lard as a fat. Back in those days, shortly after the Spanish arrived in the late 15th century, the bubbling cauldron of a hungry soldier welcomed any ingredient that was available. So a typical Spanish recipe might be transformed with yucca and pumpkin and colored with the red of achiote.

African slaves brought by the Spanish from Guinea and the Gold Coast of Africa during the 16th century to toil in the sugar fields also left their marks on the Puerto Rican table. The slaves brought plantains, bananas, pigeon peas, okra, and yams. The Taínos used corn husks to wrap foods, but the Africans replaced them with plantain leaves. The African population developed a variety of coconut-based dishes and preferred frying foods to stewing them.

Other important ingredients were the result of Spanish exploration of the world. For example, breadfruit was brought in from Tahiti and has remained a staple. But Puerto Ricans have also adopted the mango from South Asia and oranges from China.

A wooden *pilon,* which the Taínos used to mash ingredients and paints, is still used today, particularly in the preparation of *mofongo* (mashed plantains with garlic and olive oil), which is of both African and Spanish origin.

Puerto Rican cookery constantly reveals a rich, historical blend. Dishes often feature pepper, lime rind, cinnamon, cloves, fresh ginger, garlic, and the juice of the sour orange. Two popular herb seasonings are cilantro (coriander) and oregano. These ingredients, along with small sweet peppers, are commonly used to flavor soups and meats. The conventional wisdom says that the real secret of the cocina criolla depends on the use of sofrito, achiote, lard, and the *caldero* (cooking pot).

Plátanos, or plantains, are related to bananas but are larger and starchier. They are served mostly as side dishes and may be eaten green (as *tostones,* which are salty) or ripe (as *amarillos,* which are sweet). They can be fried, baked, boiled, or roasted and served either whole or in slices. Sometimes whole amarillos are served with cinnamon as a dessert. *Pasteles,* boiled plantain leaves wrapped with fillings, tamale-style, are a Christmas specialty but can be eaten anytime.

* * *

RICE IS OMNIPRESENT ON THE PUERTO RICAN PLATE. It can be served "white" with kidney beans, or prepared with *gandules* (pigeon peas) or garbanzos (chick peas); most often rice is simply served with *habichuelas* (red beans). Whatever the case, the accompaniment for rice is almost always some kind of bean, always richly seasoned. Rice stuck to the pot, known as *pegao,* is the most highly prized, full of all the ingredients that have sunk to the bottom.

Popular soups include the *sopón de pollo con arroz* (chicken soup with rice), *sopón de pescado* (fish soup), and *sopón de garbanzos con patas de cerdo* (chick pea soup with pig's feet). More than a soup, but maybe less than a stew, is the *asopao. Asopao de pollo,* the most popular variety, is made with a whole chicken, flavored with spices such as garlic, paprika, and oregano, as well with salt pork, cured ham, green peppers, chili peppers, onions, tomatoes, chorizo, and pimentos. A remarkable number of ingredients go into the *sancocho,* a hearty soup that includes vegetables, plantains, meats, and anything the poor man could find.

The *lechón asado* (a roasted or barbecued pig) is the quintessential Puerto Rican Christmas tradition. The whole pig is roasted in an open pit, a process that takes several hours. It's basted with sour orange juice and achiote coloring. The lechón asado is best when the pig's skin is golden and absolutely crisp. The traditional dressing served with the dish is the *aji-li-mojili,* a combination of garlic, sweet seeded chili peppers, vinegar, lime juice, salt, and olive oil.

Snacks—particularly different kinds of fritters—are an important part of the Puerto Rican diet. All-time favorite street snacks include *bacalaítos fritos* (deep-fried codfish fritters), *pastelillos* (deep-fried cheese and meat turnovers), and *alcapurrias* green plantain croquettes stuffed with beef or pork. *Piononos,* made from ripe bananas, are also high-ranking fritters.

Tropical fruits often wind up at the table in the form of delicious juices. A local favorite is pineapple juice from crops grown in the north of the island. Coconut, mango, papaya, lime, and tamarind are other local favorites. Puerto Rico is home to lesser known fruits that are worth trying if you find them; these include the caimito (which is also called a star apple and has a mild, grapelike flavor), quenepa (also called a Spanish lime, which has yellow sweet-tart pulp surrounded by a tight, thin skin), and zapote (a plum-size fruit that tastes like a combination of peach, avocado, and vanilla). The Plaza del Mercado in the Santurce sector of San Juan is a good place to look for the unusual.

Popular Puerto Rican desserts include the pudding or custard flan and the coconut tembleque. Guava paste or papaya cubes cooked in sugar and cinnamon must be accompanied by *queso blanco* (white cheese). *Arroz con dulce* is made of cooked rice, coconut cream, sugar, and cinnamon.

Until the 19th century, sugar and coffee were the most important of the island's crops and the backbone of the economy. Puerto Rican coffee is still the source of pride for many; Pope John-Paul II is said to like Puerto Rican coffee. A sip's worth of strong black coffee in a small cup is known as *puya*; when mixed with hot milk, it's *café con leche.*

Likewise, a source of pride is a by-product of the sugar industry: rum. Puerto Rico makes first-rate rum, including the most popular, Bacardí. The best rums can be sipped like a fine cognac, but lesser white and golden rums make great mixed drinks. The piña colada is a well-known Puerto Rican invention—a blend of coconut cream, pineapple juice, and rum. A lesser known but potent local rum specialty is *bilí,* made from quenepas soaked in rum and marinated in the bottle for weeks.

Coquito is the Puerto Rican version of Christmas rum eggnog.

Puerto Rican cuisine has been experiencing a boom of sorts, with innovative, gourmet restaurants opening around the island. Today, more chefs and restaurateurs are developing menus in the line of a Nuevo Latino cuisine. Joyfully departing from traditional Continental and Puerto Rican recipes, these chefs nevertheless include traditional ingredients and update old favorites. Traditional meats like chicken, fish, and lamb are given an added zest by sauces made from such tropical fruits as tamarind, mango, or guava. Take your palate out for a few adventures. Puerto Rican cuisine may surprise and delight you with both new and old tastes.

— Isabel Abislaimán

THE STATE OF THE ARTS IN PUERTO RICO

ALTHOUGH SPANIARDS LANDED IN PUERTO RICO in the late 15th century (Columbus was guided to the island by the Taíno Indians of Guadeloupe in 1493), several hundred years passed before what could be considered an authentically Puerto Rican art movement was born on the island in the 18th century. Notwithstanding the Taínos and their pre-Columbian works of art that are now highly prized among collectors, most of the existing paintings that came after the Spanish were part of the larger European tradition of Renaissance painting and sculpture.

A 16th-century religious mural, discovered in 1978 in Old San Juan's Iglesia de San José, is among the oldest artworks—aside from those by the Taínos, of course—to have been discovered in Puerto Rico. It is, however, widely considered insignificant in the development of the fine arts on the island. According to art historian Osiris Delgado, this anonymous repertoire of religious images continued uneventfully throughout the 17th century. In the 18th century, sculptor Tiburcio Espada (1798–1852), along with his father Felipe (c. 1754–1818), created some of the oldest surviving *santos* in the San Germán tradition (see ⇨ "Lives of the Santos" *in* chapter 3), and portrait painter José Campeche (1752–1809) begin to emerge as members of an indigenous tradition of Puerto Rican art, separate from the traditions of Europe of the time.

Another turning point for Puerto Rican artists occurred in the 19th century with the paintings of Francisco Oller (1833–1917). Oller, who was educated in Europe in the company of Gustave Courbet, Camille Pissarro, and Paul Cézanne, may be the first truly modern painter in Puerto Rico. (Oller's *El estudiante* is in the permanent collection of the Musée d'Orsay in Paris.) Unlike his peers, Oller painted realistic scenes of island life, though his use of light and color was heavily influenced by the impressionists. His most important work, *El velorio,* is the cornerstone of the collection in the Museo de la Universidad de Puerto Rico. Depicting a scene of mourning in a rural setting, the painting is one of the first attempts to create a Puerto Rican cultural identity. Such was his commitment to promoting the arts on the island that around 1870 Oller personally opened the first art gallery in Old San Juan, which exhibited his own works and those of his friends and pupils, all of whom were island natives.

Throughout the first half of the 20th century, most Puerto Rican artists followed Oller's aesthetic and grounded their works in the love of the rural landscape and lifestyle. The *jìbaro* (a poor, usually illiterate, mountain man) and the ideal of the lone house on the mountain became the affirmation of the Puerto Rican identity.

In the 1940s the government started to support the arts by providing artists with studio spaces. Shortly after, art institutions began to flourish, with the Museo de la Universidad de Puerto Rico opening in 1946. Also around this time, carvings of wooden saints (*santos de palo*) became cherished collectors items.

***

DURING THE 1950S ARTISTS BEGAN to shift their interests from the agrarian ideal toward social justice and the urban proletariat, and artists of this period focused their eyes on slums, poverty, and hardships of the city. You can see this contrast in the work Ramon Frade's *Nuestro pan* (a celebration of rural life) and Rafael Tufino's *Goyita* (focusing on dignified urban poverty). The artists of the 1950s made art with social impact and wide distribution. Murals were widely commissioned during the 1950s and '60s for government buildings and factories. One example is *La Plena,* a mural by Rafael Tufino celebrating the African roots of Puerto Rican folk music in the Centro de Bellas Artes.

The 1950s also saw two specific developments. The Instituto de Cultura Puertorriquena (ICP) was established in 1955 to promote Puerto Rican artists; today the agency oversees many museums and art programs all over the island. And in 1959, the Museo de Arte de Ponce (MAP) was founded by former governor and philanthropist Luis A. Ferré. MAP houses a private collection of more than 2,400 catalogued works from the 14th through 19th centuries, including paintings by El Greco, Goya, Rubens, Cranach, Murillo, and Delacroix. The collection is particularly strong in Italian baroque and pre-Raphaelite works, with good representation by Latin American and Puerto Rican artists from the 18th century to the present. Myrna Baez, Julio Rosado del Valle, and Antonio Martorell are included in the collection.

In the 1960s, as the art world moved away from socially committed art, Puerto Rican artists still struggled with nationalism and identity issues. Locally, this struggle resulted in a battle between abstraction and avant garde expression (with artists such as Julio Rosado Del Valle, Olga Albizu, and Luis Hernández Cruz) on the one hand, and figurative and socially minded art considered "genuinely" Puerto Rican on the other.

Finally, in the 1980s, abstract expressionists and other stylistic experimenters were granted a place at the table of Puerto Rican identity. These years opened art to the irreverent humor of Carmelo Sobrino, to the environmental activism of Carlos Marcial, and to aspects of the fantastic, as in the works of Marta Pérez, Jorge Zeno, and Rafi Trelles. Also, in the early 1980s the Puerto Rican landscape was deemed to include El Barrio in New York City and issues related to migration, poverty, colonialism, and crime. Broadening their geographic horizons also prompted Puerto Rican artists to use the self-portrait as a means to explore politics, race, the psyche, sexuality, and gender, as seen in the works of Arnaldo Roche and Mari Mater O'Neill.

By 1988 a group of artists, professors, critics, collectors, and art lovers, had come together to establish the Museo de Arte de Contemporáneo de Puerto Rico. The museum's collection comprises mostly works donated by the artists themselves. The museum finally moved to its own new building in 2003. By 1989 even the Puerto Tourism Company recognized that art can be an important way to present Puerto Rico to the world, so it began acquiring its own collection.

In the 1990s, sculpture as a medium started playing a more significant role. The most visible evidence is demonstrated by the large investments in public art in the city of San Juan and the Sculpture Symposium of the Universidad de Puerto Rico, whose works are permanently exhibited at the Botanical Garden.

Although the government has done a lot to promote the arts in Puerto Rico, it was only in 2000 that the Museo de Arte de Puerto Rico opened, becoming the first government-sponsored museum of international caliber in Puerto Rico. Since it has relatively few pieces in its permanent collection—relying largely on loans from other institutes—the museum is primarily a collection of collections. It is, however, the first government-sponsored internationally relevant museum built in Puerto Rico.

The state of the arts is looking up. Puerto Rico's Public Art Project promises to make the whole island an indoor and outdoor showcase of international and Puerto Rican art. The project consists of works in various urban and rural settings around the island—from the stations of the new Urban Train in the San Juan metropolitan area to beach benches in the shape of surfboard-petals by Aaron Salabarrias in Rincón to festive mosaic murals by Daniel Lind in Loiza.

—Isabel Abislaimán

CHRONOLOGY

ca. AD 500 The first human inhabitants arrive in Puerto Rico, apparently on primitive rafts from Florida. Known today as Arcaicos (Archaics), these hunter-gatherers live near the shore, where they subsist on fish and fruit.

ca. 1000 The Arcaico are replaced by more advanced Arawak Indians who arrive by canoe from South America. The agrarian Taíno (a subgroup of the Arawak) name the island Boriquén, and thrive there in thatched villages.

1493 Christopher Columbus, on his second voyage to the New World, meets a group of Taíno on the island of Guadeloupe. The Taínos guide him to Boriquén. On November 19, Columbus claims the island for Ferdinand and Isabella of Spain, and christens it "San Juan Bautista."

1508 Caparra, the first Spanish settlement, is founded on the south shore of the island's largest bay. Juan Ponce de León, a soldier who had accompanied Columbus on his second voyage, is appointed governor by the Spanish crown.

1510 The Spanish begin mining and smelting gold on the island. In an effort to Christianize the Taíno, they also institute a program of virtual slavery: the Indians are required to work for the settlers in return for religious instruction. In November, a group of Taíno loyal to a *cacique* (chieftain) named Urayoan set out to determine whether the Spanish are gods. By drowning a young settler in a river, the Taíno prove the Spanish to be mortal.

1511 The Spanish crown grants the island a coat of arms. The town of Caparra is renamed Puerto Rico (Rich Port). The Taíno rebel against the conquistadors, but are no match for European armament. In a brutal act of reprisal, the Spanish hunt down and kill as many as 6,000 Taíno Indians.

1512 Ferdinand II of Spain issues the Edict of Burgos, intended to protect the island's surviving Indians from abuse by the settlers.

1513 The first African slaves are introduced. Setting sail from the settlement of San Germán on the island's west coast, Ponce de León heads north across the Caribbean and discovers Florida.

1521 The island's primary town moves across the bay from its original, mosquito-plagued site. It's renamed Puerto Rico, and its capital becomes known as San Juan instead of the other way around.

1523 The first sugarcane processing plant is built.

1532 Puerto Rican gold mines cease to be profitable, and Spanish settlers leave in droves for Peru. Governor Francisco Manuel de Lando declares emigration a crime punishable by the amputation of a leg.

1539 To help protect their Caribbean trade routes from pirates and competing colonial powers, the Spanish begin building the massive fortress of San Felipe del Morro (El Morro).

1542 The coconut palm is introduced.

1595 English privateer Sir Francis Drake, assigned to disrupt Spanish colonial trade, attempts unsuccessfully to capture the town of San Juan.

1598 Another Englishman, George Clifford, 3rd Earl of Cumberland, attacks the island and occupies San Juan with 4,000 men. He's forced to withdraw a few months later when his troops are decimated by disease.

1625 San Juan is again invaded, this time by Dutch forces under Bowdoin Hendrick. The attack fails when Hendrick is unable to conquer El Morro.

1680 The town of Ponce is founded on the south coast.

1736 Coffee is first cultivated in the central highlands.

1760 The west -oast town of Mayagüez is founded.

1765 The Spanish crown sends Field Marshal Alejandro O'Reilly to inspect military and social conditions. He conducts a census and reports that Puerto Rico's races mix "without any repugnance whatsoever."

1776 Coffee becomes a major export item.

1797 When France and Spain declare war on England, 7,000 British troops under Sir Ralph Abercromby invade Puerto Rico. The British are driven back after a two-week campaign.

1809 After Napoléon Bonaparte deposes the King of Spain, the Spanish Cortes (parliament) permits representatives from Spain's New World colonies to participate in the drafting of a new constitution.

1810 Ramón Power y Giralt is selected as Puerto Rico's first delegate to Spain.

1812 The Cádiz Constitution is adopted, granting Puerto Rico and other Spanish colonies the rank of provinces and extending Spanish citizenship to colonials. A brief period of social and economic optimism reigns on the island, and Puerto Rico's first newspaper is founded.

1815 With the fall of Napoléon, the monarchy is restored in Spain, and the Cádiz Constitution is revoked. Puerto Rico reverts to being merely a Spanish colony.

1825 Notorious Puerto Rican pirate Roberto Cofresi is captured by the U.S. Navy in the Caribbean and handed over to Spanish authorities, who execute him by firing squad at El Morro.

1843 Puerto Rico's first lighthouse is constructed at El Morro. The first town is founded on the outer island of Vieques.

1868 Inspired by Puerto Rican separatist Ramón Emetrio Betances, several hundred revolutionaries attempt a coup against Spanish rule. The rebels successfully occupy the town of Lares before authorities crush the revolt. The uprising comes to be known as the Grito de Lares (Cry of Lares).

1873 Slavery is abolished on Puerto Rico by decree of the Spanish king, Amedeo I de Saboya.

1876 The mountain rain forest of El Yunque is designated as a nature reserve.

1887 Journalist and patriot Luis Muñoz Rivera helps form the Puerto Rican Autonomous Party.

1897 Just prior to the Spanish-American War, Spain approves the Carta Autonómica, granting the island administrative autonomy.

1898 In February Puerto Rico's first autonomous local government is inaugurated. In April the Spanish-American War breaks out. In July American troops invade, conquering the island in 17 days with minimal casualties. In December, after 405 years of continuous rule, Spain officially cedes Puerto Rico (along with the Philippines and Guam) to the United States. No member of Puerto Rico's autonomous government is consulted.

1899 Hurricane San Ciriaco kills 3,000 people and leaves 25% of the population homeless.

1900 The U.S. Congress passes the Foraker Act, which declares Puerto Rico to be a U.S. territory. The island's elected civil government remains under the control of a U.S.-appointed governor.

1903 President Theodore Roosevelt gives the Navy control over the out island of Culebra. The Navy later uses it as a gunnery range.

1904 Luis Muñoz Rivera establishes the Unionist Party of Puerto Rico to combat the widely unpopular regulations imposed by the Foraker Act.

1912 As dissatisfaction with American rule increases, the Independence Party is formed. This is the first political party to claim Puerto Rican independence as its primary goal.

1917 President Woodrow Wilson signs the Jones Act, which grants U.S. citizenship to Puerto Ricans.

1930 With economic conditions bleak on the island, militant separatist Pedro Albizu Campos forms the Nationalist Party. The party demands immediate independence for Puerto Rico.

1933 Cockfighting is legalized.

1935 After a visit to the island, President Franklin Roosevelt establishes the Puerto Rican Reconstruction Administration in an effort to rehabilitate Puerto Rico's economy.

1937 A decade of occasional political violence culminates with La Masacre de Ponce (The Ponce Massacre). During a Palm Sunday parade of Nationalist Party blackshirts, police open fire on the crowd, killing 19 and injuring some 100 others.

1938 Luis Muñoz Marín, son of Luis Muñoz Rivera, creates the Democratic Popular Party.

1941 The U.S. military establishes bases on Vieques and Culebra, relocating a portion of the islands' population to St. Croix, Virgin Islands.

1945 Large numbers of Puerto Ricans begin to emigrate to the mainland United States, particularly to Florida and the New York City area.

1948 The U.S. Congress grants Puerto Ricans the right to elect their own governor. In November, Luis Muñoz Marín is voted in as the island's first elected native governor. Gambling is legalized.

1950 In July President Harry Truman signs a law permitting Puerto Rico to draft its own constitution as a commonwealth, but radical nationalists are far from satisfied. In October, violence breaks out throughout the island, leaving 31 people dead. A few days later, two Puerto Rican nationalists from New York attempt to assassinate Truman in Washington.

1952 Puerto Rican voters approve the new constitution, and the Commonwealth of Puerto Rico is born. The island's flag, based on a patriotic design dating from the time of Spanish colonialism, is officially adopted.

1953 In this peak year of emigration to the U.S. mainland, nearly 70,000 people leave the island.

1961 Puerto Rican actress Rita Moreno wins an Academy Award for her performance in the hit film *West Side Story.*

1964 Luis Muñoz Marín steps down as governor after 16 years. His career is remembered as brilliantly successful: under his governorship, the percentage of Puerto Rican children attending school rose from 50% to 90%, and per capita income increased sixfold.

1967 The question of Puerto Rico's political status is put before its voters for the first time. A 60% majority votes to maintain the commonwealth, rather than push for complete independence or U.S. statehood.

1972 Beloved Puerto Rican baseball star Roberto Clemente, an outfielder for the Pittsburgh Pirates, dies in a plane crash. He's inducted into the Baseball Hall of Fame the following year.

1974 A radical nationalist organization called the Fuerzas Armadas Liberación Nacional Puertorriqueña (Armed Forces of Puerto Rican National Liberation, or FALN) claims responsibility for five bombings in New York. Over the next decade, the group commits dozens of acts of terrorism in the United States, causing five deaths and extensive property damage.

1981 Members of the Macheteros, another radical nationalist group similar to the FALN, infiltrate a Puerto Rican Air National Guard base and blow up 11 planes, causing some $45 million in damage.

1993 In a second referendum on Puerto Rico's political status, voters again choose to maintain the commonwealth.

1998 Hurricane Georges leaves 24,000 people homeless and causes an estimated $2 billion in damage. In a third referendum on the political status issue, voters once more opt to maintain the commonwealth, although the pro-statehood vote tops 46%.

1999 Puerto Ricans of all political stripes are unified in protest against the U.S. Navy bombing range on Vieques after a civilian security guard is killed by a stray bomb. Dozens of protesters occupy the range and disrupt naval exercises. President Bill Clinton offers clemency to 16 FALN members serving time in federal prisons for a string of bombings in the U.S. during the 1970s and '80s.

2000 In May, 2000, protesters encamped on the Vieques naval bombing range are forcibly removed by federal agents.

2001 In January, Sila Maria Calderón becomes the island's first woman governor. In March, Puerto Rican actor Benicio del Toro wins Academy Award for Best Supporting Actor for his role in *Traffic*. In May, beauty Denise Quiñones, from the mountain town of Lares, becomes Miss Universe. Also that month, President George W. Bush announces that the Navy will end training on Vieques by May 2003. After the September 11 terrorist attacks, however, congress passes legislation allowing the military to stay until another suitable site is found.

2002 In May, 2002, the U.S. Navy withdraws its fleet from the training grounds off the coast of Vieques.

— Stephen Fowler. Updated by John Marino.

A GAMBLING PRIMER

CASINOS ARE NO LONGER AS LARGE A PART of the tourism experience in Puerto Rico as they once were—but that's due more to growth in other areas than to a decline in the casinos themselves. If gambling is your thing, or if you're feeling yourself drawn to the "action" for the first time, Puerto Rico's resort-based casinos provide an attractive setting for trying your luck.

The most popular games have their rules, etiquette, odds, and strategies. If you're new to gambling, take a reconnaissance stroll through the casino, read up on the games here, and choose the one that best suits your style. If you take the time to learn the basics and fine points thoroughly, you'll be adequately prepared to play with as much of an edge as the game allows.

Baccarat

The most "glamorous" game in the casino, baccarat (pronounced *bah*-kuh-rah) is a version of *chemin de fer,* popular in European gambling halls. The Italian word *baccara* means "zero"; this refers to the point value of 10s and picture cards. The game is run by four pit personnel. Two dealers sit side by side at the middle of the table; they handle the winning and losing bets and keep track of each player's "commission" (explained below). The "caller" stands at the middle of the other side of the table and dictates the action. A pit boss supervises the game and acts as final judge if any disputes arise.

How to Play. Baccarat is played with eight decks of cards dealt from a large "shoe" (or card holder). Each player is offered a turn at handling the shoe and dealing the cards. Two two-card hands are dealt: the "player" and the "bank" hands. The player who deals the cards is called the banker, though the house, of course, banks both hands. The players bet, before the deal, on which hand, player or banker, will come closer to adding up to 9 (a "natural"). The cards are totaled as follows: Ace through 9 retain face value, and 10s and picture cards are worth zero. If a hand adds up to more than 10, the number 10 is subtracted from the total. For example, if one hand contains a 10 and a 4, the hand adds up to 4. If a hand holds an ace and 6, it adds up to 7. If a hand has a 7 and 9, it adds up to 6.

Depending on the two hands, the caller either declares a winner and loser (if either hand actually adds up to 8 or 9), or calls for another card for the player hand (if it totals 1, 2, 3, 4, 5, or 10). The bank hand then either stands pat or draws a card, determined by a complex series of rules depending on what the player's total is and dictated by the caller. When one or the other hand is declared a winner, the dealers go into action to pay off the winning wagers, collect the losing wagers, and add up the commission (usually 5%) that the house collects on the bank hand. Both bets have a house advantage of slightly more than 1%.

The player-dealer (or banker) continues to hold the shoe as long as the bank hand wins. As soon as the player hand wins, the shoe moves counterclockwise around the table. Players are not required to deal; they can refuse the shoe and pass it to the next player. Most players bet on the bank hand when they deal, since they "represent" the bank, and to do otherwise would seem as if they were betting "against" themselves. This isn't really the case.

Baccarat Strategy. Making a bet at baccarat is very simple. All you have to do is place your money in either the bank, player, or tie box on the layout, which appears directly in front of where you sit at the table. If you're betting that the bank hand will win, you put your chips in the bank box; bets for the player hand go in the player box. (Betting on a tie is a sucker bet.)

Because the caller dictates the action, the player's responsibilities are minimal. It's not necessary to know any of the card-drawing rules, even if you're the banker. Playing baccarat is a simple matter of guessing whether the player or banker hand will come closer to 9, and deciding how much to bet on the outcome.

Blackjack

Blackjack is the most popular table game in the casino. It's easy to learn, it's fun to play, and it involves skill, and therefore rewards those who learn its nuances. Blackjack also has one of the lowest house advantages. Because blackjack is the only table game in the casino in which players can gain a long-term advantage over the house, it's the only table game in the casino (other than poker) that can be played professionally. And because blackjack can be played professionally, it's the most written-about and discussed casino game. Dozens of how-to books, trade journals, magazines, newsletters, computer programs, videos, theses, and novels are available on every aspect of blackjack, from how to add to 21 to how to play against a variety of shuffles, from when to stand or hit to the Level-Two Zen Count. Of course, training someone to play blackjack professionally is beyond the scope of this guide. Contact the **Gambler's Book Club** (☎ 800/552–1777) for a catalog of gambling books, software, and videotapes, including the largest selection on blackjack around.

The Rules. Basically, here's how it works: You play blackjack against a dealer, and whichever one of you comes closest to a card total of 21 without going over is the winner. Number cards are worth their face value, picture cards count as 10, and aces are worth either 1 or 11. (Hands with aces in them are known as "soft" hands. Always count the ace first as an 11; if you also have a 10, your total will be 21, not 11.) If the dealer has a 17 and you have a 16, you lose. If you have an 18 against a dealer's 17, you win (even money). If both you and the dealer have a 17, it's a tie (or "push") and no money changes hands. If you go over a total of 21 (or "bust"), you lose immediately, even if the dealer also busts later in the hand. If your first two cards add up to 21 (a "natural"), you're paid 3 to 2. However, if the dealer also has a natural, it's a push. A natural beats a total of 21 achieved with more than two cards.

You're dealt two cards, either face down or face up, depending on the custom of the particular casino. Two cards go to the dealer—one face down and one face up. Depending on your first two cards and the dealer's up card, you can:

stand, or refuse to take another card.

hit, or take as many cards as you need until you stand or bust.

double down, or double your bet and take one card.

split a like pair; if you're dealt two 8s, for example, you can double your bet and play the 8s as if they're two hands.

buy insurance if the dealer is showing an ace. Here you're wagering half your initial bet that the dealer does have a natural; if so, you lose your initial bet but are paid 2 to 1 on the insurance (which means the whole thing is a push).

surrender half your initial bet if you're holding a bad hand (known as a "stiff") such as a 15 or 16 against a high up-card like a 9 or 10.

Blackjack Strategy. Playing blackjack is not only about knowing the rules—it's also about knowing *how* to play. Many people devote a great deal of time to learning strategies based on complicated statistical schemes. However, if you don't have the time, energy, or inclination to get that seriously involved, the following basic strategies, which cover more than half the situations you'll face, should allow you to play the game with a modicum of skill and a paucity of humiliation:

- When your hand is a stiff (a total of 12, 13, 14, 15, or 16) and the dealer shows 2, 3, 4, 5, or 6, always stand.
- When your hand is a stiff and the dealer shows a 7, 8, 9, 10, or ace, always hit.
- When you hold 17, 18, 19, or 20, always stand.
- When you hold a 10 or 11 and the dealer shows a 2, 3, 4, 5, 6, 7, 8, or 9, always double down.
- When you hold a pair of aces or a pair of 8s, always split.
- Never buy insurance.

Caribbean Stud

Caribbean Stud is played on a blackjack-size table. It's a poker-based game, so you need to know the ranking of hands. You are playing against the dealer, and your hand must beat the dealer's hand. You do not have to worry about beating the other players' hands.

The game starts with each player making an ante bet equal to the table minimum. This is placed in the circle marked "ante" in front of the player. At this time the player also has the option of making an additional dollar side bet for the bonus jackpot. An automatic shuffler is used, and the dealer distributes a five-card hand to each player face down. The dealer retains a hand and turns one card face up.

Players look at their cards and decide to fold and forfeit their ante bet or call by making an additional bet, which is twice the size of the ante. For example, at a $5 table your ante bet would be $5 and your call bet would be $10.

After the players have made their decision to fold or call, the dealer's hand is turned over. The dealer must qualify by having a hand with ace plus king or better. If the dealer does not qualify, the players are paid even money for their original ante bet and the second call bet is a "push," which means it does not win or lose.

If the dealer qualifies and the player wins the hand, he or she is paid even money for the ante bet, and the call bet is paid based on the winning hand on a predetermined schedule.

The player must act before the dealer. This means there will be times when you fold a hand only to have the dealer not qualify. This does not mean you should play every hand. A simple strategy is to play your hand if it contains Ace-King or better, and fold anything else.

The house edge for the main game is about 5%, but the pace of the game is fairly slow. Because of this the house edge won't hurt your bankroll too much if you play for smaller stakes.

The same is not true of the side bet for the progressive jackpot. As with all so-called bonus bets, the bonus jackpot has a high house edge. You need a flush or higher to qualify for one of the bonus payouts, and the money you win when you receive one of these hands is not close to the odds of doing so.

If for some reason you decide to make the side bet, you should know that you are eligible for the jackpot even if the dealer's hand does not qualify. You must inform the dealer immediately before they pick up the cards. Normally the dealer will pick up all the cards without turning them over. Make sure you speak up.

That is about all you need to know to play Caribbean Stud. Give it a try, but stay away from the side bet.

Craps

Craps is a dice game played at a large rectangular table with rounded corners. Up to 12 players can crowd around the table, all standing. The layout is mounted at the bottom of a surrounding "rail," which prevents the dice from being thrown off the table and provides an opposite wall against which to bounce the dice. It's important, when you're the "shooter," to roll the dice hard enough so that they bounce off the end wall of the table; this ensures a random bounce and shows that you're not trying to control the dice with a "soft roll." The layout grid is duplicated on the right and left side of the table, so players on either end will see exactly the same design. The top of the railing is grooved to hold the bettors' chips; as always, keep a close eye on your stash to prevent victimization by rail thieves.

It can require up to four pit personnel to run an action-packed, fast-paced game of craps. Two dealers handle the bets made on either side of the layout. A "stickman" wields the long wooden stick, curved at one end, which is used to move the dice around the table; the stickman also calls the number that's rolled and books the proposition bets (⇨ *below*) made in the middle of the layout. The "boxman" sits between the two dealers and oversees the game; he settles any disputes about rules, payoffs, mistakes, etc. A slow crap game is often handled by a single employee, who performs stick, box, and dealer functions. A portable end wall can be placed near the middle of the table so that only one side is functional.

How to Play. To play, just join in, standing at the table wherever you can find an open space. You can start betting casino chips immediately, but you have to wait your turn to be the shooter. The dice move around the table in a clockwise fashion: The person to your right shoots before you, the one to the left after. (The stickman will give you the dice at the appropriate time.) If you don't want to roll the bones, motion your refusal to the stickman and he'll skip you.

Playing craps is fairly straightforward; it's betting on it that's complicated. The basic concepts are as follows: If the first roll turns up a 7 or 11, that's called a "natural"—an automatic win. If a 2, 3, or 12 comes up on the first throw (called the "come-out roll"), that's termed "crapping out"—an automatic loss. Any other total on a first roll is known as a "point": The shooter keeps rolling the dice until the point comes up again. If a 7 turns up before the point does, the shooter loses. When either the point (the original number thrown) or a 7 is rolled, this is known as a "decision"; one is made on average every 3.3 rolls.

But "winning" and "losing" rolls of the dice are entirely relative in this game, depending on how you bet. There are two ways you can bet at craps: "for" the shooter or "against" the shooter. Betting for means that the shooter will "make his point" (win). Betting against means that the shooter will "seven out" (lose). (Either way, you're actually betting against the house, which books all wagers.) If you're betting "for" on the come-out, you place your chips on the layout's "pass line." If a 7 or 11 is rolled, you win even money. If a 2, 3, or 12 (craps) is rolled, you lose your bet. If you're betting "against" on the come-out, you place your chips in the "don't pass bar." A 7 or 11 loses; a 2 or 3 wins (a 12 is a push). A shooter can bet for or against himself or herself.

At the same time, you can make roughly two dozen wagers on any single roll of the dice. Besides the "for" and "against" (pass and don't pass) bets, you can also make the following wagers at craps:

Come/Don't Come: After a pass-line point is established, the come bet renders every subsequent roll of the dice a come-out roll. When you place your chips in the come box, it's the same as a pass-line bet. If a 7 or 11 is rolled, you win even money. If a 2, 3, or 12 is rolled, you've crapped out. If a 4, 5, 6, 8, 9, or 10 is rolled, it becomes another point, and the dealer moves your chips into the corresponding box on the layout. Now if that number comes up before the 7, you win the come bet. The opposite (almost) is true for the don't come box: 7 and 11 lose, 2 and 3 win (12 is a push), and if 7 is rolled before the point, you win.

Odds: The house allows you to take odds on whether or not the shooter will make his or her point, once it's established. Since the house pays off these bets at "true odds," rather than withholding a unit or two to its advantage, these are the best bets in a crap game. Odds on the 6 and 8 pay off at 6 to 5, on the 5 and 9 at 3 to 2, and on the 4 and 10 at 2 to 1. "Back up" your pass-line bets with single, double, triple, or up to 109 times odds (depending on the house rules) by placing your chips behind your line bet. For example, if the point is a 10 and your bet is $5, backing up your bet with single odds ($5) returns $25 ($5 + $5 on the line and $5 + $10 single odds); taking triple odds returns $55 ($5 + $5 on the line and $15 + $30). To take the odds on a come bet, toss your chips onto the layout and tell the dealer, "Odds on the come."

Place: Instead of waiting for a point to be rolled on the come, you can simply lay your bet on the point of your choice. Drop your chips on the layout in front of you and tell the dealer to "place" your number. The dealer puts your chips on the point; when it's rolled you win. The 6 and 8 pay 7 to 6, the 5 and 9 pay 7 to 5, and the 4 and 10 pay 9 to 5. In other words, if you place $6 on the 8 and it hits, you win $7. Place bets don't pay off at true odds, which is how the house maintains its edge (1.51% on the 6 and 8, 4% on the 5 and 9, and 6.66% on the 4 and 10). You can "call your place bet down" (take it back) at any time; otherwise the place bet will "stay up" until a 7 is rolled.

Buy: Buy bets are the same as place bets, except that the house pays off at true odds and takes a 5% commission if it wins. Since buy bets have an edge of 4.7%, you should only buy the 4 and 10 (rather than place them at a 6.6% disadvantage).

Big 6 and 8: Place your own chips in these boxes; you win if the 6 or 8 comes up, and lose on the 7. Since they pay off at even money, rather than true odds, the house edge is large—9.09%.

Field: This is a "one-roll" bet (a bet that's decided with each roll). Numbers 3, 4, 9, 10, and 11 pay even money, while 2 and 12 pay 2 to 1. The house edge on the field is 5.5%.

Proposition Bets: All proposition bets are booked in the grid in the middle of the layout by the stickman. "Hardways" means a matching pair of numbers on the dice (two 3s for a hardways 6, two 4s for a hardways 8, etc.). A hardways 4 or 10 pays 7 to 1 (11.1% edge), and 6 or 8 pays 9 to 1 (9.09%). If a 7 or a 4, 6, 8, or 10 is rolled the "easy way," hardways bets lose. "Any seven" is a one-roll wager on the 7, paying 4 to 1 with a whopping 16.6% edge. "Yo'leven" is also a one-roll wonder paying 14 to 1 with a 16.6% edge. "Any craps" is a one-roll bet on the 2, 3, or 12, paying 7 to 1 (11.1%). Other bad proposition bets include the "horn" (one-roll bet on 2, 3, 11, or 12 separately; 16.6%), and "c and e" (craps or 11; 11.1%).

Note: The players place their own pass line, field, Big 6 and 8, and come line bets. Players must drop their chips on the table in front of the dealers and instruct them to make their place and buy bets, and to take or lay the odds on their come bets. Chips are tossed to the stickman, who makes the hardways, any craps, any seven, and c and e bets in the middle of the layout.

Roulette

Roulette is a casino game that utilizes a perfectly balanced wheel with 38 numbers (0, 00, and 1 through 36), a small white ball, a large layout with 11 different betting options, and special "wheel chips." The layout organizes the 11 different bets into six "inside bets" (the single numbers, or those closest to the dealer) and five "outside bets" (the grouped bets, or those closest to the players).

The dealer stands between the layout and the roulette wheel, and chairs for five or six players are set around the roulette table. At crowded times, players also stand among and behind those seated, reaching over and around to place their bets. *Always* keep a close eye on your chips at these times to guard against "rack thieves," clever sleight-of-hand artists who can steal from your pile of chips right from under your nose.

To buy in, place your cash on the layout near the wheel. Inform the dealer of the denomination of the individual unit you intend to play (usually 25¢ or $1, but it can go up as high as $500). Know the table limits (displayed on a sign in the dealer area); don't ask for a 25¢ denomination if the minimum is $1. The dealer gives you a stack of wheel chips of a different color from those of all the other players and places a chip marker atop one of your wheel chips on the rim of the wheel to identify its denomination. Note that you must cash in your wheel chips at the roulette table before you leave the game. Only the dealer can verify how much they're worth.

The dealer spins the wheel clockwise and the ball counterclockwise. When the ball slows, the dealer announces, "No more bets." The ball drops from the "back track" to the "bottom track," caroming off built-in brass barriers and bouncing in and out of the different cups in the wheel before settling into the cup of the winning number. Then the dealer, who knows the winning bettors by the color of their wheel chips, places a marker on the number and scoops all the losing chips into his or her corner. Depending on how crowded the game is, the casino can count on roughly 50 spins of the wheel per hour.

How to Place Inside Bets. You can lay any number of chips (depending on the table limits) on a single number, 1 through 36 or 0 or 00. If the number hits, your payoff is 35 to 1, for a return of $36 on a $1 bet. You could, conceivably, place a $1 chip on all 38 numbers, but the return of $36 would leave you $2 short, which divides out to 5.26%, the house advantage.

If you place a $1 chip on the line between two numbers and one of those numbers hits, you're paid 17 to 1 for a return of $18 (again, $2 short of the true odds).

Betting on three numbers returns 11 to 1, four numbers returns 8 to 1, five numbers pays 6 to 1 (this is the worst bet at roulette, with a 7.89% disadvantage), and six numbers pays 5 to 1.

How to Place Outside Bets. Lay a chip on one of three "columns" at the lower end of the layout next to numbers 34, 35, and 36; if the winning number falls in the column you've chosen, the payoff is 2 to 1. A bet placed in the first 12, second 12, or third 12 boxes also pays 2 to 1. A bet on red or black, odd or even, and 1 through 18 or 19 through 36 pays off at even money, 1 to 1. If you think you can bet on red *and* black, or odd *and* even, in order to play roulette and drink for free all night, think again: The green 0 or 00, which fall outside these two basic categories, will come up on average once every 19 spins of the wheel.

Slot Machines

At the beginning of the 20th century, Charlie Fey built the first mechanical slot in his San Francisco basement. Slot-machine technology has exploded in the past 20 years, and now there are hundreds of different models, which accept everything from pennies to specially minted $500 tokens. Electronically operated machines known as "multipliers" accept more than one coin (usually three to five, maximum) and have flashing lights, bells, and whistles, and spin, credit, and cash-out buttons. Multipliers frequently have a variety of pay lines: three horizontal for example, or five horizontal and diagonal.

The major advance in the game, however, is the progressive jackpot. Banks of slots within a particular casino are connected by computer, and the jackpot total is displayed on a digital meter above the machines. Generally, the total increases by 5% of the wager. If you're playing a dollar machine, each time you pull the handle (or press the spin button), a nickel is added to the jackpot.

How to Play. To play, insert your penny, nickel, quarter, silver dollar, or dollar token into the slot at the far right edge of the machine. Pull the handle or press the spin button; then wait for the reels to spin and stop one by one, and for the machine to determine whether you're a winner (occasionally) or a loser (the rest of the time). It's pretty simple—but because there are so many different types of machines nowadays, be sure you know exactly how the one you're playing operates.

The house advantage on slots varies widely from machine to machine, between 3% and 25%. Casinos that advertise a 97% payback are telling you that at least one of their slot machines has a house advantage of 3%. Which one? There's really no way of knowing. Generally, $1 machines pay back at a higher percentage than quarter or nickel machines. On the other hand, machines with smaller jackpots pay back more money more frequently, meaning that you'll be playing with more of your winnings.

One of the all-time great myths about slot machines is that they're "due" for a jackpot. Slots, like roulette, craps, keno, and the big six, are subject to the Law of Independent Trials, which means the odds are permanently and unalterably fixed. If the odds of lining up three sevens on a 25¢ slot machine have been set by the casino at 1 in 10,000, then those odds remain 1 in 10,000 whether the three 7s have been hit three times in a row or not hit for 90,000 plays. Don't waste a lot of time playing a machine that you suspect is "ready," and don't think that if someone hits a jackpot on a particular machine only minutes after you've finished playing on it that it was "yours."

Video Poker

Like blackjack, video poker is a game of strategy and skill, and at select times on select machines, the player actually holds the advantage, however slight, over the house. Unlike with slot machines, you can determine the exact edge of video poker machines (or in gambler's lingo, "handicap" the machine). Like slots, however, video poker machines are often tied into a progressive meter; when the jackpot total reaches high enough, you can beat the casino at its own game.

The variety of video poker machines is already large, and it's growing steadily larger. All of the different machines are played in a similar fashion, but the strategies are different. This section deals only with straight-draw video poker.

How to Play. The schedule for the payback on winning hands is posted on the machine, usually above the screen. It lists the returns for a high pair (generally jacks or better), two pair, three of a kind, a straight, flush, full house, straight flush, four of a kind, and royal flush, depending on the number of coins played—usually 1, 2, 3, 4, or 5. (The machine assumes you're familiar with poker and its terminology.) Look for machines that pay, with a single coin played, 1 coin for "jacks or better" (meaning a pair of jacks, queens, kings, or aces; any other pair is a stiff), 2 coins for two pairs, 3 for three of a kind, 4 for a straight, 6 for a flush, 9 for a full house, 25 for four of a kind, 50 for a straight flush, and 250 for a royal flush. This is known as a 9/6 machine: one that gives a nine-coin payback for the full house and a six-coin payback for the flush with one coin played. Other machines are known as 8/5 (8 for the full house, 5 for the flush), 7/5, and 6/5.

You want a 9/6 machine because it gives you the best odds: The return from a standard 9/6 straight-draw machine is 99.5%; you give up a half percent to the house. An 8/5 machine returns 97.3%. On 6/5 machines, the figure drops to 95.1%, slightly better than roulette. Machines with varying paybacks are scattered throughout the casinos. In some you'll see an 8/5 machine right next to a 9/6, and someone will be blithely playing the 8/5 machine!

As with slot machines, it's always optimal to play the maximum number of coins in order to qualify for the jackpot. You insert five coins into the slot and press the "deal" button. Five cards appear on the screen—say, 5, J, Q, 5, 9. To hold the pair of 5s, you press the "hold" buttons under the first and fourth cards. The word "hold" appears underneath the two 5s. You then press the "draw" button (often the same button as "deal") and three new cards appear on the screen—say, 10, J, 5. You have three 5s; with five coins bet, the machine will give you 15 credits. If you want to continue playing, press the "max bet" button: Five units will be removed from your number of credits, and five new cards will appear on the screen. You repeat the hold and draw process; if you hit a winning hand, the proper payback will be added to your credits. Those who want coins rather than credit can hit the "cash out" button at any time. Some older machines don't have credit counters and automatically dispense coins for a winning hand.

Video Poker Strategy. Like blackjack, video poker has a basic strategy that's been formulated by the computer simulation of hundreds of millions of hands. The most effective way to learn it is with a video poker–computer program that deals the cards on your screen, then tutors you in how to play each hand properly. If you don't want to devote that much time to the study of video poker, memorizing these six rules will help you make the right decision for more than half the hands you'll be dealt:

- If you're dealt a completely "stiff" hand (no like cards and no picture cards), draw five new cards.
- If you're dealt a hand with no like cards but with one jack, queen, king, or ace, always hold on to the picture card; if you're dealt two different picture cards, hold both. But if you're dealt three different picture cards, only hold two (the two of the same suit, if that's an option).
- If you're dealt a pair, always hold it, no matter what the face value.
- Never hold a picture card ("kicker") with a pair of 2s through 10s.
- Never draw two cards to try for a straight or flush.
- Never draw one card to try for an inside straight.

SPANISH VOCABULARY

Words and Phrases

Basics

English	Spanish	Pronunciation
Yes/no	Sí/no	see/no
Please	Por favor	pohr fah-vohr
May I?	¿Me permite?	meh pehr-mee-tay
Thank you (very much)	(Muchas) gracias	(moo-chas) grah-see-as
You're welcome	De nada	day nah-dah
Excuse me	Con permiso	con pehr-mee-so
Pardon me	¿Perdón?	pair-dohn
Could you tell me?	¿Podría decirme?	po-dree-ah deh-seer-meh
I'm sorry	Lo siento	lo see-en-to
Good morning!	¡Buenos días!	bway-nohs dee-ahs
Good afternoon!	¡Buenas tardes!	bway-nahs tar-dess
Good evening!	¡Buenas noches!	bway-nahs no-chess
Goodbye!	¡Adiós!/ ¡Hasta luego!	ah-dee-ohss/ah -stah-lwe-go
Mr./Mrs.	Señor/Señora	sen-yor/sen-yohr-ah
Miss	Señorita	sen-yo-ree-tah
Pleased to meet you	Mucho gusto	moo-cho goose-to
How are you?	¿Cómo está usted?	ko-mo es-tah oo-sted
Very well, thank you.	Muy bien, gracias.	moo-ee bee-en, grah-see-as
And you?	¿Y usted?	ee oos-ted
Hello (on the telephone)	Diga	dee-gah

Numbers

1	un, uno	oon, oo-no
2	dos	dohs
3	tres	tress
4	cuatro	kwah-tro
5	cinco	sink-oh
6	seis	saice

7	siete	see-et-eh
8	ocho	o-cho
9	nueve	new-eh-vey
10	diez	dee-es
11	once	ohn-seh
12	doce	doh-seh
13	trece	treh-seh
14	catorce	ka-tohr-seh
15	quince	keen-seh
16	dieciséis	dee-es-ee-saice
17	diecisiete	dee-es-ee-see-et-eh
18	dieciocho	dee-es-ee-o-cho
19	diecinueve	dee-es-ee-new-ev-eh
20	veinte	vain-teh
21	veinte y uno/ veintiuno	vain-te-oo-noh
30	treinta	train-tah
32	treinta y dos	train-tay-dohs
40	cuarenta	kwah-ren-tah
43	cuarenta y tres	kwah-ren-tay-tress
50	cincuenta	seen-kwen-tah
54	cincuenta y cuatro	seen-kwen-tay kwah-tro
60	sesenta	sess-en-tah
65	sesenta y cinco	sess-en-tay seen-koh
70	setenta	set-en-tah
76	setenta y seis	set-en-tay saice
80	ochenta	oh-chen-tah
87	ochenta y siete	oh-chen-tay see-yet-eh
90	noventa	no-ven-tah
98	noventa y ocho	no-ven-tay-o-choh
100	cien	see-en
101	ciento uno	see-en-toh oo-noh
200	doscientos	doh-see-en-tohss
500	quinientos	keen-yen-tohss
700	setecientos	set-eh-see-en-tohss
900	novecientos	no-veh-see-en-tohss
1,000	mil	meel
2,000	dos mil	dohs meel
1,000,000	un millón	oon meel-yohn

Colors

black	negro	neh-groh
blue	azul	ah-sool
brown	café	kah-feh
green	verde	ver-deh
pink	rosa	ro-sah
purple	morado	mo-rah-doh
orange	naranja	na-rahn-hah
red	rojo	roh-hoh
white	blanco	blahn-koh
yellow	amarillo	ah-mah-ree-yoh

Days of the Week

Sunday	domingo	doh-meen-goh
Monday	lunes	loo-ness
Tuesday	martes	mahr-tess
Wednesday	miércoles	me-air-koh-less
Thursday	jueves	hoo-ev-ess
Friday	viernes	vee-air-ness
Saturday	sábado	sah-bah-doh

Months

January	enero	eh-neh-roh
February	febrero	feh-breh-roh
March	marzo	mahr-soh
April	abril	ah-breel
May	mayo	my-oh
June	junio	hoo-nee-oh
July	julio	hoo-lee-yoh
August	agosto	ah-ghost-toh
September	septiembre	sep-tee-em-breh
October	octubre	oak-too-breh
November	noviembre	no-vee-em-breh
December	diciembre	dee-see-em-breh

Useful Phrases

Do you speak English?	¿Habla usted inglés?	ah-blah oos-ted in-glehs
I don't speak Spanish	No hablo español	no ah-bloh es-pahn-yol

I don't understand (you)	No entiendo	no en-tee-en-doh
I understand (you)	Entiendo	en-tee-en-doh
I don't know	No sé	no seh
I am American/ British	Soy americano (americana)/ inglés(a)	soy ah-meh-ree-kah-no (ah-meh-ree-kah-nah)/in-glehs (ah)
What's your name?	¿Cómo se llama usted?	koh-mo seh yah-mah oos-ted
My name is . . .	Me llamo . . .	meh yah-moh
What time is it?	¿Qué hora es?	keh o-rah es
It is one, two, three . . . o'clock.	Es la una. . . . Son las dos, tres	es la oo-nah/sohn lahs dohs, tress
Yes, please/No, thank you	Sí, por favor/No, gracias	see pohr fah-vor/no grah-see-ahs
How?	¿Cómo?	koh-mo
When?	¿Cuándo?	kwahn-doh
This/Next week	Esta semana/ la semana que entra	es-tah seh-mah-nah/lah seh-mah-nah keh en-trah
This/Next month	Este mes/el próximo mes	es-teh mehs/el prok-see-moh mehs
This/Next year	Este año/el año que viene	es-teh ahn-yo/el ahn-yo keh vee-yen-ay
Yesterday/today/ tomorrow	Ayer/hoy/mañana	ah-yehr/oy/mahn-yah-nah
This morning/ afternoon	Esta mañana/tarde	es-tah mahn-yah-nah/tar-deh
Tonight	Esta noche	es-tah no-cheh
What?	¿Qué?	keh
What is it?	¿Qué es esto?	keh es es-toh
Why?	¿Por qué?	por keh
Who?	¿Quién?	kee-yen
Where is . . . ?	¿Dónde está . . . ?	dohn-deh es-tah
the train station?	la estación del tren?	la es-tah-see-on del train
the subway station?	la estación del tren subterráneo	la es-ta-see-on del trehn soob-tair-ron-a-o
the bus stop?	la parada del autobus?	la pah-rah-dah del oh-toh-boos
the post office?	la oficina de correos?	la oh-fee-see-nah deh-koh-reh-os
the bank?	el banco?	el bahn-koh
the hotel?	el hotel?	el oh-tel
the store?	la tienda?	la tee-en-dah

the cashier? the museum? the hospital? the elevator? the bathroom?	la caja? el museo? el hospital? el ascensor? el baño?	la kah-hah el moo-seh-oh el ohss-pee-tal el ah-sen-sohr el bahn-yoh
Here/there	Aquí/allá	ah-key/ah-yah
Open/closed	Abierto/cerrado	ah-bee-er-toh/ ser-ah-doh
Left/right	Izquierda/derecha	iss-key-er-dah/ dare-eh-chah
Straight ahead	Derecho	dare-eh-choh
Is it near/far?	¿Está cerca/lejos?	es-tah sehr-kah/ leh-hoss
I'd like . . . a room the key a newspaper a stamp	Quisiera . . . un cuarto/una habitación la llave un periódico un sello de correo	kee-see-ehr-ah oon kwahr-toh/ oo-nah ah-bee- tah-see-on lah yah-veh oon pehr-ee-oh- dee-koh oon seh-yo deh koh-reh-oh
I'd like to buy . . . cigarettes matches a dictionary soap sunglasses suntan lotion a map a magazine paper envelopes a postcard	Quisiera comprar . . . cigarrillos cerillos un diccionario jabón gafas de sol loción un mapa una revista papel sobres una tarjeta postal	kee-see-ehr-ah kohm-prahr ce-ga-ree-yohs ser-ee-ohs oon deek-see-oh- nah-ree-oh hah-bohn ga-fahs deh sohl loh-see-ohn-brohn- seh-ah-do-rah oon mah-pah oon-ah reh-veess-tah pah-pel so-brehs oon-ah tar-het-ah post-ahl
How much is it?	¿Cuánto cuesta?	kwahn-toh kwes-tah
It's expensive/ cheap	Está caro/barato	es-tah kah-roh/ bah-rah-toh
A little/a lot	Un poquito/ mucho	oon poh-kee-toh/ moo-choh
More/less	Más/menos	mahss/men-ohss
Enough/too much/too little	Sufficiente/ demasiado/ muy poco	soo-fee-see-en-teh/ deh-mah-see-ah- doh/moo-ee poh-koh

Telephone	Teléfono	tel-ef-oh-no
Telegram	Telegrama	teh-leh-grah-mah
I am ill	Estoy enfermo(a)	es-toy en-fehr-moh(mah)
Please call a doctor	Por favor llame un medico	pohr fah-vor ya-meh oon med-ee-koh
Help!	¡Auxilio! ¡Ayuda! ¡Socorro!	owk-see-lee-oh/ ah-yoo-dah/ soh-kohr-roh
Fire!	¡Encendio!	en-sen-dee-oo
Caution!/Look out!	¡Cuidado!	kwee-dah-doh

On the Road

Avenue	Avenida	ah-ven-ee-dah
Broad, tree-lined boulevard	Bulevar	boo-leh-var
Fertile plain	Vega	veh-gah
Highway	Carretera	car-reh-ter-ah
Mountain pass, Street	Puerto Calle	poo-ehr-toh cah-yeh
Waterfront promenade	Rambla	rahm-blah
Wharf	Embarcadero	em-bar-cah-deh-ro

In Town

Cathedral	Catedral	cah-teh-dral
Church	Templo/Iglesia	tem-plo/ee-glehs-see-ah
City hall	Casa de gobierno	kah-sah deh go-bee-ehr-no
Door, gate	Puerta portón	poo-ehr-tah por-ton
Entrance/exit	Entrada/salida	en-trah-dah/sah-lee-dah
Inn, rustic bar, or restaurant	Taverna	tah-ver-nah
Main square	Plaza principal	plah-thah prin-see-pahl
Market	Mercado	mer-kah-doh
Neighborhood	Barrio	bahr-ree-o
Traffic circle	Glorieta	glor-ee-eh-tah
Wine cellar, wine bar, or wine shop	Bodega	boh-deh-gah

Dining Out

A bottle of . . .	Una bottella de . . .	oo-nah bo-teh-yah-deh
A cup of . . .	Una taza de . . .	oo-nah tah-thah deh
A glass of . . .	Un vaso de . . .	oon vah-so deh
Ashtray	Un cenicero	oon sen-ee-seh-roh
Bill/check	La cuenta	lah kwen-tah
Bread	El pan	el pahn
Breakfast	El desayuno	el deh-sah-yoon-oh
Butter	La mantequilla	lah man-teh-key-yah
Cheers!	¡Salud!	sah-lood
Cocktail	Un aperitivo	oon ah-pehr-ee-tee-voh
Dinner	La cena	lah seh-nah
Dish	Un plato	oon plah-toh
Menu of the day	Menú del día	meh-noo del dee-ah
Enjoy!	¡Buen provecho!	bwehn pro-veh-cho
Fixed-price menu	Menú fijo o turistico	meh-noo fee-hoh oh too-ree-stee-coh
Fork	El tenedor	ehl ten-eh-dor
Is the tip included?	¿Está incluida la propina?	es-tah in-cloo-ee-dah lah pro-pee-nah
Knife	El cuchillo	el koo-chee-yo
Large portion of savory snacks	Raciónes	rah-see-oh-nehs
Lunch	La comida	lah koh-mee-dah
Menu	La carta, el menú	lah cart-ah, el meh-noo
Napkin	La servilleta	lah sehr-vee-yet-ah
Pepper	La pimienta	lah pee-me-en-tah
Please give me	Por favor déme	pohr fah-vor deh-meh
Salt	La sal	lah sahl
Savory snacks	Tapas	tah-pahs
Spoon	Una cuchara	oo-nah koo-chah-rah
Sugar	El azúcar	el ah-thu-kar
Waiter!/Waitress!	¡Por favor Señor/Señorita!	pohr fah-vor sen-yor/sen-yor-ee-tah

INDEX

A

A La Banda ✕, *96*
A La Brasa Steakhouse ✕, *162*
Adjuntas, *176*
Agriculture research stations, *184–185*
Aguada, *179–180*
Aguadilla, *177–179*
Aguaviva Seaside Latino Cuisine ✕, *31*
Aibonito, *126–127*
Air travel, *F28–F30*
with children, F36
discount reservations, F41
eastern Puerto Rico, 114–115
luggage limits, F50–F51
northwestern Puerto Rico, 187
San Juan, 68–69
southern Puerto Rico, 154
Airports and transfers, *F30–F31*
Aji ✕, *24–25*
Ajili Mojili ✕, *F25, 32*
Alcaldía, *10*
Amadeus ✕, *25*
Anchor's Inn ✕, *96*
Annie's ✕, *152*
Annual Criollisimo Show, *F19*
Antiques shops, *66*
Apartment and villa rentals, *F47*
Eastern Puerto Rico, 106–107
San Juan, 39–40
Architecture, *7*
Arecibo, *F22, 166–168*
Arroyo, *129–130*
Art festivals, *F19, F21, F22*
Art galleries and museums
eastern Puerto Rico, 86, 87, 90, 100, 103, 108, 112–113
San Juan, 11, 13, 17, 20, 23, 63–64
southern Puerto Rico, 130, 139, 148
Art shops, *63*
Arts, *198–199.* ⇨ *Also* under specific regions, cities, and towns
At Wind Chimes Inn 🏨, *45–46*
ATMs, *F49*
Augusto's Cuisine ✕, *33, 36*
Avocat ✕, *25*

B

Bacardi Artisan's Fair, *F19*
Bacardi Rum plant, *22*
Baccarat, *205–206*
Bahía Ballena, *143*
Bahía Fosforescente, *146*
Bahía Mosquito, *F27, 103*
Bahía Salinas Beach Hotel ✕🏨, *152*
Balneario Boquerón, *F27, 152*
Balneario Caña Gorda, *144*
Balneario de Añasco, *185*
Balneario de Carolina, *57*
Balneario de Luquillo, *F27, 94*
Balneario de Rincón, *181*
Balneario Escambrón, *57*
Balneario Pico de Piedra, *179*
Balneario Punta Guilarte, *130*
Balneario Seven Seas, *96*
Bamboo ✕, *113*
Bamboobei ✕, *82*
Banana's 🏨, *106*
Baños de Coamo, *132*
Barranquitas, *F22, 127–128*
Barranquitas Feria de Artesonia, *F22*
Bars
eastern Puerto Rico, 98, 107
northwestern Puerto Rico, 183
San Juan, 48–49
southern Puerto Rico, 153
Barú ✕, *25, 29*
Baseball, *F19*
San Juan, 58
Bayamón, *F21*
Beaches, *F23, F52*
eastern Puerto Rico, 79, 84, 87, 94, 96, 103–104, 109, 111, 113
Fodor's choice, F27
health concerns, F45
northwestern Puerto Rico, 162, 168, 170, 178, 179, 181, 185
San Juan, 7, 57–58
southern Puerto Rico, 123, 130, 131, 139–140, 143–144, 146, 152
Bebos Cafe ✕, *37*
Bella Gelato ✕, *57*
Ben & Jerry's ✕, *12*
Beside the Pointe ✕🏨, *182*
Bicycling, *F52–F53*
eastern Puerto Rico, 84, 110
San Juan, 58
Blackjack, *206–207*
Blossom's ✕, *96*
Blue Beach, *104*
Blue Macaw, The ✕, *104*
Boat and ferry travel, *F31–F32*
eastern Puerto Rico, 116–117
northwestern Puerto Rico, 187
San Juan, 69
Boat races, *F19, F21*
Boating and sailing
eastern Puerto Rico, 98–99, 107, 111, 112
southern Puerto Rico, 146
Bobbin Lace Festival, *F21*
Bookstores, *64*
Bosque Estatal Carite, *123, 126*
Bosque Estatal de Boquerón, *151–152*
Bosque Estatal de Guánica, *F27, 143*
Bosque Estatal de Guilarte, *176*
Bosque Estatal de Maricao, *176–177*
Bosque Estatal de Río Abajo, *171–172*
Bosque Estatal de Toro Negro, *174*
Bosque Estatal Guajataca, *168*
Bosque Nacional del Caribe. ⇨ *See* El Yunque
Brass Cactus Bar & Grill (Canóvanas) ✕, *86*
Brass Cactus Bar & Grill (Luquillo) ✕, *94*
Bus travel, *F32–F33*
eastern Puerto Rico, 115
northwestern Puerto Rico, 187–188
San Juan, 70
southern Puerto Rico, 154
Business hours, *F32*
Buyé Beach, *152*

C

Cabo Rojo, *151–154*
Café Berlin ✕, *24*
Café 4 Estaciones ✕, *14*
Café Media Luna ✕, *F26, 104*
Café Tompy ✕, *140–141*
Cafetería Los Chapines ✕, *152*
Cafeteria Mallorca ✕, *24*
Caja de Muertos, *139–140*
Caleta Guesthouse, The 🏨, *41*
Cameras and photography, *F33*

Camping, *F47–F48*
Canóvanas, *86*
Caparra Ruins, *23*
Capilla de Porta Coeli, *149*
Capilla del Cristo, *10*
Capitol building, *17*
Car rentals, *F33–F34*
eastern Puerto Rico, 115–116
northwestern Puerto Rico, 188
San Juan, 70
southern Puerto Rico, 154
Car travel, *F34–F36*
eastern Puerto Rico, 116
northwestern Puerto Rico, 188–189
San Juan, 70–72
southern Puerto Rico, 154–155
Caribbean Grill Restaurant ✕, *36*
Caribbean National Forest. ⇨ *See* El Yunque
Caribbean stud, *207*
Caribe Aquatic Adventures, *61*
Caribe Hilton San Juan 🏨, *42*
Caribe Playa Beach Resort ✕🏨, *131*
Carli Café Concierto ✕, *29*
Carnivales, *F19, F21*
Casa Alcaldía Antigua, *148-149*
Casa Armstrong-Poventud, *134*
Casa Bacardi Visitor Center, *22*
Casa Bavaria ✕, *128*
Casa Blanca, *10–11*
Casa Borinquen ✕, *25*
Casa Cautiño, *128–129*
Casa Cielo 🏨, *106*
Casa Cubuy Ecolodge 🏨, *112*
Casa Dante ✕, *32*
Casa de Lola Rodríguez de Tío, *148*
Casa de los Kindy, *149–150*
Casa de Ramón Power y Giralt, *11*
Casa del Caribe 🏨, *46*
Casa del Libro, *11*
Casa Jaime Acosta y Forés, *150*
Casa Vieja, *148*
Casa Wiechers-Villaronga, *134–135*
Casals, Pablo, *F21, 14, 15*
Casals Festival, *F21*
Casino games
baccarat, 205–206
blackjack, 206–207
Caribbean stud, 207
craps, 207–209
roulette, 209–210
slot machines, 210–211
video poker, 211–212
Casinos, *F23*
eastern Puerto Rico, 89, 98, 114
Northwestern Puerto Rico, 186
San Juan, 49–50
southern Puerto Rico, 142
Castillo Serrallés, *137*
Cataño, *F19*
Catedral de San Juan, *11*
Catedral Nuestra Señora de Guadalupe, *135*
Caverns, *F27*
Northwestern Puerto Rico, 166–167, 168
Cayey, *123, 126*
Cayo Caracoles, *146*
Ceiba, *F22*
Centro Ceremonial Indígena de Tibes, *137, 139*
Centro de Bellas Artes Luis A. Ferré, *17*
Centro de Información El Portal, *91*
Centro de Información Palo Colorado, *92*
Centro de Información Sierra Palm, *91*
Centro Nacional de Artes Populares y Artesanías, *11*
Centro Vacacional Punta Guilarte 🏨, *130*
Cetí Festival, *F22*
Channel Beach, *131*
Chayote ✕, *33*
Chef Wayne ✕, *87*
Che's ✕, *37*
Chez Daniel ✕, *113*
Chez Shack ✕, *104*
Chicharrón Festival, *F21*
Chicken Burger ✕, *132*
Children, attractions for
San Juan, 11, 12, 13–14, 42–43, 57
southern Puerto Rico, 126–127, 130, 136, 139, 144
Children and travel, *F36–F37*
Christmas, *F20*
Chronology, *200–204*
Chumar ✕, *112*
Chupacabra legend, *169*
Churches
eastern Puerto Rico, 85, 113
San Juan, 10, 11, 13
southern Puerto Rico, 135, 148, 149
Cielito Lindo ✕, *37*
Cigar shops, *65*
Cilantro's ✕, *151*
Climate, *F18*
Clothing shops, *65–66, 67*
Club Seaborne 🏨, *110*
Coamo, *F20, 132–133*
Coffee Harvest Festival, *F20*
Coffee industry, *F20, F26, 139, 175*
Colleges and universities, *20*
Columbus, Christopher, *15*
Combate Beach Hotel ✕🏨, *153*
Compostela ✕, *38*
Computers, *F37*
Conservation Trust of Puerto Rico, *11*
Consulates, *F43*
Consumer protection, *F37*
Convento de los Dominicos, *11*
Copamarina Beach Resort ✕🏨, *144*
Corozal, *F22*
Courtyard Isla Verde Beach Resort 🏨, *44*
Cowabunga's Ice Cream & Internet Cafe ✕, *181*
Crafts festivals, *F19, F21, F22*
Craps, *207–209*
Credit cards, *F49*
Cronopios (shop), *64*
Crow's Nest 🏨, *106*
Cruceta El Vigía, *139*
Cruise travel, *F37–F38*
Cueva del Viento, *168*
Cuisine of Puerto Rico, *F23, F42, 28, 79, 195–197*
Culebra, *100, 108–111*
Currency, *F49*
Customs and duties, *F38–F39*

D

Dance, *85*
Dance clubs
eastern Puerto Rico, 83, 107
northwestern Puerto Rico, 186
San Juan, 50–51
Dance festivals, *F19, F20, F21*
Danza Week, *F20*
David Antonio (shop), *65*
Del Mar y Algo Mas ✕, *151*
Designers, *67*
Dinghy Dock ✕, *109*
Dining, *F41–F43.* ⇨ *Also* under specific regions, cities, and towns
with children, F36
cuisine of Puerto Rico, F23, F42, 28, 79, 195–197

Fodor's choice, F25–F26
health concerns, F45
meal plans, F7
price categories, 24, 77, 122, 160
Disabilities and accessibility, *F39–F41*
Discounts and deals, *F41*
Dome's Beach, *181*
Dorado, *161–163, 166*
Dragonfly ✕, *29*
Dulce Sueño Paso Fino Fair, *F21*
Duties, *F38–F39*
Duty-free shopping, *F31*

E

Eastern Puerto Rico, *F9–F10, 76–118*
beaches, 79, 84, 87, 94, 96, 103–104, 109, 111, 113
dining, 76–77, 79, 82–83, 86, 87–88, 94–95, 96–97, 104–105, 109–110, 112, 113–114
emergencies, 116
English-language media, 116
itineraries, 77
lodging, 78, 88–89, 95, 97–98, 105–107, 110, 112, 114
mail and shipping, 117
money matters, 117
nightlife and the arts, 83, 85, 89, 98, 107
the northeast and El Yunque, F27, 78–79, 90–93
outdoor activities and sports, 79, 83–84, 86, 87, 89–90, 95, 98–99, 107–108, 110–111, 112, 114
price categories, 77, 78
safety, 117
shopping, 85–86, 90, 93, 100, 108, 111
southeastern coast, 111–114
telephones, 118
tours, 118
transportation, 114–117, 118
Vieques and Culebra, 100–111
visitor information, 118
web sites, 118
when to tour, 78
Ecotourism, *F43*
Northwestern Puerto Rico, 163
El Alcázar (shop), *66*
El Ancla ✕, *140*
El Bajo de Patillas, *131*
El Bobby ✕, *112*
El Bohío ✕, *152*
El Buen Café ✕, *167*
El Canario by the Sea 🏨, *46*
El Cañon de San Cristóbal, *127*
El Capitolio, *17*
El Combate, *F27, 152*
El Consulado 🏨, *46*
El Convento Hotel 🏨, *F25, 40*
El Dia de los Tres Reyes, *F20*
El Estoril ✕, *185*
El Fogón de Abuela ✕, *172*
El Ladrillo ✕, *162*
El Mar de la Tranquilidad ✕, *131*
El Muelle Guest House 🏨, *153*
El Museo del Cartel, *87*
El Nuevo Olímpico ✕, *167*
El Patio de Sam ✕, *29*
El Picoteo ✕, *F26, 31*
El Plátano Loco ✕ *179*
El Suarito ✕, *129*
El Tren del Sur (The Train of the South), *130*
El Tuque, *140*
El Yunque, *F27, 78–79, 90–93*
Electricity, *F43*
Embassies and consulates, *F43*
Embassy Suites Dorado del Mar Beach & Golf Resort 🏨, *162–163*
Embassy Suites San Juan Hotel & Casino 🏨, *43*
Emergencies, *F43*
and car travel, F35
eastern Puerto Rico, 116
northwestern Puerto Rico, 189
San Juan, 71
southern Puerto Rico, 155
English-language media, *F43–F44*
Eastern Puerto Rico, 116
Northwestern Puerto Rico, 189
San Juan, 72
Southern Puerto Rico, 155
Estación Experimental de Agricultura Tropical, *184–185*
Etiquette and behavior, *F44*

F

Fajardo, *F19, F21, 95–100*
Fajardo Inn 🏨, *97*
Farmacia Domínguez, *150*
Faro de Arecibo, *166*
Faro de Maunabo, *131*
Faro Punta Mulas, *101*
Ferry travel. ⇨ *See* Boat and ferry travel
Festival de Bomba y Plena, *F21*
Festival de Café, *F20*
Festival de Chiringas, *F21*
Festival de Mundillo, *F21*
Festival de Platos Tipicos, *F22*
Festival del Platano, *F22*
Festival of Puerto Rican Music, *F22*
Festival of Typical Dishes, *F22*
Festivals and seasonal events, *F19–F22, F23*
Fiesta de Flores, *F21*
Fiesta de Santiago Apóstal, *F21*
Fiesta Patronales, *F19, F22*
Film festivals, *F20*
Fishing
eastern Puerto Rico, 84, 114
northwestern Puerto Rico, 163, 183–184
San Juan, 59
southern Puerto Rico, 147
Fishing competitions, *F19*
Flower Festival, *F21*
Fodor's choice, *F25–F27*
Food festivals, *F20, F22*
Forests. ⇨ *See* Natural wonders
Fortresses
eastern Puerto Rico, 103
San Juan, F26, 12, 17, 23
Frutti Mar ✕, *31*
Fuerte San Cristóbal, *12*
Fuerte San Felipe del Morro, *F26, 12*
Fuerte San Gerónimo, *17*
Furniture shops, *66*

G

Galería Petrus, *63*
Galería Raíces, *64*
Gallery Inn 🏨, *40*
Gallery Night, *54, 63*
Galloway's ✕, *152*
Gambling. ⇨ *See* Casino games
Gardens, *20*
Gay and lesbian bars and clubs, *51–52*
Gay and lesbian travel, *F44*
San Juan, 72
Gift shops, *66*
Gilligan's Island, *144*
Golf, *F53*
eastern Puerto Rico, 79, 89–90, 98, 114
northwestern Puerto Rico, 163, 166, 179

San Juan, 59–60
southern Puerto Rico, 129, 133, 153
Great Taste Chinese Restaurant ✕, *32*
Greenhouse, The ✕, *36*
Guánica, *143–145*
Guayama, *F21, 128–129*
Guided tours, *F55*
eastern Puerto Rico, 118
northwestern Puerto Rico, 190–191
San Juan, 73–74
southern Puerto Rico, 157

H

Hacienda Buena Vista, *F26, 139*
Hacienda Margarita ✕🏨, *128*
Hacienda Tamarindo 🏨, *F25, 106*
Hampton Inn & Suites San Juan Resort 🏨, *44*
Handicrafts shops, *66*
Happy Belly's on the Beach ✕, *170*
Harbor View Villas 🏨, *110*
Hatillo Festival de los Mascaras, *F20*
Health concerns, *F44–F45*
northwestern Puerto Rico, 189
San Juan, 72
southern Puerto Rico, 155
Heineken JazzFest, *F19*
Hiking, *F53*
eastern Puerto Rico, 92
northwestern Puerto Rico, 163, 173
San Juan, 60
southern Puerto Rico, 123, 145
Hilton Ponce & Casino 🏨, *141*
Historical buildings
eastern Puerto Rico, 112–113
San Juan, 10, 11, 13
southern Puerto Rico, 128–129, 134–135, 137, 139, 149–150
Historical sites, *F26*
History of Puerto Rico, *200–204*
Hix Island House 🏨, *105*
Holiday Inn & El Tropical Casino Ponce 🏨, *141*
Holiday Inn Mayagüez and Tropical Casino ✕🏨, *186*
Holidays, *F46*
Home exchanges, *F48*
Horned Dorset Primavera ✕🏨, *F25, 181–182*
Horse fairs, *F21*
Horse racing, *60, 86*
Horseback riding
eastern Puerto Rico, 87
northwestern Puerto Rico, 166, 170, 173
southern Puerto Rico, 145
Hostels, *F48*
Hostería del Mar 🏨, *47*
Hotel Bélgica 🏨, *141–142*
Hotel Cielomar ✕🏨, *178*
Hotel La Casa Grande ✕🏨, *172*
Hotel La Playa 🏨, *46*
Hotel Meliá 🏨, *141*
Hotel Milano 🏨, *40–41*
Hotel Olimpo Court 🏨, *47*
Hotel Villa Confresí ✕🏨, *182*
Hotel Villa Real 🏨, *168*
Hotels, *F48.* ⇨ *Also* Lodging
price categories, 39, 78, 122, 160
Howard Johnson Hotel 🏨, *44–45*
Humacao, *F19, F22, 112–114*
Humacao's Fiesta Patronale, *F19*
Hyatt Dorado Beach Resort & Country Club (Dorado) ✕🏨, *162, 163, 166*
Hyatt Dorado Beach Resort & Country Club (San Juan), *59*

I

Iglesia de San Germán Auxerre, *148*
Iglésia de San José, *13*
Iglésia de San Patricio, *85*
Il Perugino ✕, *30*
Inches Beach, *131*
Indian festival, *F22*
Inn on the Blue Horizon 🏨, *F25, 105–106*
Insurance
for car rentals, F34
travel insurance, F46
Inter-Continental San Juan Resort & Casino 🏨, *41*
International Artisans' Festival, *F21*
International Billfish Tournament, *F19*
Isabela, *F21, 168, 170–171*
Isla Mata de la Gata, *146*
Island culture, *54*
Island Steak House ✕, *105*
Itineraries, *F16–F17*
for eastern Puerto Rico, 77
for northwestern Puerto Rico, 161
for San Juan, 3–4
for southern Puerto Rico, 121

J

Jardín Botánico, *20*
Jayuya, *F22, 173–174*
Jayuya Indian Festival, *F22*
JB Hidden Village 🏨, *179–180*
Jerusalem ✕, *37*
Jewelry shops, *68*
Joyuya Indian Festival, *F22*

K

Kasalta Bakery, Inc. ✕, *31*
Kayaking
eastern Puerto Rico, 84, 90, 99, 107
northwestern Puerto Rico, 168, 173
San Juan, 60
Kelly Cup Sailboat Regatta, *F21*
King's ✕, *136*
Kite Festival, *F21*
Kite surfing, *62*

L

La Bella Piazza ✕, *30*
La Bombonera ✕, *24*
La Buona Lasagne ✕, *36–37*
La Campesina ✕, *104–105*
La Casita ✕, *146*
La Casona ✕, *38*
La Casona (historic home), *148*
La Cava ✕, *140*
La Chaumière ✕*30*
La Concha ✕, *144*
La Fonda del Jibarito ✕, *F26, 25*
La Fortaleza, *12*
La Guancha, *139, 140*
La Guardarraya ✕, *145*
La Intendencia, *13*
La Llave del Mar ✕, *130*
La Mallorquina ✕, *30*
La Ostra Cosa ✕, *29*
La Parguera, *146–147*
La Patisserie ✕, *31*
La Pesqueria ✕, *114*
La Piedra ✕, *127*
La Piedra Escrita, *174*

La Playuela, *152*
La Ponderosa, *178*
La Vista Restaurant & Ocean Terrace ✕, *37*
Lace festival, *F21*
Lago Dos Bocas, *172*
Landing, The ✕, *181*
Language, *F46*
Lares, *167*
Las Cascadas Aquatic Park, *178*
Las Vegas ✕, *88*
Latin music clubs, *52–53*
Lazy Parrot ✕🏨, *182*
Lechoneras ✕, *126*
Lemontree Waterfront Cottages 🏨, *183*
L'Habitation Beach Guest House 🏨, *47*
Lighthouses
eastern Puerto Rico, 96, 101
northwestern Puerto Rico, 166, 178, 180–181
southern Puerto Rico, 131, 151
Lisa Cappalli (shop), *65*
Lodging, *F47–F48.* ⇨ *Also* under specific regions, cities, and towns
with children, F36–F37
for disabled travelers, F40
discount reservations, F41
Fodor's choice, F25
price categories, 39, 78, 122, 160
Loíza, *F21, 84–86*
Lolita's ✕, *94*
Los Fiestas de la Calle San Sebastián, *F20*
Lupita's ✕, *140*
Luquillo, *F27, 94–95*
Luquillo Beach Inn 🏨, *95*

M

Mail and shipping, *F49*
eastern Puerto Rico, 117
northwestern Puerto Rico, 189–190
San Juan, 72
southern Puerto Rico, 155–156
Malls, *63, 86*
Mamacitas ✕🏨, *109–110*
Mangére ✕, *162*
Marathon races, *F20*
Maria's Beach, *181*
Maricao, *F20, 176–177*
Marisquería Atlántica ✕, *38*
Marisquería La Dorada ✕, *38*
Markets, *63*
Mark's at the Meliá ✕, *F26, 140*
Martino ✕, *36*
Martin's BBQ ✕, *126*
Mary Lee's by the Sea 🏨, *F25, 145*
Mask-makers, *F20, 85–86, 136*
Maunabo Lighthouse, *131*
Mausoleo de la Familia Muñoz, *127*
Mayagüez, *184–186*
Mayagüez Resort & Casino ✕🏨, *186*
Meal plans, *F7*
Medicines, *F45*
Military exercises, *102*
Mirador Piedra Degetau, *126–127*
Miró Marisqueria Catalana ✕, *38*
Molino Inn ✕🏨, *129*
Mona Island, *185*
Money matters, *F49–F50*
eastern Puerto Rico, 117
northwestern Puerto Rico, 190
San Juan, 72
southern Puerto Rico, 156
Morgan's Steak & Sea Food ✕, *23*
Morse, Samuel F. B., *129–130*
Mosquito Bay, *F27, 103*
Muñoz family, *127*
Museo Antigua Aduana de Arroyo, *130*
Museo Casa Roig, *112–113*
Museo Cemí, *174*
Museo de Arte Contemporáneo de Puerto Rico, *17*
Museo de Arte de Ponce, *F26, 139*
Museo de Arte de Puerto Rico, *F26, 17, 20*
Museo de Arte y Casa de Estudio, *148*
Museo de Arte y Historia de San Juan, *13*
Museo de Arte y Historio de Francisco Oller, *23*
Museo de Historia, Antropología y Arte, *20*
Museo de la Historia de Ponce, *135*
Museo de las Américas, *F26, 13*
Museo de Nuestra Raíz Africana, *14*
Museo del Indio, *13*
Museo del Niño, *13–14*
Museo El Fortin Conde de Mirasol, *103*
Museo Histórico de Coamo, *132*
Museo Luis Muñoz Rivera, *127*
Museo Pablo Casals, *14*
Museums. ⇨ *Also* Art galleries and museums
African influences in island culture, 14
archaeology, 10–11, 20
art, 11, 13, 17, 20, 23, 87, 103, 112–113, 130, 139, 148
books, 11
Casals, 14
for children, 11, 12, 13–14, 136
in eastern Puerto Rico, 87, 91, 101, 103, 112–113
fire-fighting, 136
Fodor's choice, F26
forests, 91
history, 11, 13, 20, 23, 101, 103, 112–113, 130, 132, 135, 166
lighthouse, 101, 166
military, 12
Morse, 130
Muñoz Rivera, 127
music, 11, 135–136, 166
in northwestern Puerto Rico, 166, 174
posters, 87
Rodríguez de Tió, 148
in San Juan, 10–11, 12, 13–14, 17, 20, 23
science, 23
in southern Puerto Rico, 127, 130, 132, 135–136, 137, 139, 148, 149
sugar industry, 137
Taíno Indians, 13, 103, 135, 148, 166, 174
Tibes Indians, 137, 139
Music, *F23–F24*
eastern Puerto Rico, 85
San Juan, 7, 15, 52–53
Music clubs
eastern Puerto Rico, 83, 107
northwestern Puerto Rico, 183, 186
San Juan, 52–53
southern Puerto Rico, 142, 147, 153
Music festivals, *F19, F20, F21, F22*

N

Naguabo, *F22, 111–112*
Naguabo's fiesta patronale, *F22*

Natural wonders
eastern Puerto Rico, 78–79, 90–93, 96, 103, 109, 113
Fodor's choice, F27
northwestern Puerto Rico, 166–167, 168, 171–172, 174, 176–177, 185
southern Puerto Rico, 123, 126–127, 143, 151–152
Navidades, *F20*
Nightlife and the arts
eastern Puerto Rico, 83, 85, 89, 98, 107
northwestern Puerto Rico, 183, 186
San Juan, 47–56
southern Puerto Rico, 142, 147, 153
Nono Maldonado (shop), *65*
Northwestern Puerto Rico, *F10–F11, 159–191*
beaches, 162, 168, 170, 178, 179, 181, 185
dining, 159–160, 162, 167, 170, 172, 174, 176, 177, 178–179, 181–183, 185–186
emergencies, 189
English-language media, 189
exploring, 159–160
health concerns, 189
itineraries, 161
lodging, 160, 162–163, 168, 170, 172, 174, 176, 177, 178–180, 181–183, 186
mail and shipping, 189–190
money matters, 190
nightlife and the arts, 183, 186
north coast, 160–171
outdoor activities and sports, 163, 166, 170, 173, 179, 183–184
price categories, 160
safety, 190
shopping, 184, 186
telephones, 190
tours, 190–191
transportation, 187–189, 190
visitor information, 191
west-central inlands, 171–177
west coast, 177–186
when to tour, 160
Numero Uno 🏨, *45*

O

Observatorio de Arecibo, *167*
Oller, Francisco, *23*
Oriental Palace ✕, *32–33*
Otoki Bar & Grill ✕, *114*
Outdoor activities and sports, *F52–F53.* ⇨ *Also* specific activities
eastern Puerto Rico, 79, 83–84, 86, 87, 89–90, 95, 98–99, 107–108, 110–111, 112, 114
northwestern Puerto Rico, 163, 166, 170, 173, 179, 183–184
San Juan, 56–62
southern Puerto Rico, 123, 129, 133, 142, 145, 147, 153–154

P

Package deals, *F41*
Packing, *F50–F51*
Palacete los Moreau, *171*
Palio ✕, *87*
Palm Restaurant, The ✕, *36*
Palmas del Mar 🏨, *114*
Paradisus Puerto Rico Sol Meliá All-Inclusive Resort 🏨, *88*
Parador Baños de Coamo ✕🏨, *133*
Parador Boquemar ✕🏨, *153*
Parador El Faro ✕🏨, *178–179*
Parador El Guajataca 🏨, *170*
Parador El Sol 🏨, *186*
Parador Hacienda Gripiñas ✕🏨, *174*
Parador Joyuda Beach 🏨, *153*
Parador La Familia 🏨, *97–98*
Parador La Hacienda Juanita ✕🏨, *177*
Parador Oasis ✕🏨, *151*
Parador Villa del Mar 🏨, *146*
Parador Villa Parguera ✕🏨, *147*
Paradores, *F48*
Parks
northwestern Puerto Rico, 180–181
San Juan, 14, 20, 23
Parque Central Municipo de San Juan, *20*
Parque Ceremonial Indigena de Caguana, *172*
Parque de Bombas, *136*
Parque de las Cavernas del Río Camuy, *F27, 166–167*
Parque de las Ciencias Luis A. Ferré, *23*
Parque de las Palomas, *14*
Parque Pasivo El Faro, *180*
Parguera Blues Café ✕, *146*
Park Plaza Normandie 🏨, *45*
Parrot Club ✕, *F26, 29*
Parrots, *93*
Paso Fino horses, *F21, 87, 128*
Passports, *F51*
Patillas, *130–131*
Paul Julien's Caribbean Vacation Villa 🏨, *144*
Performing arts, *55–56*
Photography, *F33*
Pikayo ✕, *33*
Pinky's ✕, *31–32, 58*
Piñones, *79, 82–84*
Pito's ✕, *140*
Planetariums and observatories
northwestern Puerto Rico, 167
San Juan, 23
Plantain Festival, *F22*
Playa Borinquen, *178*
Playa Breñas, *162*
Playa Cerro Gordo, *162*
Playa Corcega, *181*
Playa Costa Azul, *94*
Playa Crashboat, *F27, 178*
Playa Culebrita, *109*
Playa de Isla Verde, *F27, 57*
Playa de Ocean Park, *57–58*
Playa del Condado, *57*
Playa Flamenco, *F27, 109*
Playa Gas Chambers, *178*
Playa Grande, *101*
Playa Guajataca, *168, 170*
Playa Húcares, *111*
Playa Jobos, *168*
Playa Joyuda, *152*
Playa La Pared, *94*
Playa Las Picúas, *87*
Playa Los Tubos, *162*
Playa Media Luna, *104*
Playa Montones, *168*
Playa Punta Santiago, *113*
Playa Santa, *144*
Playa Sardinera, *162*
Playa Shacks, *168*
Playa Sun Bay, *103*
Playa Table Rock, *179*
Playa Tres Palmas, *181*
Playa Wilderness, *178*
Playa Zoni, *109*
Playita Condado, *57*
Playita Rosada, *146*
Plaza de Humancao, *113*
Ponce, *133–143*
Ponce de León, Juan, *10–11, 13, 23*
Posada La Hamaca 🏨, *110*
Posada Vistamar ✕, *105*

Price categories
dining, 24, 77, 122, 160
eastern Puerto Rico, 77, 78
lodging, 39, 78, 122, 160
northwestern Puerto Rico, 160
San Juan, 24, 39
southern Puerto Rico, 122
Public art, *21*
Puerta la Bahía ✕, *132*
Puerto del Rey Marina, *95*
Puerto Rican green parrots, *93*
Puerto Rico International Film Festival, *F20*
Puerto Rico International Offshore Cup, *F19*
Puerto Rico Symphony Orchestra, *F20*
Puerto Rico Tourism Fair, *F21*
Pulpo Loco by the Sea ✕, *82*
Punta Higuera Lighthouse, *180*
Punta Jacinto, *144*
Punta Santiago Vacation Center 🏨, *114*

R

Radisson Ambassador Plaza Hotel & Casino 🏨, *44*
Rafting, *168*
Ramiro's ✕, *38*
Red Beach, *104*
Refugio de Vida Silvestre, *151–152*
Refugio de Vida Silvestre de Humacao, *113*
Refugio Nacional de Vida Silvestre de Culebra, *109*
Regata de Veleros Copa Kelly, *F21*
Rental properties, *F47*
Reserva Natural Las Cabezas de San Juan, *96*
Residencia Morales, *149*
Rest rooms, *F51*
Restaurants. ⇨ *Also* Dining
price categories, 24, 77, 122, 160
Rex Cream ✕, *129*
Ricomini Bakery ✕, *185*
Rincón, *180–184*
Rincón Beach Resort 🏨, *182*
Rincón of the Seas ✕🏨, *182–183*
Rincón Tropical ✕, *181*
Río Grande, *F21, 86–90*
Río Grande Plantation Eco Resort 🏨, *88–89*
Ristorante Otello ✕, *96*
Ritz-Carlton San Juan Hotel, Spa & Casino 🏨, *42*
Rocket Plaza, *23*
Rodríguez de Tío, Lola, *148*
Rosa's Sea Food ✕, *97*
Roulette, *209–210*
Rum distilleries, *22*

S

Safety, *F51–F52*
eastern Puerto Rico, 117
northwestern Puerto Rico, 190
San Juan, 73
southern Puerto Rico, 156
Sailing. ⇨ *See* Boating and sailing
St. James Festival, *F21*
Salinas, *131–132*
San Blas de Illescas Half Marathon, *F20*
San Germán, *147–151*
San Juan, *, F9, 2–74*
addresses, 68
architecture, 7
beaches, 7, 57–58
children, attractions for, 11, 12, 13–14, 23, 42–43, 57
climate, F18
dining, 12, 14, 20, 23–39, 53–54, 57, 58
emergencies, 71
English-language media, 72
exploring, 2, 4–20, 22–23
festivals and seasonal events, F19, F20, F21, F22, 54, 55, 63, 67
gay and lesbian travel, 72
greater San Juan, 16–20, 31–39
health concerns, 72
itineraries, 3–4
lodging, 39–47
mail and shipping, 72
money matters, 72
music, 7, 15, 52–53
nightlife and the arts, 4, 47–56
Old San Juan, 4–15, 24–25, 29–31, 40–41
outdoor activities and sports, 56–62
Paseo de la Princesa, 14
Plaza de Armas, 14
Plaza de Colón, 15
Plaza del Mercado, 20
Plazuela de la Rogativa, 15
price categories, 24, 39
public art, 21
safety, 73
San Juan environs, 22–23
shopping, 62–68
telephones, 73
tours, 73–74
transportation, 68–71, 73, 74
visitor information, 74
when to tour, 4
San Juan Bautista Festival, *F21*
San Juan Fashion Week, *67*
San Juan Marriott Resort and Stellaris Casino 🏨, *43*
San Sebastián Street Festival, *F20*
Sand and the Sea ✕, *F26, 126*
Sandy Beach ✕, *181*
Santeros (carvers), *150*
Sardinera Seven Seas ✕, *97*
Santurce, *F19*
Scuba diving and snorkeling, *F53*
eastern Puerto Rico, 84, 89, 95, 99, 107–108, 111
health concerns, F44–F45
northwestern Puerto Rico, 163, 170, 179, 183–184
San Juan, 59
southern Puerto Rico, 123, 142, 145, 147, 153–154
Senior-citizen travel, *F52*
Shimas ✕, *87–88*
Shopping, *F52*
duty-free, F31
eastern Puerto Rico, 85–86, 90, 93, 100, 108, 111
northwestern Puerto Rico, 184, 186
San Juan, 62–68
southern Puerto Rico, 143, 147
Slot machines, *210–211*
Snorkeling. ⇨ *See* Scuba diving and snorkeling
SOFO Culinary Week, *F20*
Soleil Beach Club & Bistro ✕, *82*
Southern Puerto Rico, *F10, 120–157*
beaches, 123, 130, 131, 139–140, 143–144, 146, 152
central southern region, 122–133
children, attractions for, 126–127, 130, 136, 139, 144
dining, 121–122, 126, 127, 128, 129, 130, 131, 132–133, 136, 140–141, 144, 145, 146, 147, 151, 152–153
emergencies, 155
English-language media, 155
exploring, 120–121
health concerns, 155
itineraries, 121

lodging, 122, 128, 129, 130, 131, 133, 141–142, 144–145, 146–147, 151, 152–153
nightlife and the arts, 142, 147, 153
outdoor activities and sports, 123, 129, 133, 142, 145, 147, 153–154
mail and shipping, 155–156
money matters, 156
Ponce, 133–143
price categories, 122
safety, 156
shopping, 143, 147
southwest region, 143–154
telephones, 156–157
tours, 157
transportation, 154–155, 156
visitor information, 157
when to tour, 122
Souvenirs, *F52*
Spanish vocabulary, *213–219*
Sports. ⇨ *See* specific sports
Steps Beach, *181*
Student travel, *F53*
Sugar industry, *137*
Surfing
eastern Puerto Rico, 95
northwestern Puerto Rico, 163, 183
San Juan, 60–61
Symbols, *F7*

T

Taíno Indians, *F22, 13, 103, 135, 148, 166, 172, 173, 174*
Tamarindo Estates 🏨, *110*
Tangerine ✕, *33*
Tantra ✕, *30*
Taverna Española ✕, *104*
Taxes, *F54*
Taxis
eastern Puerto Rico, 118
northwestern Puerto Rico, 190
southern Puerto Rico, 156
San Juan, 73
Teatro La Perla, *137*
Teatro Tapia, *15*
Teatro Yagüez, *185*
Telephones, *F54*
eastern Puerto Rico, 118
northwestern Puerto Rico, 190
San Juan, 73
southern Puerto Rico, 156–157
Tennis, *61*
Theater buildings
northwestern Puerto Rico, 186, 186
San Juan, 15, 17, 55–56
southern Puerto Rico, 137, 142
Thermal springs, *132*
Three Kings Day, *F20*
Tibes Indians, *137, 139*
Tierra Santa ✕, *37*
Time, *F54–F55*
Tipping, *F55*
Torre Yokahu, *91*
Tours, *F55*
eastern Puerto Rico, 118
northwestern Puerto Rico, 190–191
San Juan, 73–74
southern Puerto Rico, 157
Train rides, *130*
Train travel, *F55*
San Juan, 74
Transportation Museum, *23*
Transylvania ✕, *30*
Travel agencies, *F55–F56*
for disabled travelers, F41
for gay and lesbian travelers, F44
for tour bookings, F55
Traveler's checks, *F49–F50*
Tropical Agriculture Research Station, *184–185*
Tropical Restaurant ✕, *32*
Tu Casa Boutique Hotel 🏨, *45*
Tutti Frutti En Areyto ✕, *82*

U

Universidad de Puerto Rico, *20*
Urdin ✕, *38–39*
Utuado, *171–173*

V

Van travel, *187–188*
Via Appia ✕, *36*
Victor's Place ✕, *94–95*
Video poker, *211–212*
Vieques, *100–108*
Vieques National Wildlife Refuge, *103*
Villa Marina, *95*
Villa Montaña ✕🏨, *170*
Villa Pesquera ✕, *88*
Villa rentals, *F47*
eastern Puerto Rico, 106–107
Villas de Sotomayor ✕🏨, *176*
Villas del Mar Hau ✕🏨, *F25, 170*
Virgen del Carmen, *F22*
Visas, *F51*
Visitor information, *F56*
eastern Puerto Rico, 118
northwestern Puerto Rico, 191
San Juan, 94
southern Puerto Rico, 157
Vocabulary, *213–219*

W

Water Club, The 🏨, *43*
Water sports
eastern Puerto Rico, 90
northwestern Puerto Rico, 183–184
San Juan, 61–62
Waterfalls
northwestern Puerto Rico, 174
southern Puerto Rico, 127
Waterfront, The ✕, *83*
Weather information, *F18*
Web sites, *F56*
eastern Puerto Rico, 118
Westin Río Mar Beach Resort (Río Grande) 🏨, *88*
Westin Río Mar Beach Resort & Country Club (San Juan), *60*
Westin Rió Mar Country Club (Río Grande), *90*
Whale-watching, *184*
When to go, *F18–F22*
Wildlife preserves
eastern Puerto Rico, 103, 109
southern Puerto Rico, 151–152
Windsurfing
eastern Puerto Rico, 90
northwestern Puerto Rico, 166
San Juan, 62
Wyndham Condado Plaza Hotel & Casino 🏨, *42–43*
Wyndham El Conquistador Resort & Golden Door Spa 🏨, *F25, 97, 98*
Wyndham El San Juan Hotel & Casino 🏨, *F25, 41*
Wyndham Martineau Bay Resort & Spa 🏨, *105*
Wyndham Old San Juan Hotel & Casino 🏨, *40*

Y

Yauco, *F20, 145*
Yerba Buena ✕, *32*
Yokahu Observation Tower, *91*

Z

Zabor Creative Cuisine ✕, *33*
Zoos, *23, 184*
Zoológico Dr. Juan A. Rivero, *184*

NOTES

NOTES

NOTES

NOTES

FODOR'S KEY TO THE GUIDES

America's guidebook leader publishes guides for every kind of traveler. Check out our many series and find your perfect match.

FODOR'S GOLD GUIDES
America's favorite travel-guide series offers the most detailed insider reviews of hotels, restaurants, and attractions in all price ranges, plus great background information, smart tips, and useful maps.

COMPASS AMERICAN GUIDES
Stunning guides from top local writers and photographers, with gorgeous photos, literary excerpts, and colorful anecdotes. A must-have for culture mavens, history buffs, and new residents.

FODOR'S CITYPACKS
Concise city coverage in a guide plus a foldout map. The right choice for urban travelers who want everything under one cover.

FODOR'S EXPLORING GUIDES
Hundreds of color photos bring your destination to life. Lively stories lend insight into the culture, history, and people.

FODOR'S TRAVEL HISTORIC AMERICA
For travelers who want to experience history firsthand, this series gives in-depth coverage of historic sights, plus nearby restaurants and hotels. Themes include the Thirteen Colonies, the Old West, and the Lewis and Clark Trail.

FODOR'S POCKET GUIDES
For travelers who need only the essentials. The best of Fodor's in pocket-size packages for just $9.95.

FODOR'S FLASHMAPS
Every resident's map guide, with dozens of easy-to-follow maps of public transit, restaurants, shopping, museums, and more.

FODOR'S CITYGUIDES
Sourcebooks for living in the city: thousands of in-the-know listings for restaurants, shops, sports, nightlife, and other city resources.

FODOR'S AROUND THE CITY WITH KIDS
Up to 68 great ideas for family days, recommended by resident parents. Perfect for exploring in your own backyard or on the road.

FODOR'S HOW TO GUIDES
Get tips from the pros on planning the perfect trip. Learn how to pack, fly hassle-free, plan a honeymoon or cruise, stay healthy on the road, and travel with your baby.

FODOR'S LANGUAGES FOR TRAVELERS
Practice the local language before you hit the road. Available in phrase books, cassette sets, and CD sets.

KAREN BROWN'S GUIDES
Engaging guides—many with easy-to-follow inn-to-inn itineraries—to the most charming inns and B&Bs in the U.S.A. and Europe.

SEE IT GUIDES
Illustrated guidebooks that include the practical information travelers need, in gorgeous full color. Thousands of photos, hundreds of restaurant and hotel reviews, prices, and ratings for attractions all in one indispensable package. Perfect for travelers who want the best value packed in a fresh, easy-to-use, colorful layout.

OTHER GREAT TITLES FROM FODOR'S
Baseball Vacations, The Complete Guide to the National Parks, Family Vacations, Golf Digest's Places to Play, Great American Drives of the East, Great American Drives of the West, Great American Vacations, Healthy Escapes, National Parks of the West, Skiing USA.